Health and Environment in Sustainable Development

Five Years after the Earth Summit

World Health Organization
Geneva
1997

Table of Contents

Message from the Director-General

The Earth Summit in Rio de Janeiro in 1992 stressed that development is about meeting the needs of people, their health, their well-being, their lives and the environment on which they depend. The basic human need for a safe environment — one which provides clean water, and adequate food and shelter, and in which different people can live together in peace — is the same for all of us. Five years have passed since the Earth Summit and numerous initiatives have been launched at local, national and global level to highlight the need for health-and-environment action. So it is timely to start the analysis of how we are doing as a community of peoples in terms of meeting this need, how development can provide resources for health protection, but also how such development can threaten health through degradation of natural resources. This analysis should highlight problems, but also give examples of solutions that will bring us closer to sustainable development. The dreams and aspirations of a healthy future for the next generation can be accomplished only if we use our current knowledge wisely and take action in solidarity.

This book focuses on the health of girls and boys, women and men, many of whom are struggling to survive and live an acceptable life in a hostile environment. Each day the world has to accommodate yet more people. On average three persons are added to the global population each second, which translates into an average of 90 million more people every year. Population growth in itself creates great difficulties in providing the water, food and shelter that are required for health, especially since most population growth takes place in developing countries where resources are already insufficient. Moreover, unsustainable consumption in the most affluent countries means that the world's non-renewable resources are becoming rapidly depleted. Thus the life-supporting global environment is increasingly subject to stresses such as climate change, loss of biodiversity, desertification and deforestation. The call for sustainable development at the Earth Summit drew the world's attention to environmental issues such as these that are of profound importance for the health of this generation and future generations.

It has probably taken you about two minutes to read this section from the beginning. While you were doing so, 260 girls were born and 264 boys, most of them in developing countries. Those fortunate enough to have been born in developed countries can expect to enjoy a healthy childhood and to live for more than 70 years. But many of those born in developing countries will suffer from a variety of childhood diseases and will not live to see even their fifth birthday. Within each country, the poor and underprivileged are also experiencing the worst health conditions. Inequities of this kind must be addressed by communities and governments, both at local and national level.

Health professionals must press for adequate programmes and resources, join forces with their counterparts in the environmental sector, and establish health-and-environment concerns as a prime element in sustainable development programmes. On a broader basis, wide participation on the part of all sectors in the community must be ensured if solutions and strategies that achieve sustained improvements in health are to be formulated and implemented. Furthermore, to secure the greatest gains, the current and future needs of people, particularly the poor and vulnerable, must be focused upon. By describing environmental health problems around the world, and some potential solutions for them, this book offers ways to protect and maintain health for the benefit of all.

Hiroshi Nakajima, M.D., Ph.D
Director-General
World Health Organization

About this Book

F ive years have passed since the Earth Summit, the important United Nations Conference on Environment and Development which took place in Rio de Janeiro. A milestone has thus been reached on the path towards sustainable development. However, new directions in development can take years, if not decades, to gain a foothold. We have therefore chosen to analyse trends pertaining to health-and-environment issues from the early 1970s — the era of the first United Nations Conference on the Human Environment, held in Stockholm — up to the present, and to make projections from the present until the year 2020. In so doing we are able to provide a fifty-year perspective on health and environment within the context of social and economic development.

Specifically, this book demonstrates that environmental quality is crucial for human health. It does this in two ways: by describing the adverse health effects of environmental hazards and by showing, conversely, how a sound environment can support or "enable" health. In showing trends over time and presenting projections for the future it underscores newly emerging environmental health problems and indicates the type of local and national monitoring and assessment that would improve environmental health management.

The book's intended audience consists of decision-makers, community leaders, scientists and professionals in governmental and nongovernmental organizations who are interested in development issues. It is hoped that this book will inspire professionals working in a variety of development sectors — such as agriculture, industry, environment, aid and planning — and health professionals who wish to become more aware of environmental health issues.

The concept of the environmental cause-and-effect framework provides the book's structure. The first chapter explains the framework and introduces key issues discussed in this book. The basic driving forces behind environmental health problems, such as population growth, economic development and non-sustainable consumption, need to be addressed if we are to secure a healthy environment and sustainable development. Human activities lead to pressures on the environment from sewage, solid waste and pollution, that may eventually affect the quality or state of the environment. If exposed to unhealthy environmental conditions (state), people may experience health effects.

This framework accords with the way in which environmental health scientists have begun to extend their investigation of the environmental causes of ill health beyond the traditional focus on localized hazards to human health. This is because it is becoming increasingly accepted that many of those local hazards are the "downstream" products of large-scale environmental pollution and degradation that are linked to human-induced stresses driven by population growth, economic development and technological forces. Consequently, it is becoming evident that promotion and protection of human health may be undertaken more cost-effectively by implementing measures that limit "upstream" damage to the environment, even though such measures may take some time to yield results. Nevertheless, interventions to control individual exposures to the more down-stream hazards may still be preferable if adverse health consequences arising from existing environmental degradation are acute. But in many cases, both approaches will be needed.

The chapters in this book reflect this holistic way of thinking by following the steps of the health-and-environment cause-and-effect framework shown schemat-ically in Fig. 1.3 (see page 9). A more detailed account of this rationale can be found in Chapter 1.

This book is a contribution by WHO to the five-year follow-up to the Earth Summit. This anniversary provides an opportunity to assess the impact made by environmental health activities at local, national and global level during this peri-od. The book systematically brings together quantitative data on health-and-envi-ronment linkages at the global level, with examples from regions and countries. Health-and-environment linkages were described in the 1972 WHO report, *Health hazards of the human environment*, and in the 1992 WHO report, *Our planet, our health*, but new information and new ways of considering health and environment issues have emerged, and form the basis of this book.

The programmes on Health and Environment at WHO had the main responsi-bility for the preparation of this book. Many other programmes at WHO head-quarters and Regional Offices contributed text and illustrations. The report could not have been completed without the major efforts of a number of WHO staff members and key consultants. Special thanks are due also to the members of the Director-General's Council on the Earth Summit Action Programme for Health and Environment for their input.

Abbreviations and Acronyms

AAMA	American Automobile Manufacturers Association
AIDS	acquired immunodeficiency syndrome
ARI	acute respiratory infections
ATSDR	(US) Agency for Toxic Substances and Disease Registry
BMJ	British medical journal
BSE	bovine spongiform encephalopathy
CDC	Centers for Disease Control and Prevention (USA)
CFC	chlorofluorocarbon
CHD	coronary heart disease
COPD	chronic obstructive pulmonary disease
CSD	(UN) Commission on Sustainable Development
CVD	cardiovascular disease
DAC	Development Assistance Committee
DALY	disability-adjusted life year
DHHS	(US) Department of Health and Human Services
EC	European Commission
ECA	European Collaborative Action
ECETOC	European Chemical Industry Ecology and Toxicology Centre
ECLAC	(UN) Economic Commission for Latin America and the Caribbean
EEA	European Environment Agency
EEC	European Economic Community
EIA	environmental impact assessment
EME	established market economies
ETS	environmental tobacco smoke
EU	European Union
FAO	Food and Agriculture Organization of the United Nations
FSE	former socialist economies of Europe
GATT	General Agreement on Tariffs and Trade
GDP	gross domestic product
GEMS	Global Environment Monitoring System (UNEP/WHO)
GIS	geographic information system
GHG	greenhouse gas
GDP	gross domestic product
GNP	gross national product
GPI	genuine progress index
HCFC	hydrofluorocarbon
HFC	halogenated fluorocarbon
HICARE	Hiroshima International Council for the Health Care of the Radiation-exposed
HIV	human immunodeficiency virus
IAEA	International Atomic Energy Agency
IARC	International Agency for Research on Cancer

ICC	International Chamber of Commerce
ICLEI	International Council for Local Environmental Initiatives
ICNIRP	International Commission on Non-Ionizing Radiation Protection
ICRP	International Commission on Radiological Protection
IDRC	International Development Research Centre (Canada)
IETC	International Environmental Technology Centre (UNEP)
IFAD	International Fund for Agricultural Development
IFCS	Intergovernmental Forum on Chemical Safety
IIASA	International Institute for Applied Systems Analysis
ILEC	International Lake Environment Committee
ILO	International Labour Organisation
IMO	International Maritime Organization
IMR	infant mortality rate
INCLEN	International Clinical Epidemiology Network
IOMC	Inter-Organization Programme for the Sound Management of Chemicals
IPCC	Intergovernmental Panel on Climate Change
IPCS	International Programme on Chemical Safety (UNEP, ILO and WHO)
IPHECA	International Programme on the Health Effects of the Chernobyl Accident
IQ	intelligence quotient
ISIC	International Standard Industry Classification
ISRIC	International Soil Reference Information Centre
LAC	Latin America and the Caribbean
JAMA	Journal of the American Medical Association
LPG	liquefied petroleum gas
MARC	Monitoring and Assessment Research Centre (UK)
MEA	multilateral environmental agreement
MEC	Middle Eastern Crescent
MVA	manufacturing value added
NCRP	National Council on Radiation Protection and Measurements (USA)
NEAP	national environmental action plan
NEHAP	national environmental health action plan
NGO	nongovernmental organization
NIOSH	National Institute for Occupational Safety and Health (USA)
NRC	National Research Council (USA)
NT	neonatal tetanus
OAI	other Asia and islands
ODA	official development assistance
OECD	Organisation for Economic Co-operation and Development
ORT	oral rehydration therapy
Oxfam	Oxford Committee for Famine Relief
NT	neonatal tetanus
PAHO	Pan American Health Organization
PEEM	Panel of Experts on Environmental Management for Vector Control (WHO/FAO/UNEP/UNCHS)
PIC	prior informed consent
POP	persistent organic pollutant
SCOPE	Scientific Committee on Problems of the Environment
SDI	sustainable development indicator
SIDA	Swedish International Development Cooperation Agency

SSA	sub-Saharan Africa
SSI	small-scale industry
TT	tetanus toxoid
UN	United Nations
UNCED	United Nations Conference on Environment and Development
UNCHS	United Nations Centre for Human Settlements (HABITAT)
UNCTAD	United Nations Conference on Trade and Development
UNDP	United Nations Development Programme
UNEP	United Nations Environment Programme
UNESCO	United Nations Educational, Scientific and Cultural Organization
UNFPA	United Nations Population Fund
UNHCR	Office of the United Nations High Commissioner for Refugees
UNICEF	United Nations Children's Fund
UNICRI	United Nations International Crime and Justice Research Institute
UNIDO	United Nations Industrial Development Organization
UNITAR	United Nations Institute for Training and Research
USDA	United States Department of Agriculture
UNSCEAR	United Nations Scientific Committee on the Effects of Atomic Radiation
USEPA	United States Environmental Protection Agency
UVR	ultraviolet radiation
WARDA	West African Rice Development Association
WASH	Water and Sanitation for Health Project (USA)
WBCSD	World Business Council for Sustainable Development
WCED	World Commission on Environment and Development
WHO	World Health Organization
WHR	World Health Report
WMO	World Meteorological Organization
WRI	World Resources Institute
WSSCC	Water Supply and Sanitation Collaborative Council
WTO	World Trade Organization
YYL	years of life lost

Chemical abbreviations

Cd	cadmium
CFC	chlorofluorocarbon
Cl_2	chlorine
CH_4	methane
CO	carbon monoxide
CO_2	carbon dioxide
CS_2	carbon disulfide
DDT	dichlorodiphenyltrichloroethane
F	fluorides
F_2	fluorine
HC	hydrocarbon
HCB	hexachlorobenzene
HCFC	hydrochlorofluorocarbon
HCHO	formaldehyde
HCl	hydrochloric acid
HF	hydrofluoric acid
Hg	mercury
HNO_3	nitric acid
H_2S	hydrogen sulfide
MeHg	methyl mercury
Mn	manganese
NH_3	ammonia
NO_2	nitrogen dioxide
NO_x	nitrogen oxides
N_2O	nitrous oxide
O_3	ozone
PAH	polynuclear aromatic hydrocarbon
Pb	lead
PCB	polychlorinated biphenyl
PCDD	polychlorinated dibenzo-p-dioxin
PCDF	polychlorinated dibenzo-p-furan
PM_{10}	particulate matter with an aerodynamic diameter of less than 10 µm
POP	persistent organic pollutant
Ra	radium
Rn	radon
R-SH	mercaptan
RSP	respirable suspended particulate
SiF_4	silicon fluoride
SO_2	sulfur dioxide
SO_3	sulfur trioxide
SPM	suspended particulate matter
VOC	volatile organic compounds

Units of Measurements

billion	one thousand million
centi (c)	10^{-2}
DU	Dobson unit (2.69×10^{19} molecules/cm^2)
exa (E)	10^{18}
giga (G)	10^{9}
kilo (k)	10^{3}
mega (M)	10^{6}
milli (m)	10^{-3}
micro μ	10^{-6}
nano (n)	10^{-9}
atm-cm	atmospheres/centimetres
Bq	becquerel
g	gram
Gy	gray
ha	hectare
hr	hour
J	joule
l	litre
m	metre
Sv	sievert

Chapter 1
A New Perspective on Health

Driving Force
Pressure
State
Exposure
Effect
Action

1.1 How are we doing?

Every parent hopes that their new-born child will enjoy a healthy, happy and long life. This is nothing new. Good health has been a fundamental aim in every culture, and various rules, rites and practices to protect health have been developed throughout history. Not all of these practices worked, and some may even have had the opposite effect to the one intended. Nevertheless, the recorded experience and scientific research of the last century provide much evidence of how good health can be promoted and protected. We now know that the living environment is a corner-stone for good health and we have largely identified what makes the environment healthy. Human society is thus more able than ever before to achieve the fundamental aim of good health for each community. But how are we actually doing?

Almost all babies are born with the capacity to survive for at least seventy years. But a large percentage of them do not go on to live long lives because of the poor quality of the environment into which they are born and in which they grow up. In some of the "least developed countries", more than 20% of children die before they reach the age of 5. In a typical "developed country", however, less than 1% of children will do so (WHO, 1997a). Inherited variation cannot explain such significant differences in health status between populations. Rather, it is the case that if we *all* lived in an environment that was supportive of health and

if we enjoyed good nutrition and housing, safe water and sanitation, received vaccinations against key communicable diseases, kept peace with our neighbours and avoided unhealthy activities such as tobacco smoking, most of us would survive for at least 70 years.

Fig. 1.1 shows the remarkable sustained improvement in Sweden's infant mortality rate, thereby illustrating the continual health gains that can be made. (Sweden is used here since it has such a long history of systematic mortality records.) The improvement observed during the last 200 years has coincided with improvements in living conditions and basic sanitation initiated in the 19th Century. Sustained peace since 1809, economic growth and increasing attention on the part of the Swedish Government to basic human needs, such as good nutrition, high-quality housing, environmental protection and healthcare for all, have helped maintain this momentum up to the present.

Of course, modern affluent societies have grown accustomed not only to having their basic human needs met, but also to ready access to additional commodities and services, such as energy supply, transportation, communication systems, consumer markets and adequate healthcare. Higher standards of living and economic development mean in turn that consumption of natural resources is growing fast in many parts of the world. In developed countries it has already reached a very

Fig. 1.1

Historical trend of infant mortality in Sweden, Guinea-Bissau and Chile

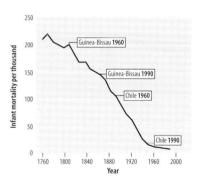

The curve shows the long and steady decline of infant mortality in Sweden, which has one of the world's longest history of births and deaths registration. The decline was initially attributable to gradual improvements in nutrition, hygiene and environmental conditions. In other words it began long before specific medical interventions such as mass vaccination and anti-bacterial therapeutics were introduced. The level of infant mortality rates in 1960 and 1990 for Guinea-Bissau and Chile are indicated, showing the large differences in infant mortality at different development stages.

Sources: based on official Swedish mortality statistics and WHO mortality database.

high level; one that could not be sustained were all countries to consume similar quantities of natural resources. Thus, increasingly, the global environment's life support functions are being stretched to the limit and, in some cases (see Section 4.9) are actually being exceeded. As a result, new threats to human health — and quite possibly the re-emergence of old threats — can be anticipated. Protection of environment and health should therefore be understood as a constantly active and vigilant process, that needs to be integrated into economic development analysis and decision-making (see Section 2.7 and Chapter 6).

The growing world population is another important health-and-environment issue. Reduced mortality, which is a sign of improved health, contributes to longer life expectancy and population growth when not accompanied by reduced birth rates. There are just under 6000 million people living on Earth today: about 80% in the developing countries (UN, 1995a). Current annual population growth is about 90 million, most of it occurring in developing countries. In many countries this increase is creating great difficulties in meeting the basic needs of populations and leading to pressure on environmental resources. There is a limit to the water, agricultural soil and other natural resources that Earth can provide. However, more equitable access to these resources and improved management of the environment would enable the needs of more people to be met.

The very large differences in the health situation of countries is illustrated in **Fig. 1.1**. In 1990, in Guinea-Bissau, the infant mortality rate (140 infant deaths per 1000 births) was at the Swedish level of 1870, while in Chile the rate (20 per 1000) was at the Swedish level of 1950. These rates will continue to improve, but special efforts will have to be made if countries such as Guinea-Bissau are to achieve in a reasonable time the "Health-for-All" target of less than 50 infant deaths per 1000 births.

The "health gap" between developing and developed countries was described in detail in the *World health report 1995* (WHO, 1995a) and is illustrated in **Box 1.1** with reference to inequities in infant mortality within the global population. In 1970, the worst-off 20% of the world's population had an infant mortality rate about 5 times higher than the best-off 20%. By 1995 this ratio had fallen to 4 and it is estimated that by 2020 it will have fallen further, assuming that current trends continue and environment and living conditions improve. **Table 1.1** illustrates a similar pattern for child mortality, and water and sanitation coverage — the latter is an important general environmental health indicator. Mortality trends for older age groups are comparable: with improvements in the living environment, and in health services, nutrition and education, mortality rates go down. Differences between countries remain, however (Feachem et al., 1992). Subsequent chapters analyse these patterns in more detail.

Reducing mortality rates obviously requires the minimization or elimination of environmental hazards. But this necessitates financial and human resources, and these are scarce in developing countries. Frequently, competing demands mean that environmental protection is neglected; the poorest countries and the poorest people in those countries are affected most (**Table 1.1**).

To illustrate the differences between countries we will categorize countries by "development level" using the United Nations classification: "least developed countries"; "other developing countries"; "economies in transition", and "developed countries". However, since available data is often based on classification by geographic region, some figures and tables use geographic rather than development classifications. That said, there is a considerable overlap between regional classifications and development level classifications (see Annex A).

Current inequities in health

Box 1.1

Infant mortality inequity curve

In the figure below, country data on population and infant mortality rates (IMRs) have been plotted as a cumulative distribution of world population. Countries have been ranked according to their IMR for 1970, 1995 and 2020. As can be seen, the gap between the two extremes — populations with the lowest IMRs and populations with the highest IMRs — is decreasing. In 1970, 20% of the global population lived with an IMR below 26 per 1000. At the opposite extreme, 20% of the global population had an IMR of more than 132 per 1000 (inequity ratio = 5.1). In 1995 the gap narrowed to below 19 and above 72 for the two extremes (ratio = 3.8). A more vertical curve, as in the estimate for 2020, shows further reduced global inequality; for this date the two extremes are 12 and 39 (ratio = 3.3). These "optimistic" projections assume that environment and living conditions will improve considerably in developing countries.

In 1970, only 30% of the world's population lived with an IMR below 50 per 1000 (which is a WHO Health-for-All target;). This improved to just above 60% in 1995. It is expected to exceed 90% by 2020.

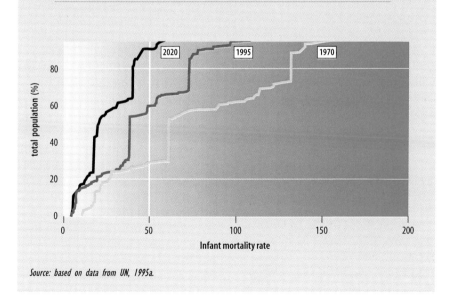

Source: based on data from UN, 1995a.

between four country categories are reflected in the differences in survival shown in **Fig. 1.2.** A child born in 1992 in a country in sub-Saharan Africa (which mainly comprises least developed countries) has a 25% risk of dying before age 15 and a 50% risk of dying before age 60, whereas in the established market economies (all of which are developed countries), the risks are 2% and 10% respectively. The survival curves for children born in Latin America and the Caribbean (representing other typical developing countries) and children born in the former socialist economies of Europe (representing typical economies in transition) are in an intermediate position (**Fig. 1.2**).

Inequity between countries is mirrored by inequity within countries. Because income level and social status are important health determinants, higher-income groups enjoy longer lives and better health than lower-income groups. Inequity within coun-

Table 1.1

Infant mortality, child mortality, water supply and sanitation coverage, and GNP per capita in six countries

Country	Infant mortality rate* (0–1 years) (per 1000)	Child mortality* (0–5 years, cumulative) (per 1000)	Access to safe water** (% of population)	Access to adequate sanitation** (% of population)	GNP per capita*** (US$)
Sweden	5	6	100	100	24 740
Chile	15	17	96	71	3 170
Philippines	39	48	84	75	850
Ghana	77	113	56	42	430
Guinea-Bissau	135	207	57	20	240
Afghanistan	159	251	10	8	(<200)+

+ estimate, data not available   *1995   **1994   ***1993

Source: compiled from data in WHO, 1996a.

Fig. 1.2

Survival curves for countries of four economic categories

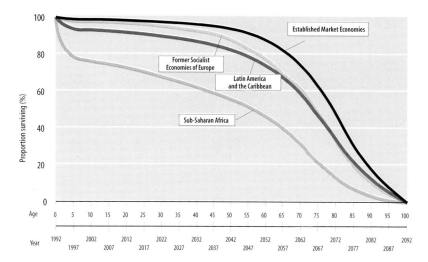

These curves were calculated on the basis of 1990 mortality rates. Projections to 2092 do not take into account future changes in mortality rates. Important differences in survival (or in its inverse form, mortality) for people from the four country categories can be seen.

Source: calculated from data in Murray & Lopez, 1996a.

(Satterthwaite et al., 1996; UNICEF, 1997).

The curves in **Fig 1.2** show the time-scale within which today's children will grow up. Children born during the year of the Earth Summit will be 28 years old in 2020 and 58 years old in 2050. So the lives of these children and their future health and welfare will be determined by social, economic and environmental conditions that lie far beyond the reach of current forecasting. Nevertheless, the environment of today will determine the health situation of tomorrow.

Answering the question "How are we doing?" is therefore not simple. A mixed message will come across in the following chapters. Global average life expectancy is increasing and some developing countries are achieving improvements in basic environmental and health conditions, supported by economic growth and development policies that protect health and the environment. But some of the least developed countries are lagging further and further behind with respect to the health status of their citizens, environmental quality and economic development. At the same time, pollution and unsustainable consumption of natural resources are pushing the global ecosystem to its limits. If it continues unabated this trend will lead to major impacts on health in developed and developing countries alike. Vigorous and sustained actions at local, national and international level must be undertaken to create a healthy environment for all.

1.2. Five years since the Earth Summit

The Earth Summit held in Rio de Janeiro, Brazil, in June 1992 heralded a new approach to national and international development, and environment planning. By adopting the principles of the *Rio Declaration* and *Agenda* 21 (UN, 1993) as the route to sustain-

tries is also seen in terms of gender, geographic area, race/ethnicity and age group and, in many instances, is worsening. Women are often especially disadvantaged and suffer an additional health burden due to discrimination, lack of opportunity and the often associated poverty (see Section 2.4). Children represent another vulnerable group, as pointed out in recent reports able development in the 21st Century, the world's leaders recognized the importance of investing in improvements to people's health and their environment as a prerequisite for sustainable development.

Sustainable development was defined by the Brundtland Commission as "development that meets the needs of the present without compromising the ability of future generations to meet their own needs" (WCED, 1987). It incorporates many elements, and all sectors, including the "health sector", must contribute to achieving it. A whole chapter (Chapter 6) of *Agenda 21* deals with the protection of human health (UN, 1993), and other chapters refer to major health determinants.

But although politicians and national planners have long viewed health-and-environment improvement as a social imperative, arguments often erupt concerning the right balance between allocation of resources for protection of environment and health, and allocation of resources for "lifestyle enhancement". This is despite the fact that scientists have been warning for many years that progress towards any development goal is slowed when populations suffer from ill health and life support-systems are degraded. During preparations for the Earth Summit, this message increased in urgency, since it had become apparent that economic growth was being constrained in many countries by water shortages and land degradation, by an increasing number of environmental health problems caused or aggravated by crowded and squalid conditions in peri-urban settlements, and by increasing amounts of domestic and industrial waste (WHO, 1992a). More recently, awareness has increased of the links between economic growth and environmental protection, and of the need to adopt sustainable development strategies that both preserve the environment and enhance quality of life (Shahi et al., 1997).

Thus during the five years since the Earth Summit, commitment to securing human health and a healthy environment has become widespread, as evidenced by a number of declarations and statements that have emanated from recent international conferences (**Table 1.2**). Moreover, this goal has been acknowledged at the highest political level, as at the G7 meeting of environmental ministers in 1996. And at national level, many countries have formulated or are in the process of formulating sustainable development plans that give increased weight to health-and-environment concerns (see Section 6.3). However, these plans need to be supported and implemented by all sectors contributing to economic development (see Section 1.9) and progress towards sustainable development needs to be monitored. Accordingly, after the Earth Summit, the Commission on Sustainable Development (CSD) was created to monitor and further promote national and international sustainable development activities (see Section 6.2). A five-year follow-up of progress regarding activities proposed in each of the chapters in *Agenda 21* has now been prepared (CSD, 1997a).

Additionally, the *Global environment outlook* report (UNEP, 1997a), which provides detailed analysis of environmental quality, has been produced. It reports progress on several fronts, particularly in the form of national and international awareness, and commitments to environmental protection. However, it notes that "from a global perspective the environment has continued to degrade" (UNEP, 1997a). Similarly, the World Bank (1997a) reports progress in the integration of environmental concerns into all aspects of development investment, but comments that "funding for environmental programmes remains inadequate". Furthermore, it remains to be seen whether the current trend towards "restructuring", "privatization" and "globalization" will be compatible with "sustainability".

It should be noted that meeting human survival needs is a theme of the

> "Human beings are at the centre of concerns for sustainable development. They are entitled to a healthy and productive life in harmony in nature"
> Rio Declaration Principle 1.

Box 1.2

From Stockholm to Rio and beyond

The Rio process had its roots in the 1972 Stockholm Conference, which was the first big UN conference on the environment. In the twenty years between Stockholm and Rio, global environmental threats and the link between environment and development and human well-being were recognized, and the concept of "sustainable development" made a mainstream issue by the Brundtland Commission (WCED, 1987). The international consultation process set in train by Rio continues, as shown in the table below.

To-day, five years after Rio, we are beginning to understand much more clearly just how much is at stake. We understand that sustainability concerns not only environment, but a whole range of social, economic and political factors. We understand that we are all responsible for the long term and that the future of humankind might be at risk if certain trends are not modified. This poses a challenge of overwhelming complexity. Among the components of sustainability, health in particular stands out. Nothing is closer to us than health or illness and no argument in favour of environmental action is stronger than that of the need to eliminate health risks. As we move on in the Rio process, health must be at the centre of concern.

Selected international conferences on health and environment and related issues since 1992

1992	UN Conference on Environment and Development (UNCED), Rio de Janeiro, Brazil
	Tenth Commonwealth Health Ministers Meeting, Nicosia, Cyprus
1994	International Conference on Population and Development, Cairo, Egypt
	Second European Conference on Environment and Health, Helsinki, Finland
	International Conference on Chemical Safety, Stockholm, Sweden
1995	UN World Summit for Social Development, Copenhagen, Denmark
	Fourth World Conference on Women, Beijing, People's Republic of China
	WHO International Conference on Health Consequences of the Chernobyl and other Radiological Accidents, Geneva, Switzerland
	Pan American Conference on Health and Environment in Sustainable Human Development, Washington, USA (PAHO)
	Second Conference on Health, Environment and Development, Beirut, Lebanon (WHO)
1996	UN Conference on Human Settlements (HABITAT II), Istanbul, Turkey
	One Decade after Chernobyl: Summing Up the Radiological Consequences, Vienna, Austria (IAEA/WHO/EU)
	World Food Summit, Rome, Italy

Source: Ambassador Bo Kjellén, Chief Negotiator, Ministry of the Environment, Sweden.

Universal declaration of human rights (UN, 1948). This states that everyone has the right to a standard of living adequate to maintaining the health and well-being of themselves and their family, including food, clothing, housing, healthcare and the necessary social services. What is more, recent international conferences (**Box 1.2**) have referred to the right of the poor and disadvantaged to receive increased priority with respect to health protection, as does the WHO *Health-for-All* policy (see Section 6.6).

All these developments at the national and international political level have promoted a new perspective on "health". Health is now a concern for almost every sector in society and not just the "health sector". Thus it is understood that appropriate developments must occur in agriculture, industry and energy if sustainable health improvements are to be attained. At the same time, though, the health sector has an important role as advocate and guide for healthy development.

1.3 Environmental threats to human health

Literally, the word "environment" refers to whatever surrounds an object or some other entity. Humans experience the environment in which they live as an assemblage of physical, chemical, biological, social, cultural and economic conditions which differ according to local geography, infrastructure, season, time of day and activity undertaken. In this book, however, we focus on the impacts of environmental conditions on health, and on the social and economic conditions that act as "driving forces" and put "pressures" on the environment. We therefore discuss other threats to health such as smoking and poor diet in brief only. This accords with the way in which environment is considered in *Agenda* 21 (UN, 1993).

The different environmental threats can be divided into "traditional hazards" associated with lack of development, and "modern hazards" associated with unsustainable development (WHO, 1992a). The changing pattern of environmental health hazards and associated health risks — moving from "traditional" to "modern" with time and economic development — has been called the "risk transition" (**Box 1.3**).

One of the differences between traditional and modern environmental health hazards is that the former are often rather quickly expressed as disease. For example, a villager drinks polluted water today and tomorrow has severe diarrhoea. Diarrhoeal incidence can accordingly be a relatively useful measure of the relevant risk and of our efforts to control it. For many modern environmental health hazards, however, a long period of time may pass before the health effect manifests itself. A cancer-causing chemical released into the environment today may not reach a person until it has passed through the food-chain for months or years, for instance, and even then may not cause development of a noticeable tumour for decades. Similarly, environmental change occurring over several decades, such as stratospheric ozone depletion due to chlorofluorocarbon emissions (see Section 4.9), may undermine Earth's life support-systems. So for modern environmental health hazards, understanding the environmental pathways through which the hazards move is particularly important.

"Traditional hazards" related to poverty and "insufficient" development include:

* lack of access to safe drinking-water
* inadequate basic sanitation in the household and the community
* food contamination with pathogens
* indoor air pollution from cooking and heating using coal or biomass fuel

* inadequate solid waste disposal
* occupational injury hazards in agriculture and cottage industries
* natural disasters, including floods, droughts and earthquakes
* disease vectors, mainly insects and rodents.

"Modern hazards" are related to rapid "development" that lacks health-and-environment safeguards, and to unsustainable consumption of natural resources. They include:

* water pollution from populated areas, industry and intensive agriculture
* urban air pollution from motor cars, coal power stations and industry
* solid and hazardous waste accumulation
* chemical and radiation hazards following introduction of industrial and agricultural technologies
* emerging and re-emerging infectious disease hazards
* deforestation, land degradation and other major ecological change at local and regional levels
* climate change, stratospheric ozone depletion and transboundary pollution.

1.4 A health-and-environment cause–effect framework

The relationship between human health and the environment is evidently highly complex. Each of the traditional and modern hazards is associated with a variety of aspects of economic and social development. Moreover, there is no single best way of organizing and viewing the development–environment–health relationship that reveals all the important interactions and possible entry points for public health interventions. So as with a physician taking X-rays from various angles, we must examine the complex relationship between health, environ-

Table 1.2

Key elements of declarations and statements of particular relevance to human health

Rio Declaration, Principle 1: *"Human beings are at the centre of concerns for sustainable development. They are entitled to a healthy and productive life in harmony with nature."*

UNCED
Rio de Janeiro, Brazil, 1992

"All countries should give priority to measures that improve the quality of life and health by ensuring a safe and sanitary living environment for all population groups through measures aimed at avoiding crowded housing conditions, reducing air pollution, ensuring access to clean water and sanitation, improving waste management, and increasing the safety of the workplace."

International Conference on Population and Development
Cairo, Egypt, 1994

"In addressing inequalities in health status and unequal access to health-care services between women and men, governments and other actors should promote an active and visible policy of mainstreaming a gender perspective in all policies and programmes, so that...an analysis is made of the effects for women and men respectively."

Fourth World Conference on Women
Beijing, People's Republic of China, 1995

"... to sustain our global environment and improve the quality of living in our human settlements, we commit ourselves to sustainable patterns of production, consumption, transportation and settlements development; pollution prevention; respect for the carrying capacity of ecosystems; and the preservation of opportunities for future generations. In this connection, we shall cooperate in a spirit of global partnership to conserve, protect and restore the health and integrity of the Earth's ecosystem."

United Nations Conference on Human Settlements,
HABITAT II
Istanbul, Turkey, 1996

"... a peaceful, stable and enabling political, social and economic environment is the essential foundation which will enable States to give adequate priority to food security, poverty eradication and sustainable agriculture, fisheries, forestry and rural development."

World Food Summit
Rome, Italy, 1996

"We decided to include this issue (i.e. health and environment) for the first time in our agenda to emphasize that the protection of public health has been and remains a fundamental objective of environmental policies."

G7 meeting of Ministers of Environment
(Canada, France, Germany, Italy, Japan, UK and USA)
Cabourg, France, 1996

Sources: UN, 1993; UN, 1995b; FAO, 1996a; UN, 1996b; UNCHS, 1996a. Chairman's summary of the Meeting of the Ministers of the Environment in Cabourg, France, 9–10 May, 1996;

Box 1.3

The environmental health risk transition

"Traditional" environmental health risks relating to unsafe food and drinking-water, inadequate sanitation, infections from animals and vectors, and poor housing, have a major influence on health when countries are at early stages of development. Industrial development introduces "modern" environmental health risks relating to air pollution, chemical exposures and traffic accidents. The term "risk transition" is used to describe the reduction in "traditional risks" and increase in "modern risks" that take place as economic development progresses. However, when environmental health risks are poorly managed (Fig. A) the "traditional risks" are not eliminated in all parts of society and remain important health threats among the poor and disadvantaged, while the "modern risks" continue unabated. But if environmental health risks are well-managed (Fig. B), the "traditional risks" can be eliminated almost completely and "modern risks" reduced through effective prevention programmes.

Favourable completion of the environmental health risk transition can be threatened by the emergence of new infectious diseases, the occurrence of old diseases in geographic areas in which they had not previously appeared, and the resurgence of old diseases that had once appeared to be under control. In some countries, the revival of traditional health risks of this type is the result of poorly-managed and inequitable development. Associated factors are wide-ranging and include destruction of pristine areas, land-use changes, resource extraction and agricultural exploitation, introduction of new agricultural and animal husbandry methods, increasing spread of drug-resistant pathogens and pesticide-resistance in vectors, increased mobility of people and foodstuffs, and changing lifestyles and eating habits.

Managing the risk transition also involves preventing or minimizing modern environmental health risks. These can arise from the very modernization activities that help lower traditional risks.

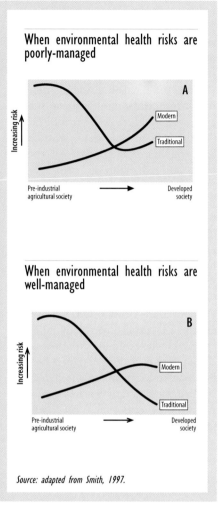

When environmental health risks are poorly-managed

When environmental health risks are well-managed

Source: adapted from Smith, 1997.

ment and development from several perspectives, to try to understand what is happening and what can best be done about it. We have chosen to relate our analysis to a "health-and-environment cause–effect framework" (**Fig. 1.3**) inspired by work on "sustainable development indicators" by OECD (1993a) and CSD (UN, 1996a). The terminology used has been adapted for analysis of health-and-environment cause–effect relationships (Briggs, Corvalán & Nurminen, 1996).

The framework in **Fig. 1.3** explicitly recognizes that although exposure to a pollutant or other environmentally mediated health hazard may be the immediate cause of ill-health, the "driving forces" and "pressures" leading to environmental degradation may be the most effective points for controlling the hazard. The "net" of connections within the framework can be used to identify cause–effect "pathways" or "trees", depending on whether the framework is used to analyse the multiple causes of a single health effect (**Fig. 1.4**), or to analyse the multiple health effects of a single driving force (**Fig. 1.5**). In some cases, a single cause–effect pathway may be identified in order to focus on a particular issue (e.g. nuclear power safety and radiation health effects), but if so, important factors that could be modified to control or eliminate the threat, may be ignored.

More generally, *driving forces* create the conditions in which environmental health hazards can develop or be averted, or that are generated by large numbers of people in their pursuit of the basics of life in terms of food and shelter, or in their appropriation and use of consumer goods. Driving forces include policies that determine trends in economic development, technological development, consumption patterns and population growth (see Chapter 2).

The driving forces therefore impose different kinds of *pressure* on the environment, in such forms as waste from human settlements, depletion of natural resources, and emission of pollutants due to mineral extraction, energy production, manufacturing, transport, agriculture and forestry. These pressures can lead to changes in the *state* of the environment, as seen when land use is changed (deforestation or drainage problems, for instance), or when discharges of toxic chemicals or other forms of waste increase concentrations of chemicals in air, soil, water or plants. The pressures are potentially associated with all stages in the life cycle of industrial products, from initial resource extraction, through transportation of raw materials, processing and distribution, to final consumption and disposal (see Chapter 3).

Whether a resultant altered state of the environment has an impact on human health depends on many factors, including the degree to which humans are actually "exposed". For exposure to occur, people must be present both at the place and at the time when the state of the environment changed and became hazardous. Exposure thus refers to the interaction between people and environmental hazards. Levels of exposure may range from harmless and acceptable to dangerous and unacceptable. The term "dose" is used to quantify the exposure as the amount of hazard actually absorbed by the body. Given known exposures and the knowledge of dose–response relationships, estimates can be made of the health risk of specific hazards, to the extent that current knowledge allows (see Chapter 4). But while "hazard" describes the potential

for causing harm to human health, it says nothing about the statistical probability that such harm will occur. "Risk" is therefore calculated to assign a quantitative value to the probability of damage associated with exposure.

Environmental hazards can lead to a wide range of health *effects*. These may vary in type, intensity and magnitude depending upon the type of hazard to which people have been exposed, the level of exposure, and the number of people affected. Most important diseases are associated with more than one type of exposure, and environmental hazards interact with genetic factors, nutrition, lifestyle hazards and other factors in causing disease (see Chapter 5). The framework (**Fig. 1.3**) is intended to highlight the important links between different aspects of development, environment and health, and to help identify effective strategies and

Fig. 1.3

Health and environment cause–effect framework

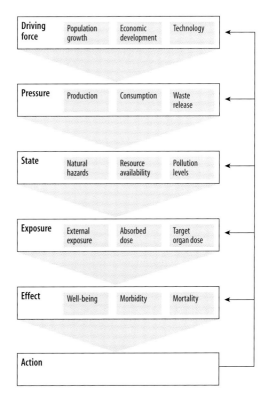

This diagram is a simplified abstraction of the complex cause–effect relationships operating between driving forces, environmental pressures, environmental states, human exposures, health effects, and actions aimed at minimizing these effects. The various boxes provide examples of factors acting at each level. Arrows mark the potential connections that exist between various causes and effects in environmental health.

Sources: modified after Kjellström & Corvalán, 1995 and Briggs, Corvalán & Nurminen, 1996.

Fig. 1.4

Health and environment cause–effect framework for ARI in children

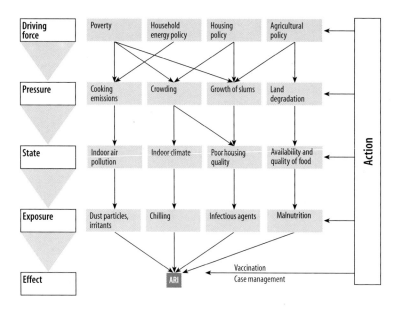

This framework, based on the model given in Fig. 1.3, provides examples of major cause–effect relationships affecting one specific group of diseases: namely, acute respiratory infections (ARI). Additional linkages could take the form of education policy and the literacy rates of mothers, both of which could increase early detection and treatment of ARI in children.

Fig. 1.5

Health and environment cause-and-effect framework for transport policy

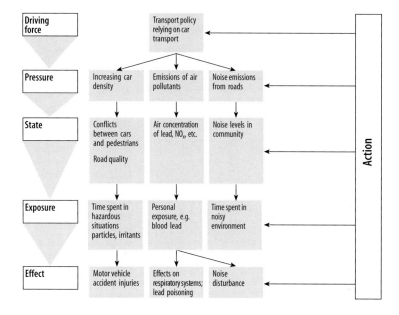

Based on the model given in Fig. 1.3, this framework highlights the major cause–effect linkages between one driving force, transport policy, and the various health outcomes that can be linked to it. Other linkages might include road encroachment on green areas and pedestrian space, and its contribution to injuries or stress.

actions (see Chapter 6) to control and prevent adverse health effects.

1.5 Relevant information for decision-making and action

Information on the health impacts attributable to environmental conditions at local and national level is needed urgently so that the implications of environmental health decisions can be assessed, the potential effects of different decisions and choices compared, and irreversible and costly health and environmental damage prevented (Briggs, Corvalán & Nurminen, 1996). The term "indicator" has been used in the identification of the types of information used for decision-making. *Agenda* 21 (UN, 1993) called for the development of "sustainable development indicators" (SDI), and a number of international agencies have collaborated with CSD to prepare a list of 130 SDIs with accompanying methodological descriptions (UN, 1996a). This list contains 12 indicators constructed on the basis of the *Agenda* 21 chapter on health, and many of the others are of direct relevance to health and environment. Environmental health indicators, from which local and national agencies can select those most relevant for their priority health-and-environment issues are also being developed (WHO, 1997a). These indicators can be applied to the different levels of the health-and-environment cause–effect framework; examples for a common hazard are given in **Table 1.3**.

Relevant information is also needed at the global level for environmental health policy development and priority setting. During the past 20 years, a number of international organizations and "think tanks" have developed annual reports containing comparative tables of international statistics related to a widening range of parameters of critical importance to health, environment and development, including population, health status, resource exploitation, trade, morbidity and mortality, personal income and wealth, aid and loan flows, government expenditures, unemployment, energy and food consumption, education and fertility (**Table 1.4**). Since 1995 WHO has also published such a report in the form of the annual report of the Director General: the *World health report* (*WHR*) (WHO, 1995a; 1996a; 1997a).

These reports commonly contain data aggregated at national and regional levels, but in recent years they have also contained information about the distribution of some factors, such as income, within nations. Frequently, data are available for at least 100 nations, sometimes for more than 150. The *WHR*, for example, lists much of its information for the more than 190 WHO Member States. A number of reports focusing on different regions of the world are also available (see, for example, PAHO, 1994; WHO, 1995p).

Obviously, the accuracy of local-level data collection affects the quality

of national, regional and global data. In many countries, more and better quality health-and-environment data are sorely needed. Furthermore, the aggregated data are often rough estimates. This explains why different reports may present different numbers, for instance, for the annual global number of people who die from malaria (see Section 5.1). In this book we therefore refer to a variety of information sources to help highlight health–environment–development linkages and trends, and to minimize bias. Every effort has been made to use as accurate estimates as possible of environmental conditions and health status.

Yet information is only a tool, which needs to be applied constructively for appropriate action. In a recent statement, the President of the UN General Assembly, Mr Razali Ismail, pointed out that, "We are all overloaded with facts, findings and figures", and pleaded for a "move from continuous strategizing and consensus-building

Table 1.3

Information for decision-making: microbiological water contamination

	Descriptive indicator	Action indicator
Driving force	Level of poverty in the community	Amount of money spent on water and sanitation improvements
Pressure	Percent of households without safe drinking-water supply	Number of unserved households provided with clean water supply each year
State	Coliforms in water	Extent of water quality surveillance and water treatment
Exposure	Percentage of population at risk	Extent of public education programmes
Effect	Morbidity and mortality from diarrhoeal diseases	Number of cases treated in hospitals and clinics

Action

Source: adapted from Briggs, Corvalán & Nurminen, 1996.

into a fully operational and action oriented phase" (Razali, 1997).

1.6 Finding solutions to environmental health problems

The previous sections have described the framework we use in this book to clarify the steps leading to the health impacts of environmental hazards. An understanding of these steps is necessary if solutions to environmental hazards are to be found and appropriate action taken. Action can be taken at each step in the framework (**Fig. 1.3**) as exemplified in **Table 1.3**. In the short term, interventions are often corrective or remedial at the level of the health effect; for example, treatment of individuals affected. In the longer term, they should be protective or preventive (for example, to prevent people from being exposed). Preventive interventions may be imple-

mented to reduce or control the hazards at the source (for example, by limiting emissions or installing flood-control systems). The most effective long-term interventions aim to eliminate or reduce the effects of driving forces, or the environmental pressures that produce the hazards (**Fig. 1.3**).

The different levels of intervention are illustrated in **Fig. 1.4**, which is based on acute respiratory infections (ARI) in children. ARI is a major cause of death in children under five in most countries (see Section 5.2). As can be seen in **Fig. 1.4**, several steps in the health-and-environment cause-and-effect framework contribute simultaneously to ARI occurrence. When quantified, this multiple-causation framework can be a powerful guide to designing cost-effective and timely interventions. It also provides a means for starting to examine possible synergies among interventions. For example, healthy child programmes that focus on dietary supplements, household ventilation and sanitation, case management, and vaccination, using the same local health team, can be a beneficial and cost-effective way of addressing ARI mortality in remote rural areas. Depending on the risk factors and ameliorative conditions at play, the same health programme could be expected also to contribute to reducing the mortality rates of several other childhood diseases, such as measles and diarrhoea. Such a framework can further be used to weigh alternatives, and to design step-by-step programmes for dealing with a particular health problem. For example, environmental improvements, incorporating air pollution control, housing improvement and nutrition programmes, might be the most effective means of controlling ARI mortality. However, they would take a relatively long time to implement, and even longer before they produced results. Alternatively, expanded vaccination programmes and improved case management could bring the problem under control more quickly. Environmental interventions would be essential,

Table 1.4

Examples of regularly published global reports containing detailed health and/or environment information

Report title	Organization	Most recent
Global environment outlook	UNEP, Nairobi	UNEP, 1997a
Human development report	UNDP, New York	UNDP, 1996
State of the world's children	UNICEF, New York	UNICEF, 1997
United Nations statistical yearbook	UN, New York	UN, 1995c
Vital signs	Worldwatch Institute Washington	Brown et al., 1996a
State of the world	Worldwatch Institute Washington	Brown et al., 1997
State of world rural poverty	IFAD, Rome	Jazairy, Alamgir & Panuccio, 1992
World development report	World Bank, Washington	World Bank, 1993*
World health report	WHO, Geneva	WHO, 1997a
World health statistics annual	WHO, Geneva	WHO, 1996b
World resources report	World Resources Institute Washington	WRI, 1996

* focusing on health

though, if a long-lasting reduction in the incidence of ARI were to be sought.

Clearly, sustainable development policies should incline us towards longer-term, broad-spectrum interventions, touching upon the driving forces operating in human society. In many developing countries this would mean tackling inequity, poverty and population growth, thereby contributing to, for example, the control of land degradation and deforestation, biodiversity loss, soil erosion, food insecurity, and decline in water quality. In developed countries, inequity also needs tackling, as evidenced by the fact that sizeable population groups live in squalor and relative poverty. Emphasis should also be placed on reducing unsustainable consumption, curbing use of non-renewable fuels and reducing generation of solid wastes to minimize transboundary pollution, toxic waste problems and global environmental change. To implement such proactive, preventive approaches successfully, development policies and planning need a long time horizon, and with health-and-environment concerns forming an integral part of the associated planning (see Section 6.3).

1.7 Supportive environments for health

Much is said in this book about the ways in which the environment, when mismanaged, can damage health. However, the environment can also be "supportive" of health, exerting a positive influence in much the same way as a healthy diet. A supportive environment for health is free from major health hazards, satisfies the basic needs of healthy living, and facilitates equitable social interaction. This concept was originally developed at the Third International Conference on Health Promotion (held in Sundsvall, Sweden in 1991) in relation to health promotion programmes. Some examples of supportive environments for health are given in **Box 1.4**.

In a health context the term "supportive environment" refers to every aspect of our surroundings (or the "setting"). It encompasses where people live, their local community, their home, and where they work and play. In accordance with this "settings" approach, programmes have been developed in a number of countries to promote Healthy Cities, Healthy Villages, Healthy Islands, Healthy Workplaces, Healthy Marketplaces, Healthy Schools, Healthy Hospitals and Healthy Kitchens (see Section 6.4).

Action to create supportive environments has many dimensions — physical, social, spiritual, economic and political — and depends upon the participation of every member of the community. It was discussed widely during the preparations for the Earth Summit in 1992, but as "primary environmental care" (Pretty & Guijt, 1992; Satterthwaite, 1996).

1.8 Power and participation for both men and women

Agenda 21 points out that sustainable development can be achieved only if the whole community is adequately represented and participates in decision-making (UN, 1993). Additionally, responsibility for preventive health-and-environment actions must rest with communities themselves, otherwise such actions may be abandoned or undermined. Representation of women is particularly important since they have key roles in all societies with respect to basic living conditions, such as housing conditions, sanitation and provision of safe drinking-water, each of which impacts on the environment.

In spite of the widespread movement towards democratization in most countries, however, women remain largely underrepresented at most levels of government, especially in ministerial and other executive bodies. They also continue to be prevented from attaining political power in legislative bodies. Globally, only 10% of the members of legislative bodies and a lower percentage of ministerial positions are held by women. In some countries, including those undergoing fundamental political, economic and social changes, significant decreases have actually been observed in the number of women holding legislative positions (UN, 1996b).

More women in politics and decision-making positions would help to redefine political priorities, place new items on the political agenda that reflect and address women's gender-specific concerns, values and experiences, and provide new perspectives on mainstream political issues (see Section 2.4). As pointed out in the report from the Fourth World Conference on Women, held in Beijing in 1995, a precautionary approach to environmental hazards should include improved analysis of women's concerns about environment and health, and follow-up action (UN, 1996b).

1.9 Intersectoral actions for a healthy environment

Given that promotion and maintenance of environmental health requires input from a wide range of sectors, an intersectoral approach is the most effective means of formulating environmental health policy (WHO 1997e). An intersectoral approach helps ensure that priorities are coherent and do not conflict with those of individual sectors.

The word "sector" is based on the notion of a division of government responsibilities with no overlap, in much the same way that a pie is cut into sector-shaped slices. The new perspective on health developed at the Earth Summit demonstrates that health can only be achieved with input from each sector. Intersectoral action thus means that each sector and each Ministry contributes to health development in a conscious and coordinated manner (**Box 1.5**).

Ministers of health and environment have key roles to play in such intersectoral activity. However, just as health-and-environment investments have been undervalued, so too have the ministries or departments responsible for them. Environment and health departments often suffer from low budgets and little influence over

---

Box 1.4

Examples of supportive environments for health

LOCAL COMMUNITY IN CHILE IDENTIFIES AND SOLVES ENVIRONMENTAL HEALTH PROBLEMS
In Conchali, a poor part of Santiago in Chile, health workers developed a community programme to improve local environmental health. This first involved requesting the community to identify what it considered to be its major environmental health problems. The leaders of eight local communities, the authorities, local people and health workers then collaborated to draw up a list of priority issues and a timeframe for solving them. During the programme's first year the local transportation system was reorganized; in its second year a local police station was established and youth and women's organizations created. Before the end of the programme's fifth year, domestic drinking-water supplies had been installed. The main lesson learned was that involving a community in identifying and prioritizing its environmental health problems stimulates community efforts to solve those problems.

HARNESSING LOCAL SKILLS TO TACKLE HOUSING AND ENVIRONMENTAL PROBLEMS IN SCOTLAND
In the city of Glasgow, Scotland, lack of investment in council housing and high unemployment are serious problems. Glasgow City Council and a nongovernmental organization (NGO) formed a voluntary organization called Heatwise. Heatwise employed local people to develop local energy conservation projects. It was later expanded to create another organization, Landwise, which used similar methods to tackle local environmental problems. Training modules were prepared with colleges of education to train local unemployed people, who implemented local community land improvement projects. Funding was obtained from the EEC social fund, the private sector and local government.

SQUATTERS IN SOUTH AFRICA SET UP COOPERATIVE TO BUILD HOMES
In a squatter area in South Africa activists from different professional sectors arranged a series of community meetings to identify and pool local human resources for construction of homes and roads. In coming together, participants — who included electricians, plumbers, builders and draughtsmen — discovered that they had many skills. A building cooperative was established with financial support from NGOs. Community empowerment was the basic strategy, with community-based resource persons as key actors. Professionals were used on "tap" (i.e. when needed), rather than being assigned authority, and came from within the community. Major achievements were a shift from dependency to independence, from individualism to empowerment, and a strengthening of cooperative spirit and local resources.

Source: adapted from Haglund et al., 1992.

economic development decisions. These problems have been compounded by division of responsibility, with health-and-environment issues split between separate ministries that have frequently done little to coordinate their activities in this area. Admittedly, the recent development of joint national plans between ministries of health and environment in certain countries and regions (see Section 6.3) is an important step forward. But much more could be achieved at national level if ministries for finance, housing, transport, energy, agriculture and industry worked closely with health and environment ministries. Joint programmes could focus on, for example, housing that provides better shelter, land planning that ensures that people are not exposed to pollution, food production that aims at good local nutrition, and workplace improvements that promote health and safety.

International agencies can also contribute to intersectoral action through collaborative assessments and policy development (see Chapter 6). Good examples in the environmental health field include the Water Supply and Sanitation Collaborative Council (WSSCC, 1996), the Inter-Organization Programme for the Sound Management of Chemicals (IOMC, 1996) and the interagency collaborative assessment of the health impacts of climate change for the Intergovernmental Panel on Climate Change (IPCC, 1996; McMichael et al., 1996). However, numerous examples exist of narrow sectoral approaches. International agencies should combat these by ensuring that their "sectoral" partners at national level are aware of the need for intersectoral collaboration.

At local and regional levels, collaboration between planners and health authorities could prevent many of the health problems, including overcrowding, the spread of communicable diseases and unacceptable pollution levels, that afflict communities in the developing world. Application of the intersec-

toral Healthy City concept (see Section 6.4) has become one of the best known and most successful examples of intersectoral collaboration (WHO, 1997e). In rural districts, closer links between, for example, school health services and health staff are ensuring that "health-promoting" schools are developed, providing children with a safer environment, adequate food and effective health education.

Intersectoral collaboration has also been one of the guiding principles of the WHO *Health-for-All* policy. Indeed, opportunities for and advantages of such collaboration are numerous and have been long identified (WHO, 1986a), particularly in the areas of nutrition, education and environment. The Earth Summit gave further support to the principle of intersectoral collaboration for health by concluding that "human beings are at the centre of concerns for sustainable development" (UN, 1993).

The health-and-environment cause-effect framework (**Fig. 1.3**) highlights the role of different sectors in dealing with driving forces, pressures on the environment and improving the state of the environment. The following chapters show that policies and actions in almost any non-health sector can have implications for environmental health.

> **Box 1.5**
>
> ### Partnership for poverty alleviation in Cebu City, the Philippines
>
> The city of Cebu in the Philippines initiated major changes in city governance to work with and provide services to urban poor communities. It established an enabling partnership between several "sectoral" departments in the city government, nongovernmental organizations and the private sector in 1988. The partnership enabled the government to address several needs of local poor urban communities, including: improvements in health, education and social services, expanded training programmes and extension of credit to the informal sector and urban poor groups. Additionally, employment and apprenticeships (in collaboration with the private sector), land tenure and security were improved markedly, and special services for street children, single mothers and the disabled developed.
>
> *Sources: UN, 1995d; WHO, 1997a.*

1.10 Health for All: the way ahead

It is clear that better health is achievable in all communities and countries currently burdened with excessive levels of disease and injury. However, better health is not an automatic outcome of economic growth. It requires guiding policies and an active contribution from government agencies, commercial enterprises and the community to secure the highest possible level of health with the resources available. Protection from environmental health hazards is a key element in such policies.

In particular, the health sector needs to show leadership by translating the preventive health message of *Agenda 21* into practical action for its own institutions and professionals, as well as for those of other sectors. The WHO Health-for-All Policy provides a framework for such action. It is currently being updated and renewed (WHO, 1997b) to enable it to meet the challenges of the 21st Century more effectively, and to light "the way ahead" for health-and-environment actions towards sustainable development.

The Health-for-All Policy and Strategy were developed during the years 1977–1979 (WHO, 1979) and subsequently adopted by all WHO Member States. They are based on primary healthcare, community involvement in healthcare delivery and the application of appropriate technology for health. These key elements remain

---

Box 1.6

Links between health and development in Health-for-All

The renewed Health-for-All policy, currently available in draft (WHO, 1997d), will be finalized at the World Health Assembly in 1998. The draft emphasizes that health is the "foundation on which all human endeavour rests" and that "health is central to development". This is in agreement with the Rio Declaration and *Agenda 21* (UN, 1993).

Health and development are linked by four key elements:

- *COMBATING POVERTY:* the health problems of the poor result from inequitable and insufficient development, and at the same time, impede development.

- *PROMOTING HEALTH IN ALL SETTINGS AND WITHIN ALL SECTORS:* the settings where people live, work, seek healthcare, play, learn, eat and rest, all provide opportunities for promoting health. The policies of all sectors that have direct or indirect effects on health should therefore be aligned to promote and protect health.

- *INCORPORATING HEALTH IN SUSTAINABLE DEVELOPMENT PLANS:* health considerations should receive the highest priority in sustainable development plans. The health sector has a leading responsibility to ensure that the linkages between health and other sectors are clearly identified.

- *GOVERNANCE TO ENSURE THAT HEALTH IS CENTRAL TO DEVELOPMENT:* the state should create an enabling environment in which partnerships for health are encouraged or stimulated. The participation of nongovernmental organizations and community-based informal networks is fundamental to health development. At the international level, a strong alliance of all organizations and institutions working for better health is needed.

Source: WHO (1997b).

corner-stones of the renewed policy, but the link between health and development has been strengthened considerably (**Box 1.6**). Many of the issues raised in this book are also referred to in the draft renewed Health-for-All Policy, which will be presented to the World Health Assembly in 1998 for worldwide adoption (see Section 6.6). The policy highlights the "health-for-all value system" which includes: health security; health as a human right; equity, and gender-sensitivity.

Additionally, it emphasizes the need to incorporate health in environment and sustainable development planning, and to create sustainable health systems (WHO, 1997b). Application of the policy will have important implications for how environment and social development is guided in the future. "Health for All" for the 21st Century requires concerted action on the driving forces behind bad health and good health. Chapter 2 provides a closer look at these driving forces. ❑

Chapter 2
Driving Forces Behind Current Health-and-Environment Trends

Driving Force
Pressure
State
Exposure
Effect
Action

2.1 The driving forces concept

Driving forces create the conditions in which environmental health threats can develop or be averted, as indicated in the health-and-environment cause–effect framework (**Fig 1.3**). These driving forces are often associated simultaneously with a number of health-and-environment issues as highlighted in **Box 2.1**. Government policies and programmes — which will vary according to the prevailing **value system** — change the direction or magnitude of driving forces and can therefore alleviate or exacerbate a broad array of environmental health threats. For example, if equitable sharing of available wealth is a part of this value system, policies will be designed to promote social equity. Similarly, if good health is a priority, resources will be channelled into health protection. The concept of sustainable development has highlighted another possible component of value systems, namely intergenerational equity which stipulates that current generations should not live in such a way that the capacities and resources required by future generations to live a decent life are threatened.

This chapter will briefly review the different driving forces identified in **Box 2.1** and other major factors in development that can be considered as driving forces. The first set of driving forces to be discussed relates to **population.** Essentially, they multiply the environmental impact of human activities — particularly consumption of natural resources and production of waste.

In other words, the more of us there are, the greater our impact on the environment. However, the level of consumption per person is also of fundamental importance since it determines the degree of such impacts.

The second set concerns **urbanization**, which is closely linked to population growth. The tendency to move away from rural areas to live in cities is a response to lack of social development and economic growth in rural areas, population redundancy in agriculture and urban demand for labour, principally in association with economic development. It is also related to growth in services and infrastructures, which tend to be concentrated in urban settings.

Poverty and inequity are further major driving forces, in terms of their influence on the environmental conditions in which people live. Marginalization of minorities and gender inequities, for instance, lead to impoverished living environments for certain groups in society.

Technical and scientific developments are also driving forces in that they may create new health-and-environment hazards, or provide means of eliminating current hazards. These developments also influence **consumption and production patterns** — driving forces that generate large-scale use of energy, water, land and other natural resources. Extraction, transportation, handling, treatment, manufacturing, distribution and disposal of basic,

Box 2.1
Elements of sustainable development

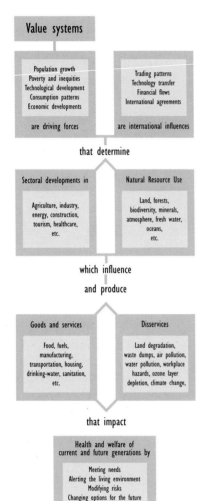

| Value systems |

| Population growth
Poverty and inequities
Technological development
Consumption patterns
Economic developments | Trading patterns
Technology transfer
Financial flows
International agreements |
| are driving forces | are international influences |

that determine

| Sectoral developments in | Natural Resource Use |
| Agriculture, industry,
energy, construction,
tourism, healthcare,
etc. | Land, forests,
biodiversity, minerals,
atmosphere, fresh water,
oceans,
etc. |

which influence
and produce

| Goods and services | Disservices |
| Food, fuels,
manufacturing,
transportation, housing,
drinking-water, sanitation,
etc. | Land degradation,
waste dumps, air pollution,
water pollution, workplace
hazards, ozone layer
depletion, climate change, |

that impact

| Health and welfare of
current and future generations by |
| Meeting needs
Alerting the living environment
Modifying risks
Changing options for the future |

Sustainable development can be described in terms of the elements in this figure, interlinking in a logical manner: the driving forces, intermediate elements and the eventual impact or effect on the health and welfare of current and future generations.

Source: Mr Nitin Desai, Under-Secretary-General for Policy Coordination and Sustainable Development, UN.

intermediate and final consumer products are major elements of resource use, and linked to economic development. Harmful environmental change can occur at any stage of **economic development**, but the latter also creates resources and opportunities for improving the quality of living conditions, which is essential for effective health protection.

2.2 Population dynamics

Population driving forces have three basic components: the total number and geographical distribution of people, age-distribution, and changes to these distributions caused by movement of people.

2.2.1 Population growth and its relation to environment

A complex interrelationship exists between population growth, environment and health. In its simplest form, increased population density leads to intensified human activities that if mismanaged contribute to environmental damage and resource depletion, both of which can have negative direct or indirect effects on human health.

Global population growth currently stands at nearly 90 million per year; which is higher than at any other time in human history. The world's population therefore grew from 5.3 thousand million in 1990, and is expected to reach 6.1 thousand million by the year 2000, and 7.7 thousand million by 2020 (UN, 1995a). Absolute annual increase is expected to peak before the year 2000 and decline thereafter (UNFPA, 1997), since the annual growth rate is declining (1.5% in 1995). Even so, the world's population is expected to have approximately doubled by the middle of the 21st Century. Pressures on the environment can be expected to increase substantially.

Population growth is not evenly distributed, however. A major determi-

nant of growth differentials is the wide variation in population density that exists between countries and regions (**Fig. 2.1**). Some 90% of future population growth will occur in the presently developing countries, many of which have difficulties in channelling adequate investments to the social sector due to current population pressures (UN, 1995a). For instance, fertility levels remain high in sub-Saharan Africa. In 17 countries of this region they are equal to or exceed six births per woman and show little or no sign of decrease (UNFPA, 1997). Given that experience shows that fertility rates are closely associated with infant mortality rates and child health in general (**Box 2.2**), a sustained global decrease in fertility will depend on general health improvements. Variation in population density is also attributable to the wide variation in birth rates and the degree to which these appear to be falling. In a number of countries where fertility was previously very high, it is now estimated to have declined significantly, due to factors such as increased access to education for girls (UNFPA, 1997).

The environmental implications of high population growth remain far-reaching for many low-income countries, particularly in southern Asia and sub-Saharan Africa, where land degradation and deforestation are most severe. Indeed, a strong relationship exists between population growth and poverty. The source of much suffering, ill health and death, poverty can act as an additional pressure on the environment. This is because, possessing few or no resources, poor people may have little choice but to exploit rather than protect their environment. At present, poorer countries are experiencing the fastest rates of population growth and changes in their population structure. Yet they have few or no means with which to manage or adapt to the environmental impacts that ensue.

Fig. 2.1

Current global population density

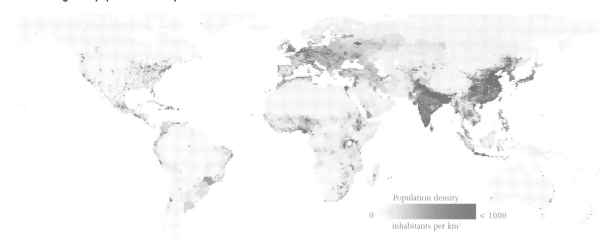

Source: Tobler et al., 1995. Courtesy UNEP/GRID, Geneva, Switzerland.

2.2.2 Population structure and changing health concerns

In many developing countries, high fertility rates coupled with decreasing mortality have created a situation where the "dependency ratio" has increased significantly, i.e. the economically active proportion of the population is relatively small compared to the economically "dependent" proportion of the population (i.e. children and the elderly). In developing countries it was not until the 1970s that the 15–64 age group began to grow at a faster rate than the under-20 group. For the least developed countries this process will not begin to take place until early in the 21st Century (**Fig. 2.2**).

Changes to population structure can be illustrated by "population pyramids", which demonstrate the age and sex composition of a population (**Fig 2.3**). Additionally, their shape indicates the potential health status of the population in question. A wide base with a narrow top, for instance, indicates a population with high mortality, especially among young children, and high fertility.

An ageing population is, of course, a sign of successful public health policy and action. But such success brings with it a different set of disease prevention

Box 2.2

Child mortality and population growth

As shown in the figure below, a clear relationship exists between infant mortality and fertility — those countries with low fertility also have low infant mortality. Indeed, a major drop in fertility always appears to be preceded by a drop in infant mortality. Programmes for reducing infant mortality are most effective in reducing fertility if they include provision of contraceptives and other actions known to reduce fertility (such as improving access to education for women and girls). Many of these actions have additional advantages for development.

Infant mortality rate (per 1000 live births) by — 1995 total fertility rate (per woman)

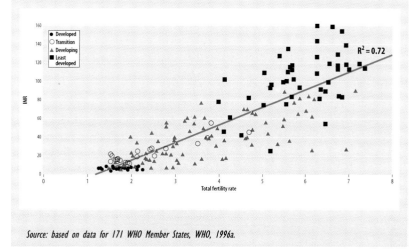

Source: based on data for 171 WHO Member States, WHO, 1996a.

Fig. 2.2

Population growth by age-group for developed, developing and least-developed countries — 1970–2020

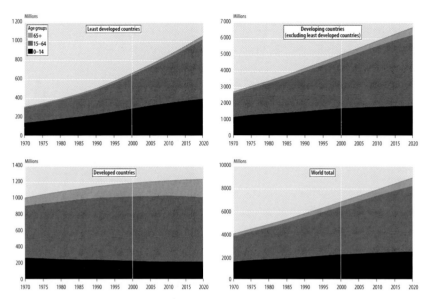

While population growth patterns show marked differences — in accordance with differing levels of economic development — the global pattern of population growth is one of an increasing proportion of adults and a growing number of persons aged 65+. The number of persons aged 65+ is increasing in all regions and particularly for women.

Source: based on data from UN, 1995a.

and healthcare needs due to changes in the relative importance of different environmental exposures. For example, diseases associated with middle and old age, such as cardiovascular diseases, cancer, chronic respiratory diseases, and mental health problems (see Chapter 5), become much more prevalent. The health effects of long-term exposures to environmental hazards will be one of the many components of this disease pattern. At the same time, because of longer individual life expectancy, the quality of housing and the community environment for elderly people becomes more important.

2.2.3 Population movement: increasing numbers

Population mobility has increased greatly due to growing affluence and international economic interdependence, both of which have promoted the development of roads and transportation systems. Large numbers of people can now move themselves from one area to another with relative ease, to the extent that both host and source

population size and structure may change considerably.

But it is important to realize that population movement takes various forms, depending on whether the population in question lives in a more or less permanent home territory. As well as one-way movements of people, two-way migrations also occur. These include the migrations of seasonal workers in economic sectors such as agriculture and forestry, the migrations of nomads, usually within a limited but nevertheless vast area, and the short-term and increasingly long-distance travels of tourists and professionals.

Population movement is seen especially in relation to rural–urban migration and rural–rural migration. Both are often associated with economic entrapment, with unemployment and hunger, which drive populations to seek a better standard of living elsewhere. Rural–urban migration is a major factor in the growth of cities and towns (see Section 2.3).

In recent decades, however, rura–rural migration has been comparable to and sometimes even greater than that from rural to urban areas. In many countries, large populations have moved from poor rural areas to new agricultural frontiers, leading to colonization of areas that previously were virtually uninhabited or only sparsely populated. Examples include the transmigration programme in Indonesia, and the expansion of the agricultural frontier in the Amazonian regions of several South American countries. Such migrations can have a strong impact on the quality of the environment (see Section 3.4) and on the sustainability of development in the host area.

Population movement also occurs as a result of warfare and environmental degradation. Warfare may displace populations by rendering territories uninhabitable, for instance, by the laying of mines (see Section 5.6). Warfare may also bring with it fear of persecution, causing populations to flee. According to most sources, at least 35 internal wars are currently taking place around the world (UNHCR, 1995) and are contributing to the rapid increase in the number of refugees (**Fig. 2.4**). The ebb and flow of considerable numbers of people displaced by conflict increases pressure on the resource bases of the receiving country or area. Land may become irretrievably damaged from overuse, as is becoming the case in some areas of African countries which have absorbed significant refugee populations (UNHCR, 1995). The displaced are therefore both victims and agents of population and environmental pressures. In extreme circumstances, human life is at risk. Refugees who often do not have access to clean and adequate fuel and water are particularly vulnerable to malnutrition and disease. In 1994, for example, the town of Goma in Zaire was strewn with the corpses of Rwandan refugees who had succumbed to such conditions (UNHCR, 1995).

The term "refugee" is also used to describe populations fleeing environmental disaster areas or destitution. "Environmental refugee", "ecological refugee" and "ecorefugee" are now commonly used epithets, although they are not recognized officially. Environmental refugees have been defined as "people who have been forced to leave their traditional habitat, temporarily or permanently, because of a marked environmental disruption — either natural or human-induced — that jeopardized their existence and/or seriously affected their quality of life" (El-Hinnawi, 1985). Such environmental disruption often involves several factors such as soil erosion, deforestation, desertification and water shortage.

2.3 Urbanization

Cities generate a large part of a nation's economic activity, offer employment opportunities, and provide entertainment and other amenities. They also create potential efficiencies not found elsewhere, as

well as advantages in the delivery of education, health and other social services. But whether concentrated in high-rise apartment buildings, or spread over large shantytown or suburban areas, their environmental impacts are considerable. In addition to instigating major land use changes for housing, roads and industry, cities consume large quantities of a nation's natural resources. Moreover, given their concentration of people and activities, and their greater levels of consumption, they produce considerable waste and pollution. And as they grow, they increasingly rely on food and other resources obtained from more distant parts of the country. Urban growth also means greater dependence on transport

Fig. 2.3

Population pyramids by economy and changes in population structure over time — 1970, 1995, 2020

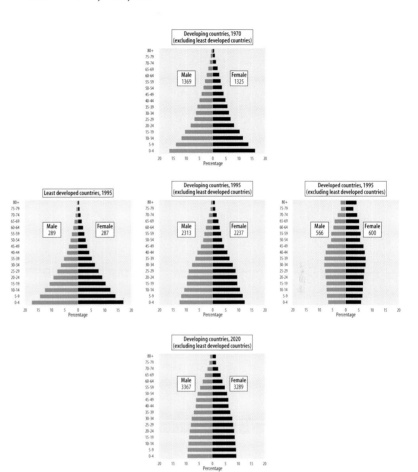

The changing mortality pattern of developing countries for the period 1975–1995 and as projected to 2020 is depicted graphically in three of the above pyramids. Note how the shape of the pyramid for developing countries for 1970 is similar to that of the least developed countries for 1995, and how projected distribution for developing countries in 2020 in turn approximates that of the more developed countries in 1995. Population size is given in millions.

Source: based on data from UN, 1995a.

Fig. 2.4

Refugees and other persons of concern to UNHCR by region — 1985, 1990, 1995

1985

Asia 5.1
Europe 0.7
Latin America 0.4
North America 1.4
Oceania 0.1
Africa 3.0

Total **10.7 million**

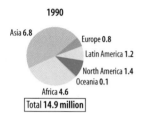

1990

Asia 6.8
Europe 0.8
Latin America 1.2
North America 1.4
Oceania 0.1
Africa 4.6

Total **14.9 million**

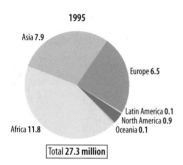

1995

Asia 7.9
Europe 6.5
Latin America 0.1
North America 0.9
Oceania 0.1
Africa 11.8

Total **27.3 million**

Source: UNHCR, 1995.

systems, generating further pollution and risk of accidents. The resultant public health challenges are daunting, but with appropriate policies and action programmes, health in cities can be improved (see Section 6.4).

2.3.1 Urban growth: scale and pace

Worldwide, cities are growing fast. In fact, the scale and pace of current urbanization are unlike that of any previous period in history; at present nearly half of humanity lives in urban areas. This urban proportion will continue to grow (UNCHS, 1996b), with most of the growth occurring in developing countries. But although the low-income countries generally are experiencing the fastest urban growth rates, the level of urbanization (or the proportion of the population that is urban) and the rate of growth are far from uniform (**Fig 2.5**). Thus the African and Asian regions have the lowest levels urbanization levels but are experiencing the most explosive urban growth rates.

Comparisons are often made with European countries, at the time of the Industrial Revolution in the 18th Century, when cities underwent very rapid growth. The scale of current urban growth in developing countries is actually greater, though, if we take into account the size of their cities, the numbers of people involved, and the number of cities that are growing. Since definitions of "urban" vary greatly, however (**Box 2.3**), statistical estimates of urban growth and the size of urban populations should be examined carefully.

Yet although most urban growth is now taking place in small- and medium-sized cities, the term "megacity", defined by the UN as a city with a population exceeding 8 million, is a commonly used index of urban growth. In 1970, 11 megacities existed, 5 of them in developing countries. By 1995, 22 megacities existed, 16 of them in developing countries (UN, 1995e) (**Fig 2.1**). But while the population growth in certain megacities is relentless,

megacities in 1996 actually incorporated less than 4% of the population of developing countries, and less than 5% of the global population.

High population density and the concentration of industry in most of the world's rapidly growing cities is leading to great pressures on local environments. Air pollution from households, industry, power stations and transportation (motor vehicles) is often a major problem (see Section 4.4). The traffic situation in Bangkok (**Box 2.4**), for example, is illustrative of the air pollution problems that many other cities in developing countries will experience, unless concerted efforts are made to provide alternatives to the motor car for transport. Water pollution and drainage (see Section 4.4), noise, crowding and poor quality housing (see Section 4.7) are other concerns for many large cities.

2.3.2 Growth of urban slums

As much as 30–60% of the urban population in low-income countries is believed to live in poor-quality housing and many case-studies undertaken in larger cities support this estimate (UNCHS, 1996b). In smaller cities the percentages may be less. The wide range reflects the complexity of the housing and health relationship. Indeed, no straightforward definition of what constitutes a "poor quality" or "unhealthy" house exists, although lack of access to piped water or a nearby stand-pipe and lack of sanitary facilities are often used as indicators (see Section 4.7). In view of this complexity, monitoring of unhealthy housing and international comparisons is difficult. Furthermore, recent research makes clear that while deficiencies in the water and sanitation facilities in houses are major factors in unhealthy housing, many others, including defects in buildings and the peri-domestic environment, inadequate drainage, poor refuse storage and collection, unsanitary food storage and preparation, and location of housing near sites of polluting and hazardous industries, or on contaminated land, must also be taken into account (see Section 4.7).

Understandably, the staggering scale and variety of problems associated with urban growth (as detailed in WHO, 1993a) has led many development planners and managers to focus on the strengthening of rural economies so that these can support a higher quality of life and better basic services, thereby reducing incentives for rural–urban migration. (Rossi-Espagnet, Goldstein & Tabidzadeh, 1991).

2.4 Poverty and inequity

As pointed out above, the most severe environmental health problems affect countries and people who lack access to economic and other resources, people who are denied opportunities to improve their lot, and people affected by warfare or other calamities. Inequity is therefore a major driving force in the health-and-environment framework. As long as large-scale inequity remains, the living environment and health status of millions of people will not improve. **Box 2.5** gives several examples of the kinds of inequity that can occur with respect to socioeconomic level, geographic area, gender and race/ethnicity. Inequity in healthcare has also been highlighted by a recent WHO report (WHO, 1996c).

The large differences in economic level, reflecting economic inequity, between the four categories of country referred to in Section 1.1 are clear in **Fig 2.6**. In this figure the height of the bars indicate the actual number of persons in each income group. About 2900 million people live in countries where per capita GNP is less than US$ 600. In contrast, about 800 million live in countries where per capita GNP is greater than US$ 9600 (the highest being Luxembourg where per capita GNP is US$ 37 320).

Poverty as reflected by global income inequity is actually increasing.

In 1970, the richest 20% of humanity had roughly 30 times more income than the poorest 20%. Today, the richest fifth receive more than 60 times as much as the poorest fifth. The wealth of the richest people in the world is stag-

Fig. 2.5

Urbanization levels and urban growth rates by region — 1970–2025

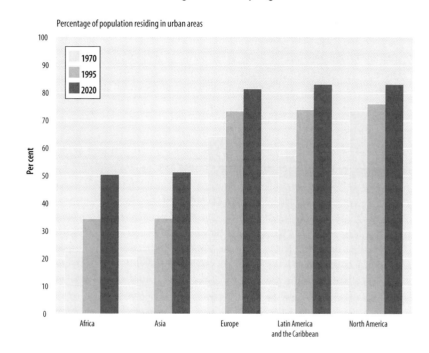

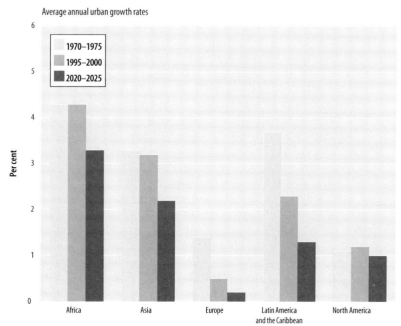

Source: based on data from UN, 1995a.

gering. The net worth of the world's 358 richest people is larger than the combined annual income of the poorest 45% of the world population (2300 million people). (UNDP, 1996).

Box 2.3
Blurred boundaries between urban and rural populations

Despite the treatment of rural populations and urban populations as separate entities, the distinction between them is becoming blurred. For instance, in all developed countries and in many others, a large part of the rural population either works in urban centres, or in what are usually considered as urban occupations (such as manufacturing or service enterprises) in facilities located in rural areas. Furthermore, different countries use very different criteria when defining settlements as urban. Many of them classify settlements with less than 2000 inhabitants as urban centres.

In fact, a country's total urban population can be increased or decreased considerably, simply by changing these criteria. This occurred recently in China, when millions of people, formerly considered as rural inhabitants, were reclassified as urban inhabitants. The population of many of the world's largest cities is therefore probably overestimated, since it includes the population of a large metropolitan region extending far beyond the city's built-up area, and significant numbers of rural inhabitants. The true proportion of the world's population living in urban centres is accordingly best considered not as a precise percentage but as ranging between 40% and 55%, depending on the criteria used to define terms such as urban centre, city or metropolitan area. Additionally, in many areas of the world, large areas are neither urban or rural, but contain a mixture of rural and urban activities and living patterns. This is illustrated by the "Kotadesasi" concept.*

Kotadesasi is a newly-created noun in the Indonesian language which combines the words for "town", "village" and "urbanization". It is used to describe the urbanization of villages, which is leading to widespread increases in peri-urban areas, often linked to an urban centre. Kotadesasi regions are characterized by rapid increases in land uses intermixed within traditional farming areas, and in the variety and concentration of their workplaces. Such development can lead to serious environmental health problems. For example, release of toxic materials from small-scale industrial activities, such as electroplating, directly into wet rice paddies, creates a particularly acute form of water pollution.

Kotadesasi regions are also characterized by high population mobility and intense traffic, increased female participation in the workforce, and uncertain, inconsistent, and incomplete governance by urban authorities. In such environments traditional risks from poor sanitation may linger on while modern risks, such as those from chemicals, are introduced earlier, but subject to less control than elsewhere. This underscores the special need to evaluate interactions between different hazards.

* This concept is reflected in development work and akin to the term "ruralization", which indicates the absorption of a rural area or village by a growing town, with the activities of the rural system continuing undisturbed by urban engulfment.

Source: adapted from Ginsburg et al., 1990.

As well as inter-country differences in economic level and income, significant intra-country social gaps have been observed. Ideally economic development helps create a better physical environment and better health, for example, through the provision of good housing, transportation systems, water supply systems, waste management and other community infrastructure. But it can also cause declines in health status through increased inequality in the distribution of wealth and the creation of poverty among people whose lives are disrupted by unsustainable economic growth (see Section 2.7).

2.4.1 The poverty–environmental degradation link

Between one-fifth and one-quarter of the world's population live in absolute poverty and this proportion is increasing (CSD, 1997b). More than 90% of this group lives in developing countries (UNCHS, 1996b) where a combination of increasing numbers of people, land given over to large-scale agribusiness, and land tenure inequality, is not only inducing population movement, but also tending to concentrate those with least opportunities in environmentally poor areas. Poverty and environmental degradation are therefore becoming more inextricably linked. The world's poorest people are found predominantly in two types of area: remote and ecologically fragile rural areas, and at the margins of expanding urban areas (Leonard, 1989). The precarious conditions of both expose poor populations to health risks from inadequate water and fuel supplies, waterborne diseases, ambient and indoor air pollution, and to natural and technological disasters (CSD, 1997b).

The recent assessment by the Commission on Sustainable Development of the progress in combating poverty since the Earth Summit (CSD, 1997b) concluded that, globally, the situation for the poor is not improving. The least developed countries have been affected by diminishing overseas development assistance and slow economic growth. Urgent investments in urban social services and in rural development have therefore been held back. Countries in transition are also experiencing increases in poverty following harsh economic reforms.

Those living in absolute poverty include a high proportion of women, children, refugees and other displaced persons who lack access to education, employment, healthcare and other basic resources (WHO, 1996a). These groups often interlink and overlap, because the fundamental cause of their condition is the same — lack of power and low status (see Section 2.4.3).

2.4.2 Displaced and impoverished groups

Wars, conflict and environmental disaster result not only in population displacement (see Section 2.2), but also create newly impoverished vulnerable groups since people lose possessions and status following flight. Some of the countries to which populations migrate are very poor and suffer from adverse environmental conditions, which are likely to deteriorate further following an influx of displaced persons. Malawi, for example, is among the twelve poorest countries in the world, yet refugees account for one in nine of its present population (Myers, 1994). In particular, its forested areas have become further degraded due to increased population demands for fuel and other forest resources. Deforestation in Malawi has now reached around 20 000 ha per year and has led to serious soil erosion, flooding and subsidence (UNHCR, 1995).

As to the future, if global warming and climate change occur as predicted, population displacement and ensuing poverty due to environmental causes such as declining agricultural productivity, sea level rise, and natural disasters such as floods, wind storms and drought, can be expected to escalate (McMichael et al., 1996). Moreover,

with resources such as water and timber diminishing, the rights to and control over them will become an increasing source of tension nationally and internationally, exacerbating environmental refugee problems (WCED, 1987). Unless action is taken to address these problems, the world is likely to experience a series of civil conflicts and refugee crises, caused by deepening poverty and environmental degradation (Oxfam, 1995).

Box 2.4
The traffic problem in Bangkok

Following continuous economic growth of 8% during the past decade, average income in Thailand has more than tripled, from US$ 800 in 1985 to US$ 2800 in 1995. As in many countries around the world, this rise in income has fuelled increased demand for motor vehicles. Since the late 1980s, motor vehicle ownership in Thailand has increased at an annual rate of 15%; in Bangkok alone 500 new automobiles are on average registered every day. By 1995, a total of 14.10 million motor vehicles had been registered throughout the kingdom. Of these, 3.24 million were registered in Bangkok, representing 22.7% of the kingdom's total registered motor vehicles.

Bangkok has a population of about 7 million and its population density is therefore high. In the absence of a mass transit system, a large number of people must rely on their own transport (usually cars or motorbikes). Bangkok today thus has one of the world's most notorious traffic congestion problems. During rush hour, traffic is able to move at only about 20 km/hr; in the inner city, the speed goes down to about 8–10 km/hr. The situation becomes worse during the rainy season when part of the city is flooded and travelling a distance of 10 km can take several hours.

The traffic problem does not end here. The air of Bangkok is heavily polluted and the physical and mental health of the population affected. Work productivity has declined as a result.

The Thai Government has responded by establishing the Office of the Commission for Management of Road Traffic, consisting of multiagency representatives. Short-term measures implemented by the Commission so far include strict enforcement of traffic regulations, rerouting of traffic to avoid traffic jams, and staggered office hours. A number of expressways and mass transit systems are being planned or are already under construction, although these will not come into operation until the end of the century.

Few people in Bangkok are under the illusion, however, that these measures will solve Bangkok's traffic problems. In the long run, decentralization of economic activities out of Bangkok will be necessary. This would not only rid the city of its traffic problems, but also help to distribute the benefits of economic growth more equitably.

Source: Dr Twatchai Yongkittikul, Secretary General of the Thai Bankers' Association, Thailand.

Box 2.5

Examples of inequity in health by socioeconomic group, geographical area, gender and race/ethnicity

BY SOCIOECONOMIC GROUP

The life expectancy at birth of the most disadvantaged population group in Mexico is 20 years less than that of its most affluent group. Adults in São Paulo, Brazil, in the late 1980s had mortality rates that were two to three times higher if they worked in nonprofessional rather than professional jobs. In Bolivia, most public spending on health goes towards care for people belonging to the upper two income quintiles, although these groups already have the best health status. Disparities in health between rich and poor are also apparent within developed countries, although they are usually smaller; wealthy groups have the most concentrated medical attention, eat better, and can afford to live in environmentally clean and disaster-free areas.

BY GEOGRAPHICAL AREA

In Nigeria, the average life expectancy in one region, Borno, is only 40 years — 18 years less than in the Bendel region. Although only 39% of the population of Côte d'Ivoire lives in cities, at least 80% of the country's public health expenditure is directed towards urban areas. In Lima, Peru, the infant mortality rate is 50 per 1000 live births, while in some rural areas it is as high as 150 per 1000.

BY GENDER

A study in India showed that female infants were almost twice as likely to die by the age of two as were males, and concluded that the most likely explanation was the different behaviour of families towards male and female children, not biological differences. Another report concluded that the death of one out of every six female infants in India, Bangladesh and Pakistan was due to neglect and discrimination. Studies in Bangladesh found that boys under 5 years of age were given 16% more food than girls the same age. Additionally, evidence is mounting that adolescent and adult women may not receive an appropriate proportion of available food within the family.

BY RACE/ETHNICITY

In Guatemala, poverty and malnutrition during the 1980s was much higher among indigenous children than among non-indigenous children. In 1990 in South Africa death rates for non-white men were double those of white men, and more than four times as much money was spent on healthcare for whites than for blacks.

Sources: Batliwala, 1987; Das Gupta, 1987; Vogel, 1988; Chatterjee & Lambert, 1989; UNPF, 1989; Gittelsohn, 1991; UNDP, 1991; Psacharopoulos et al., 1993; UN, 1993; Unidad de Análises de Políticas Sociales, 1993; World Bank, 1993; Pan American Sanitary Bureau/UN-ELAC 1994; UNDP, 1994; Yach & Harrison, 1995.

2.4.3 Status of women: poverty, patriarchy and diminishing resources

Despite rising concern about women's health status worldwide, there is a dearth of gender-disaggregated data in the health field on which to base appropriate policy and decision-making (Sims, 1994). That said, in the environment, development and health context generally, it is increasingly understood that being female is often a precondition for deprivation, neglect, and reduced access to resources and entitlements (Tomasevski, 1993; Karl, 1995). As well as lower education and status, less earning power and less access to healthcare, less obvious factors such as restricted mobility, imposed through social norms and family responsibilities also frequently contribute to poor health status. In spite of this, the life expectancy of women is generally longer than that of men. This is partly explained by the much higher injury mortality rate among men (see Section 5.6).

Local environmental conditions probably affect women more than any other group. The lives of poor women especially intersect closely with the environment on many levels. The local environment has traditionally provided women with food, fuel, fodder, plant and sources of natural medicine. But environmental degradation is creating additional pressures and increasing their workloads since their obligations and responsibilities remain unchanged. When land and water are depleted, much more labour — usually women's labour — is required to maintain the same output. The workload of children also rises, and for girls more than for boys (UNDP, 1995). When pressures on women's time and energy mount, girls are more likely to be kept from school than boys, to assist with household chores. In nearly all low-income countries, both primary and secondary school enrolments are higher among males than among females (World Bank, 1996). Trapped between poverty, patriarchy, and diminishing resources, it is poor women who first and foremost pay the price of environmental destruction.

Hastening progress towards universal attainment of at least primary education, and the elimination of illiteracy in women in particular, would help break the poverty cycle. Improvements in female education show high returns in terms of environment, health and development. Better-educated mothers have fewer, better-educated children and raise healthier families (World Bank, 1993; UN, 1995b). However, although major advances have been made in primary school enrolment in the least developed countries, net secondary school enrolments averaged only 16% (UNCTAD, 1995a). More specifically, as shown in **Table 2.1**, the average number of years of schooling among the children of poor families is much lower than among the children of the more affluent.

Thus although women's dependence on the environment provides a strong motivation for women to "manage" environmental resources sustainably, lack of influence and decision-making power in the family and community mean that their wishes and preferences are often overridden in favour of short-term benefits and increased cash income, not all of which may be spent on family care. Development policy has been slow to recognize the impacts that gender division of labour and responsibilities have on the priorities of men and women. Moreover, women often have multiple roles in the home, the family or the workplace, particularly in poor households. This combination of long duration and high intensity of work has long-term impacts on women's health and well-being (Sims, 1994).

2.5 Science and technology

During the past three decades science and technology have been two of the most decisive driving forces for economic development,

especially in developed countries. They have played, and will continue to play, a significant role not only in the search for new knowledge and more efficient means of agricultural and industrial production, but also in saving lives, improving health, improving environmental conditions and promoting human development (Barbiroli, 1996). Technological developments can be polluting and wasteful, however, and may create serious potential risks for environment and health. The prevention and reduction of such risks is thus a key issue for sustainable development.

2.5.1 Research for health and environment

Many examples exist of technologies that have helped improve health and environment, but particularly in energy, agriculture, engineering and chemistry (**Table 2.2**). Great advances benefiting human well-being have also been made in what may be loosely termed the "health sciences" (WHO, 1997c). For example, biotechnologists have developed more efficacious and easy-to-handle vaccines and techniques for prevention of infectious diseases spread via the environment, and safer and more effective methods for the biological control of disease-carrying vectors. Yet much remains to be done within the context of sustainable development to broaden "health research", so that it focuses not only on solutions to biomedical and socio-medical problems but also on identifying effective actions for health-and-environment protection, at any level in the framework of **Fig. 1.3**. A recent review of current priorities for "health research" (WHO, 1996d) provided a detailed analysis of research on interventions by the health sector and how these might be extended. Research on possible interventions by other sectors and the contributions they could make to improving health require similar attention.

Of course, if research results are to be truly useful, they must be communicated and applied. Application often

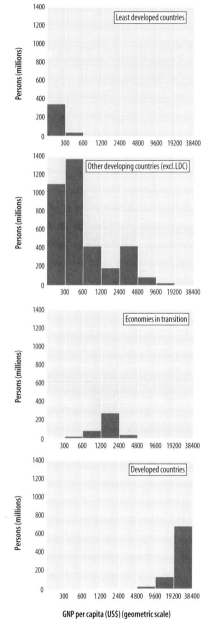

Fig. 2.6

Share of GNP per capita (US$) by population size and level of development — 1993

Source: based on data from World Bank, 1995a.

Table 2.1

Average years of schooling per capita income quintile in selected developing countries

Per capita income quintile	Guatemala	Brazil	Costa Rica	Viet Nam[a]
Highest	7.0	8.7	9.4	8.0
4th	3.5	5.7	7.1	6.5
3rd	2.3	4.3	6.2	6.1
2nd	1.5	3.1	5.6	5.7
Lowest	1.0	2.1	4.8	5.1

Note: data are for all persons 15 years and over
a: data are based on expenditure quintile

Source: World Bank, 1995a.

depends on adoption of legally enforceable standards or agreed guidelines. Economic instruments can also stimulate use of new approaches for health-and-environment improvement. The successful introduction of catalytic converters (for motor vehicles) in most industrialized countries in the early 1990s is an example of how a combination of legal standards and economic incentives can strengthen application of the results of scientific and technical research to reduce pollution (**Box 2.6**). Introducing environmental standards can also promote the use of alternative raw materials (such as water as a solvent for paint) or energy sources (such as solar power), the

recycling of finished products (such as glass bottles) or residuals (such as organic household wastes), and the development of new products that use natural resources in a more environmentally-friendly way (such as cars with low-fuel consumption).

2.5.2 Appropriate technology

The concept of "appropriate technology" was defined in the policy for primary health care developed by WHO and UNICEF (WHO, 1978) as "technology that is scientifically sound and also acceptable to those who apply it and to those for whom it is used". Evidently, what is appropriate in one community may be inappropriate in another. Local research on effective and acceptable solutions to problems of environmental pollution and health protection is accordingly required to move towards sustainable development (WHO, 1996).

Additionally, design and development of new technologies should incorporate indigenous materials, promote efficient resource use and create

Table 2.2

Examples of new technologies which have positive health-and-environment impacts

Technology	Positive impact on health and environment
Improved biomass stoves/burners	Reduced indoor/outdoor air pollution Greenhouse gas "neutral"* More efficient fuelwood use
Biogas stoves and lights	Reduced indoor/outdoor air pollution Reduced dependence on power supplies Improved recycling of organics**
Heat pump technology for space heating	Negligible indoor/outdoor air pollution No greenhouse gas emissions
Photovoltaic energy conversion systems	No indoor/outdoor air pollution No greenhouse gas emissions Reduced dependence on power supplies
Genetically improved crops	Increased yields Reduced dependence on pesticides
Catalytic converters and lead-free petrol	Reduced air pollution from cars
Electric vehicles	Reduced emission of air pollutants along roads
HCFCs and HFCs as CFC alternatives	Reduced stratospheric ozone depletion
Fibreglass cabling for telephone lines	Vastly reduced use of copper
Low water-use irrigation systems	Reduced water use and waterlogging
New alloys and plastics in manufacturing industry	Reduced waste
Biological pest control methods	Reduced use of toxic chemicals

* The growing of biomass fuel (i.e. mostly trees) absorbs exactly the same amount of CO_2 as is released in its combustion (i.e. it is neutral in terms of greenhouse gas emissions).

** Emissions produced during the production and complete burning of biogas are more oxidized and less harmful than those that would have been produced following the decay of e.g. vegetable and plant waste, and organic household waste.

minimal pollution. If not, construction materials and techniques, household energy sources, food production, cooking methods and waste disposal can all contribute to environmental health threats in attempts to satisfy basic human needs. Research to develop appropriate technologies can clearly reap many benefits. For example, local research to improve stoves for cooking and heating has provided rural people in many countries with opportunities to reduce cooking time, air pollution, injuries and burns caused by open fires, and to save on cooking fuel (WHO, 1992c). Moreover, improved stoves can be produced with local materials ensuring that they are available at low cost.

Other examples of proven "appropriate technologies" in the health-and-environment field include pesticide-impregnated bednets to reduce mosquito bites that spread malaria (Lengeler et al., 1996), agricultural technologies that reduce pesticide use (MacKay, 1993) and solar energy applications in remote communities (**Box 2.7**).

2.5.3 Technology transfer, adaptation and redesign

Technologies for food production, water supply and housing have developed differently among indigenous cultures and communities, depending on the climate, physical geography, natural fauna and flora, and availability of local materials. Many indigenous technologies were based on principles of health-and-environment protection, but their efficiency was low. Pressures from population growth and competing demands for land use created a strong impetus for change, particularly regarding food production technologies (FAO, 1996b). The "green revolution", for instance, transferred new technologies for irrigation, fertilization, pest control and seed selection on a broad scale to farmers in developing countries resulting in significant increases in food production. However, this transfer of tech-

Box 2.6

Pollution control through catalytic converters

Most developed countries and an increasing number of developing countries have introduced catalytic converters, one of the most effective technologies for controlling motor vehicle emissions. Catalytic converters operate on lead-free petrol only. Since it alters the characteristics of combustion chamber deposits, lead-free petrol emits less exhaust hydrocarbons emissions than petrol that contains lead. In addition, other pollutants are reduced by chemical reactions in the catalytic converter.

Economic incentives in the form of pricing policies are commonly introduced to encourage the use of lead-free fuel. Consumers can also be mandated to submit their vehicle for a maintenance and emissions inspection test. This encourages the service industry to undertake engine-tuning based on emissions control rather than traditional performance. (Of course, reducing the total number of vehicle miles travelled through incentives such as car pooling, increased used of mass transit, parking restrictions and petrol rationing are important additional means of reducing emissions.)

During the last 10–15 years lead-free petrol has been made the norm in most developed countries. In Latin America, the Caribbean and China, USEPA and WHO have been involved in the delivery of training courses to assist decision-makers to develop national action plans for the phasing out of leaded petrol, and in developing integrated strategies to reduce air pollution from motor vehicles. China has committed itself to selling unleaded petrol only as of the year 2000. In Central and Eastern Europe steps have been taken to phase out leaded petrol. Additionally, a European Strategy for phasing out leaded petrol is being prepared for submission to the next European Ministerial Conference planned for Aarhus, Denmark in 1998. In Russia, blood-lead surveys are being undertaken to establish a baseline against which lead-abatement activities can be measured. A lead-exposure abatement plan is also being developed for Egypt.

Recognizing the impact that lead in petrol has on the health of children in particular, the 1997 Declaration of the Environment Leaders of the Eight Major Countries (G8) on Children's Environmental Health has called for further action to reduce children's blood-lead levels, including a commitment to phase out lead in petrol, and programmes to monitor blood-lead levels in children to track progress.

Sources: Mage & Zali, 1992; USEPA, unpublished information.

nology was not without negative side-effects, such as land degradation due to overuse, pesticide poisonings, and prohibitively high costs for individual smallholder farmers resulting in concentration of land ownership in fewer hands (FAO, 1996b).

So the message is that technologies cannot simply be transferred, but must rather be adapted or redesigned to suit differing conditions. Additionally, the target groups for technology transfer should be selected carefully. For

Box 2.7
Use of solar energy technologies in primary health care

Primary healthcare facilities and clinics require only very limited amounts of energy, but many of them are situated in remote locations and do not have access to a reliable and affordable source of electricity. Increasingly, however, solar energy is playing an important role in providing energy for the key end-uses of lighting, refrigeration, water pumping, water heating and water disinfection.

LIGHTING
One of the most common applications of solar energy is to provide lighting, both in homes and in healthcare facilities. Photovoltaic elements store electricity during daylight hours, and at night provide the power for electric lights. The strength of the light can be much stronger than that of kerosene lights, the most common alternative. Moreover, the light is produced without the smoke and fumes that accompany kerosene use. The stronger light provided by solar technology also makes medical interventions much safer. The daily cost of solar lighting has been reported to be higher than that of kerosene lighting, but the cost per lux (light intensity unit) is lower for solar lighting.

REFRIGERATION
Refrigeration (mainly of vaccines), also using electricity from photovoltaic elements, is another major application of solar energy which directly supports healthcare activities in developing countries. Solar energy technology for refrigerators is now mature and fully commercialized, with more than 5000 refrigerators in use worldwide, most of them in African countries. More than 15 years of experience and evaluation have shown that solar energy refrigerators outperform kerosene refrigerators when used in large-scale immunization activities. The security provided by solar energy refrigerators and their larger storage volume permits longer-term storage of vaccines in remote areas, closer to the point of use.

WATER PUMPING, HEATING AND DISINFECTION
The 1993 World Solar Summit in Paris identified household water supply, and water pumping for clinics and health centres and hospitals, as areas where energy is critical to health. But the poorest communities often lack mains electricity supply. Solar energy thus has a potentially important role in powering water supply pumps in such areas. Information presented at the Summit clearly demonstrated the economic advantages of solar energy over diesel energy under certain climatic conditions, advantages which increase with rising water demand.

Solar energy can also be used to heat water, which would again provide another important resource for primary health services: hot water. Recent research has also developed means of disinfecting water, using sunlight irradiation of thin films of water, or reverse osmosis. The volumes of disinfected water produced are limited, however, and so these methods are not suitable for water treatment at community level.

Source: WHO, 1993b.

instance, the prospects for building genetic resistance in plants to pests and plant diseases through biotechnology are good, but the transfer of these new seed technologies to field application in developing countries should focus on those in greatest need (FAO, 1996b).

Industrial technology transfer, especially in relation to the export of hazardous industries and the transfer of "bad technology", and transfer of the harmful by-products of technology, are also of concern (WHO, 1992b). The closure of factories in developed countries using hazardous materials (e.g. asbestos, which is now banned in certain developed countries) and the transfer of production to developing countries, sometimes to factories owned by the same corporation, is just one example of the transfer or export of a hazardous industry or bad technology. International agreements on health-and-environment standards for industry, to be applied in all countries, could limit such activity, but the pressure to reduce "trade barriers" (see Section 2.7.4) is working in the opposite direction. The export of hazardous waste is an extreme example of the transfer of harmful by-products of technology (WHO, 1992b), but is now being brought under control as a result of the coming into force of the Basel Convention in 1992.

More positively, industrialization in developing countries can take the form of "jumping" directly to the most cost-efficient, energy-efficient and low-polluting technologies available. Car manufacture is one example (Greider, 1997). Recent years have seen considerable advances in the production of cars using technologies that maximize use of natural resources and minimize waste. The negative environmental impact of promoting a transport technology based on private car ownership needs to be considered, however. Many cities of rapidly industrializing countries are suffering severe air pollution due to car exhaust emissions (see Box 2.3 and Section 4.7).

Finally, it goes without saying that transfer of modern pollution control technology should be an essential feature of development cooperation, with financing integrated into the loan or aid arrangements. The policies and practices of the World Bank and other financial institutions are increasingly supporting this process (World Bank, 1995b). Wide access within industry to information about existing and new technologies is obviously essential though. The UNEP Cleaner Production programme (UNEP, 1996a) has been of great importance in this regard. Economic instruments, environmental regulations and incentives, or restrictions related to trade, can also facilitate appropriate transfer of technology (UNCTAD, 1997).

2.5.4 Information and communication technology

The information and communication field is another area of technology that has seen dramatic developments during recent years. New more advanced computer chips and CD-ROM technology, for instance, have improved the data storage and retrieval capacity of personal computers to the extent that major databases can be used conveniently in daily environmental health management. For example, information about thousands of toxic chemicals is almost instantaneous for those with access to modern computer equipment (IPCS, 1996a). Advanced computer chips are also used in new monitoring and laboratory equipment, enabling continuous and simultaneous environmental monitoring of several pollutants.

Improvements in information technology are also illustrated by use of remote sensing data from satellites in conjunction with geographic information systems to map physical characteristics of large land and sea surface areas (Washino & Wood, 1994; Savigny & Wijeyaratne, 1995). Vegetation and other changes identified in this way can be used to forecast environmental

impacts such as drought. Similarly, monitoring of the sea surface can identify algal blooms and help forecast subsequent related health problems, such as cholera (Epstein, Ford & Colwell, 1994).

New telecommunication technologies including the Internet, which is quickly being introduced and extended in developing countries, are linked to these developments. The capacity to rapidly share health-and-environment information via the Internet creates new potential for research collaboration, assistance in the interpretation of local data and the sharing of ideas on how best to instigate effective preventive action. International action is important, though, if equitable access to these modern information and communication systems is to be assured. Such access, or lack of access, is an important driving force behind the development of technical capacity at local level, particularly in relation to dealing with modern environmental health hazards.

Furthermore, many policy-makers still need to be informed how technological innovations can contribute to sustainable development. Increased dialogue between policy-makers and scientists — concerning health and environment especially — would mean that relevant research priorities could be set and solutions for pressing problems found more quickly. Improved communication between scientists and the public is also required so that science-based policies respond to public concerns. Scientists and technologists are also responsible for establishing the codes of practices and guidelines for use and advancement of scientific knowledge and methods, taking into account their cost-effectiveness and sustainability. The growing appreciation of the potential pay-offs of scientific and technological research concerning health systems and environmental protection is now matched by an understanding that this research should produce information that health providers, managers and decision-makers can use to full advantage. In the past, advanced and new technology has been appreciated but not applied effectively to solving real-life problems.

2.6 Consumption and production patterns

Affluence, by most common definitions, means increased per capita consumption of food, goods and services. This increased consumption and production depletes natural resources and produces waste, some of which can have severe effects on the environment and human health (see Chapter 3). Population increases (see Section 2.2) contribute to these developments, but more important is the already high consumption levels, due to their "lifestyle patterns", of affluent countries and the trend towards duplication of this "lifestyle" in all countries. These changes in consumption and production patterns were highlighted in *Agenda 21* (UN, 1993) as a major problem for sustainable development, and they are strong driving forces in the health-and-environment cause–effect framework (**Fig. 1.3**).

Three of the most important consumption issues in terms of sustainability are: diet (particularly the consumption of meat), consumption of certain raw materials and persistent chemicals, and the consumption of fossil fuels and associated carbon dioxide (CO_2) emissions. As pointed out in the recent CSD assessment of changing consumption patterns (see Chapter 4 in *Agenda 21*): "Over the past 45 years consumption of grain, beef and water has tripled, while paper use has risen six times. The use of fossil fuels has grown fourfold, as have CO_2 emissions" (CSD, 1997e). Inequities described in Section 2.4 are also reflected in consumption patterns: "the richest fifth of the world's population has doubled its per capita consumption of energy, meat, timber, steel and copper, and quadrupled its car ownership. The per capita consumption

of the poorest fifth has hardly increased" (CSD, 1997e).

2.6.1 Changes in diet: environmental implications

Richer populations not only consume greater variety and amounts of food, increasing the environmental effects of transport and storage of food, but also greater amounts of specific foods, which likewise has environmental implications (FAO, 1996b). Principal among these specific foods is meat, which comes from three main sources:

* hunted and gathered from essentially unmanaged wild populations — a practice now almost completely confined to marine fisheries

* animals managed but fed with food not directly usable by humans — range-fed animals and some types of aquaculture, for example

* managed animals fed with grain, fishmeal, or other products that could be directly eaten by humans — cattle feedlots and intensive poultry production are major examples.

Increased demand for meat thus:

* intensifies marine fishing, pushing some marine fisheries toward extinction and shifting the ecological balance of the oceans

* increases the demand for pasture, thus increasing the rate of deforestation and associated loss of biodiversity in some areas

* diverts more of the world's basic food supply to animals, thereby making agriculture and fishing less efficient in meeting human nutritional needs.

Fig. 2.7 illustrates the third of the above effects, for a range of countries, by depicting the proportion of locally available grain that is used for human consumption. Note that less affluent countries tend to consume much greater proportions of available grain per capita (through direct consumption) than the affluent countries, in which more than half of the grain is fed to animals to produce meat. For the most deprived populations, of course, any increase in food consumption is usually highly beneficial to health. After incomes have increased to the extent that diets become sufficient in size and nutritional balance, however, no significant health benefit attaches to greater consumption of food.

Dietary composition and food consumption per capita are therefore key driving forces for the way in which land is used for agriculture. This in turn affects water use, fertilizer application and pesticide use, all of which have impacts on environmental quality and health (see Section 3.4).

2.6.2 Consumption of raw materials and persistent chemicals

Rich countries consume a greater portion per capita of the world's raw materials. The OECD countries, for example, accounted for around 70% of global steel and aluminum production in 1994, although making up less than 15% of global population (Nriagu, 1996). Much of the resulting environmental damage arising from the extraction, transport and processing of these resources can therefore be linked to the affluence of these nations.

Environmental health risks, however, are greater for some raw materials than for others. Of particular concern are the toxic metals: lead, cadmium and mercury. Although the actual health damage produced by these metals depends on the degree to which human populations are exposed (see Section 4.10), figures for their overall production and use gives some idea of

Fig. 2.7

GDP per capita (US$) vs. percentage grain used for human consumption for selected countries — 1993

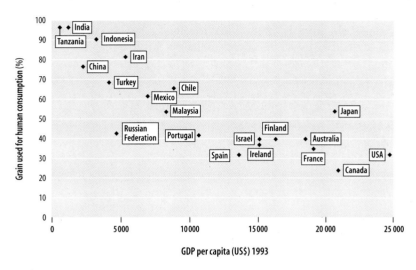

Sources: based on data from USDA, 1993; Brown et al., 1994 and FAO, 1994b.

Fig. 2.8

Global production and consumption trend for selected toxic metals

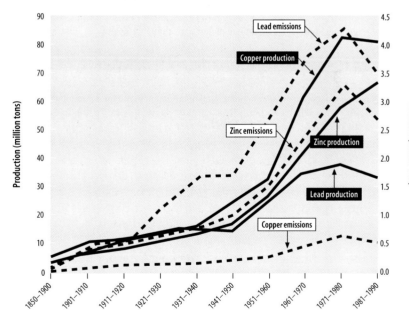

Sources: adapted with permission from Nriagu JO. History of global metal pollution. Science, 1996, 272:223–224. Copyright 1996. American Association for the Advancement of Science.

the potential for harm. **Fig. 2.8** shows production and emissions trends for selected metals. The increasing emissions of lead are of great concern (see Section 4.10).

Box 2.8

Persistent organic pollutants

Considerable political attention has recently focused on persistent organic pollutants (POPs). POPs are organic compounds that have long half-lives in the environment and undergo slow physical, chemical and biological degradation. They are able to pass through ecosystems because of their high vapour pressure and can travel great distances, both locally and globally. These characteristics mean that they may pose a special threat to the environment and human health. POPs include DDT, polychlorinated biphenyls, furans, chlordane, heptachlor, aldrin, dieldrin and endrin.

Many POPs are used in or arise from industry, agriculture and disease vector control. POPs may also be created unintentionally, as by-products. Stockpiles of unwanted POPs are significant cause for concern.

POPs have high lipid solubility and therefore bioaccumulate in the fatty tissues of living organisms. They pose a special risk to human health and the environment since they mimic the function of steroid compounds such as hormones potentially leading to disruption of the endocrine system. Human exposure to POPs occurs via diet, occupation, accidents and the indoor environment, particularly in those developing countries where POPs are used in tropical agriculture.

It is widely accepted that the use of such substances cannot be considered sustainable. Increasing evidence of the long-range transport in the environment of these substances and the consequent threats they pose to the whole globe, has prompted the international community to call for urgent global action to reduce and eliminate releases and emissions of these chemicals.

Among the twelve POPs under initial consideration for international action, DDT is the only insecticide still in use for public health purposes. The use of DDT in public health programmes, notably for malaria control, has been the subject of much controversy for many years. Vector-borne diseases — malaria is one of the most significant — are major threats to human health, and social and economic development. DDT has made a major contribution to the eradication, or virtual eradication of malaria from a number of countries and remains a most valuable tool, particularly since the options for malaria control are limited. Use of DDT has declined, however, following development of vector resistance, reduction in its global production and adverse publicity.

Further options to minimize the use and impacts of POPs include improving the availability of information and expertise on alternatives to POPs (through information exchange and education programmes) and guidance on the selection of replacements for POPs. This guidance should cover non-chemical as well as chemical alternatives, and include advice on the factors to be considered in choosing alternatives.

Sources: IPCS, 1995a; IFCS, 1996.

The production and use of chemicals that remain in the environment for long periods and cause harm have also become an environmental health issue. For instance, chlorofluorocarbons, other halocarbons and halons, have become widely used in industry (as refrigeration fluids, foam-fillers and aerosol propellants) partly because they are non-toxic to humans. But halogen radicals, which are produced following the release of halocarbons and halons, upset the balance between oxygen and ozone concentrations in the stratosphere, leading to a steady decline in ozone levels (IPCS, 1990a). As ozone filters out a major part of the ultraviolet radiation that reaches Earth from the sun, this decline has serious implications for human health (in terms of higher incidence of skin cancers and cataracts, and damaged immune response) and for the global ecological systems on which all life depends (McMichael et al., 1996).

Some persistent chemicals have more direct effects on health. For instance, DDT has been used as a pesticide for many years and is considered to have very low acute toxicity in humans. However, its long-term effects in mimicking steroid hormones make DDT an "endocrine disruptor" (Ashby et al., 1997). It is also classified as a "persistent organic pollutant" (POP) (**Box 2.8**). And because POPs remain in the environment for a considerable time, their concentrations can increase to levels that eventually cause health effects. The high DDT concentrations generally found in human breast milk in developing countries where DDT has been widely used, is an indicator of environmental accumulation of DDT (Sonawane, 1995).

2.6.3 Burning of fossil fuels

Ever since the onset of the Industrial Revolution, economic development has been steadily accompanied by changes in the composition of the atmosphere. These changes are among the more insidious signs of our unsustainable reliance on natural resources in our quest for higher living standards. Although not the only factors at play, fossil fuel combustion (for the generation of energy and transportation) is among the main culprits. Almost unnoticeably, atmospheric CO_2 levels rose from 280 ppmv in 1760 to 358 ppmv in 1994, and are projected to reach around 400 ppmv in 2020 (IPCC, 1996). Most CO_2 emissions originate in developed countries where energy consumption is high (see Section 3.6.1). Not in itself a toxic substance, CO_2 contributes to the greenhouse effect which is responsible for Earth's relatively warm climate. (Without it, the world would be some 35°C colder.)

However, increasing levels of CO_2 and other greenhouse gases (GHGs), such as methane (produced by cattle and irrigated agriculture) are suspected to be responsible for global climate change, with wide-ranging consequences for human health and wellbeing (McMichael et al, 1996). Another consequence of fossil fuel combustion, relating to sulfur content, combustion technology and emission control systems, is the release of sulfuric acid particulates. These can drift in the atmosphere over long distances until they are precipitated in the form of acid rain or snow (Whelpdale & Kaiser, 1997). The resulting widespread acidification of freshwater bodies, forests and agricultural areas is responsible for huge economic losses, mostly in industrialized countries (FAO, 1996b). Since they filter out some of the sun's heat radiation, sulfuric acid and soot particulates also cause cooling of local microclimates.

2.7 Economic development

2..7.1 Economic development as a driving force

Poverty is one of the main driving forces behind unhealthy environmental conditions (see Section 2.4). Reducing poverty through economic development that benefits the poor is clearly essential for sustainable development. Economic growth in itself is not sufficient to achieve this end, however, as recent experience has shown. In many countries, significant economic growth has occurred but has benefited mainly the rich and middle-income earners (UNDP, 1996). The poor, on the contrary, have been left behind, as growth in the economy has meant growth of inequality.

As pointed out by Mr J.G. Speth, Administrator of UNDP "the quality of growth is as important as its quantity". Indeed, "economic growth can be *jobless* rather than employment-creating, *ruthless* rather than equitable, *voiceless* rather than participatory and *futureless* rather than environmentally sound" (Speth, 1996). The Administrative Committee on Coordination of UN Agencies also expressed its concern about this issue in a statement to the 1997 Special Session of the UN General Assembly: "Sustainable development remains one of the most important challenges facing humanity as it approaches the 21st Century. Yet there is growing concern that failure to accelerate economic growth and development in vast areas of the world, to resolve burning social problems, to correct unsustainable production and consumption patterns and increasing inequity, and to halt deterioration of the environment, will irreversibly limit national capacities to respond to future challenges.".

Nonetheless, the importance of economic development for health and environment is highlighted by the fact that, overall, life expectancy and other health indicators have improved for those benefiting from economic development (WHO, 1995b). Some macroeconomic policies that have been considered necessary to achieve economic growth have had negative effects though. "Structural adjustment" policies imposed during the 1980s in a number of countries harmed social services, health services and water supply

> "The quality of growth is as important as its quantity"
>
> Mr J.G. Speth, Administrator of UNDP, 1996.

and sanitation services because they meant that governments focused instead on export industry and "privatization" (UNICEF, 1990). And even though a number of developing countries experienced rapid economic growth in the years after "restructuring", with some countries reporting significant reductions in poverty (UNDP, 1996), the problem of inequity remains in most countries. This suggests that the distribution and use of the wealth created by economic development is as relevant to a country's health-and-environment conditions as its level of economic development.

Moreover, if economic development is misguided, poorly planned or inadequately regulated, people's vulnerability to environmental health hazards is increased. For instance, investment in poorly controlled hazardous industries has led to concentrations of populations around industrial facilities, and higher levels of air and water pollution (see Sections 4.2 and 4.4). Combined, these have resulted in increased human exposure to toxic materials. Ironically, economic development aimed at modification of the environment to improve agricultural yields, and ultimately human welfare, has also had adverse effects on health and environment. Thus large water resource management projects, such as dams and irrigation schemes, have sometimes increased the health risks from vector-borne and other water-

related diseases, as well as the risks of severe flooding and dam bursts (see Section 3.6).

Economic development level is most often measured by per capita gross domestic product (GDP); large differences between groups of countries with respect to this measure are shown in **Fig. 2.7**. This economic index has frequently been criticized for assigning a positive economic value to all activities in society, irrespective of whether they are positive or negative for health, environment and social development. For instance, if a GDP measure is used, a highly polluting technology appears more economically attractive than a low-polluting technology, even though the latter may achieve the same industrial output. This is because the clean-up costs of the polluting technology would be considered to add to GDP.

In view of the somewhat misleading nature of GDP, other economic indexes such as the genuine progress index (GPI) (Cobb, Halstead & Rowe, 1995) have been developed that evaluate the negative impacts on the environment of depletion of natural resources and production of waste. Yet another measure, purchasing power parity, or "real GDP", has been developed to take into account the fact that the basic cost of living in most developing countries is lower than in developed countries (UNDP, 1996). Ideally, our methods for assessing economic

Table 2.3

Number (in thousands) of people employed in different types of economic activity — 1995

Main activities (GDP 1993, US$)	Japan 31 490	% Total	Poland 2260	% Total	Philippines 850	% Total	Myanmar* (<300)**	% Total
Total number employed	64 560	100.0	14 772	100.0	25 696	100.0	16 817	100.0
Agriculture, hunting, forestry & fishing	3670	5.7	3246	22.0	11 323	44.1	11 551	68.7
Mining & quarrying	60	0.1	480	3.2	95	0.4	87	0.5
Manufacturing	14 560	22.5	3141	21.3	2571	10.0	1250	7.4
Construction	6630	10.3	904	6.1	1239	4.8	292	1.7
Various service activities	39 640	61.4	7001	47.4	10 468	40.7	3637	21.6

*1994 data ** estimate*
Source: ILO, 1996.

development should incorporate the notion that economic progress also means progress towards a healthy environment and social equity. Economic development would then be a truly positive driving force for sustainable development.

2.7.2 Economic development trends and environmental hazards

The pressures on the physical environment that can affect health are largely due to the development of settlements, agriculture and industry, the associated use of water, land and energy, and the wastes produced by these activities (see Chapter 3). In a modern society, economic value is assigned to each of these activities and economic development becomes closely linked to the development of agriculture, various industries, services and energy systems.

In parallel with economic development and population growth, most developed countries have experienced a trend from a predominantly agricultural economy to an industrial or even post-industrial (or service) economy. This trend has been most visible in terms of the number of people engaged in different types of economic activity (**Table 2.3**) at different times. Developing countries undergoing rapid economic growth are showing a similar trend (ILO, 1996).

Subsistence agriculture in the traditional rural environment is generally the first stage of economic development and associated with particular environmental health concerns, such as provision of clean drinking-water, basic sanitation, safe housing and sufficient household fuel. As agriculture becomes more intensive and large-scale, issues relating to land degradation (see Section 3.4), use of chemicals in agriculture and occupational hazards grow in importance (see Section 4.8).

Industrial development usually follows, starting with the extraction of raw materials (through mining), and can cause major water pollution and land degradation. In addition, the industries

that refine these raw materials often create quite severe local air pollution. Also, their relatively high energy needs may serve to increase emissions from power stations. Thereafter, as industry becomes more high-technology oriented, industrial pollution problems tend to become more chemical and biological in character. Economic development may then shift again, with significant growth in the services sector, which may bring new environmental and occupational health concerns such as "sick building syndrome" and musculoskeletal "overuse syndrome" (see Section 5.12).

Economic development can therefore be an important driving force behind change in the types of environmental health hazard that are of major concern in a particular country or community. As highlighted in Section 1.3, many countries have undergone an "environmental health hazard transition" in tandem with economic development. In developing countries, though, this transition is ongoing, meaning that the "modern hazards" of industrial development become established before the "traditional hazards" of poverty have been significantly reduced. Some communities can therefore be said to live in the "worst of both worlds".

2.7.3 Trade development

A trading system that favours the optimal distribution of global production can potentially contribute to sustainable development, provided sound environmental management practices and policies are adopted. From this it follows that if developing countries earned more from their exports, they would have more resources to invest in education and development of health-and-environment protection. This would require, however, that the global trading system allow them to market their products successfully.

Trade can also have negative environmental consequences. Indeed, the potential negative impact of trade on the environment is of increasing political concern, particularly in relation to sustainable development. For example, much international trade in tropical timber has had significant adverse impacts on tropical forests.

Nevertheless, Chapter 2 of *Agenda 21* (UN, 1993) concluded that an open, equitable, secure, non-discriminatory and predictable multilateral trading system is of benefit to all trading partners and at the same time supportive of sustainable development goals. Trade liberalization and deregulation — including the Uruguay Round of multilateral trade negotiations and the establishment of the World Trade Organization — have been key components of international development in the 1990s (WTO, 1996). Much effort has been aimed at reducing trade restrictions on manufacturing trade. Further liberalization is taking place in the context of regional trade groupings, which is affecting agricultural trade and trade in commodities in particular.

Admittedly, liberalization of trade can come into conflict with health-and-environment protection goals. Trade officials often refer to any law, regulation or economic instrument that impedes trade as a "non-tariff trade barrier". For example, if a country has banned the use of asbestos for reasons of health protection, another country wanting to export asbestos-containing products to that country may label the asbestos ban a "trade barrier" which is not in line with "free trade". But it is becoming more difficult for countries to take unilateral action against products or materials that can damage health or the environment. International agreements on a common approach to health-and-environment protection are becoming increasingly important. One system that has worked well for many years is operated by the Codex Alimentarius Commission which seeks to protect the health of consumers in relation to the food trade (FAO/WHO, 1994).

Free trade, or the notion that the liberal exchange of goods between people or between countries is vital to economic development and hence to human welfare, forms the current basis for economic policy in most countries. In the absence of trade, countries would have to rely exclusively on their own production, overall incomes would be far lower, the choice of goods far less and hunger would increase (FAO, 1996b). Because trade frees resources that can be invested in environmental management and public health, it can be seen as a positive driving force for health and environment. On the other hand, too few trade restrictions can lead to increased trade in hazardous materials (going mostly from rich to poor countries) and an increased number and quantity of products manufactured using processes and production methods that may be cheap, but which inflict significant environmental damage. As total trade liberalization would be a negative driving force, various multilateral environmental agreements (MEAs) have been or are currently being negotiated (**Table 2.4**). MEAs seek to ensure that free commercial competition between countries will not lead to loss of biodiversity, environmental degradation or the accumulation of dangerous products in countries or the "global commons" (such as the oceans and the atmosphere).

Regrettably, business practices aimed at reducing costs and trade restrictions can result in a conflict of interest between business and environmental protection objectives. Each government should therefore ensure that national environmental law facilitates the discharge of its country's obligations concerning any MEA it has ratified, while at the same time providing the necessary incentives and sanctions to encourage businesses to act within the confines of such laws. Although Member States of the World Trade Organization (WTO) are under a general obligation not to raise trade restrictions or to apply discriminatory trade measures, Article 20 of the General Agreement on Tariffs and Trade (GATT) allows for exceptions if countries wish to further pursue their public health and safety and environmental goals by stipulating that additional requirements be met (WTO, 1996). In line with this, the World Business Council for Sustainable Development supports the view that businesses have a primary responsibility to develop voluntary mechanisms for health-and-environment protection and to test their effectiveness in order to minimize the need for national and international

regulatory systems (Erlam & Plass, 1996). According to WTO (1996), most conflicts arising between trade partners over whether specific Articles of GATT or MEA regulations should prevail are solved under MEA or WTO dispute settlement provisions.

2.7.4 Economic resources for health-and-environment protection

Sustainable development requires that economic resources are allocated so that health and environment are protected. This means that a balance has to be struck between overall national resources used for the "public good"

Table 2.4

The objectives of selected multilateral environmental agreements and associated trade measures

Objective(s)	Trade measures
The Montreal Protocol	
Protect the stratospheric ozone layer from destruction by human-induced emissions chlorofluorocarbons (CFCs)	Banning of trade in the regulated substances and in any products containing them, between parties of the protocol and between parties and non-parties
The Basel Convention	
Eliminate environmental risks arising from the transboundary movement of hazardous and other wastes	Prior informed consent (PIC) procedures before exporting hazardous substances, or products containing them, the use of which has been banned in the exporting country
	Each party has the right to ban the import or export of hazardous or other wastes
	Ban on trade in such wastes with non-parties
The Convention on International Trade in Endangered Species (CITES)	
Protect endangered species from continued over-exploitation	Banning trade in species of flora and fauna, or their products, listed as endangered under the rules and procedures of the convention
Biodiversity Convention	
Conservation and sustainable use of global biological diversity	Reversal of previous assumption of free access to genetic resources in developing countries
	PIC procedures when access to genetic resources is requested by another party or non-party
Trade in Chemicals: London Guidelines and FAO Code of Conduct	
Protection of countries from chemical products banned or severely restricted in their country of origin	Non-legally binding PIC procedures before exporting banned or severely restricted chemicals in the country of origin, or the country of manufacture

Source: adapted from Erlam & Plass, 1996.

"These problems have been further aggravated by the degradation of the environment, rapid urbanization, malnutrition and high levels of illiteracy exacerbated by poverty, which remains the world's deadliest disease"

Mr S.I. Shervani, President of the World Health Assembly, 1997.

and those used for "private good". The trend in the 1990s towards reduced public services and increased privatization of health-and-environment infrastructure (UNCTAD, 1995b) has tested the ability of governments to achieve such a balance.

Depending on the criteria used for assessing the outcome of privatization policies, this trend may be cautiously viewed as positive (UNCTAD, 1995b) or negative (Martin, 1993). It is clear that the poor will not, as long as they remain poor, be able to "buy" good environment or good health to the extent that the more affluent can. Redistribution of resources within the community is a prerequisite for improving equity. Such redistribution could be best implemented through public spending or creation of public services for the poor.

The World Bank recently commissioned a very detailed study of the role of "public spending" and equity (Van de Walle & Nead, 1995). Using developing country examples, it shows that public spending in the health sector can ensure improved health for the poor, but that the children of high-income households may in fact benefit more from government health spending than children of low-income households. Similarly, public investments in environmental protection may do more to improve the environment for the rich than for the poor. Conversely, targeting the poor sounds reasonable in theory but is not always best practice if health-and-environment improvements, that benefit the health of the whole community, are sought. Most developed countries that have succeeded in reducing poverty to a low level and significantly improved health-and-environment conditions have done so through creation of strong public services funded through taxation.

One means of raising resources for health-and-environment protection in developed or rapidly industrializing countries is to tax activities that pollute the environment or endanger health,

and use the money collected to support introduction of technologies that protect the environment. This approach has been used successfully in Sweden (Naturvardsverket, 1997). For instance, taxes on energy were calculated based on the potential production of SO_2, NO_x and CO_2. Environment taxes were also charged on certain pesticides, on motor vehicles according to their likely air pollution emissions, on certain other consumer products and on raw materials (such as sand), the extraction of which causes land degradation. Evaluation of these environmental taxes showed that they succeeded in reducing pollution and threats to the environment (Naturvardsverket, 1997). The money collected (56 thousand million Swedish crowns in 1996, equivalent to 3.3% of GNP) was used to finance targeted actions to reduce waste production, to introduce improved pollution control technology and to promote consumer and industrial use of "environmentally friendly" products.

The estimates of the financial resources required to carry out the various recommendations of *Agenda* 21 (UN, 1993) were generally in thousands of millions of dollars. It was hoped that much of this money would come from public sources and, in the case of some developing countries, from international development agencies. The allocation of additional and new resources for implementation of the proposals made in *Agenda* 21 has been very slow, however. The least developed countries are receiving an ever-diminishing share of the flow of financial resources that passes between developed and developing countries. In recent years, the flow of private funds has in fact passed from the least developed countries to the developed countries. As pointed out by the President of the UN General Assembly, the figures affixed to *Agenda* 21 by the Rio Conference are now pipedreams, and with them have disappeared the potential for new and additional financial resources. Official development assistance has contracted to significantly below 50% of the target of 0.7% of GNP and is dwindling further (Razali, 1997).

2.8 The foundations of sustainability

As illustrated in **Box 2.1** the driving forces described in this chapter very much determine whether a society is proceeding towards or away from sustainability. A number of "downstream" aspects of development are influenced by the driving forces of the type outlined in the diagram in **Box 2.1**. Whether it is population growth, extreme inequity or over-consumption of certain commodities, policies and actions must be implemented to guide the development process towards sustainability.

Some of the trends that have evolved since the Earth Summit are major threats to sustainable development. Population growth in itself is not bad if the country in question has the means to meet the basic needs of additional people. And if economic growth was more equitable, this would more often be the case. Enormous inequities remain, however, regarding use of energy and raw materials, food consumption and water use. Thus while the developed countries are consolidating their share of global resource use and economic development, the least developed countries lag further and further behind in human development terms. Current economic driving forces are increasing rather than decreasing inequity.

The overall result is increased pressure on land and water resources, increased household and hazardous waste, increased conflict between the economic imperatives of a "globalizing" industry and the health-and-environment protection needs of people. In Chapter 3 some of the major pressures on the physical environment that have a bearing on health will be discussed. ❑

Chapter 3

Major Human Activities Affecting Environmental Quality

Driving Forces
Pressure
State
Exposure
Effect
Action

3.1 How driving forces create environmental pressures

The atmosphere, fertile soils, fresh-water resources, the oceans, and the ecosystems they support, play a key role in providing humans with shelter, food and safe water, and the capacity to recycle most wastes. However, the pressures exerted by the "driving forces" described in Chapter 2 are in many instances increasing. Consequently, air pollution, deforestation, land degradation, deteriorating water quality and biodiversity loss are growing environmental threats (UNEP, 1997a).

Much of the problem lies with the tendency of humans to exploit natural resources with little or no regard to the waste that are produced, or to the effect of such exploitation on local and global ecosystems. Much waste created through our conversion of raw materials into products does not enter the natural cycle, or if it does, causes degradation and pollution. While such resource use has formed the basis of socioeconomic development, and has enabled a part of the global population to benefit from high-level quality of life, the remaining, much larger and more rapidly growing proportion of the global population, must often overexploit what are frequently already very impoverished natural resources in order to satisfy minimum needs. Thus the activities of rich and poor alike risk compromising the quality of life of future generations.

3.2 Household wastes

Household wastes include all gases, liquids and solids generated by domestic activity that are discarded or emitted and that are of no immediate use to others. They place great "pressure" on the environment and are closely linked to unsustainable consumption and production patterns (UN, 1993) (see also Section 2.6).

Gaseous household wastes arise mainly from heating and cooking. They contribute substantially to both outdoor and indoor air pollution (see Section 4.2). Liquid wastes, often called wastewaters, are the by-products of domestic activities, such as washing and cooking and evacuation of excreta. If these liquid wastes containing phosphates, and human faeces with pathogenic organisms, are not adequately collected, treated and/or disposed of, damage to the aquatic environment and to water resources may ensue (see Sections 4.3 and 4.4). Likewise, the inappropriate disposal of household solid wastes, comprising food scraps and other household residues, packaging and redundant and/or broken items, including household appliances such as refrigerators and washing machines, poses serious threats to aquatic and soil environments.

Population growth, especially in urban settlements, and decreasing municipal resources in many developing countries are exacerbating these problems (see Section 2.3). Moreover, with development, consumption of durable consumer goods such as batter-

Fig. 3.1

Sanitation coverage by region — 1994*

Western Asia
Urban served 44%
Rural unserved 12%
Urban unserved 20%
Rural served 24%
81 million

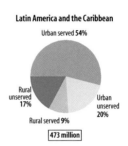

Latin America and the Caribbean
Urban served 54%
Rural unserved 17%
Urban unserved 20%
Rural served 9%
473 million

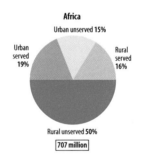

Africa
Urban unserved 15%
Urban served 19%
Rural served 16%
Rural unserved 50%
707 million

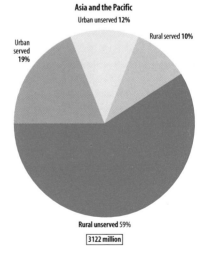

Asia and the Pacific
Urban unserved 12%
Rural served 10%
Urban served 19%
Rural unserved 59%
3122 million

* see Annex 2 for a list of countries who provided data

Source: WHO/UNICEF, 1996a.

ies, electrical appliances and motor vehicles increases, resulting in greater waste health hazards. These trends are expected to continue well into the 21st Century and could lead to a four- to five-fold increase in solid waste and associated pollution by the year 2025 (UN, 1993).

3.2.1 Human excreta: little or no treatment

Generation of human excreta

On average, human beings produce 1150 g of urine and 200 g of faeces per day (Gotaas, 1956; Wagner & Lanoix, 1958). The global urban population currently stands at about 2500 million, and the global rural population at about 3000 million. Thus, globally, every day, about 500 million kg of human faeces are generated in urban areas and about 600 million kg in rural areas, producing a total of over one million tons per day.

Most of this biodegradable organic material is disposed of with very little or no treatment, thereby polluting the environment with substances that are highly dangerous to human health. For example, faeces contain pathogens that cause diarrhoea, worm infections and enteric fevers (Feachem et al., 1983), and urine, if it enters the aquatic environment, can perpetuate the urinary schistosomiasis cycle (WHO, 1997h).

Access to sanitation services

In developed countries nearly all human excreta is collected via sewerage systems, septic systems or other sanitation systems. At the household level these provide safe sanitation. However, considerable amounts of sewage, with very little treatment, are nevertheless discharged into the environment in these countries (MOHSPE, 1994)

In developing countries, a small proportion of the total population, very roughly 10% and mainly urban, has access to sewerage systems and a slightly larger proportion, very roughly 20%,

has some type of on-site sanitation facility. But the vast majority (about 65%) of people in developing countries do not have appropriate sanitation systems (WHO/UNICEF, 1993, 1996a).

Sanitation coverage also varies enormously by region. **Fig. 3.1** shows the variability in rural and urban sanitation coverage for four major regions (WHO/UNICEF, 1996a). The best served regions are West Asia with 68% served and Latin America and the Caribbean with 63% served. These are also the regions with the smallest total population (81 million and 473 million respectively) and the most urbanized. Within Africa, sanitation coverage ranges from less than 25% to more than 75% of the total population (**Fig. 3.2**). Most of the 20 countries with the lowest sanitation coverage, and which are therefore in most need of investments in improved sanitation, are located in Africa (**Table 3.1**).

Of the unserved in developing countries (2900 million), 80% live in rural areas. Most of the faeces of the unserved are recycled for use in agriculture or deposited on land without prior destruction of pathogens, most of which eventually enter surface and

Table 3.1

20 countries where 75% to 94% of the population has no effective sanitation

Africa
Angola, Benin, Burkina Faso, Chad, Egypt, Guinea Bissau, Lesotho, Liberia, Madagascar, Niger, Sierra Leone, Sudan, Zaire, Zambia

Asia & Pacific
Afghanistan, China, Lao PDR, Papua New Guinea, Vietnam

Latin America & Caribbean
Haiti

Source: WHO/UNICEF, 1996a.

groundwaters, sometimes surviving for considerable lengths of time. For example, bucket latrines are still used (often called night-soil collection) the contents of which are collected by middlemen for direct sale to rural farmers for use in agriculture. Not surprisingly, infectious diseases such as diarrhoeal diseases, schistosomiasis and hepatitis (see Sections 5.3 and 5.5) are endemic, and sometimes epidemic in unserved areas.

On-site sanitation

Of the 20% of people in developing countries who have on-site sanitation, such as a septic system or latrine (such as pit, pour-flush or composting), some are still at risk. For example, an on-site sanitation system may protect the health of an individual household, but its design be such that pathogens are released from it and into local water bodies, causing health risks to others. The contents from pit latrines often leach into groundwater. This problem is increasing in those urban areas where groundwater resources lie beneath crowded communities not connected to sewerage systems. Additionally, in rural areas, the contents of pit latrines are deposited on fields to dry and decompose, and pathogens consequently washed into nearby water bodies (Feachem et al., 1983; Franceys, Pickford & Reed, 1992).

Other types of toilet system, such as composting and desiccating latrines, designed for the reuse of excreta in agriculture, are sometimes mismanaged. The destruction of pathogens is then not assured. However, user education and careful monitoring by health authorities could help to improve the design and management of these latrine systems and make them an excellent option for recycling human excreta (Dalhammar & Mehlmann, 1996; Winblad, 1996).

Sewerage

Most cities in developed countries are fully sewered, collecting virtually all urine and faeces and moving them away from city centres. But some of this wastewater is simply pumped out to sea with no treatment. And if the wastewater undergoes treatment, a significant proportion of faecal bacteria will nevertheless remain in the treated water, since even relatively advanced three-stage treatment plants eliminate no more than 90% of bacteria. In developing countries, cities are typically only partially sewered: the proportion of the population served may range from a small percentage to 100% in a very few cases. Treatment of discharge also ranges considerably, although in most cases developing country sewerage systems do not carry out any wastewater treatment. Data on these issues are not reliably collected, which means that obtaining an accurate picture of the situation is difficult. As for developing country rural communities, sewerage is uncommon.

Fig. 3.2

Sanitation services coverage in Africa at the end of 1994

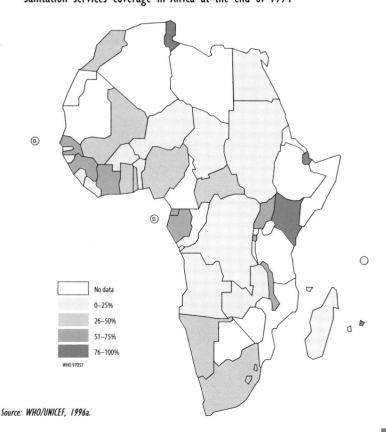

	No data
	0–25%
	26–50%
	51–75%
	76–100%

WHO 97057

Source: WHO/UNICEF, 1996a.

Fig. 3.3

Sanitation services coverage to the year 2000 in developing countries

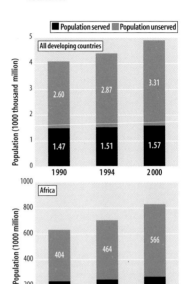

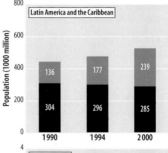

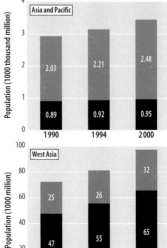

Source: WHO/UNICEF, 1996a.

The flushing of excreta into sewer water creates a tremendous amount of contaminated water. If this is not treated, but discharged directly into the environment, many pathogens are released. The average urban resident with connections to water and sewerage services frequently uses 150 litres of water per day. A household of five persons will therefore produce 750 litres of wastewater per day. Thus a city of one million people will discharge 150 000 m^3 of wastewater each day, representing a major health hazard when discharged directly into local lakes, rivers or coastal waters.

In countries where freshwater scarcity limits crop production, the economic value of wastewater increases sharply. Wastewater from urban centres is accordingly increasingly used in agriculture. In terms of recycling this trend is positive and should be encouraged by government policies. Indeed, the high organic content of wastewater may be a boon to farmers (the term "fertilization" is used for the combined fertilizer and irrigation effect of wastewater use). Too high a concentration, though, may lead to eutrophication of water bodies that receive the run-off. Chemical and biological contamination of soils can become a problem too if sewage is used to fertilize soil. Moreover, such reuse can be recommended only if the wastewater is collected in sewage or drainage systems which include adequate treatment (Mara and Cairncross, 1989).

Trends in sanitation coverage

In developing countries, provision of sanitation services by central and local governments and households themselves, is not keeping pace with population growth. **Fig. 3.3** shows coverage projected to the year 2000 for developing countries, by each major region and in total. Small increases in the number of people served are projected for all regions, except for Latin America and the Caribbean where the number served is expected

to decrease. Trends in sanitation services therefore indicate that the percentage of unserved and the total population unserved will rise, reaching a total of 3300 million unserved in the year 2000. Projections estimate that the population in developing countries will have increased by 1500 million by 2020. Most of these people will live in conditions of poor sanitation unless major investments in the necessary infrastructure and management are made.

Future development of sanitation services

Various factors complicate the task of improving sanitation in developing countries. For instance, recent urbanization has been very rapid, often consisting of the rapid growth of informal settlements at the periphery of principal settlements. Informal urban settlements are usually densely populated, suffer from poor-quality housing, and frequently lie outside the remit of the municipal waste management authority. The application of conventional waste treatment methods is obviously difficult in such conditions and innovative approaches called for instead.

The state of existing sewerage systems presents further problems. Many of the sewerage networks in developing countries, especially Africa, were constructed a century or more ago. Most of these systems have not been maintained adequately and are now in dire need of rehabilitation. Additionally, increases in population density and per capita water consumption have caused the systems to become overloaded. Sanitation planning for the future must therefore take into consideration not only the financial requirements of new systems for those as yet unserved, but also the resources needed to rehabilitate systems representing past infrastructural investments. This underscores the importance of continuous operation and maintenance to avoid later costly repairs and reconstruction works (Dalhammar & Mehlmann, 1996).

Ideally, sanitation solutions serve more than one purpose. For instance, in areas of the world where fertilizer is expensive and soil quality diminishing, techniques are being developed for safely recycling human urine and faeces back into the soil (Dalhammar & Mehlmann, 1996; Winblad, 1996). Research into the separate collection of urine and faeces and separate handling of them for reuse is under way, and trials are being carried out in many countries. As urine has the greater fertilizer value, and in most instances carries no pathogens (with the exception of *Schistosoma haematobium* in some areas), its reuse is less problematic. The pathogens in human faeces, however, must be destroyed completely by drying before reuse.

3.2.2 Solid wastes from households: levels increasing

Solid waste generation

Solid household waste consists mainly of non-hazardous waste such as paper and plastic packaging material, glass, food scraps and other residues, and garden materials. However, it generally also contains small quantities of hazardous substances such as paints, medicines, solvents, cleaning materials and batteries, making waste management more difficult and increasing the environmental risks that waste presents (UNEP, 1993).

Solid household wastes often become intermixed with wastes of similar character from shops, offices, and small-scale industrial units working with materials such as metals, timber and textiles. The resulting waste streams are commonly called municipal waste. Management of this waste can be classified into distinct phases: generation and storage; collection and handling; recycling and reuse; transfer and transportation, and treatment and disposal.

In general, the higher a country's level of industrialization, the larger its proportion of toxic, non-organic and non-biodegradable waste, particularly

Table 3.2

Examples of municipal waste composition (%) for selected cities

	UK	Delhi India	Kathmandu Nepal	Wuhan China
Vegetables	25	49	67	16
Dust, ash, other materials	18	38	10	78
Plastic, leather, rubber	7	1	<0.5	0.5
Textiles	3	3	7	0.5
Glass	10	1	1	0.5
Metals	8	1	5	0.5
Paper	29	7	7	2
Wood	n.a.	n.a.	3	2

n.a.: data not available

Source: based on data from Rushbrook & Finnecy, 1988.

packaging materials and paper (**Table 3.2**). Conversely, in low-income countries, a large proportion of municipal waste consists of organic matter and ashes or grit.

The production of household and municipal waste continues to increase worldwide, both in absolute and per capita terms. Estimated typical municipal waste production per capita increases with rising average income (**Table 3.3**); this is highlighted by the data presented for selected cities in **Table 3.4**. However, since the definition of municipal waste may differ between countries, these comparisons are very approximate. Additionally, waste generation quantities may vary greatly within a single city. In a developing country city, waste production may amount to only 0.3 kg/person/day in a poor neighbourhood, but up to 1.0 kg/person/day in a wealthy neighbourhood (UNCHS, 1996b).

Ideally, waste production should be minimized. Encouragingly, it appears that in many developed countries industry is realizing that minimization can improve efficiency and reduce costs, helping in turn to reduce waste generation at the household level. In developing countries, however, attempts to promote waste minimization have been hampered by lack of data on waste production at source, and on waste collection and disposal.

Table 3.3

Typical quantities of municipal waste production per capita

Type of country	Waste generation (Kg/capita/day)
High-income countries	0.8 to 3.0
Middle-income countries	0.5 to 0.9
Low-income countries	0.3 to 0.6

Source: based on data from UNCHS, 1996b.

Table 3.4

Municipal waste quantities generated in selected major cities

	Tons/day	Kg/capita/day
Seoul (Republic of Korea)	22 000	2.0
Singapore	4500	1.6
Buenos Aires (Argentina)	11 700	1.1
Mexico City (Mexico)	10 000	0.6
Rio de Janeiro (Brazil)	6000	0.6
Bangkok (Thailand)	2740	0.4
Metro Manila (Philippines)	2650	0.3

Source: based on data from UN, 1995e.

UNCHS is therefore assisting developing countries with data collection on waste production and devising policy options at the municipal level for waste minimization (CSD, 1997c).

Access to solid waste collection

In developed countries close to 100% of the population has access to municipal waste services. In many developing countries only a small proportion of the population has such access and thus a mere 30% of wastes are collected (UNCHS, 1996b). In low-income neighbourhoods there may be no collection at all. Instead, it must be undertaken by individuals or local communities (WHO, 1996g). Some community waste collection and management systems have proven very efficient. In fact, they are often the only satisfactory means available for waste collection and management (**Box 3.1**).

Disposal and treatment

Reliable data regarding waste disposal are very few. For developing countries they are hardly gathered at all. In developed countries the tendency is to dispose of municipal wastes in sanitary landfills or by incineration. In developing countries incineration is rarely undertaken because of its expense. Instead, collected wastes are disposed of in controlled or uncontrolled (unconfined) landfills, or, more frequently, dumped on the street, in backyards or drainage ditches, buried in gardens, or burned in open fires.

If wastes are not disposed of adequately or remain untreated, microbiological and/or chemical pollutants may affect land and air, or enter surface and groundwaters. Such pollution is rarely assessed since many sources and pollutants are often involved. Moreover, assessment is difficult because the environmental distribution and fate of such pollutants are highly complex.

Recycling

Recycling is an essential element of sustainable waste handling. In some countries it has been practised for decades, largely for economic reasons, but increasingly in response to environmental considerations. The best-known examples include reuse of scrap metals, reuse of bottles, paper recycling and composting of organic waste. Conversion of waste products into products for use in other sectors is also growing. In some countries, construction materials for roads and buildings are increasingly made from recycled waste products such as incinerator ashes and shredded automobile tyres.

In developing countries recycling often takes the form of scavenging, but this exposes waste handlers to numerous health hazards (see Section 4.3). However, since it also provides income for many poorer social groups its abolition and prohibition will prove difficult. In major cities, such as Bogota, Calcutta and Manila, more than 30 000 people (in each city) are involved in the "informal waste economy" (CSD, 1997c).

3.3 Fresh water

The saying "Water is life" is found in many cultures around the world. It underscores the fact that clean water is an absolute prerequisite for healthy living. Yet for a large percentage of the world's population, water supplies are neither safe nor adequate. Understanding the issues that affect water quantity and quality is the first step to rectifying this situation and crucial to assuring sustainable water supplies.

3.3.1 Global freshwater resources: limited, uneven and subject to pressure

The world's freshwater resources are limited. Of the total 35 million km^3 of freshwater stocks available on a long-term basis, only 90 000 km^3 (0.26%) are usable; much of this is stored in ice caps, glaciers and in permanent snow covers in the Antarctic and Arctic regions. The remainder — that is, the only fresh water which is available for use — amounts to a total global average of about 40 700 km^3 per year (Gleick, 1993). Moreover, freshwater resources are unevenly distributed over the global land mass, and about two-thirds of fresh water enters the oceans as run-off, leaving about 14 000 km^3 as a relatively stable supply (FAO, 1994a). This is equivalent to an average of approximately 2300 m^3 per person globally. Current global water use is estimated at about one-half of this available supply.

Most renewable freshwater resources are concentrated in the temperate climatic zone and in the humid tropics. In the arid and semi-arid regions, where much of the world's population lives, the already limited nature of water resources, combined with extreme uneven regional and seasonal distribution, often leads to severe water shortages. Geographical distribution of water resources is actually more important than national water availability per capita. However, water management can do much to alleviate the unevenness of freshwater distribution.

Since most future population growth will take place in the developing countries of Africa, Asia and Central and South America (see Section 2.2), per capita water availability can be expected to decrease in these regions. Currently, per capita availability is highest in South America and lowest in North Africa and the Near East. In western Europe and North America, per capita water availability is not expected to change greatly in the near future, as **Fig. 3.4** demonstrates.

3.3.2 Global freshwater use: demand inequity

Demand for water is increasing in several sectors — for drinking-water (domestic needs), food production (agriculture) and product manufacturing (industry). Water use figures differ significantly in terms of continent, region, country and area (**Fig. 3.5**) and type of use, but globally, total demand for water increased by six times between 1900 and 1990. This growth

rate was more than double the population growth rate for the same period and can be attributed to increased reliance on irrigation to achieve food security, growth in industrial water uses, and increased domestic water use per capita. The amount of water used for irrigation, for example, has increased by a factor of ten this century and plans are being elaborated for further expansion (FAO, 1994). Disparities in use within sectors are sometimes very marked. Beef production, for instance, is particularly "thirsty", requiring 100 000 litres to produce

---

Box 3.1

Community participation in solid waste management: Kalabagan, Dhaka (Bangladesh)

The City Corporation of Dhaka, Bangladesh ceased to be able to provide satisfactory waste collection and disposal services. Waste heaps began to pile up in streets and to contribute to the feeding and breeding of dogs, rats and insects, and became a source of undesirable odours and clogged drains during the rainy season. In Kalabagan, about 700 households were affected.

In response, the local community began organizing daily direct waste collection from individual houses. It engaged four waste collectors, hired two rickshaw vans with drivers, and one community member to collect payment from the households and to keep financial accounts. The two community members who initiated these activities offered honorary services to oversee management of the system.

The rickshaw van drivers organize sorting with selected waste pickers and sell recyclable waste (bones, polythene bags, paper, broken plastic and metal waste) to relevant industries. This yields extra income for the van drivers and their team. The waste collectors also receive an extra payment from those householders who do not carry their waste directly to the van. These additional gains encourage the waste collection team to follow a strict schedule for waste collection and sorting.

Lessons learned:

- The initiative of two community members was sufficient to raise community awareness concerning this issue and to set up a new waste management system.

- This approach is sustainable as evidenced by the fact that it is being replicated in the surrounding area.

- Women are prominent in the efficient operation of the system — they usually deposit the waste directly into the collection vans.

Source: WHO, 1996g.

Fig. 3.4

Per capita annual freshwater availability (km³) in 1990 and 2025 for selected countries*

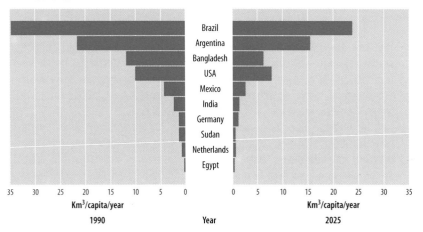

* UN medium population projection

Sources: based on data from Gleick, 1993 and UN, 1995a.

Fig 3.5

Per capita water use by continent for 1995

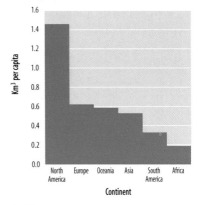

* 1987 data

Source: based on data from WRI, 1996.

just one kilogram; a kilogram of broiler chicken needs only 3500 litres of water (Pimentel et al., 1997). If water resource management and water policies aimed at more efficient water use are not implemented, unsustainable growth in water demand will continue (CSD, 1997a).

As shown in **Fig. 3.5**, water use per capita varies considerably between continents, depending mainly on population density and level of socioeconomic development. An important role is also played by hydroclimatic conditions which determine the amount of readily available water and the need for irrigation in agriculture. Estimates for 1995 suggest that Asia consumes approximately 60% of the world's water, but that North America has the highest per capita consumption rate (FAO, 1994a).

Despite trends towards stabilization of water use, and even slight decreases in a few countries (USA, Sweden, Great Britain and the Netherlands, for example), water requirements for the world as a whole are growing for all types of socioeconomic activity. Agriculture has the major share, although ultimately this will decrease in relative terms due to increasing industrial development. Agricultural water demand is mostly for irrigation and livestock watering; industrial water demand includes water

for the manufacture of goods and operation of thermal power plants. Community water use includes domestic uses in urban and rural areas. Incremental evaporation from lakes and reservoirs constitutes a large portion of unrecoverable water losses throughout the world: in total this exceeds use by industry and households combined (Gleick, 1993).

3.3.3 Freshwater scarcity: of growing proportions

Water scarcity today is mostly a local problem caused by uneven distribution of water sources, misuse, poor management and population growth. Increasingly, though, it is becoming a problem of regional and even sub-continental proportions, as seen in large parts of northern Africa, central Asia and southern India. Currently, over 1000 million people (one-fifth of the global population) do not have access to an adequate supply of safe water for household consumption (WHO/UNICEF, 1996a). The minimum basic freshwater requirement is 50 litres per person, per day, or 18 m³ per person, per year (**Box 3.2**).

Areas with greatest freshwater demand, such as large urban agglomerations, industrial complexes and agricultural areas with sizeable irrigation systems, often face severe problems in meeting freshwater demand in terms of both quantity and quality. In fact, in many regions, freshwater scarcity is increasing and leading to severe ecological degradation, which in turn is limiting agricultural and industrial production, threatening human health, and increasing the potential for international conflict over water resources. Aquifers, for instance are being overexploited. Known as "groundwater mining", and often the result of ill-planned industrial and agricultural development, this practice is reducing the quantity of groundwater in permanent storage. The mining of the sub-Saharan aquifer is one example (Gleick, 1993).

About 20 countries are suffering more or less severely from water scarcity. This number is expected to have risen by 2050 (Gleick, 1993). "Water scarcity" is not easily defined, however. The definition used here is based on an index of vulnerability — if a country's annual per capita water availability is 1000 m^3 or less it is considered to be suffering from water scarcity (Falkenmark et al., 1989). Water availability in many of the countries already suffering from water scarcity is expected to decline further (Engelman & Le Roy, 1995a) (**Fig. 3.6**).

Depending on their economic and political situation, however, countries might be able to cope with water scarcity through effective water management — for example, by improving irrigation systems, promoting safe reuse of water through construction of wastewater treatment facilities, introducing realistic water pricing, applying best available water-saving technologies in industry, and undertaking desalinization. Other proven strategies such as integrated land use and water resources management along rivers and lake basins, cultivation of crops requiring less water, agricultural reuse of wastewater and minimization of water pollution, can do much to increase water availability (Gleick, 1993). Even very scarce water supplies can be stretched through efficient management and modern technology, as has been proved in several semi-arid countries. International political and economic agreements such as those concerning international river basins can also relax pressures on water.

3.3.4 Freshwater pollution: a new problem every decade

Global freshwater resources are threatened not only by overexploitation of groundwater and surface water, and poor resource management, but also by ecological degradation. Ecological degradation of freshwater bodies has ceased to be a purely local phenomenon, encroaching along entire river systems and even into international river and lake basins.

Discharge of untreated sewage into rivers and lakes, dumping of industrial wastes, and run-off from agricultural fields treated with herbicides and pesticides, are the main sources of freshwater pollution. Industrial development, the exponential growth of human settlements and the ever-increasing use of synthetic organic substances, are also having serious adverse impacts on freshwater bodies. Many surface and groundwaters are now contaminated with nutrients, heavy metals and persistent organic pollutants (POPs), and the aquatic life they contain severely threat-

Box 3.2
Minimum basic freshwater needs

Among the concepts introduced during the 1977 UN Water Conference in Mar del Plata, Argentina — one of the earliest international efforts to address global water problems — was that of "basic needs". It was stated that "... all peoples, whatever their stage of development and their social and economic conditions, have the right to have access to drinking water in quantities and of a quality equal to their basic needs" (UN, 1977). This concept was strongly reaffirmed during the Earth Summit and expanded to include ecological water needs: "In developing and using water resources, priority has to be given to the satisfaction of basic needs and the safeguarding of ecosystems" (UN, 1993).

Implicit in the latter quotation is a reference to the basic water needed for certain human and ecological functions, and to the allocation of sufficient water resources for their discharge. Gleick (1996) defines and quantifies "basic water requirements", in terms of quantity and quality, for four basic human needs: drinking-water for survival, water for human hygiene, water for sanitation services, and modest quantities of water for household food preparation (see table below). Gleick recommends that international organizations, national and local governments, and water providers adopt a basic water requirement standard for meeting these needs of 50 litres per person per day, and to guarantee access to this quantity independently of individuals' economic, social or political status.

Basic water requirements for fundamental human needs	Litres per person per day
Drinking-water	5
Sanitation	20
Food preparation	10
Bathing	15
Total recommended	50

Sources: UN, 1977, 1993; Gleick, 1996.

Fig. 3.6

Selected countries with water scarcity (water resources less than 1000 m³ per capita per year) for 1990 and 2050

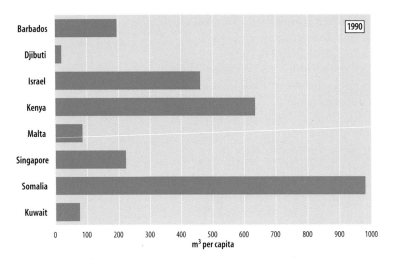

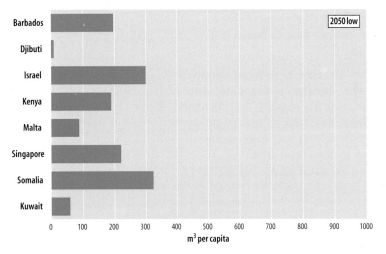

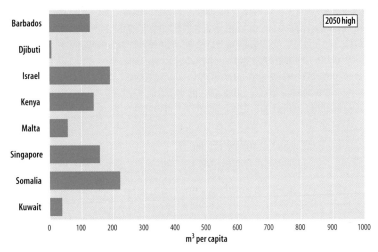

Note: figures for 2050 are given for both the low and high UN population growth projections

Source: Engelman & Le Roy, 1995a; WRI, 1996.

ened. **Table 3.5** illustrates the impact of intensive agriculture and high population density on nitrogen levels in rivers monitored by GEMS.

In fact, a new water pollution problem appears to emerge each decade in developed countries. In the 1950s concern focused on "oxygen balance" and in the 1960s on eutrophication. In the 1970s heavy metals were perceived as a serious threat to health, while in the 1980s, acidification, organic micropollutants and nitrates came to the fore. In the early and mid-1990s, groundwater contamination attracted much attention, but now appears to be shifting to POPs (see Section 2.6). Meanwhile, developing countries undergoing rapid industrialization are faced with the full range of modern toxic pollution problems, and without having resolved "traditional" organic water pollution problems associated with poor-quality water supply and lack of sanitation services.

The amounts of pollution that are discharged into watercourses often far exceed their waste-assimilation capacity. Nearly 450 km³ of wastewater enters surface waters worldwide annually and about 6000 km³ of fresh water, equivalent to two-thirds of total reliable annual run-off, are needed to dilute and carry it into the world's oceans (UNEP, 1991a). Therefore, in many parts of the world, pollution of surface water and groundwater is limiting the usable part of available freshwater significantly. Furthermore, serious health threats can arise if polluted water is used as drinking-water, for bathing or washing, for food processing or for irrigation of edible crops (see Section 4.4).

Once contaminated, water requires costly purification treatment before it can be used for community water supply or by industry. In most developed countries, municipal and industrial wastewater treatment facilities are now in place, but at considerable cost. In developing countries, growing urban centres and rural areas have few if any such facilities since the necessary water-carriage sewerage systems, which must be operated in conjunction with multi-stage wastewater treatment, are prohibitively expensive. Yet such infrastructure is likely to be increasingly necessary, given that estimates suggest a doubling of industrial water use over the next 25 years, leading to a more than four-fold increase in industrial pollution (CSD, 1997c).

3.3.5 The marine environment: land-based pressures

The health, well-being, and, in some cases, the very survival of people living along coasts are closely tied to the condition of coastal systems (estuaries and wetlands), and their associated watersheds, drainage basins and near-shore coastal waters. Most of the pollution load of the oceans, including municipal, industrial and agricultural wastes and run-off, as well as atmospheric deposition, derives from land-based activities and affects the marine environment's most productive areas. Resultant risks to marine life and human health have been identified as: sewage, POPs, radioactive substances, heavy metals, oils (hydrocarbons (HCs), nutrients, sediment mobilization and litter (UNEP, 1995a). An example of the disastrous human health consequences of the prolonged discharge of toxic chemicals in a coastal environment is provided in **Box 3.3**. Sustainable patterns of human activity in coastal areas are clearly crucial. These are not easy to attain, however, in view of population increase in coastal areas and the trend towards their further urbanization and industrialization.

In many parts of the world, pressures on marine areas are exacerbated by overfishing and climate anomalies, such as increasing frequency of El Niño episodes and rising surface-water temperatures. The combined action of these factors has already led to the collapse of previously productive fishing grounds and to increasing frequency of (toxic) algal blooms, with negative

impacts on human health (McMichael et al., 1996) (see Section 4.10).

3.3.6 Hydrology and aquatic environments: integrated planning needed

Human activity affects not only the quality and quantity of freshwater resources, but also their distribution in the environment, so much so that the nature of whole ecosystems may undergo substantial change. Of major importance in this connection are dams and impoundments, irrigation schemes, aquaculture, urban drainage and wastewater disposal (Hunter et al., 1993). Awareness is now growing, however, that healthy functioning of aquatic ecosystems requires integrated planning among several sectors, including agriculture, industry, natural resources and health. This in turn will require that we deepen our understanding of the interactions between the interface of aquatic environments, such as wetlands, and the human populations that inhabit them. The specific health risks of aquatic ecosystems for vulnerable groups within local communities also require further investigation.

The impacts of human activities on water resources may extend to remote areas. In parts of North Africa large, earth-filled dams have created marshy conditions along reservoir shores and at their base, through seepage. At the same time, the reduced run-off caused by water retention in the reservoirs has substantially impaired the replenishment of aquifers under the fertile plains at a considerable distance from the dam. So although large urban centres are benefiting from the pumped reservoir water, sometimes several hundreds of kilometres away, the water quality of the declining aquifers is deteriorating rapidly due to percolation and concentration of agrochemicals. Local farming communities must dig increasingly deeper wells for water of diminishing quality, and rely on irrigation and drainage canals for their domestic water needs. The human health impacts

Table 3.5

Nitrogen level in rivers monitored by GEMS

World region	Ammonia (µg/l)*	Nitrates (µg/l)*
All GEMS rivers outside Europe	70	250
European GEMS rivers	210	4500
Natural average for unpolluted rivers	15	100

Source: WHO/UNEP, 1987.

Box 3.3

Minamata: environmental contamination with methyl mercury

In Minamata, Japan, inorganic mercury was used as a catalyst in the industrial production of acetaldehyde. When discharged in wastewater into a small bay, it was taken up by organisms in the bottom sediments, which converted the mercury to highly toxic methyl mercury (MeHg). Eventually this contaminant accumulated in fish and other seafoods. Residents in the area who consumed large amounts of these suffered MeHg intoxication, known as "Minamata disease", first diagnosed in 1956. The mercury emissions continued until 1968.

However, even after discharge of the mercury ceased, the bottom sediment of the polluted water areas contained high MeHg levels.

Various measures were taken to deal with Minamata disease, including:
* environmental pollution control
* help for patients, including compensation for lost income, subsidized medical expenses for persons suspected of having Minamata disease, and a survey of the potential health impacts on those living in contaminated areas
* promotion of investigation and research activities.

Measures undertaken to control the environmental pollution included:
* cessation of the process using mercury
* industrial effluent control
* environmental restoration, which ultimately included removal of contaminated sediment from the bay
* restrictions on the intake of fish and other seafoods, and compensation to the fishing industry for lost revenue.

The table compares the estimated annual cost in 1990 due to Minamata disease with those for pollution prevention and control measures in the area around Minamata Bay. This figure does not include indirect costs such as the salaries of government staff. The real cost of the damage caused by Minamata disease, including healthcare subsidies and compensation for lost income, was probably 100 times greater.

	Cost million yen/year
Cost of pollution control and prevention measures	123
Damage in total	12 631
Health damage	7671
Environmental pollution damage	4271
Fishery damage	689

Minamata disease served as a turning-point: environmental protection measures have since made good progress in Japan. The Japanese Government, patients and their supporters reached agreement in 1996 and Minamata disease legal issues were finally settled, 40 years after the first outbreak. This experience demonstrates that health-and-environment considerations must be integrated into the process of economic and industrial development from a very early stage.

Source: Environment Agency of Japan, 1996.

of this transition include increased occurrence of diarrhoeal and infectious diseases (such as schistosomiasis) and prolonged exposure to hazardous chemical residues.

In response to the need for integration of water resources development planning and management, as prominently expressed in Agenda 21, many countries have started to revise their national water resources policies and strategies, with a focus on comprehensive decision-making criteria that take into account all user groups in the different public sectors and in the private sector. This has given rise to the concept of integrated river basin development and management, which aims at sustainable use of water resources in a catchment area, taking upstream and downstream effects into account (Chandiwana & Snellen, 1994; Mather, Sornmani & Keola, 1994). This is ensuring that greater attention is paid to environmental conditions, particularly vegetation cover, which influence sediment loads and flooding risk.

Implementation of integrated river basin development and management remains at an early stage, however, and opportunities to apply concepts are sometimes needlessly lost (**Box 3.4**). In addition, health sector policy and decision-makers remain insufficiently aware of the cross-cutting nature of many health issues. So although water resources planning has benefited from increased application of environmental impact assessments (EIAs), development of national EIA policies and institutional arrangements for effective decision-making procedures on these cross-sectoral issues, governments have not taken optimal advantage of new concepts, policies and strategies in water resource management. Capacity-building efforts by WHO therefore aim to promote health impact assessment as an integral part of EIA and to strengthen the abilities of managers in different sectors to effectively include health issues in intersectoral development dialogue (Birley et al.; 1996) (see also Chapter 6).

3.4 Land use and agricultural development

3.4.1 Competition for land

Competition for land appears to be intensifying between sectors and production systems. Agriculture, in particular, can be expected to become an even more dominant form of land use. In developing countries, where population growth is fastest, and consumption patterns among growing urban populations are changing, accelerated extension of areas under cultivation, expansion of irrigated agriculture, changed cropping patterns (including crop intensification) and increased chemical inputs, have been observed. Gradual substitution of rice for traditional coarse grains as the staple food of urban populations in West Africa is a good example of the intricate interrelationships between development, consumption patterns, cropping patterns and environment (**Box 3.5**).

In contrast to agricultural areas, urban areas are very small. Thus although half of the world's population lives in cities, the total amount of land dedicated to urban uses is actually only 1% of total land surface. However, cities are often located on prime agricultural land or valuable ecosystems near rivers, lakes or coasts (WRI, 1996). For instance, about 476 000 ha of arable land in developing countries are converted annually to urban uses.

In short, "cultivated" land is much greater in extent than urbanized areas, and agriculture the dominant agent of global land transformation. Around 11% (1440 million ha) of all land is arable land, of which 17% is irrigated (240 million ha). Between 1970 and 1994, arable land and crop land increased by 5% and the area of permanent grassland by 6% (Alexandratos, 1995). So while agricultural land is sometimes lost to urbanization, forest and woodlands are being converted to croplands and pasture (WRI, 1994; Alexandratos, 1995). **Table 3.6** outlines changes in land use for several regions.

Given population increase and the finite extent to which further land can be converted to agricultural uses, per capita arable land availability is becoming an issue. The minimum amount of arable land required to feed a single

---

Box 3.4

Integrated management of the Senegalese river basin: a lost opportunity

The Senegal River basin is shared by Guinea, Mali, Mauritania and Senegal, and covers 290 000 km^2; the river itself is 1790 km in length. The Organisation pour la Mise en Valeur du Fleuve Sénégal (OMVS) was established in 1972 by Mali, Mauritania and Senegal, to manage the river basin. Two dams were constructed in the 1980s: the Manantali Dam in the Upper Senegal River, in Mali, for electricity generation, and the Diama Dam, at the mouth of the river in Senegal, to prevent further saltwater intrusion into the delta area, which was affecting aquatic ecology as far as 350 km upstream.

The construction of the Diama Dam led to the formation of a large, shallow freshwater reservoir which allowed the rapid expansion of irrigated agriculture in the delta: rice production in the area between St Louis and Richard Toll, and sugar cane production around and south of Richard Toll. But this led to the largest epidemic of *Schistosoma mansoni* infections (intestinal schistosomiasis) on record in Africa, south of the Sahara.

The reservoir of the Manantali Dam reached spillway level in August 1991. Turbines and power lines have not been installed, however. The energy component continues to be a subject of negotiations between OMVS and the World Bank, with the required substantial health-and-environment representing a major obstacle to the conclusion of the loan involved. Meanwhile, the dam's impact on downstream ecology has been considerable: in the absence of annual floods, the traditional recession agriculture of the local population has had to be abandoned. The delivery of electricity for pumps which would enable farmers to practise irrigated agriculture has yet to start. Widespread malnutrition has been reported. Additionally, new fishing communities (some 1500 people) have settled along the river and are exposed to the risk of schistosomiasis.

An extensive, basin-wide health impact assessment led to the recommendation of reservoir fluctuation and artificial flooding as means of reducing the health risks and restoring the original ecology of the basin downstream from the Manantali Dam. A more controversial but apparently technically sound measure which involves letting salt water intrude into the delta, some weeks before the artificial flood reaches the mouth of the river, aims at reducing snail intermediate host populations and environmental receptivity to schistosomiasis. A proposal to carry out studies that would lead to formulation of a set of decision-making tools for dam operations, has, however, not met with sufficient agreement at the negotiating table. It now looks as if, following the recent disestablishment of OMVS (January 1997), the energy loan will be given instead to the privatized organization set up to operate the Manantali Dam. In so doing, the opportunity to arrive at a basin-wide approach for environment and health will have been lost.

Source: Diop & Jobin, 1994.

person with a largely vegetarian diet on a sustainable basis, without intensive use of fertilizers and pest control, is considered to be 0.07 ha (Engelman & LeRoy, 1995b). In 1990, arable land availability per capita was less than 0.07 ha in only a few countries: for example, Egypt, Japan, the Netherlands, South Korea and Switzerland. But as shown in **Table 3.7**,

taking into account the UN medium population projection, the number of countries with less than 0.07 ha arable land availability per capita is expected to have increased sharply by the year 2025. Countries with limited arable land are especially restricted in terms of options for managing the environment.

Competition for land also appears to be intensifying between different population groups within countries and across national boundaries, as seen in recent conflicts in the Balkans, Africa and the Middle East. Conflicts over the distribution of land and the wealth it produces contribute to the violence which forces people to abandon their homes and seek sanctuary elsewhere (Oxfam, 1995). Additionally, land degradation due to population movement — both political and environmental — is being observed in many regions (UNHCR, 1995) (see also Section 2.2.3).

Competition for land contributes to food insecurity. While outside the scope of this book, this is of grave concern and must be taken into account when considering agriculture and food supply.

Indeed, although impressive progress has been made in agricultural production during the past 25 years (**Fig. 3.7**), more than 780 million people are chronically undernourished. This is not because of inadequate global food production, but because of unequal food distribution between geographical or social groups. In Africa, the situation has been worsening for the last 20 years, both in absolute and relative terms; the number of undernourished people almost doubled from 94 million (35%) in 1970 to 175 million (37%) in 1990. Chronic undernutrition is likely to remain widespread in sub-Saharan Africa. In the year 2010 it could affect one-third of its population (some 300 million people) (Alexandratos, 1995). In South Asia and the Latin America/Caribbean regions, the absolute number of people suffering from malnutrition has increased due to population growth,

Box 3.5
Rice production in West Africa

Between 1961 and 1990, regional demand for rice in West Africa grew at an annual rate of 5.6%; it is not expected to fall below 5% in coming years. A 1985 study of consumption patterns in Ouagadougou, Burkina Faso, found that the poorest third of urban households obtain one-third of their cereal intake from rice, with the purchase of rice representing 45% of their cash expenditure on cereals.

In the last decade, regional rice production rose at an annual rate of 3.3% only, barely exceeding the rate of population growth and meeting just half of the increase in demand. Most of the increase in rice production has been due to expansion (average 2.4% annually) of the cultivated area with regional rice yields (on average amounting to only 40% of the global mean) increasing at a mere 1.5% per year.

Rice production is not only failing to keep pace with demand, but also increasing some disease risks. In Senegal, irrigation expansion following the construction of the Diama Dam at the mouth of the Senegal river (see Box 3.4), caused a massive epidemic of intestinal schistosomiasis. Admittedly, sugar cane production was the main culprit, but irrigated rice production also contributed substantially. In Côte d'Ivoire, farmers — influenced by anecdotal information on disease risks — are reluctant to expand their rice cultivation into the basses-fonds. Instead, expansion of rice-growing areas is rather moving uphill, causing serious deforestation. A study on the association between rice production systems and vector-borne diseases in West Africa is under way in Côte d'Ivoire and Mali, and seeks to identify the eco-epidemiological characteristics of different rice agro-ecosystems. The study is being carried out jointly by the West Africa Rice Development Association, the Panel of Experts on Environmental Management for Vector Control, and the Canadian International Development Research Centre.

West African governments seek to promote local rice production to reduce foreign exchange expenditures on rice imports. In recent years, rice imports, which have been rising at an annual rate of 8%, have cost the region over US$ 750 million in scarce foreign currency annually. Yet on the world market, rice prices are less than West African production costs. Governments therefore have to choose between establishing internationally unpopular tariff barriers on rice imports, and heavily subsidizing local farmers. Many West African communities engaged in irrigated rice production can barely meet their basic needs, and certainly cannot afford to invest in maintaining irrigation infrastructure. This, together with sub-optimal water management practices, is resulting in serious environmental deterioration, including waterlogging and salinization, and increasing environmental health risks.

Source: WHO, 1993c.

Table 3.6

Trends in land use during 1980–1990

Region	Domesticated land as % of total land area in 1990	Changes in cropland (%)	Changes in % of permanent pasture land	Changes in % of forest and woodland
Africa	36	+ 5	+ 0.9	-3.8
Asia	45	+ 1.3	+ 9.5	-4.9
North and Central America	30	-0.7	+ 1	+ 0.3
South America	35	+ 12.7	+ 4.4	-5.1
Europe	47	-1.8	-3.7	+ 0.9
Former USSR	25	-1.0	+ 1.7	-22.2
Oceania	57	+ 9.9	-4.8	-0.1
World	37	+ 1.8	+ 2.4	-7.8

Source: WRI, 1994.

although the relative proportion of malnourished population has declined (Alexandratos, 1995).

Much can be done, however, to ensure that land development initiatives are sustainable, and to minimize land-use conflict. Considerable experience now exists of innovative land development mechanisms that combine social, economic and environmental goals, work with rather than against land markets, and use new forms of public/private partnerships (UNCHS, 1996b). In view of the rapid urbanization now occurring (see Section 2.3) it is particularly important that such mechanisms be used in urban planning. In developing countries, even where half or more of a city's population and many of its economic activities are located in illegal or informal settlements, urban planners have sometimes relied on traditional master-planning approaches. In so doing they have restricted their role to servicing a high-income influential minority (UNCHS, 1996b). This has meant that the environment and health needs of large population groups have gone unmet.

3.4.2 Agricultural development and environmental changes

Extension and intensification of agricultural production systems, together with fluctuations in the supply of and demand for agricultural produce is causing shifts in the environmental determinants of the health status of local communities. Some of these are masked or compounded by simultaneous demographic and socioeconomic shifts. Major environmental health risk factors of agricultural development are presented in **Table 3.8**.

All agricultural development must accordingly be seen in its local ecological (and epidemiological) context. Changed land-use patterns, for instance, will have varying impacts on different environmental health issues in different parts of the world. Thus deforestation in South-East Asia has destroyed the habitat of the most important local malaria vector, *Anopheles dirus*, bringing down malaria transmission rates. Afforestation, reforestation and the development of plantation agriculture (rubber, fruit trees) are reversing this effect, though, sometimes increasing malaria transmission risks to far higher levels than occurred in the primary forest environment. In Sri Lanka, the development of pristine areas for irrigation schemes, under the Accelerated Mahaweli Development Project, has resulted in major biodiversity loss, so much so, that the malaria vector *Anopheles culicifacies* has emerged as the main representative of a previously rich mosquito fauna. Mosquito disease vector densities, biting patterns and associated transmission risks, are also influenced by the presence or absence of livestock.

Table 3.7

Countries for which arable land availability per capita is projected to be less than 0.07 ha in 2025*

Country	1960	1990	2025**
Japan	0.06	0.04	0.04
Egypt	0.09	0.05	0.03
South Korea	0.08	0.05	0.04
Switzerland	0.08	0.06	0.05
Netherlands	0.09	0.06	0.06
China	0.16	0.08	0.06
Bangladesh	0.17	0.09	0.05
North Korea	0.16	0.09	0.06
Israel	0.19	0.09	0.06
Vietnam	0.17	0.10	0.05
Kenya	0.21	0.10	0.04
Somalia	0.24	0.12	0.05
Guinea	0.21	0.13	0.05
Tanzania	0.31	0.13	0.05
Nepal	0.19	0.14	<0.07
Haiti	0.18	0.14	<0.07
Yemen	0.25	0.14	0.05
Jordan	0.28	0.14	0.05
Saudi Arabia	0.29	0.15	0.06

* ranked by 1990 availability; data from 1960 and 1990 are also shown
** UN medium population projection

Sources: based on data from Engelman & LeRoy, 1995b and UN, 1995a.

Table 3.8

Major environmental health risk factors of agricultural development

Agricultural development issue	Direct environmental changes	Secondary environmental changes	Environmental health risk factors
Irrigation development	Hydrological changes Waterlogging Salination Increased water surfaces Increased relative humidity	Increased insect populations Increased weed densities Greater chemical inputs	Introduction of new vector species Increased vector densities Changed vector population composition Prolonged transmission season Chemical poisoning
Land-use changes	Deforestation Reduced biodiversity/habitat Simplification	Changed composition of the insect fauna	Changed vector population composition Changed vector longevity
Cropping patterns	High-yielding varieties Shift from subsistence to cash crops Accelerated cropping cycle Plantation agriculture	Greater chemical inputs Greater densities of insect populations	Poisoning Reduction of predator insect densities in favour of pest and vector species
Livestock management	Changes in livestock densities and spatial distribution of livestock New breeds of livestock	Changed densities of blood-sucking insects	Changed disease transmission potential
Mechanization	Changes in livestock densities Loss of ecological features associated with draught animals	Changed densities of blood-sucking insects Reduced refuge areas for predator insects Air and water pollution	Changed disease transmission potential
Chemical inputs	Increased levels of pesticides, herbicides and/or fertilizer	Chemical contamination Eutrophication of water bodies Expansion of aquatic weeds	Poisoning Introduction of new vector species Development of insecticide resistance in vector populations

Source: Bradley & Narayan, 1987.

3.4.3 Soil degradation: sources and effects

All human development depends on the availability of soils for settlement, industry and agriculture. Even more fundamentally, soils serve as a substrate for all terrestrial ecosystems. Good quality soil is therefore essential for human health; pressures on the environment that degrade soil jeopardize sustainable development.

Severe soil degradation is occurring worldwide in the form of exacerbated wind and water erosion, physical deterioration (including compaction, reduced aeration, increases and decreases in soil pH), nutrient loss, chemical contamination, increased contamination with pathogens and salinization. All of these may involve poor management of agricultural water use. For example, mismanagement of irrigation systems has led to the salin-ization of over 10 million ha (UNEP, 1993), and may be reducing crop yields. It can even render land unusable.

The causes of human-induced soil degradation that predominated in the 1980s are presented in **Table 3.9**. As can be seen, most soil degradation during this decade was directly due to agricultural activities (such as intensive crop production), removal of vegetation (to create pasture for cattle) or overgrazing. In extreme cases, soil degradation leads to destruction of the original biotic functions of soils; about 9 million ha (1% of total land area) are now so degraded that they can be neither reclaimed nor restored.

Soil erosion is the most serious type of soil degradation since it severely diminishes the agricultural productivity of soils and can only partly be compensated by increased fertilization. Human activities can exacerbate soil erosion to such an extent that the erosion rate exceeds the rate of new soil formation, as is the case on 35% of the world's croplands. Soil lost to wind and water erosion ranges from 5–10 tonnes per ha annually in Africa, Europe and Australia, to 10–20 tonnes per ha annually in the Americas, to 30 tonnes per ha annually in Asia (Brown et al., 1996b). Erosion is particularly widespread in dryland areas.

Chemical degradation is another increasing problem, now affecting about 2% of Earth's land surface. It can be caused by nutrient loss (through soil erosion), salinization (related to poor irrigation practices), chemical pollution and acidification (for example due to acid rain; see Section 4.9). Acidification and contamination with heavy metals, pesticides and other organic contaminants (outlined below), and with hazardous and other industrial waste, are the dominant forms of chemical soil deterioration in Europe and North America, while in Asia salinization predominates. The slow mobilization of chemicals accumulated in soils, that may be caused by environmental change processes such as acid deposition, deserves attention with regard to its potential long-term health effects.

Heavy metals: In general, heavy metal concentrations in soils increase with increasing proximity to and intensity of human habitation. Metal concentrations in most soils remain below critical limits for agriculture, but may be exceeded if accumulation occurs in topsoils. Fortunately, recent reductions in atmospheric emissions (for instance, through the phasing out of leaded petrol in many countries, the removal of heavy metals from industrial emissions, and the reduction of copper in fodder and cadmium in fertilizers), mean that the accumulation rate of metals in soils is falling. Metals may also be added to soil if sewage sludge is used as fertilizer. Cadmium has been of particular concern (IPCS, 1992a).

Pesticides: Use of pesticides and fertilizers, along with irrigation and high-yielding crop varieties, has increased agricultural productivity considerably. But these substances can also have adverse effects on the environment and the resultant human exposures can be high (see Section 5.6). In the USA, studies have found about 40 pesticides in groundwater in 30 states; serious pesticide contamination of groundwater has also been reported for several other developed

Fig. 3.7

World gross agricultural production, population and production per capita

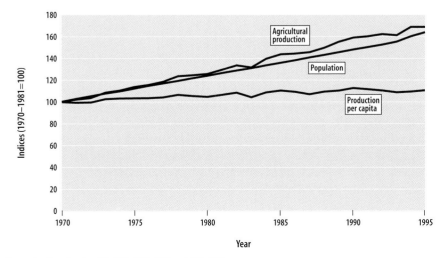

Sources: based on data from UN, 1981, 1990, 1995c and FAO, 1995.

Table 3.9

Main causes of human-induced soil degradation in the 1980s

Region	Percentage of all degraded land				
	Vegetation removal	Over-exploitation	Over-grazing	Agricultural activities	Bio-industrial activities
Africa	14	13	49	24	0
North America	11	7	24	57	0
South America	41	5	28	26	0
Asia	40	6	26	27	0
Europe	38	0	23	29	9
Oceania	12	0	80	8	0
World	30%	7%	35%	28%	1%

Source: based on data from ISRIC/UNEP, 1991.

countries. According to USEPA estimates, almost 1% of all community water systems contain potentially unsafe concentrations (WRI, 1992). The consequences of pesticide-contamination of soils for human health, in particular of the resulting potential for long-term exposure to low dosages in food, are unclear, however.

Pesticide use worldwide could be reduced by 50% by more widespread use of non-chemical pesticide controls, such as genetic improvement of host-plant resistance, crop rotation, use of biological controls, alteration of planting times, soil and water management, fertilizer management, planting of short-season varieties, tillage and improvement of pesticide application technologies (USEPA, 1994). Such a reduction in pesticide application could be achieved without any decline in crop yields and, in some cases, would actually increase yields (Lean, 1992) (see **Box 3.6**).

Organic compounds: As a result of industrial activities and the disposal of sewage sludge, numerous organic compounds of varying toxicity are discharged into the environment, ultimately accumulating in soils, threatening crop plants and grazing livestock, and possibly also affecting human health. Many of the contaminants are very persistent, for instance polyaromatic HCs, polychlorinated biphenyls (generally regarded as the most important contaminants), and polychlorinated dibenzo-p-dioxins and polychlorinated dibenzo-p-furans (PCDDs and

PCDFs). Soil data gathered in southeast England in a semi-rural plot show that PCDD and PCDF soil concentrations had increased from 31 to 92 μg/kg between 1890 and 1990 (Kjeller et al., 1991).

Fertilizers: In regions where soils are vulnerable to nitrate leaching, over-fertilization can result in very high nitrate concentrations in surface and groundwaters. For example, 25% of the population of the EU is estimated to be exposed to drinking-water with a nitrate content exceeding the maximum recommended level of 25 mg/l (WRI, 1992). Nitrate levels continue to rise, especially in some deep groundwaters. In very young babies, high exposure can lead to methaemoglobinaemia ("blue baby syndrome") (see Sections 4.4.4 and 4.6).

3.5 Industrialization: improved prospects and adverse consequences

Industrialization is central to economic development and improved prospects for human well-being. But if proper abatement technology is not used, industry becomes a major source of air and water pollution, hazardous wastes and noise (**Table 3.10**). Industrial operations accordingly have the potential to affect the health of workforces (see Section 4.8), that of the general environment, and through it the health of nearby populations, and sometimes even populations that are very far removed. It is industry's impacts on the general environment and populations that are focused upon in this section. Of concern are the routine discharges of pollutants to the environment as well as accidents with serious environmental consequences. Manufacturing industries also have environmental impacts through their use of energy and raw materials, particularly if large amounts of non-renewable raw materials are involved.

Box 3.6

Alternatives to pesticide use

Integrated pest management (IPM) and biological control (BC) have proved to be successful alternatives to pesticide use.

INTEGRATED PEST MANAGEMENT

IPM relies on a combination of techniques such as crop rotation, intercropping, careful spraying with pesticides of low toxicity (if used at all), and biological control to inhibit the proliferation of weeds, pests and pathogens. Examples of IPM include:

Country/region	Crop	Method/effects
Brazil	Soybean	Pesticide use reduced by 80–90% over 7 years
Jiangsu Province, China	Cotton	Pesticide use decreased by 90%; pest control costs cut by 84%; yields increased
Orissa, India	Rice	Insecticide use cut by 30–50%

BIOLOGICAL CONTROL

BC relies on nature's own set of checks and balances. Natural predators are introduced to keep pest populations to a minimum, or pest breeding disrupted by release of sterilized males. Examples of BC include:

Country/region	Crop	Method/effects
Equatorial Africa	Cassava	Parasitic wasp introduced to control mealy bug pest on some 65 million ha of cropland
Arkansas, USA	Rice/soybean	Commercially marketed, fungus-based "bioherbicide" used to control noxious weeds
Costa Rica	Banana	Pesticide use stopped with result that natural enemies reinvaded and banana pest populations reduced

Source: Lean, 1992.

3.5.1 Emissions, waste and natural resource use

Table 3.10 shows the types of emissions to air, water and soil that are emitted by selected sectors whose activities have significant routine environmental impacts. They include industries producing chemicals, paper and pulp, cement, glass and ceramics, iron and steel, non-ferrous metals and leather, and those involved in refining and processing petroleum. (Environmental problems relating to the energy industry are covered in Section 3.6.)

The following factors determine the type and level of industrial emissions:

- type and amount of product manufactured and manufacturing process used
- type, amount and content of raw materials used
- the use of energy, water and air

Table 3.10

Overview of significant and potential environmental impacts by industrial sectors

Sector	Air	Water	Soil/Land
Chemicals (industrial inorganic and organic compounds, excluding petroleum products)	• Many and varied emissions depending on processes used and chemicals manufactured • Emissions of particulate matter, SO_2, NO_x, CO, CFCs, VOCs and other organic chemicals, odours • Risk of explosions and fires	• Use of process water and cooling water • Emissions of organic chemicals, heavy metals (cadmium, mercury), suspended solids, organic matter, phenols, PCBs, cyanide water-quality effects • Risk of spills	• Chemical process wastes disposal problems • Sludges from air and water pollution treatment disposal problems
Paper and pulp	• Emissions of SO_2, NO_x, CH_4, CO_2, CO, hydrogen sulphide, mercaptans, chlorine compounds, dioxins	• Use of process water • Emissions of suspended solids, organic matter, chlorinated organic substances, toxins (dioxins)	
Cement, glass, ceramics	• Cement emissions of dust, NO_x, CO_2, chromium, lead, CO • Glass emissions of lead, arsenic, SO_2, vanadium, CO, hydrofluoric acid, soda ash, potash, speciality constituents (e.g. chromium) • Ceramics emissions of silica, SO_2, NO_x, fluorine compounds	• Emissions of process water contaminated by oils and heavy metals	• Extraction of raw materials • Metals soil contamination and waste disposal problems
Mining of metals and minerals	• Emissions of dust from extraction, storage and transport of ore and concentrate • Emissions of metals (e.g. mercury) from drying of ore concentrate	• Contamination of surface water and groundwater by highly acidic mine water containing toxic metals (e.g. arsenic, lead, cadmium). • Contamination by chemicals used in metal extraction (e.g. cyanide)	• Major surface disturbance and erosion • Land degradation by large slag heaps
Iron and steel	• Emissions of SO_2, NO_x, hydrogen sulphide, PAHs, lead, arsenic, cadmium, chromium, copper, mercury, nickel, selenium, zinc, organic compounds, PCDDs/PCDFs, PCBs, dust, particulate matter, HCs, acid mists • Exposure to ultraviolet and infrared radiation, ionizing radiation • Risks of explosions and fires	• Use of process water • Emissions of organic matter, tars and oil, suspended solids, metals, benzene, phenols, acids, sulphides, sulphates, ammonia, cyanides, thiocyanates, thiosulphates, fluorides, lead, zinc (scrubber effluent) water-quality effects	• Slag, sludges, oil and grease residues, HCs, salts, sulphur compounds, heavy metals soil contamination and waste disposal problems
Non-ferrous metals	• Emissions of particulate matter, SO_2, NO_x, CO, hydrogen sulphide, hydrogen chloride, hydrogen fluoride, chlorine, aluminium, arsenic, cadmium, chromium, copper, zinc, mercury, nickel, lead, magnesium, PAHs, fluorides, silica, manganese, carbon black, HCs, aerosols	• Scrubber water containing metals • Gas-scrubber effluents containing solids, fluorine, HCs	• Sludges from effluent treatment, coatings from electrolysis cells (containing carbon and fluorine) soil contamination and waste disposal problems
Coalmining and production	• Emissions of dust from extraction, storage and transport of coal • Emissions of CO and SO_2 from burning slag heaps • CH_4 emissions from underground formations • Risk of explosions and fires	• Contamination of surface water and groundwater by highly saline or acidic mine water	• Major surface disturbance and erosion • Subsidence of ground above mines • Land degradation by large slag heaps
Refineries, petroleum products	• Emissions of SO_2, NO_x, hydrogen sulphide, HCs, benzene, CO, CO_2, particulate matter, PAHs, mercaptans, toxic organic compounds, odours • Risk of explosions and fires	• Use of cooling water • Emissions of HCs, mercaptans, caustics, oil, phenols, chromium, effluent from gas scrubbers	• Hazardous waste, sludges from effluent treatment, spent catalysts, tars
Leather and tanning	• Emissions including leather dust, hydrogen sulphide, CO_2, chromium compounds	• Use of process water • Effluents from the many toxic solutions used, containing suspended solids, sulphates, chromium	• Chromium sludges

Sources: Stanners & Bourdeau, 1995; World Bank, 1997.

- size of the facility
- amount of toxic materials stored on site
- quality and efficiency of abatement technology (if used).

Another set of factors relates to the human exposures that can result from industrial emissions and includes:

- surrounding environmental conditions (rivers, wind, soil conditions, etc.)
- location of human settlement *vis-à-vis* industrial operations.

Regarding specific products, other emissions and impacts on environment and health may occur, depending on the packaging of the product, how it is distributed to consumers, the nature of consumption, and the product's eventual fate. The total impacts of industrial activity on the environment thus exceed the impacts occurring as a result of the manufacturing process alone.

Air pollution in particular has long been associated with the industrial sector and arises both from the use of fossil fuels to provide energy, and from industrial processes themselves (see Section 4.2). While the major air pollutants — suspended particulate matter, sulfur dioxide, carbon monoxide (CO), nitrogen oxides (NO_x) and HCs — are generated and emitted by a large number of industrial sectors, specific chemicals are associated with specific industries and processes (Table 3.10). Water pollution may occur following the use of water during an industrial process, following subsequent discharges, or the discharge of the product into water (see Section 4.4). Contamination of soil can also lead to water contamination if pollutants are leached from soil into groundwater.

Hazardous wastes must also be considered when assessing the health-and-environment impacts of industrial activity (see Section 4.3). Such wastes are associated with many different industries; examples range from waste oils from vehicles servicing, to expired or redundant pesticides, to mercury from chlorine production and spent catalysts, to oily refining wastes. In the absence of comprehensive regulatory systems, the most common methods for disposing of such wastes are uncontrolled discharge in water sources, uncontrolled disposal in open dumps and random disposal on land. Finally, however, major efforts are being made by some governments in developed countries and industries themselves to limit discharge of hazardous wastes through waste minimization and recycling, reclamation and reuse (CSD, 1997c), and to clean up existing hazardous waste disposal sites. At the international level, the Basel Convention restricts the transboundary movement of hazardous wastes and aims at strengthening infrastructures for hazardous waste control in developing countries (see Section 2.7).

Special attention should also be given to waste generated by the healthcare industry (**Box 3.7**). In many hospitals, wastes are segregated, the most dangerous and infectious waste being incinerated. But if mismanaged, hospital wastes may be disposed of in municipal waste dumps or in city sewers, becoming a health risk to the general population.

Resource-intensive industries are those involved in metal-smelting, food production, and pulp, paper and timber production. Energy-intensive industries include non-ferrous smelting and refining industries, cement industries, utility industries and pulp and paper industries. In Europe, industrial energy consumption increased very little in absolute terms from 1970 to 1990. However, the proportion of energy consumed by industry in Europe decreased from 49% to 41% during the same period (Stanners & Bourdeau, 1995). Energy conservation has been achieved by improving energy efficiency, diversifying into cleaner fuels, using materials more efficiently and recycling. Intensity of resource use is another major determinant of industry's health-and-environment impacts.

Water-intensive industries include non-metallic mineral industries, those involved in production of concrete products, ready-mixed concrete and motor-vehicle parts, and the pulp and paper industries. They consume large quantities of water during their production processes, principally for cooling and power generation. In high-income countries, industry accounts for 47% of total water withdrawals (WRI, 1996). However, industrial water use is expected to decline in these countries due to increased use of water-efficient technology in production processes.

The impact of resource-intensive industries could also be reduced through increased recovery of metals — including chromium, mercury and copper — and solvents. Estimates suggest that in the USA up to 80% of waste solvents and 50% of the metals in liquid waste streams could be recovered by technologies developed as long ago as the late 1970s (Postel, 1987). And in Japan, the USA and Western Europe, waste exchanges, operating on the simple premise that one industry's waste can be another's raw material, have succeeded in promoting the recycling and reuse of industrial wastes (UNEP, 1992a).

Impacts of small-scale industries

Major industrial impacts also arise from small-scale industry. In developing countries informal small-scale industries are an important part of the industrial sector. They contribute substantially to economic development, but can create problems for environment and health if environmental safeguards are not used. For example, small-scale mining, smelting, refining and manufacturing may release large quantities of toxic metals into air, water and soil (see **Box 3.8**). Electroplating of metals and recycling of lead, often carried out in small-scale facilities, also have significant potential in terms of toxic metal emissions. When such facilities are sited close to housing areas, serious human exposures can result.

Proliferation of small-scale industries is having notably adverse environmental impacts in China. For instance, many printing houses in China rely on stereotyping, which results in the recycling of huge numbers of lead-types every day (Shen et al., 1996). Since these printing houses tend to be concentrated in heavily populated cities, they represent a health risk for large populations. China's rural areas too are facing increasing lead pollution due to widespread small-scale industrialization. As the latest, environmentally-sustainable technologies are not affordable,

Box 3.7
Healthcare waste

Healthcare waste is becoming an important environmental health issue worldwide. It comprises all waste generated during healthcare provision and research and is generated mainly by:

* healthcare facilities
* nursing homes
* domestic environments where healthcare is being undertaken
* medical laboratories and research institutes
* mortuary/autopsy centres.

About 80% of wastes generated by healthcare providers is non-hazardous, and comparable to municipal waste. The remainder is hazardous and can pose a variety of health risks. Hazardous healthcare waste comprises:

* pathological waste: blood, body tissue, body organs, body parts and animal carcasses

* infectious waste: waste suspected to contain pathogens in sufficient quantity to cause infection in susceptible hosts

* sharps: needles, syringes, scalpels, broken glass and any other items that could cut or puncture human skin

* pharmaceutical waste and chemical waste: spilled pharmaceutical products and drugs, and pharmaceutical products and drugs which have reached their expiry date, or which are no longer required, and discarded solid, liquid and gaseous chemicals from, for example, laboratory work, disinfecting procedures and cleaning

* radioactive waste: solid, liquid and gaseous waste contaminated with radionuclides (radioactive isotopes) generated by investigative and therapeutic procedures.

many small mines, smelters and other lead industries operate with few environmental controls (Shen et al., 1996).

Combined health-and-environment impacts

Box 3.9 lists the industry sectors considered by the Panel on Industry of the WHO Commission on Health and Environment, Panel on Industry (WHO, 1992b) to be the most likely to have adverse health-and-environment impacts. Of course, the activities of different industrial sectors should not be considered in isolation: many have complex links with the activities of other industrial sectors and have cumulative, interlinked rather than individual, purely additive impacts on ecosystems. They may also combine with those caused by other sectors such as transportation and agriculture.

The rapid speed at which industrialization and economic development has occurred during the past twenty years, especially in many developing countries, is another factor to be considered, since it has meant that too little thought has been given to industry's potential adverse impacts. Singling out the contribution of industrial pressures as distinct from other factors such as transportation, is difficult, though, because many factors contribute to the state and quality of the environment. In addition to a higher proportion of small informal enterprises, for example, weak infrastructure, inadequate pollution control and inappropriate technologies are also rendering developing country populations vulnerable to the environmental hazards caused by unplanned, rapid industrialization. Moreover, developed countries have exacerbated the environmental problems now being experienced by developing countries through transfer of hazardous wastes, industries and technologies.

3.5.2 Industrial accidents and health-and-environment impacts

Accidental releases of hazardous substances from industrial installations are a

---

Box 3.8

Human exposure to mercury in South America due to gold-mining

The upsurge in gold prices in 1979 led to a huge increase in gold-mining activities using mercury amalgamation in many South American countries, including Bolivia, Brazil, Colombia, Guyana, Peru and Venezuela. In the Amazon River basin especially, the gold rush has reached immense proportions: over 650 000 goldminers are estimated to be working at more than 2000 mining sites.

In the Amazon region, metallic mercury is used to recover fine gold from gravel. Approximately 100 tons of gold are produced annually, and at least 130 tons of mercury released into the environment during the gold recovery process. About 40% of this mercury is released directly into river systems during amalgamation, and the remaining 60% into the atmosphere during the burning and re-burning of the mercury-gold amalgam.

Populations living in the Amazon region are exposed to mercury via two pathways. First, goldminers and gold-shop workers are exposed occupationally to inorganic mercury due to direct inhalation of mercury vapour during the gold recovery process. Second, some of the mercury released into the river system is methylated, after which it accumulates in fish. Populations who consume fish caught in these rivers are therefore exposed to methyl mercury. Blood and hair tests have shown that exposures can be high in either instance. Both inhalation of mercury vapour and ingestion of methylmercury can cause serious nervous system disease. Attempts to reduce exposures and prevent poisonings, through introduction of new mercury recovery techniques, are under way.

Sources: IPCS, 1989, 1990b; Malm et al., 1990; Akagi, Malm & Branches, 1996.

major contributor to environmental damage and can cause serious adverse health effects among local populations. Fires are of particular concern because of their potential to spread to neighbouring areas. A listing of major industrial accidents for 1970–1992 (**Table 3.11**) shows that they have occurred in all regions of the world and are often linked to explosions. More up-to-date data have not been published. The number of dead and injured (**Table 3.11**) does not reflect the full health impact of these disasters, as the indirect effects of dislocation, economic losses, stress and social upheaval in the community may be of even greater proportions (Mitchell, 1996). Countries in the early stages of industrialization usually experience more frequent accidents, since they often lack trained engineers, operators and equipment maintenance staff, as well as regulatory personnel. Industrial accidents can be prevented, however, by incorporating technical checks into the production

Box 3.9

Examples of industrial sectors most likely to have adverse health-and-environment impacts

The Panel on Industry of the WHO Commission on Health and Environment considers the following 16 sectors as the most likely to have adverse health-and-environment impacts on the general population and on workers:

* asbestos and human-made fibres
* organic and inorganic chemicals
* cement, glass and ceramics
* electronics
* iron and steel
* rubber and plastic products
* metal products
* mining of metals and minerals
* non-ferrous metals (e.g. lead, zinc, copper)
* pesticides, paints and pharmaceuticals

* petroleum products
* pulp and paper
* textiles and leather
* wood and furniture
* service industries (e.g. tourism and leisure, hospitals and healthcare, dry-cleaning urban waste control)
* miscellaneous (e.g. construction, recycling, military industries).

Source: WHO, 1992b.

system and running effective managerial systems that focus on safety (ILO, 1988; ILO, 1991).

3.5.3 Industrial activity trends

Trends in industrial production can be measured in terms of manufacturing value added (MVA) (see glossary), which quantifies the actual industrial input into a country's economy. The MVA share of global gross domestic product (GDP) was estimated at 22% for 1994 (UNIDO, 1995).

During 1970–1995, industrial production continued to increase in all regions other than the countries of Eastern Europe and the former USSR (**Table 3.12**). But in almost all regions, annual growth rates were higher between 1970 and 1980, than between 1980 and 1990, or between 1990 and 1995. In fact, the annual growth rate decreased substantially in Eastern Europe and the former USSR in the

1990s. Conversely, a noticeable increase was observed in China.

During 1990–1995, the fastest growing industries were plastic products (3.16% annual growth rate), tobacco manufacturing (3.14%), professional and scientific goods (2.76%) and other chemical products (2.76%) (**Table 3.13**). However, machinery (electronic and non-electronic), transport equipment and chemicals dominate world manufacturing. Industries of major importance in terms of environmental impacts (industrial chemicals, petroleum refineries, and iron and steel and non-ferrous metal production) experienced slow or no growth during 1990–1995 (UNIDO, 1995).

3.5.4 Industry and sustainable development: evolving together

Three elements are crucial to achieving more environmentally sound industrial development. Firstly, environmental considerations must be incorporated into all aspects of planning for new industry. Secondly, techniques must be developed which more easily and flexibly control pollution within a legal framework which provides strong incentives, particularly economic incentives, to minimize the release of pollutants and the production of waste, and which places greater emphasis on the "polluter pays" principle. Thirdly, producers of hazardous products should be required to be responsible for these products "from cradle to grave", i.e. from production to safe disposal. The approach to comprehensive control of industrial environmental hazards is being promoted as "cleaner production" (UNEP, 1996a).

Integrated preventive and proactive environmental management practices, such as the "front-end approach", are being promoted in preference to the "end-of-pipe" control approach implemented in the 1980s (**Box 3.10**). The former emphasizes the fundamental importance of primary prevention, including use of appropriate control

Table 3.11

Serious industrial accidents, worldwide — 1970–1992*

Year	Country	Place	Origin of accident	Product(s) involved	No. of deaths	No. injured
1970	Indonesia	Java	Tank fire	Kerosene	50	0
	Japan	Osaka	Explosion (subway)	Gas	92	0
1973	Indonesia	Jakarta	Fire, explosion	Fireworks	52	24
1974	UK	Flixborough	Explosion	Cyclohexane	28	104
1977	South Korea	Iri	Explosion (rail transport)	Dynamite	57	1300
1978	Japan	Sendai	Storage	Crude oil	21	350
	Spain	Los Alfaques	Road accident	Propylene	216	200
	Mexico	Xilatopec	Explosion (road accident)	Gas	100	200
1979	USSR	Novosibirsk	Factory accident	Chemicals	300	—
	Pakistan	Rawalpindi	Explosion	Fireworks	)30	100
	Thailand	Phangnga	Collision and fire (bus/lorry)	Oil	50	15
1980	India	Mandir Asod	Factory explosion	Explosives	50	—
	Thailand	Bangkok	Explosion, munitions	Explosives	54	353
	Iran	Deh-Bos Org	Fire, explosion	Dynamite	80	45
	Turkey	Danaciobasi	Bottled gas explosion	Butane	107	0
	Spain	Ortuella	Explosion at school	Propane	51	90
1981	Mexico	Montanas	Derailment	Chlorine	28	1000
1982	Venezuela	Tacoa	Storage tank explosion	Fuel oil	)153	500
1983	Egypt	Nile River	Explosion (transport)	LPG	317	44
	Brazil	Pojuca	Fire, explosion	Gasoline	42	)100
	India	Dhulwari	Explosion	Gasoline	41	)100
	India	Dhurabari	Fire	Oil	76	)60
1984	Brazil	Cubatao	Pipeline explosion	Gasoline	89	—
	Mexico	St. J. Ixhuatepec	Storage tank explosion	LPG	)500	2500
	India	Bhopal	Leakage at factory	Methyl isocyanate	2800	50 000
	Pakistan	Ghari Dhoda	Pipeline explosion	Natural gas	60	—
	Romania		Factory	Chemicals	100	100
1985	India	Tamil Nadu	Road transport	Petrol	60	—
1986	USSR	Chernobyl	Reactor explosion	Radioactivity	31	299
1988	Pakistan	Islamabad	Explosion (storage)	Explosives	)100	3000
	USSR	Arzamas	Explosion (rail transport)	Explosives	91	744
	UK	North Sea (Scotland)	Explosion, fire (platform)	Oil/gas	167	0
	Mexico	Mexico City	Explosion	Fireworks	62	87
1989	China	Henan	Factory explosion	Fireworks	27	22
	USSR	Acha Ufa	Pipeline explosion	Gas	500	700
	USA	Pasadena	Explosion	Ethylene	23	125
1990	Thailand	Bangkok	Explosion (truck at house)	LPG	63	100
	India	near Patna	Explosion (train)	Gas	100	0
	Nepal	Katmandu	Polluted drinking-water		100	0
	USSR	Voronej-Rostov	Fire after multiple collision	Gasoil	55	14
1991	Thailand		Explosion (road transport)	Dynamite	171	100
	Italy	Livorno	Explosion (tanker in harbour)	Oil	140	0
1992	Senegal	Dakar	Explosion (tank)	Ammonia	41	403
	Mexico	Guadalajara	Explosion (sewage pipeline)	Petrol, hexane	>200	1500

* selection criteria: 50 or more deaths or 100 or more injured, exclusive of accidents at sea

Sources: based on data from OECD, 1992; WHO, 1992b.

technology to eliminate or reduce pollution arising from industrial processes and operations, both in and out of the workplace, in order to protect the general environment and the health of workers and surrounding communities. Full application of control technology comprises not only its design and

Box 3.10

Green industry: towards sustainable practices

The green factor: Visible, environmentally responsible behaviour is becoming an essential element of business success. Businesses in some parts of the world are adopting more sustainable practices, realizing the substantial market potential of environmentally-friendly products. However, the business community must take a proactive role so that it can set its own agenda of industrial transformation and manage change in a manner that makes economic sense.

Cleaner industry: Reducing waste or pollution at the source is good business since it is cheaper and more efficient than trying to clean up polluted environments. In contrast to traditional, "end-of-pipe" approaches, the "front-end approach" entails attacking the source of waste by adjusting process technologies and controls, cleaning and handling practices, product design and packaging, and even transportation practices, following a hierarchy of waste management options: reduce waste at the source; reuse or recycle waste that is produced, preferably on site and directly back into the production process; or treat waste that cannot be prevented or recycled with the latest technology to detoxify, remove, or destroy it.

Cleaner production: The continuous application of an integrated preventive environmental strategy to process, products and services increases eco-efficiency, reducing health-and-environment risks. Cleaner production requires changing attitudes, ensuring responsible environmental management, creating appropriate national policy environments, and evaluating technology options.

Green design: Introducing environmental consciousness into the design phase of products and processes is one of the most effective methods of preventing pollution since this stage sets the parameters for the manufacturing process, determining the kind of waste produced. The focus should therefore shift from product performance and ease of production at minimum cost, to minimization of the environmental impact of a product throughout its life cycle.

Industrial ecology: Industrial sustainability can be achieved by practising pollution prevention, green design, and closed-loop materials cycling on a system-wide basis. This approach seeks to mimic the efficient and sustainable flows of material and energy that characterize natural ecosystems, and requires close cooperation between suppliers, producers, distributors, users and waste recovery or disposal entities.

Greening the marketplace: Sustainable industry can be achieved only if the necessary adjustments are made to global economic markets so that product prices reflect full environmental costs. Companies are often cushioned from the costs of the environmental degradation caused by their activities. These costs are frequently borne instead by individuals not directly responsible, or by the global community as a whole. Moreover, markets generally offer little incentive for environmentally sound behaviour. But if companies are made to internalize costs, market forces will begin to penalize industrial practices that harm the environment. Government involvement in adjusting tax and regulatory policies to intervene in markets on behalf of the environment will be necessary, though.

Sources: WRI, 1994; UNEP, 1996a.

implementation, but also its operation, maintenance and management. Incorporating environmental considerations into the design phase of products and processes can also do much to prevent and minimize pollution (**Box 3.10**). Additionally, environmental impact assessment and environmental auditing should be integrated into strategic business planning and the overall environmental management cycle.

Quite apart from the environmental benefits, adoption of integrated environment management systems has many competitive advantages for companies. Clean industry not only saves on pollution control costs but also helps make manufacturing more efficient and cost-effective. So there are compelling economic, humanitarian and ecological reasons why industry should embrace sustainable practices (UNEP, 1994b; WRI, 1994).

The rise in consumer awareness of the need to maintain a healthy environment is also encouraging businesses to adopt sustainable practices. Simultaneously, the emergence of the so-called "green factor" has prompted businesses to realize the significant market potential for environmentally-friendly products. The International Chamber of Commerce has therefore developed guideline principles in an effort to promote the concepts of sustainable industrial development and to encourage, wider adoption of good environmental management practices (Stanners & Bourdeau, 1995). However, industrial sustainability cannot be achieved by companies acting in isolation: governments must also be involved. Ministers responsible for health and for the environment must ensure that they have significant input into decisions related to industrial development at all levels, ranging from initial policy development to means of monitoring environmental health effects (see Chapter 6).

3.6 Energy

3.6.1 Energy dependency

Energy plays a critical role in basic human survival. Too little energy, therefore, through its effect on nutrition and food safety, and on chilling, has important implications for health (**Box 3.11**). Energy is also crucial to transportation and industrial processes. However, production and use of energy, if not properly controlled, may be accompanied by adverse health-and-environment impacts.

Although approximately half of the world's population is dependent on biomass fuels (fuelwood, animal dung and crop residues) for cooking and heating, 1995 estimates showed that, in terms of total world energy, biomass fuel contributed only 10–15%, compared to 33% for oil, 23% for coal, and about 19% for natural gas. Nuclear energy contributed about 6% and hydropower, along with minor sources such as wind and geothermal power, supplied 7%. **Fig 3.8** depicts the changes in the world's energy mix that have occurred since 1850. **Fig. 3.9** illustrates the differences in fuel use, and the huge difference in energy use per capita, between developed and developing countries.

Projected increases in global primary energy production for the next two decades range from 30% to 50% encompassing increases of up to 100% in developing countries and small increases in developed countries. The world has a variety of energy sources (oil, coal, natural gas, uranium, biomass, oil shale, hydro and solar energy), sufficient to meet projected needs well into the next century (WHO, 1992e). These resources are not uniformly distributed, however, nor of equal quality. It is thus not so much physical global supply limitations that will constrain energy exploitation, but rather geographic, economic and health-and-environment constraints.

Table 3.12

Growth rates and share of world manufacturing value added (MVA) in individual regions — 1970–1995 (percentage)

MVA	Average annual growth rates			Share in total
Region	1970–1980	1980–1990	1990–1995	1994
North America	2.3	2.5	2.58	24.9
Western Europe	2.6	1.5	0.48	32.2
Japan	5.2	5.8	0.56	16.9
Eastern Europe & former USSR	6.9	1.4	-12.06	2.9
Latin America & Caribbean	6.2	-0.1	2.88	5.2
Tropical Africa	2.1	2.6	1.46	0.3
North Africa	6.1	5.6	1.78	0.5
Western Asia	8.8	5.1	5.38	2.9
Indian subcontinent	4.3	6.9	3.8	1.4
China	10.2	8.7	15.8	4.8
East & South-East Asia	11.4	8.5	7.3	5.6

Note: MVA is valued in national currencies at 1990 prices, but has been converted to 1990 US$

Source: based on data from UNIDO, 1995.

Table 3.13

Growth rates and shares of world MVA for 28 industries — 1970–1995 (percentage)

MVA	Average annual growth rates			Share in total
Country and ISIC* sector	1970–1980	1980–1990	1990–1995	1994
311 Food	3.2	1.9	2.28	10
313 Beverages	2.1	1.2	2.04	2.3
314 Tobacco manufacture	1.4	3.9	3.14	1.7
321 Textiles	1.2	-	-0.64	3.8
322 Wearing apparel	2.3	-0.2	0.88	2.1
323 Leather and fur products	1.6	0.1	-0.28	0.3
324 Footwear, excluding rubber or plastic	1.9	-1.8	0.98	0.5
331 Wood and cork products	2.7	-0.4	-0.02	1.6
332 Furniture and fixtures	3.9	0.7	1.08	1.4
341 Paper and paper products	2.7	2.3	0.34	3.1
342 Printing and publishing	3.2	3.6	1.06	5
351 Industrial chemicals	2.5	2.9	0.24	5.2
352 Other chemical products	2.4	4.3	2.76	5.7
353 Petroleum refineries	6.3	-1.2	1.36	2.7
354 Miscellaneous petroleum and coal products	5.2	-0.2	-0.52	0.3
355 Rubber products	1.9	1.6	0.22	1.3
356 Plastic products	6.2	5.2	3.16	3
361 Pottery, china & earthenware	3.7	0.4	0.88	0.4
362 Glass and glass products	2.5	1.4	0.5	0.9
369 Other non-metallic mineral products	3.3	0.8	0.58	2.8
371 Iron & steel	1.9	-0.9	-0.72	3.7
372 Non-ferrous metals	2.7	0.7	-1.02	1.5
381 Metal products, excluding machinery	2.4	1.3	0.46	5.7
382 Non-electrical machinery	3.5	2	-0.96	10.4
383 Electrical machinery	3.6	3.2	1.24	10.4
384 Transport equipment	3.7	2.6	1.14	10.2
385 Professional & scientific goods	4.5	3.8	2.76	2.7
390 Other manufactures	2.8	2	0.22	1.4

Note: MVA is valued in national currencies at 1990 prices, but has been converted to 1990 US$
* International Standard Industrial Classification of all economic activities (revision 2)

Source: based on data from UNIDO, 1995.

Box 3.11

Too little energy is a health hazard

If people do not have sufficient energy for heating and cooking purposes, adverse health impacts ensue. This is seen in places where women and children must walk long distances to obtain wood and other biomass fuels, expending considerable time and energy in the process, and placing themselves at increased risk of assault and natural hazards such as leeches and snakes.

A study in Malawi found, additionally, that nutrition was negatively affected if families had to walk long distances to gather cooking fuel. And when seasonal changes resulted in longer fuel-collection times, families were unable to compensate for this by reducing the time spent on agricultural activities. Rather, the time was subtracted from resting and food preparation. Moreover, inferior fuels, such as twigs and grass, that were used as a substitute in times of shortage required more attention from the women during cooking, keeping them from other tasks. These fuels also produce more health-damaging smoke and are inadequate for processing some of the more nutritious kinds of food, such as cereals and beans (since they have long cooking times). Statistically significant correlations were found between the amount of fuel available and the caloric intake from cereals and other cooked foods during periods of fuel shortage. The figure outlines some coping strategies adopted by households to deal with fuel shortages and the health consequences.

Household strategies to cope with fuelwood shortage and their nutritional and health implications

COPING STRATEGIES	NUTRITIONAL AND HEALTH IMPLICATIONS
Increase in time spent on fuelwood collection	Fuel harvesting
Substitution of fuelwood by:	increased caloric needs
• inferior biomass fuels	increased risk of assault and injury
• commercial fuels	increased risk of natural hazards
Economizing on fuelwood	Cooking with inferior biomass fuels
Consumption (less cooking)	increased air pollution
	increased tending time
	decreased consumption of foods requiring long cooking times
	Food supply
	decreased food production
	decreased food purchase
	decreased food preservation and storage
	Time allocation
	decreased income-generating activity
	decreased rest time
	decreased space and water heating and other hygiene-related activities
	Food preparation and distribution
	decreased frequency of food preparation
	increased consumption of warmed-up food
	decreased preparation of special foods for children and pregnant/lactating women

Sources: Agarwal, 1985; Brouwer, 1994; figure modified from Brouwer, 1994.

The environmental implications of future energy growth will depend greatly on the mix of technologies and fuels that are chosen today. Experience shows that making major shifts in energy systems quickly is difficult. Rather, they may take decades as indicated in **Fig. 3.8**. The lesson is that if we are to have clean and safe energy systems in thirty years time, we must start to move towards them today. It must be remembered also that the health-and-environment impacts of energy use occur not only at the point of final use, but along the entire energy chain — from exploration and primary production to the disposal of residues (**Box 3.12**).

3.6.2 Household use of biomass and coal: impairing indoor air quality

In developing countries, biomass accounts for about one-quarter of all energy use (**Fig. 3.9**). In some of the least-developed countries as much as two-thirds of the population depend on biomass (**Fig. 3.10**). Open fires are commonly found in dwellings in rural and peri-urban areas in developing countries. Used for cooking and heating, such fires may be set in a hole in the ground, among stones on which the cooking-pot is placed, in a three-sided brick or stone platform, or in a simple clay or metal stove (Smith, 1993). The stove is often at floor level, adding to the risk of accidents, and jeopardizing food hygiene. Usually there is no chimney to remove pollutants. Additionally, solid fuels such as biomass do not burn completely in simple household stoves. So even though solid fuels do not contain large quantities of non-combustible contaminants, pollutant emissions per meal are very high compared to those of other fuels (**Fig. 3.11**).

Household use of fossil fuels for space and water heating, and for cooking, is also widespread in many developed countries. Bituminous coal and lignite are particularly damaging since they burn inefficiently, emitting considerable quantities of air pollu-tants. In fact, small-scale coal burning produces the same pollutants as burn-ing of biomass fuels, plus sulfur oxides and other toxic elements, such as arsenic, fluoride and lead. Even if unprocessed, coal and biomass burn more completely, releasing less pollu-tion, if burnt in large furnaces and boilers rather than in individual household systems (Smith, 1993).

If emissions are high and ventila-tion poor, household use of coal and biomass can severely impair indoor air quality. This is indeed the case in many parts of the world. And as people are always present or nearby, large human exposures and health effects result (see Section 4.2). Yet biomass and coal can be processed — for example as char-coal and biogas or smokeless coal and coalgas — to make them cleaner. (But the expense this entails may prevent the poor from using cleaner fuels.) Generally, environmental pollution arising from combustion of processed solid fuel is much less than that arising from combustion of raw fuel. However, fuel processing creates new sources of pollution, for example, at the kiln or coal-processing facility.

Fig. 3.8

Historical development of sources of energy supply since 1850

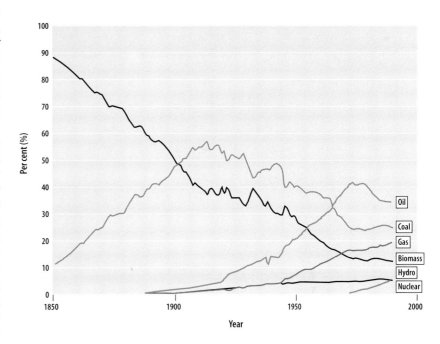

Note: these curves indicate percentages of global use, not absolute amounts, and that it takes many decades for any one new source to achieve a significant percentage of the total

Source: adapted from Nakicenovic & Grubler, 1996.

Fig. 3.9

World primary energy consumption — 1995

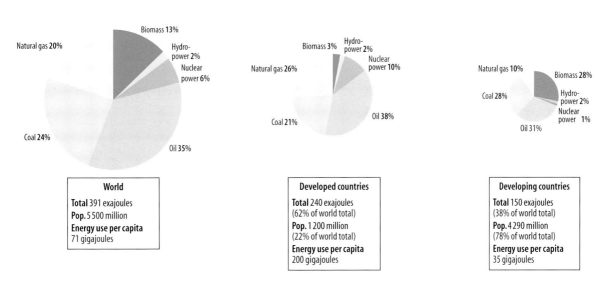

World	
Total 391 exajoules	
Pop. 5 500 million	
Energy use per capita 71 gigajoules	

Developed countries	
Total 240 exajoules (62% of world total)	
Pop. 1 200 million (22% of world total)	
Energy use per capita 200 gigajoules	

Developing countries	
Total 150 exajoules (38% of world total)	
Pop. 4 290 million (78% of world total)	
Energy use per capita 35 gigajoules	

Source: based on data from Hall, Rosillo-Calle & Woods and British Petroleum statistical review, 1996.

Fig. 3.10

Number of people using different household fuels by region — 1990s

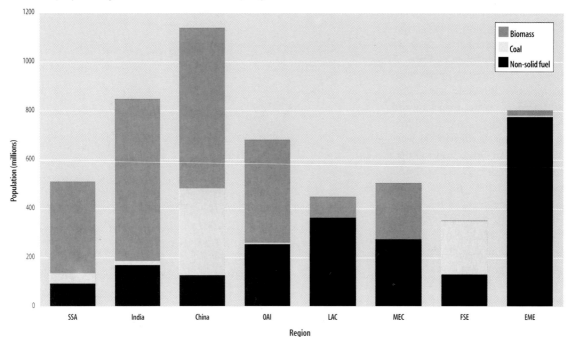

Source: based on data from Smith & Figuero, 1997.

3.6.3 Pollution from use of fossil fuels in power stations, industry and transport

Several major health-and-environment effects are associated with the production and use of fossil fuels. They occur throughout the fuel cycle, from initial harvesting to final waste disposal, and include the following direct effects:

- indoor and outdoor air pollution
- emission of greenhouse gases (GHGs)
- contamination of water bodies and land by atmospheric fallout of emissions
- occupational health-and-safety risks.

The combustion of fossil fuels in power plants and by industries, in motor vehicles and by households, is the largest source of atmospheric pollution, giving off huge quantities of sulphur and NO_x, heavy metals, HCs, particulates, CO, and other highly toxic pollutants (see Section 4.2), and is also the chief source of human-generated GHGs in the form of carbon dioxide and methane (see Section 4.9.2). In general, the level of air pollution arising from fossil fuel combustion depends on the level of non-combustible material contained in the fuel. Thus natural gas burns cleaner than oil, which burns cleaner than coal. The

Fig. 3.11

Emissions per meal for household cooking fuels

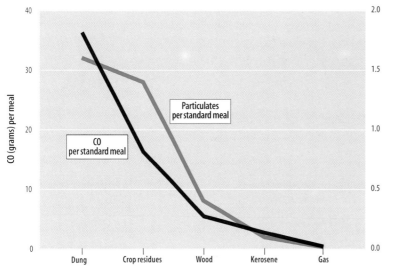

Source: adapted from Smith, 1991.

extent to which pollution *potential* is translated into actual pollution also depends on the type of burning technology and pollution control equipment that are employed. Additionally, the pollutant concentrations due to emissions will be influenced by meteorological and geographical conditions.

Regrettably, as has often been proved by environmental control efforts, reduction of pollution in one medium may cause an increase in another. For instance, contamination of water and land can occur if the waste fly-ash and scrubber sludge from smokestack desulphurization equipment is not disposed of carefully. Of particular concern are the trace elements such as arsenic, beryllium, cadmium, chromium, lead, and selenium that are found in coal ash.

Pollution from energy use in transport

Around the world, the need for increased transport of people, food, industrial raw materials, industrial products, and waste of different types, combined with rising incomes and increased demand for personal mobility, have led to rapid increases in motor vehicle ownership. During the past three decades the annual growth rate in the world vehicle fleet has been 3%, leading to a total of nearly 800 million vehicles in 1995 (**Fig. 3.12**). This growth rate has been faster than that of either the world population or economy. In 1965 there were fewer than 60 vehicles per 1000 people in the world. Today there are more than 140 per 1000 people (AAMA, 1996). Fossil fuel use for transport has therefore increased dramatically. In addition to the gaseous pollutants emitted by petrol-powered vehicles, those with poorly maintained diesel engines emit fine particulates; these appear to have serious health implications.

In common with household stoves, vehicles can have a disproportionate effect on actual human exposures to pollutants, since their emissions are released close to the ground. For exam-

---

Box 3.12

Fuel-cycle analysis for environmental assessment

Fuel used in a house, vehicle or factory often comes from far away and has undergone several processing and transport stages. This chain from harvesting through to use and on to waste disposal is called the "fuel cycle". Evaluating the overall impact of a particular type of energy use, therefore, involves consideration of the environmental health impacts that occur at each stage of the fuel cycle. This is particularly important for the modern fossil and nuclear fuels, the extraction, refining, further upgrading and use of which may each occur in different countries. Conversion to electricity involves yet another stage. In the case of some fuels, e.g. coal and uranium, waste disposal must also be incorporated in fuel-cycle analysis. In addition, transport and storage activities may be undertaken between stages, with further impacts.

An example of fuel-cycle analysis might be consideration of the health impacts of substituting kerosene for wood as household fuel in an Indian village. Since kerosene burns so much more cleanly, the comparison might appear to be an easy one to make. Unlike wood, however, the kerosene fuel cycle is long, perhaps starting with an oil well in the Persian Gulf, and continuing with shipment across the Arabian Sea, processing in a refinery in Bombay, transport by train to the nearby state capital, and finally, transport by truck to the village. Environmental health impacts are created at every stage of this fuel cycle. In terms of air pollution, kerosene is probably still cleaner than wood, but not as much as would be indicated by looking only at the fuel's end use. And like biomass, the use of kerosene entails risks of fire, and also of poisoning. Even more difficult to estimate, but no less important, might be the extra international security risk that comes from increased dependence on petroleum imports. On the other hand, use of wood as fuel may lead to ecosystem disruption from over-harvesting and other risks in some regions. Balancing these different direct and indirect health risks is not easily done, but essential to overall long-term planning for sustainable development.

---

ple, vehicles tend to influence CO levels near streets considerably. They also contribute to the formation of secondary (photochemical) pollutants, such as ozone, which are becoming a widespread urban problem (see Section 4.2). Given the high growth rates of vehicle fleets in many developing countries, vehicle-generated environmental problems have the potential to increase steadily in the next decade.

Significant lead pollution has also been caused by petrol use. The decision to allow lead to be used as an additive to petrol to enhance performance has been called one of the worst environmental health mistakes of the century (Shy, 1990). Recently, however, much progress has been made in removing lead from vehicle fuels worldwide (see **Box 2.6**). In the early 1970s, nearly all petrol contained lead, but by 1995, little more than one-quarter of the petrol burned globally contained lead as an additive (Walsh, 1997).

3.6.4 Hydropower: population dislocation and ecological change

Hydroelectric power currently accounts for about 2% of total energy supply (**Fig 3.9**) and about 25% of the world's electricity output; worldwide potential is estimated at roughly twice today's value. Most of the remaining potential lies in Asia and South America. The impacts of hydropower on health include:

- stress and other impacts on populations displaced by the filling of reservoirs
- occupational accidents during construction of dams and reservoirs
- catastrophic floods due to dam failure

- changed environmental conditions for waterborne diseases
- contamination of fish, and GHG emissions due to flooded forest and vegetation

The actual process of generating hydropower, however, does not produce significant amounts of waste or pollution. The displacement of populations living in areas scheduled to be flooded following hydroelectric dam construction is a major concern, though, particularly in developing countries with high population density. Examples include large dam projects in India, China and South-East Asia. The filling of large shallow dams, and the subsequent effects of rotting forests and vegetation that were not cleared before filling, are also problematic. In Northern Canada this has led to a rapid increase in the mercury concentration of fish in lakes that have become part of a reservoir system (Environment Canada, 1987). In Brazil, large shallow reservoirs have been shown to emit significant methane emissions due to trapped rotting vegetation (Pearce, 1996a). (Methane is a powerful GHG (see Section 4.9.2). Additionally, changed environmental conditions, such as altered flow and distribution of water bodies, have also resulted in increased transmission of waterborne diseases (see **Box 3.5** and Section 4.6.6).

3.6.5 Nuclear energy: maintained vigilance needed

In mid-1996, 437 power-generating nuclear reactors were in operation in 26 countries (see **Fig. 3.13**) and a further 39 units under construction. About two-thirds of total generating capacity is found in only four countries: France, Germany, Japan and the USA. Nuclear power for civilian purposes grew rapidly in the 1980s, but has now slowed to nearly zero growth and may even decline slightly after the turn of the century. This is largely due to the anticipated decline in nuclear

Fig. 3.12

Growth of world motor vehicle fleet — 1930–1995

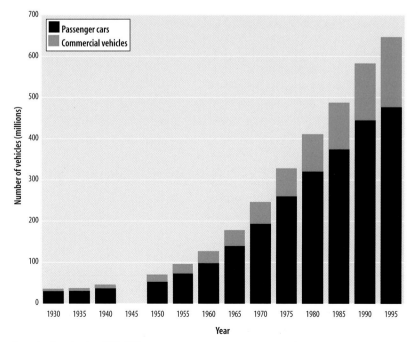

Source: based on data from AAMA, 1996.

Fig. 3.13

Nuclear power plants around the world

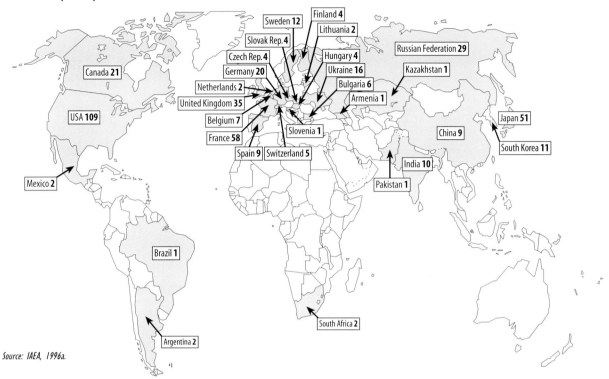

Source: IAEA, 1996a.

capacity the USA. Older US reactors are being retired and no new ones are planned, although more nuclear power plants may be constructed in the USA early in the next century if current efforts to design and commercialize a new generation of "inherently safe" reactors are successful. This may also stimulate faster growth in the rest of the world. Among developing countries, only China is currently experiencing significant growth in nuclear capacity, but from a small base.

The principal environmental concerns in connection with nuclear power systems are:

- the potential for reactor accidents releasing large amounts of radioactivity, as occurred at Chernobyl in 1986 (see Section 4.2.6 for further discussion of the health risks of radiation)
- the potential diversion of material from the nuclear fuel cycle for production of weapons of mass destruction

- radioactive releases from long-term disposal of nuclear waste.

Just as with other fuels (**Box 3.12**), obtaining a comprehensive picture of the hazards of nuclear fuels requires consideration of its entire fuel cycle, including mining and milling of uranium ore, fuel enrichment and fabrication, reactor operation, spent fuel storage and transport, fuel reprocessing, disposal of radioactive waste, and decommissioning of reactors. Emissions and the potential for accidents vary according to the stage of the cycle.

Exposure to ionizing radiation can also occur when radionuclides are released into the air during uranium mining and milling, reactor operation, and fuel reprocessing However, total emissions are fairly small compared to those emitted by natural sources (UNSCEAR, 1996). Given the large inventories of radioactive materials in operating reactors, accidental release of radionuclides is the biggest potential hazard posed by nuclear power plants.

> "Despite progress on several fronts, from a global perspective the environment problems remain deeply embedded in the socio-economic fabric of nations in all regions"
>
> UNEP, 1997a.

Fortunately, the reactor types thought to be least safe, namely those in Chernobyl and elsewhere in Eastern Europe and the former Soviet Union, are no longer being built (WHO, 1992e). Closure of all remaining plants of these types as soon as possible would be judicious, but the high cost of alternative sources of power remains a significant obstacle.

The sharpest decreases in the health risks associated with nuclear energy are, however, due to the end of the Cold War and the resultant reductions in nuclear weapons forces. Along with these reductions has come a great decrease in the activity of military nuclear facilities that provided the fissile material for weapons and the fuel for nuclear naval vessels. This has also reduced environmental risks, for it has been revealed in recent years that the operation of these military facilities in the former Soviet Union, and to a lesser extent in the West, was extremely hazardous, leading to severe local and, in some cases, regional radioactive contamination.

But the welcome nuclear disarmament activities that are now in progress, are not without health risk themselves. The many thousands of kilograms of plutonium that are being extracted from dismantled weapons must be handled appropriately, not only to prevent environmental contamination, but also to prevent terrorist groups and others capable of building bombs or other devices of mass terror from obtaining it.

3.7 Considerable threats to environmental quality and health

In this chapter we have illustrated how and to what extent human activities put "pressure" on the environment. The adverse effects are many and seem to be growing in intensity, at least in some parts of the world, and affecting larger and larger areas. Where once there was no chemical pollution, there is now.

Where solutions had been found for controlling urban wastes, new problems have been identified. The ever-increasing need for more and more water, the production of growing quantities of waste, and unsustainable use of mineral and other natural resources of all kinds, continue apace. The onslaught on the environment stems from many quarters — from households and agriculture, to industrialization and energy production and use.

Domestic or household wastes pose a significant problem for health and environment. Most of the excreta generated globally is not collected, and even if collected through on-site sanitation or sewer systems, is often not treated before being discharged into the environment. Other household wastes in liquid or solid form are similarly often discarded without proper collection and treatment. In developing countries, two-thirds of the population do not have access to sanitation. It is estimated that by the year 2000 as many as 3300 million people may be in this category. With an anticipated additional 1500 million people in developing countries by 2020, major investments are required to improve access to sanitation.

Population growth, and agricultural, industrial and energy development demand more and more water resulting in increased water scarcity in some areas, as well as increasing pollution of surface and groundwater. The number of countries experiencing water scarcity is expected to have risen from 20 to 45 countries by 2050. Estimates also suggest a doubling of industrial water use over the next 25 years leading to a more than four-fold increase in industrial pollution.

While food production has increased substantially, the absolute number of people suffering from malnutrition has increased in most regions, most notably in Africa. Chronic undernutrition is likely to remain severe in sub-Saharan Africa and to affect as many as 300 million people by 2010. Increased agricultural production has had severe environmental impacts, ranging from increased conversion of land for cultivation, and over-cultivation resulting in soil degradation, to the use of large quantities of irrigation water, fertilizer and pesticides. Increased water pollution is a major problem.

Industry is a major user of Earth's resources (mineral deposits, water and energy) and industrial production is growing worldwide, with the developed countries maintaining an overwhelming lead in global industrial production (about 75%). Machinery (electronic and non-electronic), transport equipment and chemicals dominate world manufacturing. Industries of major importance in terms of environmental impact (industrial chemicals, petroleum refineries, and iron and steel and non-ferrous production) experienced very slow or zero growth during 1990–1995.

Energy production and use can have severe adverse impacts on the environment and consequently on human health. The use of fossil fuels for energy production in power plants, industry and for transportation is the largest source of air pollution and increasing. Use of biomass for cooking and heating is a major source of indoor air pollution, affecting hundreds of millions of people. Other forms of energy production — hydropower, nuclear power and solar power — are not as prevalent, and their environmental impacts less pronounced, although there is grave concern about the possibility of accidents in the nuclear power industry and the disposal of radioactive waste.

All of these current and future potential "pressures" on the environment have implications for health. These are described in subsequent chapters. Influenced by the "driving forces" of population growth, urbanization, consumption and production patterns, and economic growth, these "pressures" are increasing in many countries. Some progress has been made in promoting and applying technologies and policies that reduce natural resource use, emissions and waste production, but much more needs to be done in order to reduce human exposures and health risks. ❏

Chapter 4
Poor Environmental Quality, Exposures and Risks

Driving Force
Pressure
State
Exposure
Effect
Action

4.1 The human dimension to environmental quality

The driving forces active in the world today are leading to pressures on the environment in the form of pollutant emissions, resource depletion, land-use changes and others, as described in Chapter 3. These pressures affect environmental quality (the "state" of the environment), as can be seen from the health-and-environment cause–effect framework (**Fig. 1.2**). Degradation of environmental quality can, in turn, lead to adverse human exposures and eventual health effects. The extent of such exposures, however, depends not only on their level, but also on the proximity of populations to them. Thus even relatively small amounts of pollution can have major health impacts if released close to human communities.

Air, water and food are the principal exposure routes of environmental health hazards. Also heavily implicated are the manner in which household wastes and sewage are handled, the environmental conditions in which people live and work, and soil quality. Evidence is growing too that the changing global environment will impact adversely on human health and well-being. This chapter describes how environmental quality in each of these media and settings affects human health. While data are not plentiful or comprehensive, they do provide a useful overview as to the current situation and some indication of future prospects.

4.2 Air pollution

Air pollution is a major environmental health problem affecting developed and developing countries alike (see Sections 3.5 and 3.6). Concern now focuses not only on the ambient air quality of cities but also on indoor air quality, in both rural and urban areas. In fact, the highest air pollution exposures occur in the indoor environment in developing countries.

Air pollution and its effects on health is a very complex subject since there are many different pollutants and their individual effects on health are difficult to discern. But it is known that air pollution impacts heavily on exposed populations. When inhaled, air pollutants affect the lung and respiratory system; they are also taken up by the blood and transported throughout the body. Furthermore, air pollutants are deposited on soil and plants and in water, thereby further contributing to human exposure if contaminated food and water are ingested.

The emphasis in this section is on suspended particulate matter (SPM). Information, in some detail, is presented on global human exposures to this pollutant and of the increased mortality associated with such exposures. The reasons for this focus are that:

- particulate pollution affects more people globally on a continuing basis than any other pollutant

- more monitoring data are available globally on particulate pollution concentrations than on any other pollutant

- more epidemiological evidence has been collected on particulate pollution exposures and their health effects than on any other pollutant and its health effects.

Table 4.1

Common atmospheric pollution sources and their pollutants

Source category	Source	Emitted pollutants
Agriculture	Open burning	SPM, CO, VOC
Mining and quarrying	Coalmining	SPM, SO_2, NO_x, VOC
	Crude petroleum and natural gas production	SO_2
	Non-ferrous ore mining	SPM, Pb
	Stone quarrrying	SPM
Manufacturing	Food, beverages and tobacco	SPM, CO, VOC, H_2S
	Textiles, leather industries	SPM, VOC
	Wood products	SPM, VOC
	Paper products, printing	SPM, SO_2, CO, VOC, H_2S, R-SH
Manufacture of chemicals	Phthalic anhydride	SPM, SO_2, CO, VOC
	Chlor-alkali	Cl_2
	Hydrochloric acid	HCl
	Hydrofluoric acid	HF, SiF_4
	Sulfuric acid	SO_2, SO_3
	Nitric acid	NO_x
	Phosphoric acid	SPM, F_2
	Lead oxide and pigments	SPM, Pb
	Ammonia	SPM, SO_2, NO_x, CO, VOC, NH_3
	Sodium carbonate	SPM, NH_3
	Calcium carbide	SPM
	Adipic acid	SPM, NO_x, CO, VOC
	Lead alkyl	Pb
	Maleic anhydride, terephthalic acid	CO, VOC
	Fertilizer and pesticide production	SPM, NH_3
	Ammonium nitrate	SPM, NH_3, HNO_3
	Ammonium sulfate	VOC
	Synthetic resins, plastic materials, fibres	SPM, VOC, H_2S, CS_2
	Paints, varnishes, lacquers	SPM, VOC
Manufacture of chemicals	Soap	SPM
	Carbon black, printing ink	SPM, SO_2, NO_x, CO, VOC, H_2S,
	Trinitrotoluene	SPM, SO_2, NO_x, SO_3, HNO_3
Petroleum refineries	Miscellaneous products of petroleum and coal	SPM, SO_2, NO_x, CO, VOC
Non-metallic mineral products manufacture	Glass products	SPM, SO_2, NO_x, CO, VOC, F
	Structural clay products	SPM, SO_2, NO_x, CO, VOC, F_2
	Cement, lime and plaster	SPM, SO_2, NO_x, CO,
Basic metal industries	Iron and steel	SPM, SO_2, NO_x, CO, VOC, Pb
	Non-ferrous industries	SPM, SO_2, F, Pb
Power generation	Electricity, gas, steam	SPM, SO_2, NO_x, CO, VOC, SO_3, Pb
Petrol retail trade	Fuel storage, filling operations	VOC
Transport	Combustion Engines	SPM, SO_2, NO_x, CO, VOC, Pb
Community services	Municipal incinerators	SPM, SO_2, NO_x, CO, VOC, Pb

Source: adapted from Economopoulos, 1993.

It must be remembered, however, that the presence of other pollutants in air is closely linked to particulate pollution, and that these other pollutants contribute to the adverse health effects that are observed. Additionally, some specific health effects, such as cardiovascular disease from exposure to carbon monoxide (CO), are primarily attributable to exposures to pollutants other than SPM. A brief mention is therefore also made of the ambient concentrations of other pollutants and of their health effects.

4.2.1 Urban ambient air quality: often poor

The largest sources of human-created air pollution are transportation, energy generation and energy-intensive industrial operations (see Section 3.6). The concentration of these activities in or around cities means that they heavily pollute the outdoor air of many urban areas.

Air pollutants consist of SPM (dust, fumes, mist and smoke), gaseous pollutants and odours. SPM and gaseous pollutants are emitted by a wide range of sources (**Table 4.1**). In recent years, attention has shifted to that portion of SPM made up of particles that are so small that they can penetrate deeply into the lung. These particles are more closely linked to the health effects of SPM than larger size particles (WHO, 1997f). Accordingly, many countries now monitor and regulate particles smaller than 10 µm (PM_{10}) (see, for example, USEPA, 1996).

Depending on their source and interactions with other components of air, particles can have quite different chemical compositions and health impacts. Yet until recently, understanding of the relationship between the chemical composition of particles and health impacts was limited. As a result, particles have often been treated as a single group. A major exception to this is lead particles, which are known to be especially hazardous to children's health

(IPCS, 1995b). Consequently, stringent health-based standards for airborne lead have been established in some countries. Chemical components of SPM that are of concern also include arsenic, nickel, cadmium and those present in diesel exhaust (IPCS, 1996b).

Other health-damaging pollutants include gaseous inorganic pollutants such as sulphur dioxide (SO_2), CO, and nitrogen dioxide (NO_2), as well as hydrocarbons (HC), such as benzene and butadiene, other volatile organic compounds (VOCs) (see **Table 4.1**), and secondary pollutants. Secondary pollutants are formed by chemical reactions in the atmosphere. For example, SO_2 can oxidize and dissolve in water to form sulphuric acid mist. Reactions between nitrogen oxides (NO_x) and HCs in the presence of sunlight produce ozone (O_3), the major health-damaging component of photochemical smog (Mage & Zali, 1992; Stanners & Bourdeau, 1995; WHO, 1995d; Loomis et al., 1996).

A major review of air pollution in megacities was undertaken by WHO and UNEP (WHO/UNEP, 1992). Where possible, this information has been updated; the most recent data for 17 large cities are presented in **Fig. 4.1**.

In developed countries the general picture is one of decreasing SO_2 and SPM concentrations, and constant or increasing NO_x and O_3 concentrations. In many countries in transition and in developing countries, however, not only are SO_2 and SPM concentrations rising due to growing fossil fuel combustion, but so too are NO_x and O_3 concentrations, as a result of increases in traffic exhaust emissions and industrial HC emissions (Schwela, 1996a).

Very severe local air pollution problems involving specific types of pollutants can occur around point sources. Also, periods of dangerously high air pollution levels can occur in areas whose topographical features constrain atmospheric dispersion of pollutants. Under certain meteorological conditions, such as temperature inversion and

Fig. 4.1

Air pollution in 17 large cities around the world

City	SO₂	SPM***	Pb	CO	NO₂	O₃	Year in which data is collected
Athens	low	No data	No data	low	serious	low	1995
Bangkok	low	serious	low	No data	low	No data	1995
Beijing	serious	serious	No data	No data	No data	No data	1994
Bucharest	low	moderate	serious	No data	moderate	No data	1995
Calcutta	low	serious	No data	No data	low	No data	1995
Caracas	low	moderate	serious	No data	moderate	No data	1995
Delhi	low	serious	No data	No data	moderate	No data	1995
Johannesburg	low	low	serious	low	low	low	1994
London	low*	low*	low*	low*	moderate*	low*	1995
Los Angeles	low*	moderate	low	moderate	moderate*	serious*	1995
Mexico City**	moderate	serious	No data	No data	serious	serious	1993
Santiago	low	serious	No data	moderate	moderate	moderate	1995
Sofia	low	serious	low	No data	serious	No data	1995
Shanghai	moderate	serious	No data	No data	No data	No data	1994
Sydney	No data	low	low	low	low	low	1995
Tokyo	moderate	moderate	low	moderate	moderate	low	1995
Xian	moderate	serious	No data	No data	No data	No data	1994

The data used in this table are for commercial sites and city centres unless marked *
* data from residential sites
** for Mexico City, the type of site is unknown but for the five different sites, the values belong to the same category of pollution rate
*** 1987 air quality guidelines were used (*Source: WHO, 1987.*)

No data available or insufficient data for assessment

 Low pollution WHO guidelines are normally met (short-term guidelines may be exceeded occasionally)

Moderate to heavy pollution WHO guidelines exceeded by up to a factor of two (short-term guidelines exceeded on a regular basis at certain locations)

 Serious problem WHO guidelines exceeded by more than a factor of two

Source: based on unpublished data from WHO Air Management Information System.

HEALTH AND ENVIRONMENT IN SUSTAINABLE DEVELOPMENT

Box 4.1
Oil well fires and air quality: Kuwait

Towards the end of the Gulf War in 1991, hundreds of oil wells, tank farms and related oil facilities in Kuwait were destroyed and ignited by the retreating Iraqi forces. Nine million barrels of stored crude oil and refined products were burned immediately, and about 6 million barrels of oil and 100 million m^3 of natural gas burned daily until the fires were extinguished about 10 months later. Some 6–65 thousand tons of SO_2 and 500–3000 tons of NO_x were emitted daily.

Most of the plumes from the fires consisted of dense black smoke, although some were white because of their higher water vapour content and those burning only gas were clear. The combined plumes sometimes reached 3000 m in height and 15 km in width. Most of the plumes emitted at the edge of the oil field were drawn inward toward the centre of the field by winds resulting from the intense "heat island" created by the fires. In calm meteorological conditions, the plumes resulted in dense smoke levels in Kuwait City; visibility dropped markedly and blue skies became heavily overcast. The smoke was frequently trapped between an elevated atmospheric inversion high over the city and the normal nocturnal inversion layer near ground level. At night this entrapment acted as an umbrella over the city, protecting the inhabitants from the worst of the pollution. When north-west winds blew, the smoke was carried to other countries in the region and some of it was even precipitated with snowfall in the Himalayas.

Source: Dr Abdul Rahman Al-Awadi, Executive Secretary, Regional Organization for the Protection of the Marine Environment, Kuwait.

low wind speed, high air pollution levels can persist for several days or more. Such situations occur periodically in many locations (Mage & Zali, 1992).

Fires are another source of air pollution and can lead to severe problems if the smoke is blown into populated areas (**Box 4.1**).

4.2.2 Indoor air pollution: "rule of one thousand"

Indoor air pollution can be particularly hazardous to health because it is released in close proximity to people. The "rule of 1000" states that a pollutant released indoors is 1000 times more likely to reach people's lungs than a pollutant released outdoors. The major source of indoor air pollution in developing countries is household use of biomass and coal for heating and cooking, usually involving open fires or stoves without proper chimneys (see

Section 3.6). Pollutant concentrations can be extremely high, exceeding WHO guidelines by more than a factor of 100. Women and children are affected most. It has been estimated that as many as 1000 million people, mostly women and children, are regularly and severely exposed to such concentrations (WHO, 1992f).

In addition to fumes from combustion, indoor pollutants originate from building materials, paints, solvents used in the home and environmental tobacco smoke. Indoor air quality is also affected by outdoor pollution sources. Principal pollutants and their sources are given in Table 4.2

4.2.3 Human exposures to particulate air pollution

Health effects are likely to occur if people are exposed to air pollution for a significant amount of time. In terms of health risk assessment, the duration of exposure is therefore as important as the level of air pollution. Thus if the total exposure of the world's population to air pollution is estimated by relating total person-time spent in different types of setting (i.e. developed or developing country, rural or urban setting, indoor or outdoor) to the average air pollution concentration of these settings, a comparison of total population exposures in different settings can be made, and the populations and settings with the highest health risk identified.

The distribution of the total person-time of the world population in different settings is shown in **Fig. 4.2**. Few data, however, are available, particularly for developing countries, on the indoor:outdoor time distribution of populations. The information presented in **Fig. 4.2** is therefore a gross approximation; it suggests that more than 70% of person-time is spent indoors. The percentage of the population involved in agricultural activities in developing countries was used to estimate the time spent outdoors and indoors in those countries (Smith, 1993).

In addition to time-distribution data, the estimation of human exposures requires information on typical SPM concentrations in different settings, which is provided below.

Urban outdoor: To obtain an indication of human exposure to SPM as a function of the level of development, information on urban SPM concentrations was organized according to the level of national development (**Fig. 4.3**). Urban outdoor SPM concentrations do not decrease uniformly with development; the peak occurs in the mid-development group as highlighted by the location of cities with high SPM levels (**Fig. 4.1**). The picture for total exposures is different. These are seen to decrease with increased development levels since the contribution of severe indoor air pollution decreases (**Fig 4.3**).

Urban indoor: The relationship between outdoor and indoor air pollution is important for estimating human exposure since urban indoor concentrations are substantially influenced by outdoor concentrations (**Table 4.2**). Consequently, depending on the kind of household fuel used and amount of tobacco smoke present, they are often as high or higher than outdoor concentrations, sometimes even in developed countries. In many developing country urban areas, particularly in South Asia and East Asia, biomass fuels are commonly used (see **Fig. 3.10**). In Africa, for instance, many urban households use charcoal, producing substantially lower particulate emissions than wood, but still emitting high CO levels. Fossil fuels are also a major source of urban indoor air pollution. In China, most urban households use coal, often in unvented appliances. Selected indoor air pollution concentrations for China are shown in **Table 4.3**.

Rural indoor: Although many people associate air pollution with outdoor

Table 4.2

Principal pollutants and sources of indoor air pollution, grouped by origin

Principal pollutants	Sources: predominantly outdoor
SO_2, SPM/RSP	Fuel combustion, smelters
O_3	Photochemical reactions
Pollens	Trees, grass, weeds, plants
Pb, Mn	Automobiles
Pb, Cd	Industrial emissions
VOC, PAH	Petrochemical solvents, vaporization of unburned fuels

Principal pollutants	Sources: both indoor and outdoor
NO_x, CO	Fuel burning
CO_2	Fuel burning, metabolic activity
SPM/RSP	ETS, resuspension of dust, condensation of vapours and combustion products
Water vapour	Biological activity, combustion, evaporation
VOC	Volatilization, fuel burning, paint, pesticides, insecticides, fungicides
Spores	Fungi, moulds

Principal pollutants	Sources: predominantly indoor
Ra	Soil, building construction materials, water
HCHO	Insulation, furnishing, ETS
Asbestos	Fire-retardant, insulation
NH_3	Cleaning products
Polycyclic hydrocarbons, arsenic, nicotine, acrolein	ETS
VOC	Adhesives, solvents, cooking, cosmetics
Hg	Fungicides, paints, spills or breakages of Hg-containing products
Aerosols	Consumer products, house dust
Allergens	House dust, animal dander
Pathogenic organisms	Infections

Source: adapted from WHO, 1995p.

Fig. 4.2

Distribution of time spent by the world population

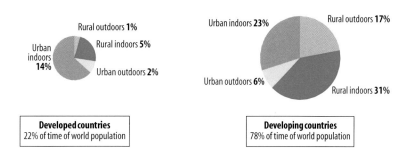

Developed countries
22% of time of world population

Rural outdoors **1%**
Urban indoors **14%**
Rural indoors **5%**
Urban outdoors **2%**

Developing countries
78% of time of world population

Urban indoors **23%**
Rural outdoors **17%**
Urban outdoors **6%**
Rural indoors **31%**

Here is shown the average time spent during one year in the eight most important environmental settings in the mid–1990s. Note that only about 2% of all people's time is spent outdoors in developed country cities where the vast bulk of air pollution control efforts have taken place.

Source: Schwela, 1996.

Fig 4.3

Air pollution trends with development

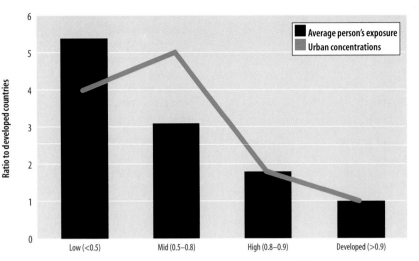

Countries grouped by level of development (HDI)

The line shows that urban outdoor SPM concentrations tend to rise in the first stages of development and then fall at later stages. As shown by the bars, however, actual exposures to city dwellers fall at every stage because indoor sources dominate exposure at early stages of development. Countries have been categorized into four groups according to the Human Development Index (HDI).

Source: Schwela, 1996.

Table 4.3

Indoor particulate air pollution from coal burning in China (sample studies)

Place	Urban/rural	Particulates µg/m3
Shanghai	Urban	500–1000
Beijing	Urban	17–1100*
Shenyang	Urban	125–270
Taiyuan	Urban	300–1000
Harbin	Urban	390–610*
Guangzhou	Urban	460
Chengde	Urban	270–700*
Yunnan	Rural	270–5100
Rural Beijing	Rural	400–1300
Jilin	Rural	1000–1200*
Hebei	Rural	1900–2500
Inner Mongolia	Rural	400–1600*

* particles less than 10 µm in size

Source: adapted from WHO 1995c.

urban environments, some of the highest concentrations actually occur in rural, indoor environments in developing countries (**Table 4.4**). These high concentrations are often due to the burning of unprocessed biomass fuels (wood, crop residues, dung) that emit considerable quantities of pollutants (see **Fig. 3.11**). In China, coal burning is a major source of indoor air pollution (**Table 4.3**). Indeed, so much pollution can be produced by indoor air pollution sources that the outdoor air quality of entire local neighbourhoods and adjoining areas may be highly polluted. Indoor air pollutant concentrations can be high even if ventilation is relatively good. In developed countries, air pollution in rural indoor environments is influenced less by type of cooking fuel than by type of heating stove and the extent of tobacco smoking.

Rural outdoor: In general, SPM concentrations in rural outdoor environments in developed and developing countries are considerably lower than in the other environmental settings. This is because population density is lower than in cities, and large combustion sources generally absent. High levels of air pollution generally

occur only on those few days when large-scale agricultural burning is undertaken. Exceptions include village environments influenced by emissions from local households, especially in continental areas with ground-level atmospheric inversions, and communities affected by dust blown from desert or dry areas. Metal smelters, chemical industries and power stations in rural areas may also cause significant local outdoor air pollution.

Total global exposure: Typical SPM concentrations for each of the above types of setting, for developed and developing countries, are listed in **Table 4.5**. Also shown are the estimated proportions of global human exposure (obtained by combining the typical concentrations of the particular environment with population and time-distribution data) that occur in each setting. Note that about three-fifths of total global exposure apparently occurs in the rural areas of developing countries. The relative level of exposure to SPM from all sources is decreasing as development increases (**Fig. 4.3**). Changing household energy sources would be the primary means of reducing exposures in developing countries.

4.2.4 Health risks of air pollution

Particular air pollution

In recent years a large number of studies of the health impacts of suspended particulate air pollution have been undertaken in developed country cities (WHO, 1997f). These studies show remarkable consistency in the relationship observed between changes in daily ambient suspended particulate levels and changes in daily mortality. Hopefully, future studies will consider indoor/outdoor differences and also be carried out in developing countries. In the meantime, we can only estimate the health risks of air pollution in these countries. Several uncertainties are involved in such estimation, as explained in **Box 4.2**, which describes how estimations — using two different methods — were made for this report. The results obtained using Method 1 are shown in **Fig. 4.4**, in the form of an estimate of total global mortality from suspended particulate air pollution exposures.

Divided into the environmental settings presented in **Table 4.5**, **Fig. 4.4** shows that, given the assumptions listed for Method 1 in **Box 4.2**, about 3 million deaths are due to suspended particulate air pollution globally each year: 2.8 million due to indoor exposures and 0.2 million due to outdoor exposures. In developing countries about 1.9 million deaths each year may be due to indoor exposures in rural areas and 0.6 million to indoor exposures in urban areas. In **Table 4.6** estimates based on Method 2 in **Box 4.2** of the annual global number of deaths due to air pollution are presented for eight major economic regions. This method arrives at a similar total number (2.7 million). The largest number of deaths is estimated to occur in India, followed by sub-Saharan Africa. The results using either method show clearly that indoor air pollution in developing is most probably the major cause of total excess deaths from exposure to air pollution.

The estimated 2.7–3 million deaths due to air pollution represent about 6% of the 50 million global deaths that occur annually (see Section 5.1). However, the uncertainty of these estimates is perhaps a factor of two in either direction. In other words, the estimate of the number of deaths attributable to air pollution ranges from 1.4–6 million annually. As noted in Section 5.2, many of these deaths are due to acute respiratory infections (ARI) in children. Cardiovascular diseases, lung cancer and chronic respiratory diseases in adults also contribute to these deaths (see Sections 5.8 and 5.10). Since there are interactions with other risk factors for all these diseases, a reduction in the number of deaths following improvement in one factor

Table 4.4

Indoor particulate concentrations from biomass combustion in developing countries

Region	No. of studies	Duration	µg/m³
Pacific	2	12 h	1300–5200
South Asia	15	Cooking period	850–4400**
		Cooking	630–820
		Non-cooking	880**
		24 h	2000–2800**
		Various	2000–6800
		Urban infants, 24 h	400–520**
China	8	Various	2600–2900
		Various	1100–11000**
Africa	8	Cooking/heating	800–1700
		Cooking/heating	1300**
		24 h	1300–2100**
		Urban area, 24 h	400–590**
Latin America	5	Cooking/heating	440–1100**
		24 h	720–1200**

* rural unless otherwise stated   ** particles less than 10 µm in diamter

Source: adapted from Smith, 1996.

Fig. 4.4

Estimated global annual deaths due to indoor and outdoor pollution exposure

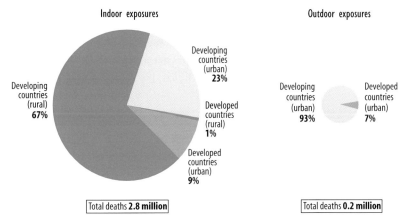

Source: Smith, 1996.

Table 4.5

Particulate concentrations and exposures in the eight major global environmental settings

Region	Concentration (µg/m³)		Exposure (%) of global total		
	Indoor	Outdoor	Indoor	Outdoor	Total
Developed					
Urban	100	70	7	1	7
Rural	80	40	2	0	2
Developing					
Urban	250	280	25	9	34
Rural	400	70	52	5	57
Total(%)			86	14	100

Note: Population exposures are expressed as a percentage of the world total. Here exposure is defined as equal to the number of people exposed, multiplied by the duration of exposure and the concentration breathed during that time.

Source: updated from Smith, 1993.

Box 4.2

Two approaches to determining the global number of deaths due to particulate exposures

The methods used in this book for estimating excess mortality caused by suspended particulate matter (SPM) are presented below.

METHOD 1: ENVIRONMENTAL SETTINGS (FIG. 4.4)

The health risks from particulate air pollution exposures have been estimated by Smith (1996), by applying the mean risk per unit ambient concentration determined from the results of a number of urban epidemiological studies (WHO, 1996h; Hong, Corvalán & Kjellström, 1997). The range of risk was found to be 1.2–4.4% increased mortality per 10 $\mu g/m^3$ incremental increase in the concentration of suspended particulates below 10 μm in diameter (PM_{10}). The total risks were calculated using the mean SPM concentration estimated for the major environmental settings listed in Table 4.5 together with population data and the incremental risk factors. The following assumptions were made.

* the risks determined for ambient levels are appropriate for total exposures
* risk factors determined for developed-country urban populations are appropriate for other populations
* the health risk is proportional to the exposure
* the true risk is at the lower end of the range of available studies, i.e. 1.2% increased mortality per each incremental increase of 10 $\mu g/m^3$
* at high concentrations, i.e. above 150 $\mu g/m^3$, the risk is reduced by 50%
* PM_{10} levels are half of those indicated for total suspended particulates in Table 4.5s.

METHOD 2: GEOGRAPHIC/ECONOMIC REGIONS (TABLE 4.6)

GEMS/AIR data, combined with data for individual cities from the new WHO Air Management Information System were used by Schwela (1996a, 1996b) to estimate excess mortality caused by exposure to SPM, by economic grouping, for different regions of the world. The model used to estimate the number of excess deaths due to air pollution incorporates the number of people at risk, the number of deaths per 100 000 without air pollution influences, and the percentage increase in deaths due to air pollution. The number of people at risk was assumed to be the number of people exposed to SPM concentrations that exceeded the 1987 WHO guidelines for annual mean SPM concentration. Data pertaining to increases in total mortality associated with incremental increases of 100 $\mu g/m^3$ in SPM in urban areas for China, Central/Eastern Europe, and established market economies, were used (Hong; Corvalán & Kjellström, 1997). The percentage increases in deaths per 100 $\mu g/m^3$ of SPM were assumed to be approximately the same for China, India, and the South-East Asian/Western Pacific region, while those for Established Market Economies were assumed to be approximately half of those in the eastern Mediterranean, Central/Eastern Europe and Latin America.

might reduce the number attributable to air pollution, and vice versa. A combination of preventive actions would be the most effective and sustainable means of reducing the number of such deaths.

Health impacts of other types of air pollution

In addition to particulates, other "classic" air pollutants of concern from a health point of view, include O_3, NO_2, SO_2, and CO. O_3 and other photochemical oxidants are formed by the action of short-wave radiation from the sun on NO_2. A continuum of health effects at different levels of exposure to O_3 may occur, including respiratory symptoms, changes in lung function and airway inflammation. O_3 exposure has also been associated with increased hospital admissions for respiratory conditions, including the exacerbation of asthma. Factors such as the time spent outdoors and people's activity level will influence the type of health outcome which may result at a particular concentration level.

Evidence for a clearly defined concentration–response relationship is lacking for NO_2. For acute exposures, only very high concentration levels affect healthy people. Asthmatics and people with chronic obstructive lung disease are more susceptible to acute changes in lung function, airway responsiveness and respiratory symptoms. Epidemiological studies of chronic exposures suggest a range of effects.

The acute effects of SO_2 include lung function changes, increases in specific airway resistance and symptoms such as wheezing and shortness of breath. Long-term effects have been more difficult to ascertain as SO_2 exposure is most often combined with exposure to SPM.

CO combines with haemoglobin to form carboxyhaemoglobin, which reduces the oxygen carrying capacity of the blood. The binding with other haeme proteins is directly related to changes in the functioning of affected organs, such as the brain and cardiovascular system, and the developing fetus. Neurobehavioural effects of CO include impaired concentration and cognitive performance at certain exposures. In the fetus, the affinity of haemoglobin for CO is increased, and birth weight may be affected.

Health effects have also been demonstrated for many inorganic pollutants including arsenic, cadmium, lead, mercury, manganese and nickel. The health effects of volatile organic pollutants have also been studied. The aforementioned health effects of the "classic" air pollutants, inorganic pollutants, volatile organic pollutants and other classes of air pollutant are discussed in the revised air quality guidelines for Europe, which are due to be published by WHO shortly (WHO, 1996f). In reality, of course, people are exposed to various mixtures of air pollutants, with additive, synergistic or antagonistic effects (see Section 4.10).

4.2.5 Environmental tobacco smoke: on the increase

Active tobacco smoking is a major cause of ill-health (WHO, 1996s). Concern is also increasing about the effects of passive smoking, i.e. exposure to environmental tobacco smoke (ETS). ETS is that portion of tobacco smoke

Table 4.6

Estimated global annual deaths (in thousands) from air pollution by environmental setting and region*

Environmental setting	Economic regions*								Total
	LAC	China	FSE	MEC	EME	India	OAI	SSA	
Rural indoor	180	320	n.a.	n.a.	0	496	363	490	1849
Urban indoor	113	53	n.a.	n.a.	32	93	40	32	363
Urban ambient	113	70	100	57	47	84	40	n.a.	511
Total	406	443	100	57	79	673	443	522	2723

na = not available
* according to World Bank classification

Source: Schwela, 1996.

released into the surrounding air, either directly (side-stream smoke) or after being exhaled by smokers. It is much less damaging per unit of emissions than the mainstream smoke inhaled directly by the active smoker. But since it is often emitted in spaces inhabited by non-smokers, it can have a large impact per unit of emissions even compared to large outdoor sources. **Table 4.7** shows the consumption of tobacco per capita across the world and gives an approximate indication of the relative emissions and exposures to ETS for different countries and regions.

Over 4000 components of cigarette smoke have been identified; many are established carcinogens or other types of toxin. Those of health concern include SPM, CO, nicotine, nitrosamines, benzene, formaldehyde and benzo[a]pyrene. Studies show that the extent of ETS exposure and its health

Table 4.7

World tobacco consumption per capita (adults 15 years and over)

	Cigarettes per adult (over 15 years of age)			Annual % change
	1970–1972	1980–1982	1990–1992	1980–1982 to 1990–1992
More developed countries	2860	2980	2590	-1.4
Established market economies	2910	3000	2570	-1.5
Formerly socialist economies of Europe	2450	2830	2770	-0.2
Less developed countries	860	1220	1410	1.4
China	730	1290	1900	3.9
India	1010	1310	1370	0.4
Other Asia and islands	780	1130	1190	0.5
Middle Eastern Crescent	950	1240	1200	-0.3
Sub-Saharan Africa	410	490	500	0.2
Latin America and the Caribbean	1430	1540	1310	-1.6
World	1410	1650	1660	0.1

Source: based on data from WHO, 1996s.

Box 4.3

Successful examples of air quality management in developed countries: USA and Germany

Health-oriented environmental pollution control programmes aim to promote a better quality of life by reducing pollution to the lowest level possible. Environmental pollution control programmes and policies, whose implications and priorities vary from country to country, cover all aspects of pollution (air, water, etc.) and involve coordination among sectors involved in industrial development, city planning, water resources development and transportation planning.

Some countries, such as the USA and Germany, have based air pollution management on a clean air implementation plan, consisting of the following elements:

- description of area with respect to topography, meteorology, socioeconomic conditions
- emissions inventory
- comparison of emission concentrations with emission standards
- air pollutant concentrations inventory
- simulated air pollutant concentrations
- comparison of air pollutant concentrations with air quality standards
- inventory of air pollution impacts
- causal analysis of compounds and sources responsible for observed effects
- control measures
- cost of control measures
- cost of public health and environmental effects
- cost–benefit analysis of control measures versus public health and environmental effects
- transportation and land-use planning
- enforcement plan
- resource commitment
- projections for the future regarding population, traffic, industries, fuel consumption
- follow-up strategies.

The impact of clean air implementation plans in the USA and Germany (known as State Implementation Plans in the former) have resulted in the following reductions in air pollution:

USA	1985 → 1994	Germany	1975 → 1994
National average CO levels	28% ↘	SO_2	75% ↘
National total CO emissions	15% ↘	NO_2	20% ↘
Pb concentrations in urban areas	86% ↘	Suspended particulate (PM_{10})	40% ↘
Total Pb emissions	75% ↘	Lead	80% ↘
Total NO_x emissions	3% ↘	Cadmium	80% ↘
Highway vehicle NO_x emissions	9% ↘		
Fuel combustion emissions	8% ↘		
National composite mean for O_3	12% ↘		
Exceedances of the ozone National Ambient Air Quality Standard	56% ↘		
Particulate (PM_{10}) (1988–1994)	20% ↘		
Estimated PM_{10} emissions from traditional inventories	12% ↘		
National annual mean SO_2	25% ↘		
National total SO_2	9% ↘		

Source: adapted from Schwela & Köth-Jahr, 1994.

effects are determined by the number of cigarettes smoked in indoor environments. Rough estimates of population exposure to ETS may be inferred from smoking prevalence.

In adult non-smokers, chronic exposure to ETS increases mortality from lung cancer by between 20–30% (US EPA, 1992) (see also Section 5.9). Other likely health effects may also ensue, such as cardiovascular disease, chronic respiratory disease, pulmonary lung function reduction in adults, and ARI in children. This implies that about 3% (100 000) of the global air pollution deaths in **Fig. 4.4** could be attributed to ETS exposure. As smoking rates are rising in many developing countries (**Table 4.7**), the health risks of ETS can be expected to increase.

4.2.6 Ionizing radiation: natural and human-caused exposure

The contribution of natural, medical and industrial sources of radiation to human exposure is shown in **Table 4.8**. Exposure to ionizing radiation can occur due to uranium mining and milling, reactor operation and fuel reprocessing, when radionuclides are released into air. However, total emissions are small compared with those

Table 4.8

Annual average adult radiation doses

Source of exposure	Annual effective dose (mSv)	
	Typical	Elevated*
Natural sources		
Cosmic rays	0.39	2.0
Terrestrial gamma rays	0.46	4.3
Radionuclides in the body (except radon)	0.23	0.8
Radon and its decay products	1.3	10.0
Total of natural sources	2.4	16.9
Sources related to human activities		
Medical	0.3	1–2
Occupational	0.001	10
Nuclear power	0.001	0.02
Large fuel reprocessing plants	0.2	0.5
Nuclear tests	0.005	0.2

* elevated values are representative of large regions; even higher values occur locally

Source: based on data from UNSCEAR, 1993.

emitted by natural sources (UNSCEAR, 1996). Of course, the converse can be true in the event of a nuclear accident. (see Section 3.6)

The health effects of ionizing radiation exposures have been studied intensively, but uncertainty remains about the exact health risks at low exposure rates (see also Section 5.9.6). If it is assumed that an increase in mortality is proportional to exposure all the way down to natural levels, then the current pattern of (non-radon) human-caused exposure (mostly medical X-rays and medical use of radioactive isotopes) implies an attributable global number of cancer deaths of 0.12 million per year (ICRP, 1990).

In some areas of the world, such as the Arabian Sea coast of Kerala in India and the Atlantic coast of Espírito Santo in Brazil, high natural ionizing radiation dose rates in air of up to 4000 n Gy/h (due to the thorium or uranium content of mineral sands) have been recorded.

Only in recent years has the extent of the largest naturally-occurring exposure — radon in residences — been realized (UNSCEAR, 1996). Radon gas (^{222}Rn) is radioactive, has a half-life of 3.8 days, and can accumulate in homes. Elevated indoor radon levels in buildings originate from radon in underlying rocks and soils, and sometimes from outdoor air. Radon levels may also be elevated due to the presence of radon in building materials, tap water or domestic gas supplies. National surveys have shown that the average indoor radon concentration in residences ranges from 10 to 140 Bq/m^3 (EC, 1995b), with maximum concentrations greater than 100 000 Bq/m^3 having been detected in individual dwellings in some countries. Remedial action is recommended if radon exposure in dwellings exceeds a yearly average concentration of 200–600 Bq/m^3 of ^{222}Rn in air (ICRP, 1990; IAEA, 1996).

Radon exposure increases the risk of lung cancer (UNSCEAR, 1996) (see Section 5.9.6). Quantifying the health impact from radon exposure is diffi-

cult, though, because the risk due to radon exposure interacts heavily with the risk due to active smoking. In the USA, for example, most lung cancer due to radon exposure seems to occur in the 25% of the adult population who smoke. Applying the US risk ratios to the world population indicates that approximately 0.2 million lung cancer deaths (80% in smokers) could be attributable to radon exposure (UNSCEAR, 1996). (The health effects

---

Box 4.4

Successful air quality management in a developing country: Chile

The Chilean government has restructured its environmental legislation. New legislation is based upon the Framework Environmental Law, which is intended to provide the basis for a gradual improvement in environmental quality, but avoiding conflict between industry, government and pressure groups.

Specific measures already implemented to reduce industrial emissions of air pollutants include the Ministry of Mining Decree 185. Adopted in 1992, this decree seeks to drastically reduce SO$_2$ emissions, to ensure that air quality meets United States Environmental Protection Agency standards in the mining areas in the north of the country, and the strict Scandinavian standards for the protection of forests in the south. An estimated 90% of SO$_2$ emissions in Chile originate from copper smelting, a process which is also responsible for high ambient concentrations of heavy metals, such as arsenic.

Pollution in the capital city

It is generally agreed that diesel vehicle emissions represent an important source of air pollution in Santiago, and have increased significantly since the deregulation of the city's bus services in the 1980s. Poor engine maintenance and the use of second-hand engine parts has exacerbated the problems created by the doubling of bus numbers between 1980 and 1988. Vehicle bans are applied during air pollution episodes; the more severe the air pollution, the more rigorous the ban. In addition to restrictions on vehicle use during air pollution episodes, the emergency bans also stipulate 20–50% cuts in industrial emissions and in the use of polluting domestic fuels. These measures have been implemented on several occasions but their success is hard to evaluate. Chile has also established a number of ambient air quality standards which are very similar to US National Ambient Air Quality Standards.

Overall, Santiago has good and improving air quality management capabilities with an excellent monitoring network, an emissions inventory and improving regulatory and administrative structures. The proliferation of highly polluting sources in the city combined with extremely unfavourable meteorological and topographical features continue, however, to result in high concentrations of a number of pollutants.

Source: adapted from MARC, 1996.

of non-ionizing radiation are discussed in Section 5.9.7.)

4.2.7 Air quality management: many factors

Air quality management aims at the elimination or reduction to acceptable levels of airborne pollutants whose presence in the atmosphere can adversely affect human health, animal or plant life, the environment and materials of economic value.

Beyond considerations of emissions from fixed or mobile sources, air quality management programmes should also take into account a wide variety of factors, including topographical and meteorological conditions which influence pollutant concentration levels in particular localities, the sociodemographic characteristics of exposed groups, and community and government participation in air pollution control efforts. For example, meteorological conditions can greatly affect ground-level pollutant concentrations. Additionally, air pollution sources may be scattered over a community or a region and their control may necessitate the involvement of more than one administrative or political unit.

Comprehensive air pollution control programmes that adopt a multidisciplinary approach, and that are based on the collaborative efforts of different entities, both private and governmental, are therefore called for. These will normally need to be based on inventories of emissions and sources, knowledge of concentration levels of pollutants, their potential health-and-environment effects, and so on. Comprehensive monitoring programmes need to be in place which yield information on trends in pollutant concentrations over space and time, and which are relevant also to likely exposures. Proposed source control measures and abatement strategies need to take into account their technical feasibility, as well as social, economic and other considerations. Various

technical, legal, and economic instruments can be used to control pollution, in combination with improved administrative and jurisdictional arrangements that aim at more coordinated and integrated air pollution control. Generally, the various sectoral responsibilities for aspects of control at different tiers of government must be clarified, and communities and the private sector involved in control strategies.

Examples of air quality management and some of the factors that such activity should take into account are given in **Boxes 4.3 and 4.4**.

The management of indoor air quality is usually left primarily to building occupants. This is in direct contrast to protection of the ambient environment, which is usually considered a government responsibility (Krzyzanowski, 1995). The decisions of the latter tend to be driven by the household economics, convenience or habits, rather than a desire to minimize health risks relating to specific activities and materials used indoors. Expecting that all health hazards will be eliminated from households and that adverse health impacts will be avoided completely, following optimal decisions taken by the individuals involved, is therefore unrealistic. Instead, public health professionals must identify the most prevalent conditions adversely affecting health in a given population and propose coordinated efforts for reducing the health risks, using the most efficient means. In developed countries, legislative and economic mechanisms are already in place to encourage individuals and building administrators, to manage indoor environments in a health-promoting way. In developing countries, the actual air quality situation should be assessed in order to inform policy-makers, create awareness of indoor air problems, assess their magnitude, provide information on health effects, and develop remedial actions and education programmes.

4.3 Household wastes

Poorly managed wastes — specifically excreta and other liquid and solid wastes from households and the community — represent a serious health threat (see Section 3.2). For example, in neighbourhoods that lack sanitation, waste heaps become mixed with excreta and contribute to the spread of infectious diseases. Equally, in areas that do have sewerage systems, sewage may nevertheless be discharged untreated into the environment, resulting in the contamination of water sources used for drinking purposes, sometimes far downstream of the point of discharge, and potentially leading to contamination of shellfish and other aquatic life.

Waste from industries and agriculture can also cause serious health risks. The main problems of industrial waste were presented in Section 3.5 and the associated contamination of water and soil will be discussed in Sections 4.4 and 4.6.

4.3.1 Health risks of inappropriate excreta disposal

Human excreta consists of urine and faeces. As discussed in Section 3.2.1, urine is relatively harmless, other than with respect to the spread of schistosomiasis in tropical countries. But human faeces are dangerous to human health everywhere because of the pathogens they contain. Pathogens enter the human body via contaminated drinking-water and contaminated food, via hands contaminated with faecal matter, and, in the case of some helminthic worm infections, directly through the skin. Ingestion of faecal pathogens can cause diarrhoeal disease, cholera, intestinal worm infections and typhoid fever (see Section 5.3). If a dangerous pathogen, such as *Vibrio cholerae*, is introduced into a community with poor sanitation, poor water supply and poor food safety, epidemic cholera may

Box 4.5

Cholera: a consequence of unsanitary conditions

The cholera epidemic that began in Peru in 1990 and spread to 16 other countries in Latin America is the most striking demonstration in recent history of the health effects of lack of sanitation facilities, lack of safe drinking-water and poor food hygiene. *Vibrio cholerae* — the pathogen that causes cholera — is thought to have reached the Peruvian coast in a contaminated ship's hull or via contaminated sea plankton (see Section 5.3.2). Coastal shellfish and fish were contaminated in turn and people who consumed these foodstuffs then became infected themselves. A total of 378 488 cholera cases were reported in Latin America during 1991, most of them in Peru. By 1995 the number of new cases was decreasing. But the epidemic still prevails throughout the continent, with 85–809 cases reported by 15 countries in 1995. Cholera incidence in the Americas represented 41% of all cholera cases officially reported to WHO that year.

In Peru, where the outbreak was most severe, the abrupt halt in tourism and agricultural exports cost the Peruvian economy US$ 1000 million in just 10 weeks. The total economic cost to Peru was more than three times the total national investment in water supply and sanitation improvements made in the 1980s.

Cholera is a worldwide problem. A total of 208 755 cholera cases and 5034 deaths were officially reported to WHO in 1995. The number of cases reported from Africa in 1995, totalling 74 105 cases, including 3024 deaths, represented about 34% of all cases.

Although cholera incidence is falling in all regions, the epidemic is expected to persist in the long term if water supply and sanitation problems in the developing world remain unsolved. Cholera can only be reliably prevented by ensuring that all populations have access to adequate excreta disposal systems and safe drinking-water. Special attention should be paid to refugee camps where large concentrations of people and poor hygienic conditions combine to generate major health risks. In Zaire, for example, 58 057 cases of cholera were reported in 1994. Most of these cholera cases occurred in refugee camps near the Rwandan border and most of them could have been avoided by ensuring potable water, adequate means of excreta disposal and safe food. A dramatic decrease in Zaire to 553 cases in 1995 reflected the stabilization of refugee movement.

Sources: : World Bank, 1992; WHO, 1996.

Table 4.9

Relationship between inadequate water supply and sanitation and selected diseases

Disease	Relationship
Diarrhoeal diseases	Strongly related to unsanitary excreta disposal, poor personal and domestic hygiene, and unsafe drinking-water
Schistosomiasis	Strongly related to unsanitary excreta disposal and absence of nearby sources of safe water
Dracunculiasis	Strongly related to unsafe drinking-water
Trachoma	Strongly related to insufficient face washing, often in the absence of nearby sources of safe water
Dengue fever	Related to unsatisfactory solid waste management, water storage, operation of water points and drainage
Infection with intestinal helminths	Strongly related to unsanitary excreta disposal, and poor personal and domestic hygiene

ensue, as in South America in the early 1990s (**Box 4.5**).

In the developing world, low sanitation coverage, poor construction of on-site facilities and the discharge of untreated or partially treated sewage means that the human environment is often highly contaminated with pathogens. **Table 4.9** illustrates the relationship between poor sanitation conditions and selected diseases. The sustainable way to break these cycles of disease is by improving sanitation coverage, treating wastewaters discharged by sewer systems, and educating the populations at risk.

In urban areas, sanitation improvements are the responsiblity of water and sanitation authorities, but ultimately depend upon political will and adequate investments in sanitation and hygiene education. In rural areas, sanitation improvements usually rest with district authorities. But in developing countries they generally do not have adequate financial and human resources for such activity. Community participation and empowerment, however, can become the key to initiating and sustaining the necessary improvements, in urban and rural areas alike (**Box 4.6**).

4.3.2 Health risks of solid waste

Solid wastes can come into direct or indirect contact with human beings at several stages in the waste cycle (see Section 3.2). The groups at risk are therefore broad and numerous and include: the population of unserved areas, especially pre-school children; waste workers; workers in facilities that produce infectious and toxic material; people living close to waste disposal facilities, and populations whose water supplies have become polluted due to waste dumping or leakage from landfill sites. Additionally, industrial dumping of hazardous waste that has become mixed together with household solid waste can expose populations to chemical and radioactive hazards.

The health risks of uncollected solid waste are obviously most severe for those actually living in unserved areas. Notably, pre-school children are at risk of injury, intoxication or infection since they are likely to be exposed to uncollected waste in streets or at unofficial dump sites. Uncollected organic domestic wastes in particular pose seri-

---

Box 4.6

Community empowerment for water and sanitation development

Dharma Vijaya Foundation, a national non-governmental organization, started a social development programme in Ginnaliya Village, Sri Lanka, in 1990. By 1993, a trained community facilitator had been assigned to live in the village and to help the community improve its water and sanitation facilities. A participatory approach was used to involve all members of the community in the process. A household survey conducted by village members showed that 90% of households lacked an adequate water supply and that about 70% lacked basic sanitation facilities.

The community was highly energized by these findings and formed a community organization to continue the participatory process, which included the drawing up of a plan to improve water and sanitation conditions in the village. But at this point, Dharma Vijaya Foundation advised that it did not have the technical resources that the community organization needed to plan and undertake improvements.

This announcement had major adverse effects. First, the community started to lose its sense of purpose, people ceased to be interested in the plans, the organizational structures developed during the project started to disintegrate, and the planning for improvements stopped. People felt let down by the outside agency.

A year later though, in 1994, the community decided to take action itself. The participatory process they had already undergone in 1993 inspired them with sufficient confidence to approach another organization, Sathmaga Participatory Development Forum (SPDF), for help. SPDF agreed to assign a representative, also a trained community facilitator, to live in the village and help reactivate the programme.

Progress was slow at first. The mistrust and disappointment generated by past efforts had to be overcome. The SPDF worker started to organize the community using existing village structures. A programme to win back the villagers' confidence and to reestablish the small groups started by the Dharma Vijaya Foundation, and re-orient the community organization, was initiated.

Rapid progress was made and SPDR was able to. provide a full-time technical officer to provide the input the community organization needed to plan its own improvements.

Ginnaliya Village now has two gravity schemes, 20 shallow wells and 125 toilets. This success has empowered the community to make more plans for improvements in other areas of their lives, including a development package for an agricultural credit scheme and an agroforestry project.

Source: WHO, 1995e.

ous health risks since they ferment, creating conditions favourable to the survival and growth of microbial pathogens, and especially if they become intermixed with human excreta due to poor sanitation. Organic wastes also provide feeding stock and a natural environment for insects, rodents and other animals which are potential carriers of enteric pathogens (**Table 4.10**). Uncollected solid wastes can also obstruct stormwater run-off, resulting in flooding or creation of stagnant water bodies which become habitats and breeding places for waterborne vectors of tropical diseases.

But even if solid waste is collected, it may create health risks for large numbers of people if disposed of improperly. Groundwater used for drinking purposes for instance, can become chemically or microbiologically polluted if wastes are disposed of in or near water sources. Direct dumping of untreated solid wastes in rivers, lakes or seas can also result in accumulation of toxic substances in the food-chain due to their uptake by plants and animals. Infectious diseases spread by poorly-managed solid waste are listed in **Table 4.10**.

Handling of solid waste obviously entails health risks, potentially leading to infectious and chronic disease and accidents. **Box 4.7** outlines those relating to waste workers.

Disposal of healthcare wastes requires special attention since it can create major health hazards, the best documented of which is the transmission of viral infections, such as hepatitis B and C, through wounds caused by discarded syringe needles. All too often, infectious wastes from hospitals, other healthcare establishments, medical laboratories and research centres, and small scattered sources (such as clinics, and households where healthcare of a family member is undertaken) are disposed of together with regular waste. The people most at risk are healthcare workers, waste handlers and hospital maintenance personnel.

Table 4.10

Selected infectious diseases associated with solid waste

Type of waste	Diseases by cause		
	Bacteria	Virus	Parasite/fungus
Infected sharp waste	Staphyloccosis	Hepatitis B	
	Streptococcosis	Hepatitis C	
	Tetanus	AIDS	
Waste-generated infected dust	Anthrax	Trachoma*	Mycosis
		Conjunctivitis	
	Pneumonia	Pneumonia	
Vectors living or breeding in waste-generated ponds		Dengue	Malaria filariasis
		Yellow fever	Schistosomiasis
Stray animals and rodents feeding on waste	Plague	Rabies	Leishmaniasis
			Hydatidosis

* by chlamydia

Source: based on data from UNEP/IETC, 1996.

Waste treatment and disposal sites themselves have the potential to create health hazards for neighbouring populations. Landfills are a source of fires, dust, smoke, noise and disease vectors such as insects, rodents and stray animals, and incinerators cause air pollution through emission of particulates, toxic chemicals and heavy metals such as cadmium, lead, mercury and zinc. Ideally, waste treatment and disposal sites should be controlled and located at an adequate distance from human settlements, and the boundaries of landfill sites confined and sealed so that drinking-water sources are protected from infiltration of leachate or run-off.

Recycling, too, although in principle a good approach to waste management, carries health risks if proper precautions are not taken. Waste workers dealing with recycling of waste that has a high metal or chemical content may experience toxic exposures, while in developing countries "scavengers" who comb waste sites for articles that can be recycled and reused may sustain injuries and come into direct contact with infectious dusts and disease vectors such as rats and flies (see Section 3.2.2). Scavengers and their families are also at risk because they often build their homes very close to, if not on, landfill sites. As well as being exposed to a wide variety of waste health hazards they are also frequently subject to social and economic abuses from waste

> ## Box 4.7
> ### Occupational hazards associated with waste handling
>
> *INFECTIONS*
> - skin and blood infections resulting from direct contact with waste, and from infected wounds
> - eye and respiratory infections resulting from exposure to infected dust, especially during landfill operations
> - zoonoses resulting from bites by wild or stray animals feeding on wastes
> - enteric infections transmitted by flies feeding on wastes.
>
> *CHRONIC DISEASES*
> - incineration operators especially are at risk of chronic respiratory diseases, including cancers resulting from exposure to dust and hazardous compounds.
>
> *ACCIDENTS*
> - musculoskeletal disorders resulting from the handling of heavy containers
> - wounds, most often infected, resulting from contact with sharp items
> - poisoning and chemical burns resulting from contact with small amounts of hazardous chemical waste mixed with general waste
> - burns and other injuries resulting from occupational accidents at waste disposal sites, or from methane gas explosion at landfill sites.
>
> *Source: adapted from UNEP, 1996c.*

recycling traders. Health surveys show that their health status is very poor and their life expectancy far below national averages (Kungskulniti et al., 1991).

4.4 Water

Adequate supply of safe drinking-water is universally recognized as a basic human need. Yet more than 1000 million people do not have ready access to an adequate and safe water supply, and a variety of physical, chemical and biological agents render many water sources less than wholesome and healthy. (Water availability problems are described in Section 3.3.) Health hazards in the aquatic environment and waterborne epidemics are mostly due to inadequate or even incompetent management of water resources, although adverse natural conditions are sometimes causative factors too. Examples of the latter include areas where the natural geochemical compo-

sition of water supplies can lead to severe health impairments. Fluorosis in the Rift Valley and in central Asia, and skin cancer due to arsenic intoxication, particularly in Asia and Central America are just two examples.

Today's perception of water problems in the world is based largely on the idea of a North:South dichotomy. This holds that developed countries are rich and highly industrialized and, as far as water is concerned, mostly preoccupied with chemical pollution. Conversely, developing countries are held to be poor and mostly agriculturally-oriented, and to suffer water pollution problems caused by contamination of watercourses with bacteria, parasites and a host of microbial disease vectors. These are oversimplifications however.

Developed countries are by no means protected from communicable diseases. General mobility and tourist travel render populations of these countries vulnerable to all sorts of biologically transmitted diseases, including waterborne (and foodborne) gastrointestinal disorders. Recent outbreaks of *Cryptosporidium*, affecting entire cities, have caused considerable alarm at many waterworks in North America and Europe (MacKenzie et al., 1994; Solo-Gabriele & Neumeister, 1996) (see Section 5.3.3). And many small community water supplies and family wells are not of an acceptable microbiological quality.

Meanwhile, the concern of many developing countries about water quality goes far beyond microbes. Chemical pollution of water sources, for instance, is increasing with industrialization and because of widespread use of agricultural chemicals (see Sections 3.3 to 3.5). This double-edged problem is most pronounced, however, in the newly industrializing countries and in countries in economic transition where the traditional problems of domestic sewage collection, treatment and disposal have not yet been resolved because creation and maintenance of sanitation infrastructure have not kept pace with industrial and urban development. Investments in drinking-water supply, treatment works and distribution networks have not matched population growth and socioeconomic development, and industrial expansion has been accompanied by inadequately treated or uncontrolled discharge of wastewaters. Consumers are thus not protected sufficiently, if at all, from microbial and chemical water contamination.

Safe water supplies for all populations can only be guaranteed when access, equity and sustainability are assured. Access can be defined as the number of people who have access to sufficient quantities of safe drinking-water for meeting basic personal health and hygiene needs. Equity refers to equitable distribution of water supply sources between countries, as well as between rich and poor populations and rural and urban areas within countries. Sustainability is a newer concept, but one which is at the heart of successful development.

4.4.1 Water supply access and equity

The number of people without access to safe water (i.e. unserved) dropped from around 1600 million in 1990 to around 1100 million in 1994 (WHO/UNICEF, 1996a). Currently, more than 800 million of those unserved live in rural areas. At the same time, the number of urban unserved is actually rising sharply in developing countries due to rapid urbanization, much of which is occurring in peri-urban and slum areas. **Fig. 4.5** shows trends in development of water supply services in developing countries for 1990–2000. **Table 4.11** lists countries with low access to safe water. **Table 4.12** illustrates the change in drinking-water supply coverage that occurred between 1990 and 1994 in selected countries.

Although per capita water availability is being reduced continuously due to increasing population density, and water scarcity looms in many regions

(see Section 3.3), urban water utilities have been able to achieve at least partial coverage. The future outlook is rather bleak, however, with a water crisis predicted for many countries for the first half of the next century. Large-scale agricultural and industrial use will make it more difficult, and certainly much more costly, to supply urban areas with drinking-water in an increasingly competitive water market.

As discussed in Section 3.3, global figures mask regional variations. Although the number of people without a safe water supply dropped by around 470 million during 1990–1994, the number unserved in Africa and in Latin America and the Caribbean has actually increased; almost all of the coverage gains have been in Asia and the Pacific (WHO/UNICEF, 1996a). Disparity between countries within regions also exists as can be seen in **Fig. 4.6** which shows water supply coverage for reporting countries in Africa.

Wide variation occurs within countries too. For instance, urban areas generally have higher coverage than rural areas (**Table 4.11**). Even within areas, inequitable distribution can be very marked. In cities water is often supplied to districts whose populations can pay for services. That said, wealthier areas often benefit from subsidized tariffs, with the result that water is used for non-essential purposes such as washing cars, watering lawns and filling swimming pools.

Meanwhile, in poorer areas, thousands of people may only have access to standpipes which are poorly and/or intermittently supplied and at which they must queue for long periods. Or even worse, they may have to buy water of doubtful quality from private vendors at prices that may be 10 to 20 times higher than average inner city water tariffs. The health consequences resulting from the deprivation caused by this inequity are sometimes considerable, as evidenced by the infant mortality rates of rich and poor — which

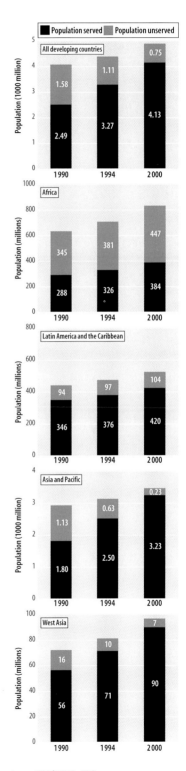

Fig. 4.5

Development of water supply services in developing countries 1990–2000

Source: WHO/UNICEF, 1996a.

Table 4.11

25 countries where half or more of the total population had no safe drinking-water supply in 1994

Country	Percentage without safe drinking-water		
	Urban	Rural	Total
Afghanistan	61	95	88
Central African Republic	82	82	82
Chad	52	83	76
Zaire	63	77	73
Papua New Guinea	16	83	72
Haiti	63	77	72
Madagascar	17	90	71
Liberia	42	92	70
Angola	31	85	68
Mozambique	83	60	68
Sierra Leone	42	79	66
Uganda	53	68	66
Vietnam	47	68	64
Mali	64	62	63
Myanmar	64	61	62
Lao PDR	60	61	61
Nigerai	37	74	61
Swaziland	59	56	57
Iraq	—	—	56
Nepal	34	59	56
Zambia	36	73	57
Malawi	48	56	55
Sri Lanka	57	53	54
Benin	59	47	50
Sudan	34	55	50

Source: based on data from WHO/UNICEF, 1996a.

Table 4.12

Trends in drinking-water supply coverage among countries reporting low coverage in 1990

Country	% coverage 1990	% coverage 1994	% change
Large gains			
Equatorial Guinea	35	95	60
Maldives	49	89	40
Bhutan	34	64	30
Moderate gains			
Uganda	21	34	13
El Salvador	47	55	8
Lao PDR	35	39	4
Madagascar	23	29	6
Burundi	49	52	3
Senegal	48	50	2
Sudan	48	50	2
No gain			
Sierra Leone	41	37	-2
Angola	36	32	-4
Mali	41	37	-4
Vietnam	42	36	-6
Haiti	38	28	-10

Source: based on data from WHO/UNICEF, 1996a.

may vary between two and ten times in magnitude — and the large numbers of urban poor who are at high risk from epidemic diarrhoeal diseases such as cholera (see Section 5.3).

Future prospects

Full coverage remains a difficult goal everywhere as all regions must contend with rapidly growing populations. Globally, by the year 2000, the majority of the unserved (627 million, or 59% of the total) will reside in Asia and the Pacific. By that date, unserved populations will have increased over those of 1994 in both the African Region and the Latin American and Caribbean Region. Most of the growth in the unserved will occur in rural areas in Africa and in the urban areas of Latin America.

Given current trends in urban water supply coverage, safe drinking-water will probably be available for all people in urban areas in Western Asia by 2000, and all populations in Latin America and the Caribbean by 2020. In rural areas, no region is likely to reach full coverage by 2020, although rural areas in Asia and the Pacific are likely to make the greatest statistical gains.

The direct effects of improved water and sanitation services on health are most clearly seen in the case of water-related diseases, which arise from the ingestion of pathogens from contaminated water or food, and from exposure to insects or other vectors associated with water. Esrey et al. (1991) (**Table 4.13**) calculated that access to sustainable safe drinking-water and sanitation services for populations currently at risk would result in:

- 200 million fewer diarrhoeal episodes
- 2.1 million fewer deaths caused by diarrhoea
- 76 000 fewer dracunculiasis cases
- 150 million fewer schistosomiasis cases
- 75 million fewer trachoma cases.

.4.2 Sustainability of water supply and sanitation services

Water supply sustainability involves: ensuring the continuous availability of sufficient quantities of water of sufficient quality, within adequate institutional frameworks; applying sound management practices, appropriate technologies, and full-cost accounting, and effectively maintaining facilities and equipment. In developing countries, however, management of water supply and sanitation systems is often poor, resulting in interruptions in the provision of services and sometimes in the complete collapse of systems. When the latter happens, users may be obliged to resort to traditional water sources which may be contaminated.

Contamination of distribution pipelines due to intermittent supply, low water pressure in the distribution network, inadequate wastewater collection systems and leaking pipes are also common problems in developing countries. If contaminated water penetrates distribution mains, water that has already been treated and disinfected may become re-contaminated.

Unaccounted for water is another major water supply problem. In many large developing country cities it has been reported as amounting to more than 50% of supplies. Most of this water is lost through leaking pipes or overflowing service reservoirs after abstraction, pumping or treatment, or during distribution. Those who suffer most from this inefficiency are populations living in impoverished, outlying urban areas. But if measures to ensure the sustainability and organization of facilities were implemented, extension of coverage to the fringe and poor areas of large cities would be possible. This would bring about considerable improvements in health. At the same time, the need to expand treatment and distribution facilities would be minimized, in effect releasing resources for other development activities.

4.4.3 Environmental health risks of water pollution

Water quality is closely linked to type of water use and level of economic development. This was clearly seen in developed countries in the mid-18th Century, at the start of industrialization, when cities expanded, became densely populated with crowded inner city slums, and excreta was discharged untreated into urban watercourses. The resultant faecal contamination of surface waters created serious health problems, including cholera and typhoid epidemics. Since drinking-water was drawn from the very same rivers or groundwater sources into which excreta was discharged, water-borne disease outbreaks became a regular occurrence.

Incidence of waterborne diseases has been reduced substantially in developed countries, but cholera and endemic diarrhoeal disease outbreaks remain frequent elsewhere (see **Box 4.5** and Section 5.3). Moreover, rapid industrialization in developing country cities, and intensive agriculture, have added a further dimension to water pollution in the form of chemical contamination. Urban populations, particularly in developing country megacities are therefore now exposed to hazardous chemicals as well as to infectious agents in surface and groundwaters.

Aspects of water pollution which have a direct bearing on human health are summarized below. The health effects of selected specific chemicals in drinking-water are described in Section 4.4.4.

Sewage

Untreated or inadequately treated municipal sewage is a major source of surface and groundwater pollution throughout the developing world (see Section 3.2). This is cause for considerable concern since the biological degradation of organic material that is discharged with municipal sewage into watercourses uses substantial amounts of oxygen (so-called biochemical oxy-

Fig. 4.6

Water supply services coverage in Africa at the end of 1994

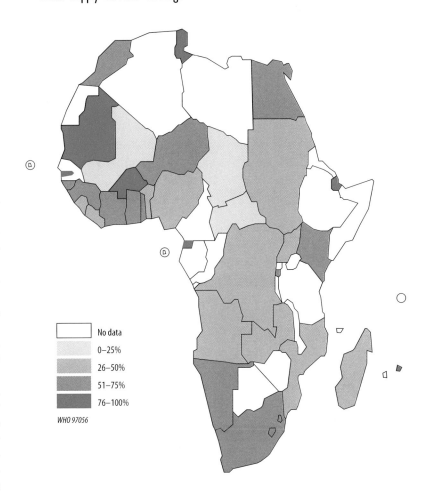

	No data
	0–25%
	26–50%
	51–75%
	76–100%

WHO 97056

Source: WHO/UNICEF, 1996a.

gen demand), upsetting the ecological balance of rivers and lakes. Sewage also carries microbial pathogens; faecal coliform levels may be very high in sewage-contaminated rivers. In developed countries, drinking-water usually receives extensive multi-stage treatment before it is supplied to the consumer. But elsewhere treatment is often unreliable and services intermittent. In many regions, therefore, peri-urban residents and the rural poor often consume water that is untreated or that is not controlled for drinking-water quality.

Nutrients

Domestic wastewater, agricultural drainage waters and much industrial

Table 4.13

Results of studies of contribution of improved water supply and sanitation to reductions in disease morbidity and mortality

	Number of studies reviewed	Median reduction (%)
Diarrhoea morbidity	19	26
Diarrhoea mortality	3	65
Dracunculiasis	7	76
Schistosomiasis	4	73
Trachoma	13	50
Overall impact on child mortality	9	60

Source: adapted from Esrey et al., 1991.

Table 4.14

12 POPs of greatest concern

PCDDs	Aldrin
PCDFs	Dieldrin
PCBs	Endrin
DDT	Hexachlorobenzene (HCB)
Chlordane	Toxaphene
Chlordane	Toxaphene
Heptachlor	Mirex

Source: adapted from UNEP, 1993.

effluence contain phophorus and nitrogen. They thus serve as a source of additional nutrients for aquatic organisms and can cause severe eutrophication of lakes and rivers, and ultimately of estuaries and coastal waters (see Section 3.2). A recent survey showed that in the Asia/Pacific region, 54% of lakes are eutrophied; the figures for Europe, Africa, North America and South America are 53%, 28%, 48% and 41% respectively (ILEC & Lake Biwa Research Institute, 1988–1993). Intensive fertilizer use in agriculture has also contaminated groundwater sources with nitrates, with the result that nitrate levels in drinking-water often far exceed the safe levels recommended by WHO (50 mg/l of nitrate).

Synthetic organics

Although data on water quality are sparse, evidence is growing that many

of the 100 000 synthetic compounds in use today find their way into the aquatic environment and accumulate in the food-chain (see Section 3.3.4). Persistent organic pollutants (POPs) represent the most harmful group for ecosystems and human health (Section 2.6.2). An international list of the twelve most dangerous POPs has been compiled, including industrial chemicals and agricultural pesticides (see **Table 4.14**). These chemicals can bioaccumulate in fish and shellfish to levels that are hazardous to human health. If pesticides are used on a massive scale, groundwaters may become contaminated, leading to chemical contamination of drinking-water.

Acidification

Acidification of surface waters, primarily lakes and reservoirs, has become one of the major adverse environmental

Figure 4.7

Global risk of surface water acidification

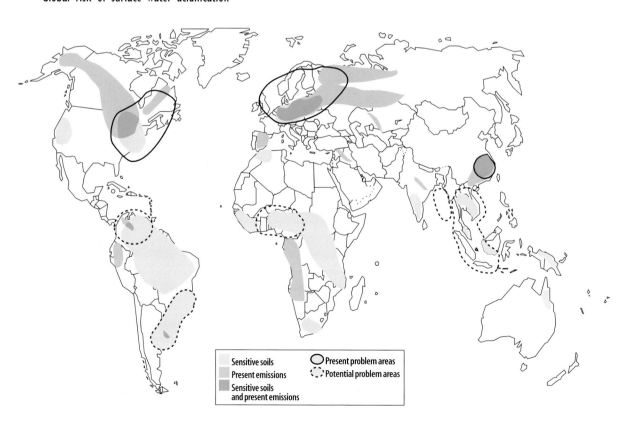

impacts of long-range atmospheric transport of air pollutants such as SO_2, emitted by power plants, smelters, other heavy industry and motor vehicles. The problem is severe in North America and Europe (see **Fig. 4.7**). Many surface-water systems in developing countries are also vulnerable to acidification and can be expected to suffer in the same way if industrial development occurs without air pollution control. Once groundwater has become acidified, metals in soils and water distribution pipes are mobilized and the level of heavy metals in drinking-water rises. In most developed countries concerned with the problem, the necessary control equipment has now been installed. But in developing countries, industrial development and growing use of fossil fuels are increasing acidification potential (see also Sections 3.4, 3.6 and 4.9.4).

4.4.4 Chemicals in drinking-water

Both naturally-occurring and human-made chemical substances in drinking-water can have serious effects on health. A variety of acute and chronic health effects have been reported. Actual risks are determined by the chemical concentration in drinking-water. Thus many toxic substances, if present below a certain threshold level, do not pose a health hazard. When assessing the potential health risk of a chemical constituent, identification and quantification of all the major routes of exposure (i.e. the total human exposure) (see Section 4.10), is important. This is because the tolerable level of the chemical in drinking-water (i.e. which permits lifelong consumption without risk of measurable health impairments) can then be determined.

Fluoride

Fluoride levels of 0.5 to 1 mg/l provide substantial protection against dental caries. However, the margin between beneficial and toxic levels of fluoride is rather narrow and higher levels of fluoride in drinking-water have led to adverse health effects, ranging from unsightly dental fluorosis to crippling skeletal fluorosis (IPCS, 1984d). Waters with significant natural fluoride content are usually found at the base of high mountains and in areas with geological deposits of marine origin. Typical examples are the geographical belt running from Syria through Jordan, Egypt, and the Libyan Arab Jamahiriya, and from Algeria to Morocco; the Rift Valley running through Sudan and Kenya, and the geographical belt stretching from Turkey through Iraq, the Islamic Republic of Iran and Afghanistan, to India, northern Thailand and China. Similar areas are also found in the USA and Central and South America.

Arsenic

High concentrations of arsenic in drinking-water are found in specific parts of Argentina, Canada, Chile, China, Japan, Mexico, the Philippines and the USA. Adverse health effects, including skin cancer, other skin effects, peripheral neuropathy and peripheral vascular disease ("blackfoot disease") have been observed in populations ingesting arsenic-contaminated drinking-water (IPCS, 1981).

Recently, arsenic contamination of groundwater, the main source of drinking-water, was detected in six districts of West Bengal, India and in several villages in Bangladesh that border India. Levels up to 70 times higher than the national drinking-water standard of 0.05 mg/l have been measured in both countries. The contamination is due to the natural soil composition of the region. While the true extent of the problem is not yet known, it has been estimated that some 30 million people may be at high risk from arsenic exposure. Meanwhile, evidence of chronic arsenic toxicity in the population is accumulating and includes incidence of melanosis (abnormal black-brown pigmentation of skin), hyperkeratosis (thickening) of palm and sole, gangrene of the lower extremities and skin cancer. In West Bengal alone, 200 000 people have been reported to be suffering from arsenical skin lesions. The Governments of Bangladesh and India are committed to finding solutions to the arsenic problem as rapidly as possible. Priority areas for action include development of alternative safe drinking-water sources, appropriate water treatment technology for arsenic removal, treatment of patients and development of public awareness (Bagla & Kaiser, 1996; Hoperhayn-Rich et al., 1996).

Lead

The pipes, solder, fittings and service connections of some household plumbing systems contain lead and cause contamination of drinking-water supplies. Lead is hazardous to health. It accumulates in the body and its effects on the central nervous system can be particularly serious (see also Sections 4.6 and 4.10.2). The fetus, infants, children and pregnant women are most at risk. Numerous epidemiological studies have demonstrated associations between childhood exposure to lead and a decreased intelligence quotient (IQ), and other health effects (IPCS, 1995b).

Nitrates

Drinking-water contaminated with nitrates can lead to serious, even fatal, consequences, especially for infants fed with formula prepared with such water. Most often the nitrate comes from fertilizer added to agricultural soil. In the human body, nitrate is converted to nitrite which then combines with haemoglobin to form methaemoglobin. Since methaemoglobin cannot bind with oxygen, transport of oxygen in the blood is impeded. In very young children severe cyanosis ("blue baby syndrome") follows and can cause death (see also Sections 3.4.2 and 4.6). In 15 European countries 0.5–10% of the population is exposed to nitrate levels exceeding 50 mg/l in drinking-water (ECETOC, 1988).

Technology to remove nitrate from drinking-water is expensive, but good agricultural practice can do much to prevent nitrate contamination. However, breast-feeding is by far the best means of avoiding exposure of infants to water contaminated with nitrates.

Pesticides

Groundwater is especially susceptible to contamination with pesticides that are mobile in soil such as alachlor, aldicarb, atrazine, bentazone, carbofuran, isoproturon, ethylene dibromide and simazine. Pesticide concentrations in many groundwater sources now exceed WHO guideline values. Some of these pesticides are believed to be carcinogenic to humans, but all are of concern with respect to future generations because of their persistence in soil and water.

4.4.5 Public health risks from recreational use of water

Untreated sewage, industrial effluents and agricultural waste are frequently discharged into inland waterways, lakes and coastal zones, endangering the use of these water bodies for recreational purposes such as swimming, canoeing and windsurfing. Recreational exposure to polluted waters can cause diarrhoea, respiratory infections, skin irritation and other diseases depending on the specific pollutants involved.

Numerous studies on the health consequences of bathing in polluted coastal waters have been undertaken, but very few can be considered as constituting scientific risk assessment (Pruess, 1996). Many epidemiological studies concentrate on populous Mediterranean beaches such as those in Egypt (Cabelli, 1983). Others have been undertaken in Hong Kong (Cheung, 1990) and in South Africa.

Estimating the overall public health consequences from recreational use of polluted water is difficult, but we do know that in the Mediterranean basin only about 41% of municipal sewage undergoes a secondary treatment and that 33% is not treated at all (UNEP, 1996b). The 150–200 million tourists that the Mediterranean basin attracts each year (representing about 35% of international tourism worldwide) and the 130 million inhabitants of the area, may be exposed (Stanners & Bourdeau, 1995). Bathing-induced epidemics are thus a possibility on many coastlines.

In the EU, 3000 bathing areas (17%) do not comply with EC quality standards or are insufficiently monitored for compliance. For inland bathing areas, the situation is even less satisfactory, with only 30% complying with minimum requirements (*World Water and Environmental Engineering*, 1996).

The environmental health conditions of some developing country coastlines are also cause for concern; coastal beaches in megacities are sometimes tainted with sewage and industrial effluents, while tourist resorts along ocean shores lack sanitation facilities and sewage outfalls and are not reliably monitored for water quality and food safety. Yet because rigorous scientific evidence of the associated health impacts is lacking, a false sense of security has arisen. Given that disease outbreaks do occur in these areas, this is by no means justified.

Control of land-based pollution sources is evidently the most effective means of preventing discharge of sewage into rivers, lakes, coastal beach areas and other marine waters used for recreation. Additionally, intensive bacteriological monitoring is recommended for public beaches and recreational areas. The economic benefits of control measures is well proven. In many European tourist resorts investments have been made in sewage treatment and construction of long ocean outfalls to carry wastewater beyond coastal waters used by bathers. The regional and local governments of the Italian Adriatic coast, for example, have invested heavily in such infrastructure (WHO, 1994j). Coastal bathing water quality in

the area has now improved and tourist numbers have accordingly increased.

4.4.6 Water-related vector-borne diseases

The aquatic environment provides an essential habitat for the mosquito vectors and intermediate snail hosts of parasites that cause human diseases. Among these diseases, malaria outranks all others in severity and distribution (see Section 5.5). Vector-borne diseases have, of course, always affected humans, even in pristine environments, But the accelerated development of water resources that started in the 1960s has led to habitat modifications and ecological conditions that favour certain disease vectors. Health issues linked to irrigation development have become a particular focus of attention, but increased transmission is also linked to the construction of dams and reservoirs, to changes in land-use patterns (with indirect effects on local hydrology and relative humidity) and to poor water management in urban areas (see also Sections 3.3.6 and 3.4).

Lack of financial resources has often been implicated in mismanaged water resources development. In the case of irrigation, rising costs have often obliged planners to omit certain components (most notoriously the drainage component) to make proposed schemes economically viable. Poor intersectoral collaboration has been another contributory factor. Many countries have no established procedures for involving the health sector at the planning and design stages of water resources development. Moreover, prolonged post World-War II reliance on residual insecticides for vector control has resulted in neglect of public health and hygiene issues among civil engineers. This has reduced the apparent need for engineers and public health experts to collaborate on water resources projects.

The most important water-related vector-borne diseases affected by development projects in recent decades include:

- **malaria:** in the Amazon region due to development in urban areas; in Africa and South Asia due to poor water management; in South-East Asia due to deforestation, afforestation and reforestation, and in many parts of the lowland tropics due to expansion or intensification of irrigated agriculture

- **schistosomiasis:** mainly in sub-Saharan Africa, in association with irrigation schemes and reservoirs

- **dengue fever:** in urban but also increasingly in some rural tropical areas where general solid waste problems have combined with inadequate household storage of drinking-water

- **filariasis:** in tropical urban areas due to the vectors breeding in organically-polluted water, i.e. in open sewage canals, blocked drains and in wastewater collected for reuse in peri-urban agriculture

- **Japanese encephalitis:** in irrigated rice-growing areas in South and East Asia following changes in cropping patterns and agricultural practices.

Box 4.8

Malaria and irrigation schemes: more questions than answers

Studies carried out in the Sahelian part of Africa (in the Gambia and Burkina Faso) indicate a paradoxical phenomenon associated with local hydrological changes following introduction of irrigated rice production. With an expansion of the breeding places for mosquito vectors, their densities increase. Transmission could also be expected to increase since, in other parts of the world where transmission is less intense, a linear relationship has been observed between mosquito population density and transmission level. Yet in Gambia and Burkino Faso, malaria vectors increase in number in areas under rice irrigation, but malaria transmission decreases. In Gambia, the regular peak in mosquito densities at the end of the rainy season has been observed to be followed by a major peak in irrigated areas, but not accompanied by a peak in transmission. In the highland setting of Burundi in central Africa, on the other hand, irrigated rice production has prolonged and intensified the malaria peak. This has been attributed to increased relative humidity, which enables mosquitos to live longer and, therefore, to be more effective vectors. Longevity is a key determinant of vectorial capacity: with time, the chance of a female mosquito picking up the malaria parasite with subsequent blood meals increases, as does the chance of the parasite completing its life cycle in the mosquito and being transmitted back to a human host.

The Sahelian paradox has not yet been resolved. Candidate attributable factors associated with irrigated areas include genetic shifts in the mosquito population influencing vectorial capacity, changes in livestock densities and distribution (which has the effect of reducing the number of human blood meals), widespread use of mosquito nets as a result of higher densities of nuisance insects, and increased access to health services due to economic progress and improved infrastructure. A Consortium Research Project with study sites along a north-south transect through Mali and Côte d'Ivoire is currently being undertaken by the West Africa Rice Development Association, the Panel of Experts on Environmental management for Vector Control. Canada's International Development Research Centre. This project, with studies in three different ecozones, including the Sahel, is expected to shed new light on the association between rice production systems and vector-borne diseases from a strictly ecological and sociocultural perspective (see also Box 3.5).

Sources: Coosemans, 1985; Carnevale et al., 1991; WHO, 1991b.

The annual million deaths due to malaria, the 200 million people infected globally with schistosomiasis, and the tens of thousands of dengue fever cases (see Section 5.5), illustrate the cost of water-related vector-borne diseases, both in terms of human suffering and healthcare costs. Yet attributing a specific number of disease cases to poor water management, especially if the disease was endemic before hydrological changes occurred and the relevant vector ecology complex, would be difficult. Solid assessment of hydraulic systems and breeding places which contribute most to disease transmission risks is called for. Intensified multidisciplinary research to redesign hydraulic structures and adapt water management practices to reduce these risks would then be possible.

4.5 Food

Food is essential to a healthy life, but it can also be a major exposure route for many pathogens and toxic chemicals. These contaminants may be introduced into food during cultivation, harvesting, processing, storage, transportation and final preparation. Inspection and monitoring of food quality is therefore necessary to ensure food safety. However, the increasing interdependence and complexity of our food supply means that even the best control systems are becoming strained. Foodborne disease is now a widespread and growing threat to human health, and a major cause of reduced economic productivity (WHO, 1997g). Health impacts range from mild indisposition to life-threatening illness. The people most affected by unsafe food are the poor, who are also vulnerable to lack of food and undernutrition (see Section 3.4).

Food contamination was therefore acknowledged as an important health issue by the Earth Summit in 1992 and by the FAO/WHO International Conference on Nutrition in the same year. Long before these conferences, however, the FAO/WHO Codex Alimentarius Commission had recognized the major impacts that toxic chemicals have on the international food trade, and established several subsidiary bodies for addressing these impacts. The World Trade Organization plans to refer to Codex in the arbitration of trade disputes involving food health-and-safety requirements, provided these are used as the basis of non-tariff barriers. Food contamination monitoring will thus become an increasingly important feature of food control programmes in both developed and developing countries.

Biological and chemical agents in food represent the two major types of foodborne hazard. Biological agents tend to pose acute hazards with incubation periods of a few hours to several weeks before the onset of disease, whereas chemical hazards usually involve long-term, low-level exposures. Nevertheless, acute poisonings have been reported for many chemicals (see Section 5.6.4). While most biological hazards can be controlled by appropriate cooking, chemical agents often remain in food unless specifically deactivated or removed.

Generally, the public health impact of foodborne disease is more serious in developing countries than in developed countries. However, foodborne pathogens are not distributed equally among developing countries. Incidence varies between them and even from place to place within individual countries, depending on many environmental and social factors such as food consumption and cooking patterns, recreational activities and food control infrastructure.

4.5.1 Biological hazards in food

Sources of biological contamination of food are diverse and include polluted water (e.g. wastewater, irrigation and household water), dirty hands, flies, pests, domestic animals, dirty cooking pots and utensils, and human and animal excreta. Foods themselves are also frequently the source of contaminants, as they may harbour pathogens naturally or may have been derived from infected animals. Cross-contamination of foods can also occur.

Table 4.15 lists biological agents by type that are known to cause major foodborne disease in humans. A large proportion of diarrhoeal diseases may be foodborne and due to these pathogens (Esrey & Feachem, 1989; Esrey, 1990) (see Section 5.3). Infection due to pathogenic strains of *Escherichia coli* is probably the most common cause of diarrhoea in developing countries, constituting up to 25% of diarrhoeal diseases in infants and children, and has been associated specifically with weaning foods (Motarjemi et al., 1993).

Cholera which is acquired by ingesting food or water contaminated with *V. cholerae* also affects several hundred thousand people each year in Africa, Latin America and Asia (see **Box 4.5** and Section 5.3.3). A new strain of

Table 4.15
Biological agents of important foodborne diseases and main epidemiological features

Agents	Important reservoir/carrier	Transmission[a] by — Water	Food	Person-to-person	Multiplication in food	Examples of food that can become contaminated
Bacteria						
Aeromonas spp.	Water	+	+	-	+	
Bacillus cereus	Soil	-	+	-	+	Cooked rice, cooked meats, vegetables, starchy puddings
Brucella spp.	Cattle, goats, sheep	-	+	-	+	Raw milk, dairy products
Camplylobacter jejuni	Chickens, dogs, cats, cattle, pigs, wild birds	+	+	+	-[b]	Raw milk, poultry
Clostridium botulinum	Soil, mammals, birds, fish	-	+	-	+	Fish, meat, vegetables (home-preserved), honey
Clostridium perfringens	Soil, animals, humans	-	+	-	+	Cooked meat and poultry, gravy, beans
Escherichia coli						
Enterotoxigenic	Humans	+	+	+	+	Salads, raw vegetables
Enteropathogenic	Humans	+	+	+	+	Milk
Enteroinvasive	Humans	+	+	0	+	Cheese
Enterohaemorrhagic	Cattle, poultry, sheep	+	+	+	+	Undercooked meat, raw milk, cheese
Listeria monocytogenes		+	+	-[c]	+	Soft cheese, raw milk, coleslaw, paté
Mycobacterium bovis	Cattle	-	+	-	-	Raw milk
Salmonella typhi and *S.paratyphi*	Humans	+	+	+/-	+	Dairy products, meat products, shellfish, vegetable salads
Salmonella (non-typhi)	Humans, animals	+/-	+	+/-	+	Meat, poultry, eggs, dairy products, chocolate
Shigella spp.	Humans	+	+	+	+	Potato/egg salads
Staphylococcus aureus (enterotoxins)	Humans	-	+	-	+	Ham, poultry and egg salads, cream-filled bakery products, ice cream, cheese
Vibrio cholerae, O1	Humans, marine life?	+	+	+/-	+	Salad, shellfish
Vibrio cholerae, non-O1	Humans, animals, marine life?	+	+	+/-	+	Shellfish
Vibrio parahaemolyticus	Seawater, marine life	-	+	-	+	Raw fish, crabs and other shellfish
Vibrio vulnificus	Seawater, marine life	+	+	-	+	Shellfish
Yersinia enterocolitica	Water, wild animals, pigs, dogs, poultry	+	+	-	+	Milk, pork, poultry
Viruses						
Hepatitis A virus	Humans	+	+	+	-	Shellfish, raw fruit and vegetables
Norwalk agents	Humans	+	+	-	-	Shellfish, salad
Rotavirus	Humans	+	+	+	-	
Protozoa						
Cryptosporidium parvum	Humans, animals	+	+	+	-	Raw milk, raw sausage (non-fermented)
Entamoeba histolytica	Humans	+	+	+	-	Vegetables, fruits
Giardia lamblia	Humans, animals	+	+/-	+	-	Vegetables, fruits
Toxoplasma gondii	Cats, pigs	0	+	-	-	Undercooked meat, raw vegetables
Helminths						
Ascaris lumbricoides	Humans	+	+	-	-	Soil-contaminated food
Clonorchis sinensis	Freshwater fish	-	+	-	-	Undercooked/raw fish
Fasciola hepatica	Cattle, goats	+/-	+	-	-	Watercress
Opisthorclis viverrini/felinus	Freshwater fish	-	+	-	-	Undercooked/raw fish
Paragonimus spp.	Freshwater crabs	-	+	-	-	Undecooked/raw crabs
Taenia saginata and *T. solium*	Cattle, pigs	-	+	-	-	Undercooked meat
Trichinella spiralis	Pigs, carnivora	-	+	-	-	Undercooked meat
Trichuris trichiura	Humans	0	+	-	-	Soil-contaminated food

a   Almost all acute enteric infections show increased transmission during the summer and/or wet months, other than infections due to rotavirus and *Yersinia enterocolitica*, which show increased transmission in cooler months.

b   Under certain circumstances, some multiplication has been observed. The epidemiological significance of this observation is not clear, however.

c   Vertical transmission from pregnant women to their fetus(es) occurs frequently.

+ = yes; +/- = rare; - = no; 0 = no information

Sources: based on data from WHO, 1992d and Adams and Moss, 1995.

Fig 4.8

Foodborne trematode infections vary according to local environmental conditions and food habits

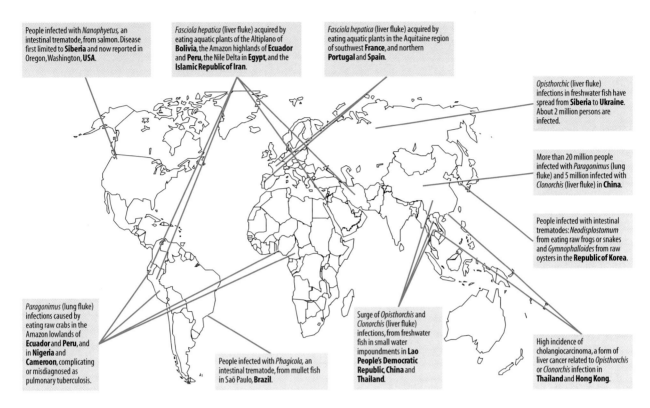

People infected with *Nanophyetus*, an intestinal trematode, from salmon. Disease first limited to **Siberia** and now reported in Oregon, Washington, **USA**.

Fasciola hepatica (liver fluke) acquired by eating aquatic plants of the Altiplano of **Bolivia**, the Amazon highlands of **Ecuador** and **Peru**, the Nile Delta in **Egypt**, and the **Islamic Republic of Iran**.

Fasciola hepatica (liver fluke) acquired by eating aquatic plants in the Aquitaine region of southwest **France**, and northern **Portugal** and **Spain**.

Opisthorchic (liver fluke) infections in freshwater fish have spread from **Siberia** to **Ukraine**. About 2 million persons are infected.

More than 20 million people infected with *Paragonimus* (lung fluke) and 5 million infected with *Clonorchis* (liver fluke) in **China**.

People infected with intestinal trematodes: *Neodisplostomum* from eating raw frogs or snakes and *Gymnophalloides* from raw oysters in the **Republic of Korea**.

Paragonimus (lung fluke) infections caused by eating raw crabs in the Amazon lowlands of **Ecuador** and **Peru**, and in **Nigeria** and **Cameroon**, complicating or misdiagnosed as pulmonary tuberculosis.

People infected with *Phagicola*, an intestinal trematode, from mullet fish in Saô Paulo, **Brazil**.

Surge of *Opisthorchis* and *Clonorchis* (liver fluke) infections, from freshwater fish in small water impoundments in **Lao People's Democratic Republic, China** and **Thailand**.

High incidence of cholangiocarcinoma, a form of liver cancer related to *Opisthorchis* or *Clonorchis* infection in **Thailand** and **Hong Kong**.

Source: WMO, 1995f.

V. cholerae, known as O139, recently emerged in Bangladesh (see **Box 5.1**) and could be transmitted to other regions of the world by travellers. Evidence is growing that food is an important route of transmission.

Other common foodborne pathogens that cause diseases frequently accompanied by diarrhoea include *Bacillus cereus*, *Staphyloccocus aureus* and *Clostridium perfringens*. Their incidence could be much higher than reported, but the infections are not a focus of public health attention as they are often self-limiting. On the other hand, infection due to *Clostridium botulinum* is rare but attracts much public attention due to its high case-fatality rate. Most cases of botulism occur as a result of faulty preservation or processing of food in the home. In China, 745 reported outbreaks of botulism involving 2861

cases with 421 deaths were reported in 1989. Over 60% of the cases were caused by contaminated home-made fermented bean products stored in earthernware jars and other containers (Gao et al., 1990).

Among viral infections, hepatitis A is of world importance and estimated to affect between 10 and 50 people per 100 000 annually. Hepatitis A epidemics frequently occur in South and South-East Asia: in China in 1988, nearly 300 000 people, of whom 32 died, became infected due to consumption of contaminated clams (WHO, 1996a). Food handlers are a major source of contamination. Infection with hepatitis A is therefore often associated with eating at a restaurant, particularly in hot tropical areas.

Infections due to helminths are another common problem and usually

Box 4.9

Health impacts of foodborne trematode infections

Foodborne trematode infections are a serious and growing public health problem. An estimated 40 million persons worldwide are already affected, and 10% of the world's population at risk of infection. Trematode infections are linked to several serious diseases, including cholangiocarcinoma in *Opisthorchis* infections, cholangiocarcinoma and gallstones in *Clonorchis* infection, and severe clinical liver disease in *Fasciola* infection. Transmission to humans occurs mostly via consumption of raw or inadequately processed freshwater fish and shellfish cultivated in endemic areas, as well as via contaminated aquatic plants.

Fascioliasis caused by *Fasciola hepatica* or *F. gigantica* — a major livestock parasite — is the best known liver fluke infection. In humans, over 300 000 clinical cases may have occurred in more than 55 countries in Europe, the Americas, Asia, Africa and the Western Pacific since 1970.

Liver infections are also caused by Oriental flukes — *Clonorchis sinensis, Opisthorchis viverrini* and *O. felineus. C. sinensis* is widely distributed in most densely-populated provinces of China (over 5 million persons infected), Korea, Viet Nam, Japan, and in overseas Chinese communities. *O. viverrini* is mainly prevalent in South-East Asia, particularly in north-east Thailand, Laos and Cambodia. More than 7 million persons are estimated to be infected in Thailand. *O. felineus* is mostly confined to Eastern Europe and the former USSR where about 2 million persons are infected. Originally localized in Siberia, the disease has now spread to many river basins of the former USSR as a result of economic development and extensive migration.

Cholangiocarcinoma, a form of liver cancer, is frequent in areas where *Clonorchis* and *Opisthorchis* flukes are endemic. In endemic countries incidence is at least 2 per 100 000. In some areas of Thailand annual incidence can be as high as 135 per 100 000.

Paragonimiasis, or lung fluke disease, caused by several different species, is endemic in most Asian countries, but especially in China, Japan, Korea, Thailand, and in some West African countries, mainly Cameroon, Nigeria, Liberia, Equatorial Guinea and Gabon. About 22 million persons are estimated to be infected.

Prevention of food contamination, which depends upon environmental control, may be impractical in developing countries, especially if large bodies of water are involved. It is therefore important to concentrate on prevention and control measures aimed at inactivation of metacercariae (the infective stage of these parasites). Heat treatment, freezing and irradiation would be appropriate control measures.

Source: : WHO, 1995f.

acquired following consumption of raw or uncooked meat. They can cause significant public health problems in areas where raw meat or fish is habitually consumed. Ascariasis is also a common parasitic infection transmitted via contaminated food. Prevalence is estimated at over 1000 million people (Warren et al., 1989) (**Fig. 4.8** and **Box 4.9**).

Multidrug resistant *Salmonella typhimurium* DT 104 in cattle, poultry, sheep, pigs and horses is another food-borne biological hazard that is fast becoming a serious public health issue. Antimicrobial therapy is now used extensively to combat *S. typhimurium* in animals but evolution of the DT 104 strain, which is resistant to the commonly-used antibiotics, has made infections in food animals difficult to control. Preliminary evidence suggests that DT 104 may have spread widely in the USA during the past two or three years and could result in a marked increase in human illness in the near future. With antimicrobial agents continuing to lose their effectiveness, microbial resistance is expected to grow (WHO, 1995y) (see also Section 5.3.2).

A recent problem that has caused major concern is the transmission of animal diseases to humans via food, for example, BSE or "mad cow disease" (WHO, 1997n), which was diagnosed in more than 1000 cows in the UK and is thought to have spread via meat to a small number of people.

4.5.2 Chemical and radioactive hazards in food

Many chemical hazards in food are produced naturally by organisms in the environment, such as *Aspergillus flavus,* which produces aflatoxin. Others are inherent components of food itself, as in the case of poisonous mushrooms. Yet other potentially hazardous chemicals are produced during processing. Polynuclear (polycyclic) aromatic hydrocarbons, (PAHs), for instance, are produced during charcoal grilling of meat. Pollutants such as lead, cadmium and polychlorinated biphenyls (PCBs) in air, water and soil can also lead to high levels of toxic chemicals in food (**Table 4.16**).

Some chemicals are used intentionally in food production. They include food additives, pesticides, animal drugs, and other agrochemicals, such as fertilizers. Food additives are used both

Table 4.16

Chemical hazards of public health importance frequently found in food residues

Chemicals	Examples	Chemicals	Examples
Pesticides	Organochlorine	Mycotoxins	Aflatoxin, ochratoxin A, patulin, fumonisi
Heavy metals	Lead, mercury, cadmium	Plant toxins	Pyrrolizidine alkaloids
Radionuclides	Iodine-131, caesium-137	Marine biotoxins	Ciguatera, *Alexandrium tamarense* (a cause of paralytic shellfish poisoning)
Other contaminants	PCBs, DDT, veterinary drugs and vaccines		

Source: based on data from WHO, 1995g.

in the home and by the food industry to facilitate processing, preserve quality and improve palatability and appearance. Nutritional supplements are also added to certain foods in order to improve their nutritional quality.

Pesticides

Studies in laboratory animals, and incidents involving human exposure to pesticides and their residues, have confirmed that many pesticides can cause different types of health effect, ranging from nausea, vomiting, sensitization and impaired immune function, to birth defects, neurotoxicity and cancer (WHO, 1990a). These effects can be aggravated further by poor nutrition and dehydration, which lower the body's ability to respond.

However, although foods introduced into international trade sometimes contain high levels of pesticide residues, the residues detected in most analysed foods have fallen within established maximum limits. Similarly, GEMS/Food data and various studies indicate that in developed countries long-term dietary exposure to pesticides is well within the acceptable range. In developing countries, though, consumers may be exposed to high levels of some pesticides in their diets since regulations and enforcement to ensure safe pesticide use are often lacking.

In most developed countries, restrictions have now been placed on the use of the older organochlorine pesticides, such as DDT, hexachlorobenzene and heptachlor, and exposure to these pesticides is accordingly below

tolerable intakes (see **Box 2.8**). Nevertheless, breastmilk in both developed and developing countries has been found to contain relatively high levels of organochlorine pesticides. A significant number of breast-fed infants may be exposed to higher than tolerable levels for a short time (Jelinek, 1992).

Exposure to organophosphorus pesticides via food has been reported by only a few countries (see Section 5.6.4). Exposures are mostly a few percent of their corresponding acceptable daily intakes because these pesticides tend to degrade rapidly in the environment. Exceptions include reported fenitrothion intakes in Australia that have reached 45% of the maximum recommended dietary level for adults (Jelinek, 1992).

Heavy metals

Ingestion over extended periods of time of foods contaminated with heavy metals such as lead, cadmium or mercury can have serious health effects. Even small daily doses of heavy metals can be significant. For example, chronic exposure to low levels of lead can lead to irreversible health effects, especially in children (Steinhart, Doyle & Cochrane, 1995). When lead pipes or lead-lined water storage tanks are used, the resultant lead exposure from drinking-water can increase lead intake from food appreciably (CDC, 1994) (see also Section 4.4.4). Household drinking-water from bulk storage tanks has resulted in lead poisoning in children in Arizona and southern California (CDC, 1994). Release of lead from lead-glazed ceramics and crystal can also increase dietary lead exposure (Rojas-Lopez, 1994). Similarly, use of lead-soldered cans can result in high lead levels in food. Many developed countries have eliminated use of lead-soldered cans, resulting in significantly decreased exposure (UNEP, 1988).

Mercury, especially in the form of methyl mercury, has been shown to have serious effects on the nervous system, particularly in children. In severe cases these can be irreversible. Fish is the major dietary source of exposure. A notorious example of mercury poisoning occurred in the 1950s and 1960s when methyl mercury was discharged in industrial waste into Minamata Bay, Japan, and accumulated in fish and other marine animals that were later consumed by local populations (IPCS, 1990b) (see **Box 3.3**). Elevated mercury levels have been found in freshwater and coastal fish, especially predatory fish. Major sources of mercury include soil, especially in acidic areas, and industrial pollution (see Section 3.5 and **Box 3.3**).

Like lead, cadmium can have health effects at relatively low exposure levels. Since it is a cumulative toxin it affects the kidneys. Exposure occurs mainly via food which has been grown on soils that have become contaminated due to mining activities and use of phosporus fertilizers. For example, contamination of rice with cadmium discharged from nearby mines in Japan caused "Itai-itai" disease in the local population (see below). While shellfish and animal organs (such as the liver and kidneys) contain the highest cadmium levels, cereals and vegetables are frequently the main sources of exposure since consumption of these foods is often high (IPCS, 1992a).

Naturally-occurring chemicals

Mycotoxins, plant toxins and marine biotoxins can contaminate food and be hazardous to health. Mycotoxins are widely present in the food supply and have a variety of toxic effects (IPCS,

1990c). Aflatoxin is probably the best known mycotoxin and attacks the liver, while the naturally-occurring mixture of aflatoxins and aflatoxin B1 has been classified as a human carcinogen (IARC, 1993) (see also Section 5.9.5). Aflatoxin production is associated with environmental factors, including certain weather conditions and poor post-harvest handling. Outbreaks of acute aflatoxin poisoning, often with high mortality rates, have been reported (Krishnamachari, et al., 1975; Dhatt, et al., 1982; Chao, Maxwell & Wong, 1991). Ochratoxin A is another important mycotoxin. Found mainly on wheat and rye it has been associated with Balkan endemic nephropathy, a fatal kidney disease prevalent in several Balkan countries (Castegnaro & Chernozemsky, 1987).

Examples of plant toxins include many wild mushrooms and many plants which can grow as weeds among food crops (see **Box 5.3**).

Intoxication by marine biotoxins such as ciguatera (IPCS, 1984c) and paralytic shellfish poisoning caused by marine algal blooms are also of growing public health concern. The geographic distribution and frequency of the latter appears to be increasing worldwide (Bird & Wright, 1988).

Other contaminants

PCBs were formerly used for a variety of industrial and electrical applications. Large amounts of these contaminants continue to exist in old equipment and at industrial waste sites. Evidence of the toxic effects of PCBs in humans derives from two large-scale incidents involving consumption of contaminated oil (Yoshimura, 1974; Masuda, 1985). The associated disease outbreaks showed that PCBs have both acute and long-term effects. In particular, it has been observed that if a woman experiences high exposures to PCBs during pregnancy, her child's intellectual functioning will suffer long-term impacts (Jacobson & Jacobson, 1996). Level of exposure to

PCBs depends on the level of consumption of fish or dairy products with a high fat content. Dietary exposure appears to have declined in many countries and to fall below guideline levels. However, biological monitoring of human breastmilk has indicated that levels of PCBs, polychlorinated dibenzo-p-dioxins and polychlorinated dibenzo-p-furans have decreased only slightly (IPCS, 1996b).

Radionuclides

Contamination of foodstuffs by radionuclides is rare but can occur following an accidental release of radioactivity. After the accident at the Chernobyl Nuclear Power Plant in 1986 (see also Sections 3.6.5, 5.7.3, 5.7.4 and 5.9.7), human populations were exposed to radionuclides in air and on soil, and following consumption of food contaminated with iodine-131, caesium-134 and caesium-137 (WHO, 1996j). Due to weather conditions, especially rainfall, the areas and foods affected varied considerably. Initial high exposures were due to contamination with radionuclides of iodine, which were found in dairy products and which accumulate in the human thyroid.

Iodine nuclides are short-lived (the half-life of iodine-131 is 8 days) and so the contamination they cause lasts a few months only. Isotopes of caesium, on the other hand, have a half-life of approximately 30 years and are therefore a longer-term concern. In Europe, wild mushrooms and game meat continue to be contaminated with caesium-137 because of nutrient cycling in forest topsoils (Grossklaus, 1988). In most countries, however, the estimated average dose acquired from eating foods contaminated as a result of the Chernobyl accident only slightly exceeded the dose normally received from background radiation (see Section 4.2.6). In areas directly affected, however, contaminated food is now the major source of radiation exposure. In these areas, limited agricultural activity only is permitted (WHO, 1996j).

4.6 Soil

Exposure to hazards in soil can occur, for instance, when farmers till agricultural soil, when children play in schoolyards, or when dust from dry fields is blown into populated areas. Additionally, deposition of biological, chemical or radioactive hazards on or in soil (see examples in Chapter 3) can lead to indirect exposures following use of contaminated groundwater for drinking-water, or consumption of food grown on contaminated soil. Only a few examples of the health problems associated with direct or indirect exposure to hazards in soil will be given here, however.

More generally, agriculture and human nutrition are heavily influenced by soil quality. Section 3.4 describes how soil can be degraded in such a way that its capacity for food production is seriously reduced. (**Tables 3.8 and 3.9** list some of the poor land management practices that are causing land degradation.) Reduced local food production and subsequent undernutrition is a major health risk to millions of subsistence farmers in developing countries, and likely to be the greatest global health risk associated with soil degradation. Most of the 780 million people who are chronically undernourished (Alexandratos, 1995) live in areas severely affected by drought or degraded soil conditions.

Specific hazards

Intestinal worm infection is very common in developing countries, particularly among children. Direct contact with soil or soil dust that has been contaminated with helminth eggs is a major source of exposure (Warren et al., 1993). In a study undertaken in Zanzibar, the faeces of over 95% of children were found to contain helminths (Albonico et al., 1994). Very few of the children were aware of their infection. However, certain intestinal worms can eventually lead to serious ill health such as anaemia or serious liver disease (Stolzfus et al., 1997). Poor sanitation is a major cause of the spread of intestinal worm infections in developing countries.

Soil can harbour many other parasites and microbes, which can survive for long periods in spite of large variations in soil temperature and humidity. Common examples of associated diseases include tetanus and polio (see Section 5.4). Tetanus spores infect humans through direct contact with soil or dirt; in developing countries, childbirth in impoverished conditions often leads to tetanus (Steinglass, Brenzel & Percy, 1993). Polio is contracted via indirect contact, after the virus has spread to water from soil (Jamison et al., 1993). In both cases, hygiene and environmental action contribute to the reduction of the health risks, but immunization is required to bring the diseases under complete control (see Section 5.4).

Chemical contamination of soil results from a number of activities and can lead to water contamination. For instance, run-off from soils to which agricultural fertilizers have been applied can lead to high levels of nitrates in groundwater and wells (see **Section 3.3**). Human exposure to nitrate can cause methaemoglobinaemia ("blue baby syndrome") (see Section 3.4.2). A recent study in Romania showed that this problem occurs in intensively-farmed areas where drinking-water is drawn from local wells (Iacob & Tarase, 1996). The nitrate from fertilizers that is found in groundwater has in effect been wasted, as the purpose of the fertilizer is to increase availability of nitrogen to agricultural crops. Reduction of fertilizer applications and better agricultural management could control the problem.

Chemical contamination of soil can also result from water pollution caused by industry and use of industrially polluted water for irrigation. One of the most notorious examples concerns cadmium pollution that occurred in several areas of Japan in the 1950s and 1960s. Pollution from mining and smelting industries resulted in accumulation of cadmium in irrigated soils. Rice grown on these soils then became a source of cadmium poisoning (Friberg et al., 1985, 1986; IPCS 1992a). Similar poisoning incidents have also been reported recently from China (Cai et al., 1995).

Mining and smelting activities can also result in lead contamination of soil. More commonly, though, contamination with lead is due to air pollution from motor vehicles, or to the weathering of lead-containing paint, particles of which may fall on soil, in the form of dust (WHO, 1995j). Very young children can be exposed if they "mouth" objects within their reach and ingest small amounts of soil, dust or paint flakes. Since dust and soil may contain as much as 10% lead, high exposure and poisoning can result from even very small ingested amounts (about 10 mg of lead per day) (IPCS, 1995b). Lead exposure in young children has been of particular concern in the USA (US Department of Health and Human Services, 1995).

Contamination of soil at waste dumps or at the sites of hazardous industries has also received considerable attention in recent years. Some exposure sites such as Love Canal and Times Beach have become infamous, yet in spite of numerous studies at different hazardous waste sites in the USA, major health impacts have rarely been documented (Batstone, Smith & Wilson, 1989).

Even if soil is not chemically contaminated, its chemical composition may be such that dust blown from dry areas into populated areas is hazardous. Cities close to deserts, such as Kuwait and Sian, China, have some of the world's highest dust levels in air (see Section 4.2); local industrial sources of air pollution cannot account for them. In China concern has been expressed about the high silica content of the fine dust blown in from deserts.

Radioactive contamination of soil, such as the iodine and caesium contamination resulting from the Chernobyl accident (WHO, 1996j), can cause significant human exposure too if it enters the food-chain (see Section 4.5.2). Iodine-131 deposited on soil (and on grass) during and just after the accident led to high iodine-131 intake in cows and soon after to high iodine-131 concentrations in milk. This exposure route is the most likely cause of the dramatic increase of thyroid cancer observed in children in the most contaminated areas around Chernobyl (WHO, 1996j). In the initial period after the accident, 144 000 ha of agricultural land and 492 000 hectares of forested land were taken out of use, and a further 26 000 km^2 declared unfit for human habitation.

4.7 Housing

4.7.1 The importance of housing for health

Housing is of central importance to quality of life. Ideally it minimizes disease and injury, and contributes much to physical, mental and social well-being. Over and above its basic purpose to provide shelter against the elements and a focus for family life, the home environment should afford protection against the hazards to health arising from the physical and social environment. The principles of "healthy " housing are listed in **Table 4.17**

The majority of the world's population, however, livex in shelter that does not meet even basic health requirements. For increasing numbers of people, available shelter not only fails to protect them, but also exposes them to health risks which are largely preventable (WHO, 1988). Perhaps surprisingly, although a great deal of attention has been given to examining the ways in which hazards in the work environment impact on workers' health, much less attention has been given to health hazards in the home environment. Of course, increasingly, in many parts of the world, the home

environment is also the work environment, posing additional potential hazards to health.

Numerous factors in the home environment may influence health negatively. Lack of access to piped water or a nearby stand-pipe and lack of sanitary facilities are often considered key indicators of "unhealthy" housing, leading to high disease burdens, in both urban and rural areas. Housing factors such as high levels of noise, poor air quality, inadequate refuse storage and collection facilities, poor food storage and preparation facilities, temperature extremes and high humidity, overcrowding, poor lighting, inadequate or inappropriate construction materials, building defects and pests may also influence health significantly.

Given the array of housing factors that affect health, a simple definition of what constitutes "poor quality" or "unhealthy" housing is not possible. Furthermore, demonstrating conclusive relationships between individual aspects of housing and health is difficult, due to the role of other factors associated with poor housing which have significant influences on health, such as inadequate healthcare services and poverty. In Table 4.18, though, some indicators of unhealthy housing conditions are presented.

Levels of exposure to unhealthy housing conditions vary. Evidently, low-income groups are generally most affected. But among these groups, women are more likely than men to be exposed to health hazards in the home environment since they spend more time there, and the activities (such as cooking) that they engage in, may involve exposure to health hazards (such as pollution due to burning of coal or biomass) (see Section 3.6 and 4.2). Also, inadequate provision for water, domestic hygiene and food preparation may increase women's labour, and take their toll on vitality and resistance to disease.

Table 4.17

Principles of healthy housing

Protection against communicable diseases through:
* safe water supply
* sanitary excreta disposal
* disposal of solid wastes
* drainage of surface water
* personal and domestic hygiene
* safe food preparation
* structural safeguards

Protection against injuries, poisonings and chronic diseases through attention to:
* structural features and furnishings
* indoor air pollution
* chemical safety
* use of the home as a workplace

Reduction of psychological and social stress through:
* adequate living space, privacy and comfort
* personal and family security
* access to recreation and community amenities
* protection against noise

Access to a supportive living environment through provision of:
* security and emergency services
* health and social services
* access to cultural and other amenities

Protection of populations at special risk:
* women and children
* displaced and mobile populations
* the aged, ill and the disabled

Source: adapted from WHO 1989e.

Table 4.18

Indicators of unhealthy housing conditions

Principal risk factor	Communicable diseases	Non-communicable diseases	Psychosocial disorders
Defects in buildings	Insect-vector diseases Rodent-vector diseases Geohelminthiases Diseases due to animal faeces Diseases due to animal bites Overcrowding-related diseases	Dust- and damp-induced diseases Injuries Burns	Neuroses Violence Delinquency and vandalism Drug and alcohol abuse
Defective water supplies	Faecal–oral (waterborne and water-washed) diseases Non-faeco-oral water-washed diseases Water-related insect-vector diseases	Heart disease Cancer	
Defective sanitation	Faecal–oral diseases Geohelminthiases Taeniases Water-based helminthiases Insect-vector diseases Rodent-vector diseases	Stomach cancer	
Poor fuel/defective ventilation	Acute respiratory infections	Perinatal effects Heart disease Chronic lung disease Lung cancer Fires/burns	
Defective refuse storage and collection	Insect-vector diseases Rodent-vector diseases	Injuries Burns	
Defective food storage and preparation	Excreta-related diseases Zoonoses Diseases due to microbial toxins	Cancer	
Poor location (near traffic, industry, etc.)	Airborne excreta-related diseases Enhanced infectious respiratory disease risk	Chronic lung disease Heart disease, cancer Cancer Neurological/reproductive diseases Injuries	Psychiatric organic disorders due to industrial chemicals Neuroses

Source: adapted from Mara & Alabaster, 1995.

4.7.2 Extent of the problem

The wide range of estimates of the number of people living in poor quality or unhealthy housing reflects the complexity of the housing and health relationship. This complexity makes monitoring of unhealthy housing and international comparisons of unhealthy housing very difficult. Particular groups within urban and rural areas face serious housing-related health problems — for instance, people living in overcrowded conditions or in makeshift shelters without basic services.

Even in developed countries, some cities, towns and other human settlements contain pockets of housing that have deteriorated into slums. In EU countries, millions of people live in dwellings without toilets, bathrooms or showers In the early 1990s, around 18 million EU citizens were homeless or extremely badly housed, including 1.8 million who during the course of a year depended on public or voluntary services for temporary shelter or who lived in illegal settlements ("squats") (Avramov, 1995).

Forms of tenure and the risk of eviction vary widely, but overall, between 30% and 60% of the housing units in most cities in developing countries are illegal, in that they contravene land ownership laws or building and planning laws and codes. Many contravene both (UNCHS, 1996b).

Information on rural housing conditions is often sparse, but rural areas in many developing countries frequently lack piped water supplies or sanitation, and may be overcrowded.

The homeless (those who "sleep rough", in a night shelter, or in temporary accommodation) should also be taken into account when undertaking housing assessments. There is a direct relationship between deficiencies in the quantity of housing provision, homelessness and inadequate housing quality (Burridge and Ormandy, 1993).

4.7.3 Crowding

In many poor households, individuals may have less than $1m^3$ of space each. In the most extreme cases, even small rooms are subdivided to allow multiple occupancy, as in Hong Kong, where many people live in beds stacked three high in dormitories, with each bed surrounded by a cage, for privacy and protection against robbery. In Calcutta, a so-called "hotbed" system operates whereby bunks stacked one above the other in tiny rooms are available for rent by the hour.

Such crowded, cramped conditions characterize the homes and neighbourhoods of poorer groups and facilitate transmission of diseases including tuberculosis, influenza, meningitis, ARI, diarrhoeal diseases and measles (see Section 5.4.2). Moreover, their inhabitants are often malnourished and their immune systems subsequently weakened, increasing susceptibility to disease. In children, malnutrition combined with diarrhoeal diseases can so weaken the body that measles and pneumonia and other childhood diseases become major killers. Children living in overcrowded households are also susceptible to ARI (see Section 5.2). Frequency of contact, density of the population, and the concentration and proximity of infective and susceptible people, promote transmission of the infective organisms (WHO, 1992f). Nevertheless, the evidence linking crowding to specific diseases and poor health is uncertain, given that crowding is related in turn to a range of other factors associated with poor health, such as poor sanitation.

Some evidence suggests that women's health is more likely to be adversely affected by crowding than that of men. In particular, women living in crowded conditions with pre-school children are more likely to experience psychological distress (Gabe & Williams, 1993). Lack of privacy and peace in the home due to crowding and insufficient living space also impacts negatively on the development of children who may have no place to study uninterruptedly. Problems such as incest and violence in the home may be negatively associated with overcrowding too (see also Section 5.6.5).

4.7.4 Accidents and injuries

If crowding combines with poor-quality housing materials, incidence of injuries and accidents rises significantly. Many accidents happen in shelters made of flammable materials, and when protection (especially of children) from the dangers of open fires or stoves is neglected (UNCHS, 1996b).

Environmental hazards associated with home accidents are also related to faulty design, poor maintenance of dwellings, and use of defective or improperly installed equipment and appliances. Falls, burns and poisonings frequently result from inadequate storage of poisonous substances and dangerous items (such as medicines and cleaning products), poorly sited or maintained heat sources (such as open fires, wood, oil, gas or kerosene burners), poor-quality floor coverings and surfaces (particularly in bathrooms), poorly designed stairways or storage areas, and improperly designed or located windows. Many accidents occur in kitchens, which are often "unhealthy" in design.

Indeed, although it is generally accepted that more people die in vehicle accidents than in home accidents, in some countries (the USA for example), far higher numbers of people sustain disabling injuries in home accidents than in vehicle accidents. Falls account for a high proportion of deaths in and around the home, as do fires. Home accidents are a major cause of death among children under the age of five years, and among the elderly (Mood, 1993).

4.7.5 Building materials and construction-related problems

Building design, materials and construction techniques, and certain household products have important implications for housing. High-rise buildings may present special hazards, some of which may increase directly with building height, particularly if building standards are weak and enforcement lax. Structural weaknesses can be a direct threat and upper story residents in high rise blocks at extreme risk in case of fire or explosion. Gas explosions are likely to be much more dangerous in high-rise buildings, particularly since resultant fires may spread rapidly via duct systems. High-rise buildings are also problematic because their maintenance costs are very high. Essential services may break down and building faults occur which tenants generally cannot rectify (Freeman, 1993). Vandalism, crime and degradation of the immediate environment often follow.

High-rise buildings and aspects of housing design and town planning have been studied in relation to mental ill-health in occupants (see Section 5.7.2). Although it would be simplistic to suggest a causal relationship between mental conditions such as depression, and living in a high-rise building, evidence nevertheless suggests that residing in a high-rise building can affect mental health negatively (Freeman, 1993). People living on the upper floors of such buildings appear to experience an increase in the prevalence of various psychosocial problems, particularly feelings of social isolation (WHO, 1988). There is also some evidence that children may fail to acquire a sense of security, curiosity and a later ability to explore and experiment.

Not only type of construction but also building materials themselves can harm health. Building materials may contain potentially hazardous materials such as asbestos, radioactive radon gas and urea foam insulation which contains formaldehyde, and may cause eye and respiratory irritations. Asbestos dust may be produced during remodelling or demolition "do-it-yourself" activities carried out under inadequately controlled conditions, or as a result of damage to asbestos panels and other products through abrasion. Radon may be drawn into homes from underlying soils, and building materials themselves, such as granite, alum shale stone, clay bricks, or concrete containing uranium mine tailings, may release radon into the home environment (see also Section 4.2.6).

Damp housing may harbour viral and bacterial agents, as well as house dust mite, which can cause respiratory problems, especially wheeze. Damp conditions also encourage the growth of mould, long considered to be a source of respiratory allergens (Hunt, 1993). Damp housing is also thought to be a contributory factor to rheumatism and arthritis (WHO, 1988). It should be emphasized, however, that not all studies have reported a relationship between damp housing and poor health, and that the relationship is complex.

Chagas disease is strongly associated with housing quality. Transmitted by insects that live and breed in cracks in the walls of mud or wooden houses, it affects around 18 million people in Latin America (WHO, 1997h). Lead poisoning is also strongly associated with housing quality and is particularly prevalent among children living in old, deteriorating housing which has flaking lead-based paint or old lead plumbing systems (see Section 10.5.2).

Other factors such as the efficiency of heating and ventilation systems, and insulation and housing design features, impact on the indoor microclimate. Extremes of hot and cold can have marked impacts on peoples' health. Construction and design of buildings can also have a significant impact on noise levels in and around the home, which, at high levels, can lead to various health effects such sleep disruption and psychological stress.

4.7.6 Indoor air pollution

High levels of indoor air pollution arising from the use of open fires, unsafe fuels and inefficient stoves for cooking and/or heating probably represents the single most serious health impact from air pollution worldwide. The domestic combustion of biomass fuels, coal, and kerosene by poor communities both in developing and developed countries, can lead to extremely high levels of indoor air pollution (especially particulates). This poses special risks to the respiratory health of women and young children who are most exposed and vulnerable (see Section 4.2). Even the use of gas stoves may result in increased levels of NO_2 inside homes.

Indoor air pollutants other than those associated with fuel combustion are also of concern in some circumstances. They include asbestos fibres from insulation materials or asbestos cement organic solvents used in building materials, wood preservatives and cleaning agents, and radon gas. The use of household cleaning products, stains, paint strippers and thinners, and other volatile organic substances can lead to toxic concentrations of certain pollutants. Exposure to such pollutants is difficult to quantify and depends on ventilation rates and personal behaviour. Environmental tobacco smoke is another major factor influencing the quality of indoor air and the health of individuals in the indoor environment (see Section 4.2.5).

Pollution from traffic and industry may also influence the quality of indoor air in urban areas.

4.7.7 Pests

Techniques for control of household pests have developed relatively slowly compared to those for controlling agricultural pests or outdoor disease vectors such as mosquitos. Pests associated with housing include lice, bedbugs, fleas, flies, cockroaches, ticks and mites, as well as rats and mice. Recent studies have demonstrated that allergic sensitivity to cockroaches may be widespread among people living in infested housing (Howard, 1993). Cockroaches can infest a variety of building types, and thrive in dark, warm, moist conditions, particularly if food is available and waste-disposal systems are poor. In houses which become infested with rats (often in urban areas) dead spaces in walls and behind panelling provide nesting sites. Rats in rural areas may also be common and are frequently associated with farming activities. Rats transmit a large number of diseases (such as plague), and parasitic infections, commonly carrying roundworm and tapeworm parasites. In urban areas they may also act as disease vectors. In developed countries such as the UK, the number of rats appears to be increasing in urban areas.

4.8 The workplace

Other than the home environment, the workplace is the setting in which many people spend the largest proportion of their time. Indeed, for many people, particularly in developing countries, the boundary between their home and workplace environments is blurred, since they often undertake agricultural or cottage industry activities within the home. Growth of the latter has often been spurred by population growth and rapid urbanization (see Sections 2.2 and 2.3), in combination with eco-

Table 4.19

Working population (millions) in the world — 1990 and 2000

Region	1990	2000	Growth 1990-2000
Africa	230	302	31.3
Asia	1410	1646	16.7
Europe	380	400	5.3
South and Central America	158	199	25.9
North America	180	200	11.1
Total	2358	2747	16.5

Source: WHO 1995i.

nomic development, and in parallel with larger, more conspicuous industrial development.

In favourable circumstances, work contributes to good health and economic achievements. However, the work environment exposes many workers to health hazards that contribute to injuries, respiratory diseases, cancer, musculoskeletal disorders, reproductive disorders, cardiovascular diseases, mental and neurological illnesses, eye damage and hearing loss, as well as to communicable diseases (see Section 5.12)

The current global labour force stands at about 2600 million and is growing continuously (**Table 4.19**). Approximately 75% of these working people are in developing countries. The officially registered working population constitutes 60–70% of the world's adult male and 30–60% of the world's adult female population. Each year, another 40 million people join the labour force, most of them in developing countries. Workplace environmental hazards are therefore a threat to a large proportion of the world population.

4.8.1 The workplace environment and economic development

In some of the least developed countries, up to 80% of the workforce is employed in agriculture, mining and other types of primary production (see Section 2.7.2). Heavy physical work, often combined with heat stress, occupational accidents, pesticide poison-

ings, organic dusts and biological hazards are thus the main causes of occupational morbidity and mortality in these countries (WHO, 1995i). Additionally, numerous non-occupational factors such as parasitic and infectious diseases, poor hygiene and sanitation, poor nutrition, general poverty and illiteracy aggravate these occupational health effects.

The informal sector and small-scale industries (SSIs), in particular, are subject to numerous workplace hazards. Many migrants find work in the informal sector and SSIs since these offer easy entry for newcomers, and often do not require formal trade skills, or large amounts of capital or machinery. Estimates suggest that over 1000 million people worldwide are employed by small-scale industries (Rantanen, Lehtinen & Mikheev, 1994). In some countries, such as Thailand, SSIs may account for the majority of registered industries. However, SSIs are not subject to occupational health-and-safety provisions. Even in the advanced economy of the USA, 90% of all work sites, covering 40% of the country's total workforce of 110 million, are not inspected regularly and/or do not have access to occupational health services. Many of those working in SSIs therefore suffer adverse health impacts due to exposure to dusts, heat stress, toxic substances, noise, vibration and poor hygiene.

In rapidly-industrializing countries occupational health problems often arise due to use of technologies that are less advanced and more hazardous than those favoured by developed countries. Moreover, managing all aspects of production — for example, health and safety at work and the health of the work environment, as well as the external environment — can be difficult when technical and financial resources are limited, as is often the case (WHO, 1995i). In such circumstances, occupational accidents, traditional physical and ergonomic hazards, and occupational injuries and diseases become major problems. Their true extent is unknown, however, since many occupational injuries and diseases are neither notified nor registered.

Evidently, the panorama of workplace hazards varies in accordance with the stage of economic development that has been reached and approaches to health protection should take this into account. The basic principles of occupational health remain the same, however, and are laid out in the *Declaration on Occupational Health for All* (WHO, 1994b).

4.8.2 Workplace exposures

Workplace health hazards generally differ from those found in the general environment. Furthermore, because workers are often exposed in confined spaces, exposures to workplace hazards are often much higher than exposures to hazards in the general environment. In developing countries, workers may be exposed simultaneously to workplace hazards, to an unsafe housing environment, and a polluted general environment. The following summary of major workplace hazards has been extracted from the Global Strategy on Occupational Health for All (WHO, 1995i), which was adopted by the World Health Assembly in 1996.

Mechanical hazards, unshielded machinery, unsafe structures in the workplace and dangerous tools are some of the most prevalent workplace hazards in developed and developing countries. In Europe, about 10 million occupational accidents happen every year (some of them commuting acci-

dents) (EC, 1995a). Adoption of safer working practices, improvement of safety systems and changes in behavioural and management practices could reduce accident rates, even in high-risk industries, by 50% or more within a relatively short time (WHO, 1995i).

Approximately 30% of the workforce in developed countries and between 50% and 70% in developing countries may be exposed to a **heavy physical workload** or **ergonomically poor working conditions**, involving much lifting and moving of heavy items, or repetitive manual tasks. Workers most heavily exposed to heavy physical workloads include miners, farmers, lumberjacks, fishermen, construction workers, storage workers and healthcare personnel. Repetitive tasks and static muscular load are also common among many industrial and service occupations and can lead to injuries and musculoskeletal disorders (see Section 5.12). In many developed countries such disorders are the main cause of both short-term and permanent work disability and lead to economic losses amounting to as much as 5% of GNP (WHO, 1995i).

Exposure to some 200 **biological agents**, (viruses, bacteria, parasites, fungi, moulds and organic dusts) occurs in selected occupational environments. The hepatitis B and hepatitis C viruses and tuberculosis infections (particularly among healthcare workers), asthma (among persons exposed to organic dust) and chronic parasitic diseases (particularly among agricultural and forestry workers) are the most common occupational diseases resulting from such exposures. Blood-borne diseases such as HIV/AIDS and hepatitis B are now major occupational hazards for healthcare workers.

Physical factors in the workplace such as noise, vibration, ionizing and non-ionizing radiation and microclimatic conditions can all affect health adversely. Between 10% and 30% of the workforce in developed countries, and up to 80% of the workforce in developing and newly-industrializing countries, are exposed to such physical factors. In some high-risk sectors such as mining, manufacturing and construction, all workers may be affected. Noise-induced hearing loss is one of the most prevalent occupational health effects in both developing and developed countries (WHO, 1995i).

About 100 000 different **chemical products** are in use in modern work environments and the number is growing. High exposures to **chemical hazards** are most prevalent in industries that process chemicals and metals, in the manufacture of certain consumer goods, in the production of textiles and artificial fibres, and in the construction industry. Chemicals are also increasingly used in virtually all types of work, including non-industrial activities such as hospital and office work, cleaning, and provision of cosmetic and beauty services. Exposure varies widely. Health effects include metal poisoning, damage to the central nervous system and liver (caused by exposure to solvents), pesticide poisoning, dermal and respiratory allergies, dermatoses, cancers and reproductive disorders. In some developing countries, more than half of the workers exposed to silica or other dust in certain high-risk industries (such as mining and metallurgy) are reported to show clinical signs of silicosis or other types of pneumoconiosis (WHO, 1989a).

Reproductive hazards in the workplace include around 200–300 chemicals known to be mutagenic or carcinogenic. The reported adverse effects include infertility in both sexes, spontaneous abortion, fetal death, teratogenesis, fetal cancer, fetotoxicity and retarded development of the fetus or newborn. Organic solvents and toxic metals, biological agents, such as certain bacteria, viruses and zoonoses, as well as heavy physical work, are also associated with an increased risk of reproductive disorders. The reproductive hazards of ionizing radiation are now well-established, while hazards

from non-ionizing radiation are under intensive study. Both male and female workers may be affected by these hazards, but protection of women of fertile age and pregnant women is of particular concern.

About 300–350 substances have been identified as **occupational carcinogens**. They include chemical substances such as benzene, chromium, nitrosamines and asbestos, physical hazards such as ultraviolet radiation (UVR) and ionizing radiation, and biological hazards such as viruses. In the EU alone, approximately 16 million people are exposed to carcinogenic agents at work (EC, 1995). The most common cancers resulting from these exposures are cancers of the lung, bladder, skin, mesothelium, liver, haematopoietic tissue, bone and soft connective tissue (see Section 5.9). Among certain occupational groups, such as asbestos sprayers, occupational cancer may be the leading factor in ill-health and mortality. Due to the random character of effect, the only effective control strategy is primary prevention that eliminates exposure completely, or that effectively isolates the worker from carcinogenic exposure.

Exposure to the estimated 3000 **allergenic agents** in the environment is mainly occupational. In the work environment, such hazardous agents enter the body via the respiratory tract or the skin.

Occupational asthma, is caused by exposure to various organic dusts, microorganisms, bacteria, fungi and moulds, and several chemicals. The increased number of people who develop an allergic response, coupled with high numbers of occupational allergenic exposures and improved diagnostic methods, has led to a steady growth in the registered numbers of occupational asthma cases in several industrialized countries (see Section 5.11). Occupational respiratory diseases should therefore be the focus of any occupational health programme.

Psychological stress caused by

time and work pressures has become more prevalent during the past decade. Monotonous work, work that requires constant concentration, irregular working hours, shift-work, work carried out at risk of violence (for example, police or prison work), isolated work or excessive responsibility for human or economic concerns, can also have adverse psychological effects.

Psychological stress and overload have been associated with sleep disturbances, burn-out syndromes, depression, cardiovascular disorders and hypertension. Severe psychological conditions (psychotraumas) have been observed among workers involved in serious catastrophes or major accidents during which human lives have been threatened or lost.

Social conditions of work such as gender distribution and segregation of jobs and equality (or lack of) in the workplace, and relationships between managers and employees, raise concerns about occupational stress. Many service and public employees experience social pressure from customers, clients or the public, which can increase the psychological workload. Measures for improving the social aspects of work mainly involve promotion of open and positive contacts in the workplace, support of the individual's role and identity at work, and encouragement of teamwork (WHO, 1995i).

4.8.3 Occupational health impacts

The great variety of occupational health hazards makes quantification of their associated health risks and impacts at the global level very difficult (Mikheev, 1994). Some estimates have been based on the occupational injuries and diseases reported in official statistics (Leigh et al., 1996). But a large number of injuries and diseases caused by workplace hazards are not reported. Adjustment is therefore necessary. Making such adjustment, WHO (1995a) and ILO (1997) estimate that there may be as many as 125 million

cases of occupational injury and disease each year, resulting in 220 000 fatalities.

Due to the changes in occupational distribution with development (see Section 2.7.2), many countries have experienced a shift from the hazards that characterize work in agriculture, mining and other primary industries, to those that characterize manufacturing industries and disease service industries. Following such a shift, occupational injuries and diseases could be expected to fall in number and the severity of those that do occur to be less. But, in fact, new occupational disease problems have emerged (see Section 5.12), leading to an increase in reported occupational disease in certain developed countries.

In addition to the specific workplace hazards discussed above, work and health are associated in other ways, creating possibly even greater impacts on health. Working conditions, type of work, vocational and professional status, and geographical location of the workplace and employment have a profound impact on the social status and social well-being of workers. Historically, occupational health programmes have developed with attempts to improve the social conditions of underserved and underprivileged occupations. In many countries, social policy and social protection are closely linked with employment and unemployment. As the mobility of workers increases, leading to high numbers of migrant workers in some countries, their health, well-being and social support will require special attention. These are key issues for sustainable development.

4.9 The global environment

4.9.1 From local pressures to global impacts

In an interdependent world, significant environmental impact in one place will affect environmental quality elsewhere.

Fig. 4.9

Possible major types of impact of climate change and stratospheric ozone depletion on human health

Mediating process	Health outcomes

Direct

| Exposures to thermal extremes | ➤ Altered rates of heat- and cold-related illness and death |
| Altered frequency and/or intensity of other extreme weather events | ➤ Deaths, injuries, psychological disorders; damage to public health infrastructure |

Temperature and weather changes

Indirect

Disturbances of ecological systems

Effects on range and activity of vectors and infective parasites	➤ Changes in geographic ranges and incidence of vector-borne diseases
Altered local ecology of waterborne and foodborne infective agents	➤ Changed incidence of diarrhoeal and other infectious diseases
Altered food (especially crop) productivity, due to changes in climate, weather events, and associated pests and diseases	➤ Malnutrition and hunger, and consequent impairment of child growth and development
Sea level rise, with population displacement and damage to infrastructure	➤ Increased risk of infectious disease, psychological disorders
Levels and biological impacts of air pollution, including pollens and spores	➤ Asthma and allergic disorders; other acute and chronic respiratory disorders and deaths
Social, economic and demographic dislocations due to effects on economy, infrastructure and resource supply	➤ Wide range of public health consequences; mental health and nutritional impairment, infections diseases, civil strife
	➤ Skin cancers, cataracts, and perhaps immune suppression; indirect impacts via impaired productivity and agricultural and acquatic systems

Stratospheric ozone depletion

Source: McMichael et al., 1996.

For instance, pollution is transported across boundaries by winds and water flows, and plant and animal diseases follow the trade routes between continents. People too may carry latent infectious disease agents, spreading them around the globe through long-distance travel. At the same time, though, several types of environmental impact have become concentrated or aggravated in specific places as a result of regional or global economic or political factors. For example, deforestation, desertification and overfishing — often caused, in part, by poverty or lack of environmental controls — may also be strongly determined by regional and global trade arrangements and market demands for natural products (see Chapters 2 and 3).

As a result of the combined action of these driving forces at local and regional levels, environmental change is gradually becoming "globalized". Major examples of global environmental change include: climate change, stratospheric ozone depletion, trans-boundary air and water pollution, acid precipitation, loss of biodiversity, desertification and deforestation. Solutions to global environmental problems require increased international cooperation, particularly through implementation of international laws and conventions. International agencies such as WHO are playing an important role in creating international consensus on how global environmental health problems can best be tackled.

4.9.2 Climate change

Human-induced climate change is due primarily to accumulation of "greenhouse" gases (GHGs) in the atmosphere, resulting from activities such as combustion of fossil fuels, large-scale deforestation and the rapid expansion of irrigated agriculture (see Sections 3.3 and 3.4). The principal GHGs are carbon dioxide (CO_2), methane (CH_4), nitrous oxide (N_2O), ozone (O_3) and chlorofluorocarbons (CFCs) (see Section 4.9.3), concentrations of which have been increasing since the mid-18th Century (McMichael et al., 1996).

It is estimated that, due to the accumulation of GHGs, global mean surface temperature will have risen by between 1.5° and 4.5°C (with a "best" estimate of 2.5°C), by the year 2100 (IPCC, 1996). Uncertainties exist but the average rate of warming is expected to be greater than any experienced during the past 10 000 years (McMichael et al., 1996). It is also anticipated that night-time temperatures will rise more than day-time temperatures.

Both direct and indirect health

impacts can be expected to occur as a result of climate change (**Fig. 4.9**). Direct effects, such as a potential increase in the number of deaths due to greater frequency and severity of heat waves, are ostensibly easier to predict than indirect effects. Indirect effects, mediated by ecosystem disturbance, could include changes in food production levels, which could affect nutritional status, or in distribution patterns of vector populations, which could affect incidence of malaria and other vector-borne diseases in large parts of the world, including some currently free from such diseases. Increased air pollution levels, especially in cities, because of the combined effects on photochemical reactions at ground level of higher UVR levels and higher temperatures, would be an example of indirect effects not mediated by ecosystem change. Indirect effects are particularly difficult to estimate given the number and diversity of the variables involved. Moreover, the different components of climate change would vary in their relative importance for different health impacts (**Table 4.20**) (McMichael et al., 1996).

Climate change and potential direct effects on human health

Increased mortality during heat waves and other extreme weather events is anticipated as the principal direct health effect of climate change. The elderly, the very young and those with incapacitating diseases such as chronic respiratory and cardiovascular disorders appear to be disproportionally affected by such weather extremes, probably due to their lesser physiological coping capacity. Those living in cities with greater exposure to "heat islands", where temperatures tend to be significantly higher than those of surrounding regions, would be particularly at risk if temperatures rose. Higher temperatures in cities would also lead to increased concentrations of ground-level O_3 (since higher temperatures increase chemical interaction

Fig. 4.10

Estimated excess mortality among Chicago residents — July 1995

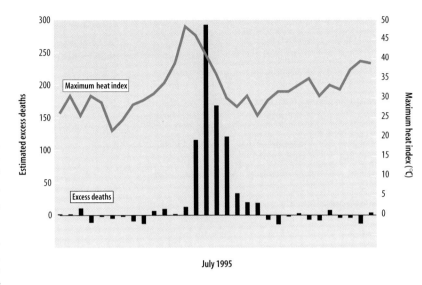

Source: Daley, 1995.

among the pollutants that form this chemical), thereby exacerbating air pollution problems (see Section 4.2). Indoor air quality, which depends to a considerable extent on the prevailing outdoor climate, could also decline.

Climate change is also anticipated to manifest itself as change in weather variability (IPCC, 1996). Relatively small changes in climate variability or

Table 4.20

Likely relative impact on health outcomes of the components of climate change

Health outcome	Change in mean temperature, etc.	Extreme events	Rate of change of climate variable	Day–night difference
Heat-related deaths and illness		+++		+
Physical and psychological trauma due to disasters		++++		
Vector-borne diseases	+++	++	+	++
Non-vector-borne infectious diseases	+	+		
Food availability and hunger	++	+	++	
Consequences of sea level rise	++	++	+	
Respiratory effects:				
• air pollutants	+	++		+
• pollens, humidity	++			
Population displacement	++	+	+	

++++ = great effect; + = small effect; empty cells indicate no known relationship

Source: McMichael et al., 1996.

Table 4.21

Major tropical vector-borne diseases and the likelihood of change in their distribution as a result of climate change

Disease	Vector	Present distribution	Likelihood of altered distribution with climate change
Malaria	Mosquito	Tropics/sub-tropics	+++
Dengue	Mosquito	Tropics/sub-tropics	++
Schistosomiasis	Water snails	Tropics/sub-tropics	++
Yellow fever	Mosquito	Tropical South America and Africa	++
Onchocerciasis	Blackfly	Africa/Latin America	++
Lymphatic filariasis	Mosquito	Tropics/sub-tropics	+
Leishmaniasis	Phlebotomine sandfly	Asia/southern Europe/ Africa/Americas	+
American trypanosomiasis	Triatomine bug	Central and South America	+
African trypanosomiasis	Tsetse fly	Tropical Africa	+
Dracunculiasis	Crustacean (copepod)	South Asia/Middle East/ Central and West Africa	?

+ = likely; ++ = very likely; +++ = highly likely; ? = unknown

Source: adapted from McMichael et al., 1996.

mean climate could produce relatively large changes in the frequency of "extreme" events. If the frequency of extreme weather events increases, the deaths, injuries, stress-related disorders and the many adverse effects associated with the social disruption, enforced migration and settlement that these events entail, would also increase. The impacts of extreme weather events would obviously be greatest on communities with the fewest technical and social resources.

Spread of infectious diseases

Many of the biological organisms and processes linked to the spread of infectious diseases are especially influenced by fluctuations in climate variables, notably temperature, precipitation and humidity. Disturbances of ecological systems by climate change are expected to cause widespread shifts in the distribution and incidence of a number of infectious diseases and in foodborne intoxications. For example, the net increases anticipated following climate change in the geographic distribution (both altitude and latitude) of insect vectors would increase the potential for transmission of many vector-borne dis-

eases (WHO 1997h). Climate change would also alter the life-cycle dynamics of vectors and infectious parasites, further influencing transmission potential.

Distribution of disease agents that are neither transmitted by vectors, nor otherwise dependent on animal hosts, will probably also be affected by climate change. The relevant diseases include other foodborne diseases, and infections spread directly from person to person, such as measles and tuberculosis.

The impacts of changes in disease incidence would be felt particularly in developing countries. For instance, since vector-borne diseases such as malaria, schistosomiasis and yellow fever (see **Table 4.21**) are a major cause of illness and death in developing tropical countries, climate change could have significant adverse impacts on the health status of their populations (see Section 5.5).

Sea level rise

Higher temperatures would cause sea level to rise, mostly as a result of thermal expansion of the oceans and melting of mountain glaciers (IPCC, 1996). The "best" estimate of current ocean and climate models is that sea level will have risen by around half a metre by the year 2100 and will continue to rise thereafter, even if GHG levels are stabilized (Wigley, 1995). This estimate thus predicts a rate of sea level rise, for the period between now and 2100, that is two to three times greater than that of the past 100 years (McMichael et al., 1996).

Sea level rise could cause considerable disruption in coastal and estuarine areas through increased erosion and damage to important ecosystems such as wetlands and coral reefs. In each case, the damage caused will be additional to that associated with human activities such as sediment removal and development of canals, dikes and levees. Given that more than half of the world's population now lives within 60 km of the sea and that the average growth rate of this coastal population is higher than that of the global population, impacts on human populations could be immense (IPCC, 1996).

In common with climate change generally, sea level rise would have both direct and indirect impacts on human health (**Table 4.22**). Direct impacts would include additional death and injury caused by more frequent or more intense flooding. Indirect impacts would result from geohydrological changes along coastlines, such as coral reef destruction, salt-water intrusion into ground-water reservoirs and coastal wetlands, and reduced gravitational drainage in low-lying lands. Population displacement may be inevitable and could cause serious problems in densely-populated delta areas and in island states. If coastal protection systems are not strengthened, a 50 cm rise in sea level by 2100 would place 80 million people at risk of being flooded more than once a year, as compared with 46 million people under present climate and sea level conditions (Baarse, 1995).

Effects on air pollution

It is well established that exposure to air pollutants can have many serious health effects, especially if severe pollution episodes occur (see Section 4.2). Climate change could increase the number of such episodes by influencing the dispersion of primary air pollutants through its impact on the circulatory motion of the atmosphere. Climate change could also increase air pollution levels by accelerating the atmospheric chemical reactions that produce photochemical oxidants (see Section 4.2), particularly O_3, due to higher air temperatures and increased UVR at ground level. Additionally, if extreme weather conditions such as high temperature and humidity become more common, the health impacts of air pollution may be heightened. However, the synergistic impacts of weather and pollution on morbidity and mortality are not yet well understood.

Climate change could also alter the production and dispersal of plant aeroallergens, resulting in shifts in the pattern of various seasonal allergic disorders, especially hay fever and asthma. Altered pollen production would principally reflect shifts in the natural and agriculturally-managed distribution of many plant species, including birch trees, grasses, ragweeds, and various crops such as rape.

4.9.3 Stratospheric ozone depletion and its health effects

Significant stratospheric ozone depletion has occurred at middle and high latitudes (**Fig. 4.11**), catalysed by trace amounts of hydrogen, nitrogen and halogen free radicals. These chemical compounds occur naturally but their concentrations have increased greatly in recent years due to industrial activities. The excess halogen free radicals derive from halocarbons — particularly CFCs (see Section 2.6) — and halons. These human-made gases have been used extensively as refrigeration fluids, blowers in foam-making, aerosol propellants, solvents, and in fire extinguishers.

Although stratospheric ozone depletion and climate change are separate phenomena, they are linked by a number of processes. For instance, several GHGs, especially CFCs, also destroy stratospheric ozone. As ozone itself is also a GHG, reduction of its levels in the stratosphere causes the stratosphere to cool, while increased ground-level ozone contributes to higher temperatures in areas with heavy motorized traffic.

Table 4.22

Potential effects on health of sea level rise

- death and injury due to flooding (as a result of greater susceptibility to extreme events)
- effects on nutrition of loss of agricultural land or changes in fish catch
- reduced availability of fresh water due to saltwater intrusion
- contamination of water supplies via disruption of sanitation, e.g. by microorganisms such as *Vibrio cholerae*, or pollutants from submerged waste dumps
- changes in distribution of disease vectors (e.g. *Anopheles sundaicus*, a saltwater vector of malaria).
- effects of local economic decline on mental and physical health
- health impacts associated with population displacement

Source: McMichael et al., 1996.

Fig. 4.11

Monthly global average stratospheric ozone values — 1964–1980 vs. 1984–1993

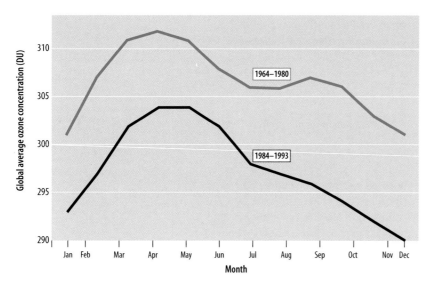

Source: Bojkov, 1995.

Fig. 4.12

Ozone layer depletion around the North Pole; mean reduction of ozone levels (%) during the months of February and March during 1992–1997

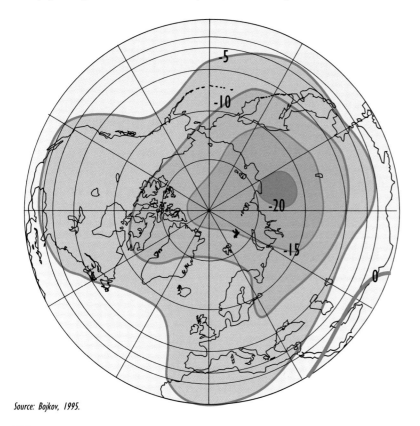

Source: Bojkov, 1995.

Stratospheric ozone depletion first became evident in the 1970s. In the early 1980s, the Antarctic "ozone hole" was discovered. Ozone trends in the Arctic are less well elucidated, but a further, more serious ozone decline can be expected in northern subpolar latitudes if atmospheric levels of chlorine and bromine compounds continue to increase (WMO/UNEP, 1995).

The most extreme stratospheric ozone depletion occurs in the polar regions and at the end of winter and early spring. In the Antarctic, depletion is most pronounced in September and October, when ozone concentration falls to 200–220 matm-cm (the "ozone hole" threshold). This is a reduction of over 40% from 1957–1979 levels. The first time this occurred at the southern pole was in the early 1980s, and each year the duration of the period of ozone depletion lengthens. In 1996, an "ozone hole" of more than 10 million km^2 persisted for more than 80 days (Bojkov et al., 1997). This is a clear sign of the progressive ozone layer depletion. Since the early 1990s, the northern polar region has also shown considerable ozone depletion (Bojkov et al. 1997). **Fig 4.12** shows the average depletion for February and March 1992–1997. The depletion is significant as far south as Northern Europe and North America.

The principal result of stratospheric ozone depletion is that an increasing proportion of solar UVR is reaching Earth's surface. Higher UV exposure is expected to lead to a number of direct impacts on human health (Table 4.22), such as an increase in the incidence of skin cancer (especially non-melanoma skin cancers) in light-skinned populations (see Section 5.9.8). It could also increase the incidence of eye lesions, such as cataracts (Table 4.22). Some 12 to 15 million people are blind from cataracts. WHO has estimated that up to 20% of cataracts or 3 million per year could be due to UV exposure (WHO/UNEP, 1995). Given that in the United States alone it costs US$ 3400 million for 1.2 million cataract operations per year, substantial savings in healthcare costs could be made by prevention of, or delay in the onset of cataracts (WHO/UNEP, 1995).

UV exposure is also thought to cause suppression of the immune system (Table 4.23). UV-induced immune suppression may have adverse impacts on infectious disease immunization programmes, particularly in areas where UV intensities are high. The possibility that UVR will cause progression of various diseases (as in the case of HIV-positive patients) remains to be elucidated. Many such important issues need to be resolved as a matter of urgency (WHO/UNEP, 1995).

Increased ground-level UVR may also affect human health indirectly via adverse effects upon animal and plant biology, and in particular by impairing terrestrial and aquatic food-chains, leading to the collapse of subsistence economies or increased food insecurity (SCOPE, 1993; IASC, 1995).

4.9.4 Transboundary air pollution and movement of hazardous waste

The transboundary movement of hazardous wastes and long-range transport of air pollution are two environmental problems of great international concern. Both of these issues have been the subject of international negotiations resulting in the adoption of international conventions.

Developed countries, motivated by economic as well as technical factors, commonly move their hazardous waste across frontiers. Chemical waste, for instance, may be sent to another country for recycling and reuse by other industries, or for treatment and disposal in special facilities not available in the country of origin. In developed countries the shipment and related transactions are normally carried out within a prescribed regulatory framework.

There have, however, been many instances of hazardous waste being shipped to developing countries in

Table 4.23

Summary of the main effects of solar UVR on the health of human beings

Nature of effect	Direction of effect	Strength of evidence
Effect on immunity and infection		
Suppression of cell-mediated immunity	Harmful (?)	Sufficient
Increased susceptibility to infection	Harmful	Inadequate
Impairment of prophylocating immunization	Harmful	Inadequate
Activation of latent virus infections	Harmful	Inadequate
Effects on the eye		
Acute photokeratitis and photoconjunctivitis	Harmful	Sufficient
Climatic droplet keratopathy	Harmful	Limited
Pterygium	Harmful	Limited
Cancer of the conjunctiva	Harmful	Inadequate
Lens opacity (cataract)	Harmful	Limited
Uveal melanoma	Harmful	Limited
Acute solar retinopathy	Harmful	Sufficient (?)
Macular degeneration	Harmful	Inadequate
Effects on the skin		
Malignant melanoma	Harmful	Sufficient
Non-melanotic skin cancer	Harmful	Sufficient
Sunburn	Harmful	Sufficient
Chronic sun damage	Harmful	Variable
Photo dermatoses	Harmful	Sufficient
Other direct effects		
Vitamin D production	Beneficial	Sufficient
Other cancers	Beneficial	Inadequate
General well-being	Beneficial	Inadequate
Indirect effects		
Effects on climate, food supply disease vectors, air pollution, etc.	Probably harmful	Inadequate

Limited = suggestive but not conclusive evidence
? = some uncertainty about assigned classification

Source: Armstrong, 1994.

order to take advantage of inadequate environmental regulations and cheaper prices. Under such circumstances waste is likely to be disposed of in ways that can damage health and contaminate the environment. Attempts to rectify this situation culminated in the adoption in 1989 of the Basel Convention on the Control of the Transboundary Movement of Hazardous Wastes and their Disposal (see Section 2.5.3). The Convention came into force in 1992 and limits the transboundary shipment of hazardous wastes and prescribes conditions for any such shipments.

The main concern relating to long-range transport of air pollution is deposition of harmful substances and reduced air quality in locations far removed from the original sources of pollution. Acid deposition is a regional air pollution problem, caused by emissions of SO_2, NO_2, ammonia and their oxidation products (see Section 4.4). While acidification of water bodies and soils is largely an environmental threat, human health may also be affected owing to the mobilization of heavy metals. Long-range transport of air pollutants has been recognized as a major problem in Europe and North America for several decades. The European Convention on Long-range Transboundary Air Pollution was adopted as early as 1979. More recently, long-range transport of air pollutants and ensuing acidification and other effects have been observed in other parts of the world.

4.9.5 Dealing with global environmental health problems

Global environmental change is occurring via numerous mechanisms. If it continues at its current rate, future generations may be unable to sustain healthy and productive lives. Scientists must therefore adopt both a descriptive role and a predictive role. They must not only monitor and characterize the impacts of humankind's current activities on ecosystems, but also anticipate and quantify the consequences of its future activities with respect to ecosystem health. In performing these roles scientists can assist governments and policy-makers in shaping and adopting social and economic policies that promote sustainable development.

Science itself may need to find new ways of handling problems relating to uncertainty and the need to predict future events. Essentially, science's traditional reliance on empirical knowledge is not of any help in such situations. Political decision-making must also change. It is no longer fair to demand ultimate proof from scientistsbefore moving into action on a future threat.

Moreover, much more effort needs to be made to incorporate considera-

tion of potential harm to human health, and loss of human lives, into the cost-effectiveness calculations that govern policy formulation and planning. And in the view of the vast health inequities found in many parts of the world today, the most acceptable ways of dealing with expected future problems might well be those that also deal with current problems; in other words, better healthcare systems, better disease surveillance systems, improved environmental health monitoring systems and greater integration of public health concern in economic planning. Such a "no regrets" approach would decrease society's vulnerability to environmental changes without compromising the health status of the present generation.

4.10 Combined exposures from a variety of sources

In this chapter we have examined human exposures to environmental hazards according to environmental media or setting (e.g. air, water, housing, workplace). Many of these hazards occur in more than one of these media or settings. Their control, therefore, requires an understanding of the relative contribution made by each medium or setting. This has led to development of the total human exposure concept. A brief overview is provided in the following of multi-media and multi-setting exposure to different hazards. This is followed by a more detailed analysis of exposure to lead and its effects.

4.10.1 The concept of total human exposure

It is clear from the descriptions of the health risks related to different exposure routes and different settings that the environment is of importance to health at all stages of economic development. Each specific exposure situation may create specific health problems, but some health effects can be induced by exposures via several routes. For instance, the microbes that cause diarrhoeal diseases can spread via water or food (see Sections 4.3 to 4.5 and 5.3). A chemical such as lead can be found at high levels in drinking-water, food, soil or air (IPCS, 1995b). Similarly, the elevated radiation exposure that occurred after the Chernobyl accident (WHO, 1995o) was due to contamination of all compartments of the environment.

Therefore, in order to develop effective preventive actions, all relevant exposures must be identified and "total human exposure" assessed for the hazards of concern. The cholera epidemic in Latin America (see **Box 4.5**) is an example of an environmental health disaster, for which the source of the hazard was initially unclear. Potential exposure routes included seafood that had become contaminated in the sea, poor quality drinking-water and foodstuffs contaminated by household water. Investigations concluded that the original source was in the sea (see Section 5.3), but that the cholera bacteria was also spread via faecal contamination of drinking-water. Control of this epidemic required multiple actions to prevent exposures from each potential source. But because access to proper sanitation and safe drinking-water remains poor in many communities in Latin America, it will be difficult to eradicate cholera in this region.

Exposure to organochlorine pesticides such as DDT and hexachlorobenzene (HCB) may also occur via several routes (see **Box 2.8**). For instance, these chemicals are found in food with high fat content, particularly dairy products and human milk, but exposure also occurs via air and drinking-water. The same is true of PCBs which have been widely used as dielectric and heat-exchange fluids, and in a variety of applications. Human exposure to PCBs has resulted largely from the consumption of contaminated food, but also from inhalation and skin absorption in workplaces.

PAHs, another group of organic compounds that accumulate in fat, are produced by fossil fuel combustion, incineration, and open burning (see Section 3.6). These chemicals contaminate indoor and outdoor air, drinking-water, and various foods, thus leading to human exposure from a variety of sources.

Some chemical pollutants occur in only one environmental medium. NO_2, for example, is found only in ambient air (see Section 4.2). However, human exposure to NO_2 occurs not only in the outdoor environment but also in the workplace and in the home. Assessment of total human exposure to NO_2 must therefore consider exposure in each of these settings. The large percentage of time people spend indoors at home, at work or commuting is another major factor in exposure assessment. The fluctuation of indoor to outdoor ratios of NO_2 concentrations has been demonstrated by an international exposure study conducted in 17 cities in 13 countries (Spengler, et al., 1996). Indoor:outdoor ratios were found to be higher in Asia (at least 1.0, except in China) than in Europe or North America (below 1.0).

4.10.2 The example of lead

Of all the pollutants to which exposure occurs via multiple pathways, lead is probably the best known and most studied (IPCS, 1995b). People are exposed to lead every day. It is naturally present in soil and commonly introduced into the environment by industries and through exhaust fumes from leaded petrol. Lead is also found in batteries, solder, dyes and insecticides and can be transferred to food through direct contact with the object that contains lead, or indirectly, through contamination of the environment. In the home, lead may be present in drinking-water if lead pipes or lead-based solder have been used for domestic plumbing. The lead content levels of soil, water and air are now one or two orders of magnitude above those estimated to have prevailed before industrialization in the 18th and 19th Centuries.

In countries where lead additives are permitted in gasoline, about 90% of lead in air derives from this source. While inhalation of lead in air contributes only 1–2% of the total lead intake of humans, indirect exposure to atmospheric lead via ingestion and inhalation of lead in dust, soil, food and water can contribute up to 50% of total lead intake (IPCS, 1995b). Reductions in the use of leaded petrol in the USA resulted in parallel reductions in air-lead levels and in the blood-lead level of the general population (Annest et al., 1983). Leaded petrol has now been phased out in many developed countries and some developing countries, including Brazil and Colombia (Pearce, 1996b). A global effort to further reduce the use of lead in petrol is under way (OECD, 1993b).

Lead-based paint, which has been used in millions of homes worldwide, can also be a major source of lead in soil and dust. This represents a particular problem for young children who put flakes and chips of paint into their mouths. Although the use of lead in paint and petrol and of lead solder in cans of food and drink has been severely restricted or banned in many developed countries, these sources of lead are still a major concern in less developed countries. Traditional cosmetics such as kohl and surma and traditional medicine, for instance, are additional sources of lead exposure, especially for women and children. Exposure can occur by dermal absorption; children are at high risk because they often wipe their eyes and suck their fingers, thereby introducing lead into their digestive system (IPCS, 1995b).

The developmental effects of chronic low-level lead exposure in early life include reduced birth weight; impaired mental development in the first two years of life; disturbances in sensory pathways within the central nervous system persisting for five or more years, and IQ deficits in school-age children. Low-level exposure to lead can be of major importance on a population basis (IPCS, 1995b). Even a small shift downwards in the population distribution of IQ will substantially increase the number of subjects with low IQ, and decrease the number of subjects with high IQ. In adults, commonly-occurring blood-lead concentrations could have the potential to increase blood pressure and cardiovascular disease and cause myocardial infarction, stroke and early death. Epidemiological evidence is still lacking, however (see Section 5.8).

Although decreasing in many countries, lead exposure remains a major public health issue, especially in cities and industrialized areas in developing countries. In order to improve this situation, lead has to be eliminated from all the world's petrol and reduced or eliminated from lead-based paints, ceramics, cosmetics and cans. Public health programmes should be developed to enhance data collection for food, air, water and soil so that total exposure can be assessed accurately and high-risk populations identified. The collected data in turn should be used in improved procedures for health risk assessment. Further research is needed to develop easily measurable biomarkers (e.g. bone-lead levels), for collecting health effect data at low exposure levels, and to improve interventions for cleaning up contaminated areas.

4.11 Multiple challenges for health protection

Contaminated air, water and food affect thousands of millions of people worldwide, contributing in different degrees to human exposure and subsequent effects on health. In many situations, human exposure to environmental health hazards occurs simultaneously so that they impact collectively on human health.

Air pollution is a problem of global proportions. WHO air quality guidelines are exceeded, at times by large margins, in many locations. The high indoor exposures in the developing countries are the most damaging to health, severely affecting more than 1000 million people.

As major causes of contamination of water and food, lack of sanitation and inadequate treatment or disposal of sewage are responsible for much disease incidence. The number of people without adequate sanitation continues to increase and will surpass 3000 million by the year 2000. Only 10% of the sewage in developing countries receives any type of treatment before being discharged into the environment. Inadequate collection and disposal of solid wastes is an added problem in urban areas in developing countries, contributing to infections, injuries and vector-borne diseases.

While over 800 million people gained access to safe drinking-water between 1990 and 1994, population growth meant that net gain (in terms of percentage covered) was much smaller. Water pollution due to discharge of sewage and industrial waste remains a major problem and leads to adverse human exposures due to contamination of drinking-water supplies. Contamination of coastal waters is also of concern at too many locations. Estimates suggest that provision of safe water and appropriate sanitation for populations currently at risk would reduce diarrhoeal deaths by 2 million and reduce prevalence of schistosomiasis and trachoma by 150 million and 75 million cases respectively.

The incidence of vector-borne diseases such as malaria, schistosomiasis and dengue fever has increased substantially as a result of poor management of water resources and agricultural development. Intersectoral cooperation, with strong inputs from the health-and-environment sectors during the planning and implementation of such projects, will be paramount if past mistakes are to be avoided.

Inadequate sanitation contributes greatly to food contamination which in turn is a major cause of diarrhoeal diseases. Contamination of foods by chemicals is a growing concern in developing countries. Statistics show that foodborne disease, primarily of microbiological origin, is increasing worldwide.

The contamination of soil by pathogens as well as by chemicals is a major contributor to human exposure to environmental health hazards. Contamination due to poor sanitation, application of agricultural chemicals, improper disposal of hazardous wastes and deposition of air pollutant particles, such as lead, is of particular concern. Soil contamination leads to groundwater pollution and uptake of contaminants by crops.

The contribution of inadequate housing to poor health figures prominently in the disease burden of populations. The absence of a safe and secure structure, lack of sanitation facilities, overcrowding and lack of tenure and security, combine to impact negatively on the health of inhabitants. Poor housing is a problem in urban and rural areas. An indication of its seriousness is the statistic that around 50% of the urban poor in developing countries live in conditions of extreme deprivation.

Environmental health hazards in the workplace are severe, affecting the health of a significant portion of the workforce. They include physical injuries, infections and chronic ailments. As many as 125 million cases of occupational injury and disease may occur each year.

The rather recent discovery of global climate change or ozone layer depletion points to further adverse effects on the health of populations due to environmental hazards. Among the hazards forecast are increasing severity of heat waves, changes in the areas affected by vector-borne diseases, and an increase in UV exposure resulting in more skin cancer and cataracts.

As was described in Section 1.6, different environmental factors can contribute simultaneously to the occurrence of a given disease, for instance, ARI in children (see **Fig. 1.4**), which is linked to indoor air pollution exposures, crowding and poor housing conditions, and malnutrition. Bacteria or viruses that lead to this type of infection are common in the environment of children. For disease to actually develop, though, a combination of exposures to the other factors must generally occur. Effective prevention of ARI therefore depends on a combination of interventions targeted at the different contributing exposures.

Table 4.24 summarizes the multiple linkages between exposure situations described in this chapter and major ill health conditions that they can cause. It is seen that most of these health conditions are potentially related to several environmental exposure situations. The following chapter will review the importance of each health condition with respect to the global health situation and the relative contribution that environmental exposures make to the global burden of disease and injury. ❑

Table 4.24

Potential relationships between exposure situations and health conditions

Health conditions of concern	Polluted air	Excreta and household wastes	Polluted water or deficiencies in water management	Polluted food	Unhealthy housing	Global environmental change
Acute respiratory infections	●				●	
Diarrhoeal diseases		●	●	●		●
Other infections		●	●	●	●	
Malaria and other vector-borne diseases		●	●		●	●
Injuries and poisonings	●		●	●	●	●
Mental health conditions					●	
Cardiovascular diseases	●					●
Cancer	●			●		●
Chronic respiratory diseases	●					●

Source: based on data from WHO, 1995g.

Chapter 5
Health Conditions in an Environmental Context

Driving Force
Pressure
State
Exposure
Effect
Action

5.1 Estimating the burden of disease

Chapter 1 argues that, as with a physician taking X-rays from various angles, the complex relation between health and environment must be looked at from different perspectives to better understand how best to intervene to improve human health. A conceptual framework was proposed to guide the viewing process. This framework took as its starting point those driving forces which, through pressures of one kind or another, significantly alter the state of the environment. The dynamics of these relationships were explored in Chapters 2 and 3.

Chapter 4 went on to consider specifically how lowered environmental quality can lead to increased levels of exposure and risk to human health. Different degraded environments were shown to be associated with specific health outcomes. For example, the role of air pollutants in provoking respiratory diseases and cancers, and the role of contaminated water and food in causing diarrhoeal disease were discussed. However, many environmental health hazards are associated with more than one health problem (Table 4.23) and certain hazards interact, making quantification of environmental health impact difficult.

In this chapter we look at environmental health problems from the viewpoint of the burden of death, disease and disability, and analyse the relative importance of the different environmental factors discussed earlier.

Needless to say, this exercise is fraught with uncertainty. Not only is the state of death, sickness and disability reporting very incomplete and often even arbitrary, but rarely is any effort made to report contributing factors, be these environmental, nutritional or otherwise. Statistics on the "cause of death" and the classification of diseases focus on the body organ in which disease is found and the pathological processes within that organ. Thus the causal role of any factor cannot be derived directly from routinely-recorded mortality and morbidity statistics. Instead, approximations of the role of different factors must be sought which are consistent with the known epidemiology of disease and disability.

In addition, as stated in the WHO Constitution, health is not only the absence of disease, but a state of complete physical and mental well-being (WHO, 1946). Many of the environment and development problems described in previous chapters impact on human well-being beyond actual "disease". The deprivations of a life in poverty, of being a refugee or war victim, or of living and working in an insecure or polluted environment have been highlighted. But the limitations of "health status" data mean that this chapter must focus on death, disease and disability. Regrettably, in so doing, the real impact of environmental factors on health is likely to be underestimated.

Table 5.1 shows two different estimates for the total number of deaths for the major causes of death for 1990–1993. The numbers in the right-hand column have been taken from the *World health report* (WHO, 1995a), and are based primarily on routinely-recorded mortality statistics. In the left-hand column, numbers from the *Global burden of disease study* (Murray & Lopez, 1996b) are presented. Some of these numbers have been adjusted as described below. The specific diseases in **Table 5.1** account for nearly 83% of all deaths. The biggest "killers" (cancer, heart disease and cardiovascular diseases) mainly affect elderly people and are the most common causes of death in developed countries. Many of these deaths can be considered "natural"; in many countries "senility" rather than a specific disease would be ascribed as cause of death. Deaths from infectious diseases, such as acute respiratory infections (ARI), diarrhoeal diseases and vaccine-preventable infections (**Table 5.1**) mainly affect children in developing countries. Important conditions in the group of "other identified diseases" include digestive diseases, congenital malformations, maternal conditions and different tropical diseases.

Each of the two estimation methods used to produce **Table 5.1** involves judgements about the best sources of mortality data, which explains the differences between the two columns for certain disease categories. The estimates by Murray & Lopez (1996b) in the left-hand column are based on the assumption that all of the deaths from "unknown causes" in older age groups are in fact from cardiovascular and other non-communicable diseases.

Murray & Lopez (1996b) have also analysed the different estimates of global deaths for specific diseases in order to avoid "double counting" of deaths. For instance, the sum of all the estimates of early childhood deaths for specific diseases (such as malaria) should not exceed the total number of deaths in this age group. The numbers in the left-hand column of **Table 5.1** have been adjusted to take this into account, which explains the lower estimated number of deaths for malaria, tuberculosis and perinatal conditions in the left-hand column.

To clarify the relative importance of different causative factors the analysis must take into account the age at which death occurs, or even better, the number of "years of life lost" (YLL). Furthermore, not all negative health outcomes are expressed only in terms of mortality. Morbidity and disability are important outcomes that ideally should be taken into account as well. In recent years much attention has been given to comparing different approaches that seek to incorporate years lost due to death, as well as years lost due to morbidity or disability. One such approach which has generated a comprehensive picture of the "burden of disease" covering all major disease and injury categories is the disability-adjusted life years (DALYs) concept (Murray & Lopez, 1996b). We will use estimates of burden of disease based on this approach in the following sections, as these estimates include all diseases of interest to our analysis and all regions of the world. Furthermore, the esti-

Table 5.1
Estimated global number of deaths — 1990–1993

Disease	A. Deaths (thousands)	(%)	B. Deaths (thousands)	(%)
Cardiovascular diseases	14 327	28	9676	19
Cancer	6024	12	6013	12
Acute respiratory infections	4380	8.7	4110	8.1
Unintentional injuries	3233	6.4	2915	5.7
Diarrhoeal diseases	2946	5.8	3010	5.9
Chronic respiratory diseases	2935	5.8	2888	5.7
Perinatal conditions	2443	4.8	3180	6.2
Vaccine-preventable infections	1985	3.9	1677	3.3
Tuberculosis	1960	3.9	2709	5.3
Intentional injuries	1851	3.7	1082	2.1
Malaria	856	1.7	2000	3.9
Mental health conditions	700	1.4	–	–
Other identified diseases	6827	13.5	3616	7.1
Unknown causes	–	–	8124	16
Total	50 467	100	51 000	100

Sources: A. deaths in 1990 according to Murray and Lopez, 1996b; B. deaths in 1993 according to WHO, 1995a.

mates relate to what is considered "preventable".

Any estimate of the burden of disease that purports to combine the health lost due to a combination of death, disease and disability is going to be very approximate due to the incompleteness of data and lack of agreement on measurement methodologies (WHO, 1997a). Murray & Lopez (1996b) made every effort to overcome these problems and to produce representative estimates for different diseases and regions. For the broad descriptions and comparisons intended in this book, the DALY approach is likely to give the current best estimate of the "true" burden of disease.

Each DALY indicates the loss of a year of healthy life — that is, time lived with a disability or time lost through premature death. The number of DALYs in different regions provides a guide to the relative distribution of disease burden: the higher the DALYs, the greater the burden. For example, the number of DALYs per 1000 people in sub-Saharan Africa in 1990 was about five times greater than in the established market economies, indicating how much greater the burden of disease is in least developed countries.

To calculate disease burden in DALYs, data on premature mortality and disability are combined. The number of YLL is assessed as the difference between the actual age at death and the age at which the person could have been expected to die, given the average age of mortality of an advanced developed country (82.5 years for women and 80 years for men). Next, the incidence of disability due to disease or injury is estimated on the basis of available information pertaining to each community. Different weights are assigned to different disability conditions, according to severity. Finally, discounting and age-weighting systems are incorporated because this methodology assumes that future years of life lost contribute less to the burden of disease than current ones. In total, 500

Table 5.2

Global YLL and DALYs for major health conditions — 1990

	YLL (thousands)	(%)	DALY (thousands)	(%)
Infectious and vector-borne diseases				
Acute respiratory infections	110 992	12	116 696	8.5
Diarrhoeal diseases	94 434	10	99 633	7.2
Vaccine-preventable infectious diseases	67 104	7.4	71 173	5.2
Tuberculosis	34 308	3.8	38 426	2.8
Malaria	28 038	3.1	31 706	2.3
Chronic diseases and injuries				
Injuries and poisoning	132 519	15	208 647	15
Unintentional injury	84 536	9.3	152 188	11
Intentional injury	47 983	5.3	56 459	4.1
Mental health conditions	10 424	1.1	144 950	11
Cardiovascular diseases	116 325	13	133 236	9.7
Cancer	64 837	7.2	70 513	5.1
Chronic Respiratory Diseases	24 755	2.7	60 370	4.3
Total: all diseases and injuries	906 501	100	1 379 238	100

Source: based on data in Murray & Lopez, 1996b.

different conditions or disease sequelae have been separately evaluated. These have been grouped into 96 detailed causes and a variety of cause groups or clusters (Murray & Lopez, 1996b).

While most of the DALY burden is due to premature death, the disability component is important for chronic illnesses which are present over many years. This is seen in **Table 5.2** where the early death component of DALYs (i.e. years of life lost —YLL) is presented along with the DALYs for selected causes. The DALY for diarrhoeal diseases, for instance, is only 5% greater than the diarrhoeal YLL (**Table 5.2**), but for chronic respiratory diseases, the DALY is more than double the YLL. The difference is even more dramatic for mental health conditions: DALYs exceed YLL by a factor of nearly 14. This is not surprising given that mental disease patients often suffer long periods of illness before they die.

Some diseases, such as acute respiratory infections (ARI) and diarrhoeal diseases, are of particular importance to children's health. Thirty percent of the estimated number of deaths for all diseases occur before 15 years of age (**Table 5.3**), but for ARI and diarrhoeal diseases specifically, the percentage is 67% and 88% respectively. (Conversely,

Table 5.3

Proportion of global burden of deaths and diseases occurring in children under age 15 — 1990

Disease	Deaths, age 0–14 (thousands)	(%)*	DALYs, age 0–14 (thousands)	(%)**
Acute respiratory infections	2918	67	105 077	90
Diarrhoeal diseases	2585	88	93 408	94
Perinatal conditions	2443	100	92 311	100
Vaccine-preventable infections	1897	96	69 147	97
Tuberculosis	139	7	5314	14
Malaria	699	82	27 151	86
Unintentional injuries	1065	33	74 620	49
Intentional injuries	258	14	10 415	18
Mental health conditions	96	14	11 000	8
Cardiovascular diseases	441	3	16 259	12
Cancer	163	3	6052	9
Chronic respiratory diseases	185	6	15 440	26
Total	15 073	30	655 112	48

* % of all deaths in this disease category
** % of all DALYs in this disease category

Source: Murray & Lopez, 1996b.

only 3% of the deaths from cardiovascular diseases (CVD) and 3% of the deaths from cancer occur in the 0–14 years age group (**Table 5.3**). The child proportions of DALYs are greater: 48% for all diseases and more than 90% for ARI and diarrhoeal diseases (**Table 5.3**). This is because the estimated years of healthy life lost are greater when a child dies than when an adult dies. As this chapter will show, the diseases that particularly affect children are also influenced by environmental quality.

In the following sections the different health conditions are discussed in the order in which they appear in **Table 5.2**, with the aim of further clarifying the importance of specific environmental conditions to each category. The conditions discussed are responsible for about 70% of the total global DALY burden and are those for which the environment is a major factor (see Section 4.10).

5.2 Acute respiratory infections

5.2.1 One of the greatest threats to child health

ARI include viral and bacterial infections of the lungs and respiratory tract, the most severe and fatal being bacteri-

al pneumonia (Shann, 1986). Certain of the vaccine-preventable infectious diseases (such as measles and whooping cough) can include severe symptoms affecting the respiratory tract and contribute to the global burden of these diseases.

Most ARI episodes are mild and self-limiting and do not require specific treatment, but some progress to pneumonia. Pneumonia incidence is sufficiently high to make it the biggest cause of childhood mortality. It is also the cause of death in many elderly people. Approximately 2.7 million of the estimated 11 million deaths that occur every year in children under the age of 5 are due to pneumonia (WHO, 1996a). This does not include the one million or so who die as a result of measles or whooping cough, although most of these deaths are also ARI deaths. Most pneumonia deaths occur in developing countries in infants under one year of age. In fact, children are most susceptible to ARI during their first month of life; thereafter the risk falls steadily (Garenne, Ronsmans & Campbell, 1992).

The large variation in the burden of disease due to ARI among countries at different stages of economic development is shown in **Fig. 5.1**. In sub-Saharan Africa (SSA), ARIs cause about 300 DALYs per 1000 children, compared to about 3 DALYs per 1000 children in the established market economies (EME). Therefore, each year in SSA countries, 30% of children's potential healthy life is lost due to ARI. The very low per capita DALY rate in the EME countries indicates what can be achieved through interventions. **Fig. 5.1** shows that "other developing countries", represented by Latin America and the Caribbean (LAC), have per capita ARI disease burdens that are about 5 times lower than those of the "least developed countries" (represented by SSA) and an additional 3 times lower than "economies in transition", represented by the former socialist economies of Europe (FSE). Thus the per capita disease burdens correspond to the level of economic development (see Chapter 2).

5.2.2 Historical trends and risk factors

Although childhood bacterial pneumonia is a major public health problem in virtually all developing countries, it is rare in developed parts of the world such as Europe and North America. This has not always been the case. Data from North America for the beginning of this century shows that at that time bacterial pneumonia was the major cause of childhood mortality, and responsible for a burden of illness and death comparable to that seen in rural Africa today (Holt, 1913; Lindner & Grove, 1943). The development of sulphonamides and penicillin in the 1930s made pneumonia a readily treatable condition and dramatically lowered the case-fatality rate.

The bacteria responsible for pneumonia are still ubiquitous, however, and frequently cause middle ear infection and meningitis, although rarely pneumonia. The genetic make-up of populations in developed countries can hardly have changed appreciably, so the reduction in pneumonia incidence must be attributable to environmental factors. Those which have emerged from case–control studies as possible explanations include nutritional factors, crowding and indoor air quality (Berman, 1991).

Malnutrition and low birth weight are recognized risk factors for pneumonia, particularly fatal pneumonia, and we are now more aware of the importance of subclinical deficiencies of micronutrients such as zinc in determining susceptibility to childhood infections. Crowding also plays a role (see Section 4.7), although not all studies have substantiated this, and many children in developed countries still live in crowded conditions. Perhaps the biggest and most relevant environmental change that has taken place is the improvement in indoor air quality. In the early part of this century most households in Europe and North America used wood or coal for domestic cooking and heating, and contained smoke from combustion of these fuels most of the time. Today, almost all households in these regions use gas or electricity for heating and cooking purposes; any smoke present is generally from tobacco-smoking. In many developing countries, though, indoor exposure levels to pollutants that damage the respiratory tract and the lungs can be extremely high because wood and coal continue to be the major types of fuel used for domestic purposes (see Section 3.6).

Despite the reduction in childhood pneumonia rates, respiratory disease remains the most frequent childhood medical problem in developed countries. Upper respiratory tract infections, middle ear infections and asthma have replaced pneumonia as a leading childhood respiratory infection, and while mortality is very low, morbidity is substantial. In some developed countries as many as 30–40% of schoolchildren have some form of asthma, and asthma prevalence is increasing (see Section 5.11). It appears then that in developed countries a transition has taken place — from a childhood respiratory disease pattern dominated by pneumonia to one dominated by asthma. Evidence of a similar transition is now appearing in the rapidly developing economies of Asia and Latin America (Lai et al., 1996). This coincides with an increase in motor vehicle air pollution, which is associated with asthma (see Section 4.2).

It is not known whether or not the disappearance of pneumonia and the emergence of asthma are linked, but an association with changes in children's environments is likely. Children exposed to severe indoor air pollution in developing countries (see Section 4.2) are likely to suffer a significantly increased risk of ARI. Estimates suggest that approximately 60% of the global ARI burden of disease is associated with indoor air pollution and other environmental factors (see Section 5.13).

Fig. 5.1

Acute respiratory infections among children aged 0–4years, by region — DALYs per 1000 children (log scale)

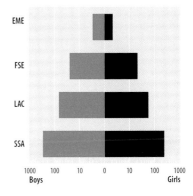

Source: Murray & Lopez, 1996b.

5.2.3 Current control strategies

In most developing countries, control of pneumonia mortality relies on early, effective case-management. This is achieved by training primary health workers to recognize the simplest signs of pneumonia (such as fast breathing) and to treat such cases with oral antibiotics (WHO, 1995k). The effectiveness of this approach is limited, however, if the availability of antibiotics, training of primary health workers and access to health facilities are poor. The growing problem of resistance to antibiotics which is becoming increasingly prevalent among bacteria-causing pneumonia could further undermine this approach.

Efforts to reduce ARI incidence in children also depend upon the reduction of indoor air pollution exposures to biomass and coal smoke (see Section 4.2). Other preventive strategies include improving nutrition, reducing occurrence of low birth weight and reducing the risk of neonatal pneumonia (as the risk in the newborn is highest) (Stoll, 1997). Effective case-management and improved parental awareness of the need to seek health care are also essential.

A vaccine against the most virulent serotype of *Haemophilus influenzae* has virtually eliminated meningitis due to this bacteria in developed countries. This vaccine has the potential to prevent pneumonia caused by this bacteria in developing countries (Mulholland et al., 1997), but its high cost is a significant obstacle. A vaccine against *Streptococcus pneumoniae* using similar technology is currently being developed and may become available within the next 3–5 years.

If current trends continue, middle class communities living in cities of the rapidly developing economies of Asia and Latin America can be expected to experience improved living conditions and access to healthcare during the next two decades. They can therefore be anticipated to move increasingly towards ARI patterns seen in developed countries today. Thus the risk of pneumonia will probably recede for their children, while asthma becomes more prevalent. Meanwhile, the poorer children of Asia and Latin America, and most of the children in sub-Saharan Africa, will continue to be at risk of bacterial pneumonia. For these children, the likelihood of receiving adequate treatment for pneumonia may even diminish. The antibiotics currently used in developing countries are cheap drugs that have either never been patented, or are off-patent and manufactured by generic producers. If resistance renders these drugs ineffective, more sophisticated and more expensive drugs may be the only alternative. But poor people will not be able to afford them. However, if future community developments are able to specifically address the environmental factors responsible for childhood pneumonia, reduced incidence of the condition may offset the rising cost of treatment, eventually leading to genuine sustainable control of this health problem.

5.3 Diarrhoeal diseases

5.3.1 The devastating results of poor sanitation

Diarrhoeal diseases are closely associated with poor sanitation and hygiene, and resultant contamination of water and food with faecal matter (see Sections 3.2, 4.3 and 4.4). Not surprisingly, the regions of the world suffering the highest morbidity and mortality due to these diseases are those where sanitation services are least developed and poverty most deeply embedded.

Diarrhoeal episodes occur in all types of country but are 5 to 6 times more common in developing countries (WHO, 1987a). The total number of diarrhoeal episodes each year may be as high as 4000 million (WHO, 1996a) and each year 3 million deaths due to this disease may occur (**Table 5.1**).

Fig. 5.2

Diarrhoeal diseases among children aged 0–4 years, by region — DALYs per 1000 children (log scale)

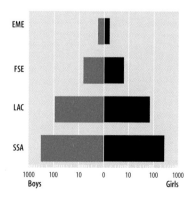

Source: Murray & Lopez, 1996b.

Table 5.4

The burden of some tropical and vector-borne diseases

Disease	People at risk (millions)	People infected (millions)	Mortality	Morbidity/disability	Number of countries affected
Malaria	2020	> 500	1.5–2.7 million	300–500 million clinical cases	> 90
Dracunculiasis	100	> 0.15	Exceptional	High disability	18
Chagas disease	100	18	> 45 000	3 million	21
Schistosomiasis	600	200	< 20 000	20 million	74
Foodborne trematode infections	730	40	>10 000	Liver disease or diarrhoea	> 100
Intestinal parasites	4000	3500	Helminths: 135 000 Protozoa: 90 000	Helminths: 450 million Protozoa: 48 million	> 100 All
Lymphatic filariasis	1100	120	Excess mortality among those with elephantiasis	44 million with chronic disability	73
Onchocerciasis	120	18	Excess mortality among the blind	270 000 blind	34
Leishmaniasis	350	12	Visceral: 75–80 000 Cutaneous: very low	Visceral: very high Cutaneous: multiple lesions	88
Dengue and dengue haemorrhagic fever	2500–3000	> 10	20–30 000	Millions of cases	> 100
Sleeping sickness	55	> 0.3	20 000	> 300 000 cases; high disability	36

Note: Figures are provisional, subject to change as and when more current data become available. Some people may be infected with more than one disease. Figures have been rounded up.

Source: WHO, 1997h.

Children under the age of 5 are at highest risk, but diarrhoeal disease can also be fatal among the elderly and frail (Huttly, 1996). The relationship between economic development level and per capita DALYs in diarrhoeal disease among children under age 5 is shown in **Fig. 5.2**. The pattern is similar to the one seen in **Fig. 5.1** for ARI. The poorest countries suffer from per capita DALYs that are about 200 times higher than those of the richest countries. Diarrhoeal diseases account for 12% of the global total YLL and 8% of the global total DALYs (**Table 5.2**).

The diarrhoeal diseases of main concern are cholera, typhoid fever, paratyphoid fever, salmonella, shigella, giardiasis, non-human *Escherichia coli* infection and a variety of other diseases caused by bacteria, parasites and viruses. The specific pathogens of greatest importance to public health vary according to the geographic setting and age of the patient. Thus rotavirus is a significant cause of severe diarrhoea in children under two years of age in developing countries, and salmonella and campylobacter are primary causes of severe diarrhoea among adults in developed countries who consume poultry raised in factory-farms

(Martines, Phillips & Feachem, 1993).

Most of the global burden of diarrhoeal diseases occurs in children in developing countries (Murray & Lopez, 1996b) and it is estimated that approximately 90% of the diarrhoeal disease burden is related to the environmental factors of poor sanitation and lack of access to clean water and safe food (see Section 5.13).

5.3.2 The example of cholera

Cholera is one of the most deadly diarrhoeal diseases. In the middle of the last century, Snow's recognition of a link between faecally-contaminated water and cholera enabled him to undertake pioneering epidemiological research into the disease (Snow, 1849). Research into cholera continues to provide new and important insights concerning the relationship between its distribution, incidence and environmental factors.

The 1991 Latin American cholera epidemic (see **Box 4.5**) demonstrated relationships between occurrence of cholera and lack of sanitation, lack of safe drinking-water and poor food hygiene (see also Section 4.3). *V. cholerae* is believed to have been introduced into

Box 5.1

Cholera and environmental change in Bangladesh

An extensive study was conducted in Bangladesh from 1987 to 1990 to determine the source and host of *V. cholerae* in the environment. Samples of water and plankton were collected at ten stations every two weeks. The results showed that *V. cholerae* levels increased with increased abundance of copepods.

These findings led to an examination of the seasonal distribution of copepods, ocean currents and cholera epidemiology. Significant copepod egg production was found to occur only when concentrations of diatoms and other large phytoplankton were high. These in turn were at their highest levels when sea temperatures were high. When sea surface-temperature rose from slightly below 25°C in January to just below 30°C in May, cholera cases doubled. Subsequent rises and falls in temperature correlated with corresponding changes in the number of cholera cases.

Source: Colwell, 1996.

Fig. 5.3

Mortality trend for diarrhoeal disease among children under 5-years of age in Mexico — 1978–1993

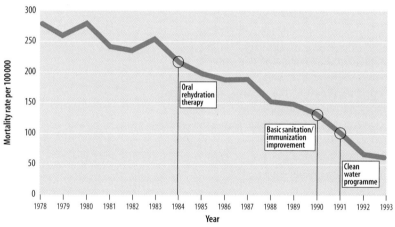

Source: Gutiérrez et al., 1996.

(Colwell, 1996). The epidemic also highlighted relationships between global environmental changes and human health (Colwell, 1996).

New methods of detecting the cholera vibrio when present at extremely low concentration — for example, as few as one to two cells per litre of water — have demonstrated that, contrary to past belief, *V. cholerae* cells do not die off or decay in the environment. Instead, they survive in association with aquatic life such as plankton crustacean copepods, water hyacinths and blue-green bacterium. Survival of *V. cholerae* in seawater for more than 50 days has been demonstrated. It can survive under unfavourable environmental conditions in a dormant state, in which it is viable although nonculturable. It can thus remain infectious and contribute to the occurrence of seasonal cholera epidemics (**Box 5.1**). Interestingly, at the time of the cholera outbreak in Peru a warming event related to the 1990–1995 El Niño in the tropical Pacific took place. This could have resuscitated dormant *V. cholerae* present in coastal algae bloom, which would account for the extraordinarily rapid development of the epidemic in coastal communities far from Lima.

5.3.3 Impact of interventions

No evidence exists of a fall in global incidence rates of diarrhoea during the past 15 years, but mortality due to diarrhoeal diseases appears to have dropped substantially during this time period, implying falling case-fatality rates (Martines, Phillips & Feachem, 1993). Data from Egypt and Costa Rica indicate that this reduction has at the same time been accompanied by reductions in general childhood mortality rates, suggesting that diarrhoea has not been replaced by other causes of death (Martines, Phillips & Feachem, 1993).

Time trends are also evident for Mexico. In June 1991, fear of the dev-

the harbour at Lima, Peru, when bilge water was dumped from a ship that had arrived from Asia (Lederberg, Shope & Oaks, 1992). The bacteria rapidly contaminated fish and shellfish in the harbour, trigging the most explosive cholera epidemic since the 1961 seventh pandemic in Sulawesi, Indonesia. However, evidence suggests that the near simultaneous appearance of cholera along the near 2000 km Peruvian coastline would not have occurred, had *V. cholerae*-infested plankton blooms not also been notably present in the area at the same time astating effects of cholera prompted the Mexican Government to undertake widespread chlorination of water for human consumption and prohibit use of sewage water for irrigating fruit and vegetables. The annual mean number of diarrhoeal episodes among under five-year olds decreased from 4.5 to 2.2 between 1991 and 1993, and the corresponding mortality rate fell from 102 to 63 per 100 000 (Gutiérrez et al., 1996). The usual summer peak in mortality was not observed during these years, leading investigators to conclude that improved sanitation had decreased the incidence of bacterial infections, but not of rotavirus, which more frequently occurs during winter months.

A 6.4% reduction per year in childhood diarrhoeal disease mortality rates had already been reported in Mexico before these environmental sanitation measures were introduced (**Fig. 5.3**). It has been ascribed to the implementation of a nationwide programme promoting oral rehydration therapy (ORT) in 1984.

Each diarrhoeal pathogen is associated with specific environmental routes and conditions. Environmental conditions are most in evidence when transmission occurs via the faecal–oral route (see Section 4.3). A number of studies have focused on how improving environmental conditions can reduce incidence of diarrhoeal diseases among children under 5 years old. But the success of intervention projects aimed at improving provision of clean water supplies and excreta disposal facilities has varied considerably. Analysing the impact of such interventions, Esrey et al. (1991) estimated, from 19 studies considered to have followed a rigorous methodology, a median reduction of 26% (range 0–68%) in diarrhoea morbidity in this age group. Data from another three studies, not considered rigorous, indicated a median reduction of 65% (range 43–79%) in diarrhoea mortality (see **Table 4.13**).

The range of impact seen is perhaps not surprising given the variability in the types of intervention and the different settings in which the projects studied took place. In an earlier review, Esrey, Feachem & Hughes (1985) presented data which suggested that improvements in water quantity and in excreta disposal facilities may be more important than improvements in water quality. This pattern was less clear in their later review (Esrey et al., 1991), although it has been observed when comparisons have been made of sub-groups within a study (Victora et al., 1988; Aziz et al., 1990; Daniels et al., 1990; Gorter et al., 1991; Huttly et al., 1990).

A recent analysis of data from demographic and health surveys conducted in 8 countries demonstrated that improvements in sanitation had a greater impact on diarrhoea prevalence than improvements in water (Esrey, 1996). The provision of sufficient amounts of water for good hygiene practices may be as or more important than simply providing good-quality water. Installation of sanitary hardware such as boreholes and latrines should be combined with appropriate promotion of the use of these facilities and relevant behaviours (see Sections 3.2 and 4.3). But to be effective these actions should be part of large-scale efforts to improve socioeconomic and environmental conditions (Timaeus & Lush, 1995)

In developed regions of the world, contaminated food is probably the major transmission route for sporadic diarrhoea outbreaks, particularly in institutions. Concern has been expressed that increased consumption of processed foods and use of ever-more sophisticated food processing technologies will cause diarrhoeal disease incidence to increase, as has been observed for salmonella infections (**Fig. 5.4**). Improved reporting is believed to be contributing to this trend, however, making quantification of the real increase difficult.

Contaminated municipal water-supply systems are another major source of diarrhoeal diseases in devel-

Fig. 5.4

Incidence of salmonellosis — 1970–1995

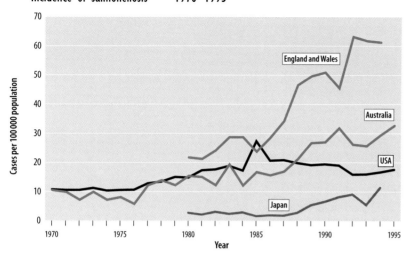

Source: WHO Programme on Food Safety.

oped regions. In 1993, for example, the USA suffered the biggest outbreak of diarrhoea in its history when more than 400 000 people in the city of Milwaukee became ill with watery diarrhoea for an average of 10 days (MacKenzie et al., 1994; Solo-Gabriele & Neuneister, 1996). The cause of this outbreak was infection with the parasite *Cryptosporidium parvum*. Commonly found in cows and their excreta, this parasite was washed into the river system by a particularly heavy flood. (Climatologists believe that this and other unusual weather events that occurred during 1986–1995 are attributable to global climate change (see also Section 4.9.2).) The small size of the *Cryptosporidium* cyst enables it to pass through most filtration systems. Moreover, it is resistant to chlorine disinfection (see also Section 4.4).

5.4 Vaccine-preventable infections diseases

5.4.1 When immunization helps stop environmental transmission

The major vaccine-preventable diseases (measles, neonatal tetanus, poliomyelitis, diphtheria and pertussis) account for nearly 15% of the total disease burden of the 0–4 age group (Murray & Lopez, 1996b). But, in common with ARI, incidence varies dramatically between the world's regions (see Section 5.2). Most of the disease burden occurs in developing countries. The number of DALYs per capita for the least developed countries is about 500 times greater than for developed countries (Murray & Lopez, 1996b). Measles accounts for slightly over 50% of this disease burden, followed by tetanus and pertussis, at 25% and 19% respectively.

All of these diseases have been included in national immunization programmes. Progress in immunizing the world's children has been rapid since the inception of the WHO Expanded Programme on Immuni-zation in 1974 (WHO, 1997a). However, the transmission of these diseases — especially measles, tetanus and poliomyelitis — is associated with poor living conditions, crowding and other environmental factors. Effective and sustainable elimination of these diseases will therefore depend on both immunization and environmental improvements. It is estimated that environmental improvements could contribute 10% of the potential reduction in the global burden of these diseases (see Section 5.13), taking into account the effectiveness of immunization programmes. We have included a brief description of some vaccine-preventable diseases in this book to highlight the fact that the distribution of many of them is associated with environmental conditions, and that vaccinations are often effective but not the only method available for controlling them.

5.4.2 Measles

Measles is a highly infectious viral disease transmitted via droplets produced by the cough or sneeze of an infected individual. An extremely small dose of virus particles in air is sufficient for transmission. Its spread is therefore facilitated in places, such as schools, crowded living quarters and even hospitals where people congregate in close proximity.

Before cities were established (3–4000 years ago), the measles virus was restricted to hunter-gatherers who roamed in search of food. The virus would have been transmitted only if an infected group met another group within the virus period of infectivity (around 14 days). However, the emergence of urban settlements changed this dynamic and facilitated rapid transmission. Urban populations would have been constantly replenished by non-immune individuals, either from the cohort of newborns, or from the constant stream of visitors from other cities or outlying country areas.

The poor in developing countries continue to be at risk. They live close together and have very limited access to health services, particularly immunization services. Many children are therefore not immunized and the cycle of infection thus maintained. Research has shown that a child who goes to market on his or her mother's back can become infected even if exposed only briefly (Aaby et al., 1988). On returning home, the infected child may sleep close to siblings and even neighbours' children, ensuring their prolonged exposure to the virus throughout the night. In this setting, all children not previously infected are likely to contract the disease. Also, because they are exposed to a much higher infecting dose than was the primary case, they may suffer a worse, perhaps lethal attack of the disease. Crowding and poor living conditions are clearly key environmental factors contributing to the spread of the disease (Byass et al., 1995).

Thus although better housing and sanitation have contributed to reduction of measles incidence, they are not sufficient in themselves to eradicate this disease. Massive investment in vaccine and immunization services is also necessary. Increasing coverage with measles vaccine has already led to a steady decline in disease incidence

(**Fig. 5.5**). Indeed, because of the virus' ability to seek and infect non-immune individuals, no country has made progress in measles control without use of the vaccine.

5.4.3 Neonatal tetanus

Neonatal tetanus (NT) is caused by the toxin of tetanus spores living in anaerobic conditions in damaged or dying tissue such as the umbilical cord. Contamination of tissue occurs after contact with soil or animal droppings containing the spores. Once a widespread disease among newborns, the bulk of NT cases in the world now occurs in areas where most babies are born in non-sterile conditions at home.

Tetanus spores will always be with us and if domesticated animals are present, the risk increases. Efforts to eliminate spores from the environment would therefore be impractical. Instead, preventive measures must aim to prevent contamination of the umbilical cord through improved hygiene, and to protect the newborn child with antibodies generated through tetanus toxoid immunization of the mother and passed across the placenta before birth.

Fig. 5.5

Global immunization coverage of measles vaccine and numbers of reported measles cases — 1983–1995

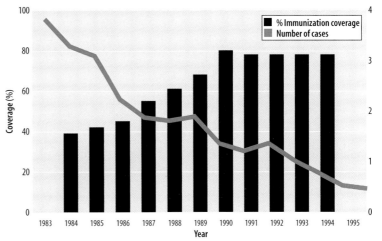

Source: *WHO Global Programme for Vaccines and Immunization.*

Fig. 5.6

Global annual reported polio cases — 1988–1996*

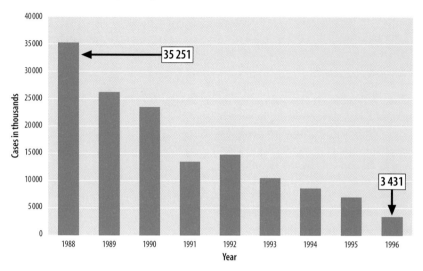

* 1996 data received as of 11 April 1997

Source: WHO Global Programme for Vaccines and Immunization.

5.4.4 Poliomyelitis

Poliomyelitis (commonly known as polio), like the diarrhoeal diseases, is essentially transmitted via the faecal–oral route. Unsafe drinking-water and poor sanitation promote its spread. Starting as an infection of the intestines, the polio virus can also infect the spinal cord and cause permanent paralysis, most often in the legs. The majority of polio cases occur in children under 5 years of age.

Polio was a problem worldwide until the 1960s. Development of an effective vaccine in the 1950s and its use for mass vaccination have since virtually eliminated polio in developed countries. Provision of adequate sanitation and clean drinking-water have also contributed to the reduction of disease incidence, but are not sufficient to ensure eradication. Global polio eradication is feasible, though, because the virus which causes polio affects only humans, immunity is lifelong, and there are no long-lasting environmental sources of polio virus. In 1988, the World Health Assembly designated the eradication of polio by the year 2000 as one of its main targets. This target was endorsed subsequently by the World Summit for

Children in 1990 (UNICEF, 1990b). Remarkable progress towards that goal has been made, to the extent that the target will be met in the year 2000 (**Fig. 5.6**).

5.4.5 Other vaccine-preventable diseases

A few other vaccine-preventable infectious diseases will be mentioned here briefly as their causation is associated with environmental and living conditions.

By the middle of the 20th Century tuberculosis was well on the decline in developed countries, and without much assistance from a vaccine or drugs. Improved housing conditions (see Section 4.7) and diet were undoubtedly the key factors in this fall in incidence. Control of the disease cannot be achieved by environmental improvements alone, however. Vaccination and effective treatment are therefore particularly important among poor communities in developing countries where the disease remains a major health problem (Rodriguez & Smith, 1990). WHO has launched a global strategy to promote "directly-observed treatment, short-course" (DOTS) as a means of ensuring that each patient receives effective treatment and that the spread of the disease is halted (WHO, 1995x). The disease's recent resurgence has been largely due to the emergence of HIV infection (Anon, 1995).

Pertussis and diphtheria, while declining in prevalence before widespread use of vaccines, also declined dramatically in incidence in developed countries once high vaccine coverage had been achieved.

In the former USSR, diphtheria control has recently broken down, resulting in massive outbreaks, death and disability (WHO, 1996a). The fall-off in vaccine administration following political upheaval in the early 1990s is to blame. So even though improved living conditions and better health services have contributed significantly to diphtheria control, vaccination remains the most important factor in eliminating this disease.

Meningococcal meningitis is another example of a disease which has been controlled partly by improving environmental conditions, but largely by administration of the vaccine. It was traditionally known as a disease acquired by young adults in dormitories and military barracks. Improved sleeping conditions and nutrition helped to reduce high mortality from the bacterium and further progress in protection was made with development of the vaccine. Epidemics of the disease continue to occur, however, particularly in developing countries (WHO, 1996a). Modern outbreak control consists of a combined approach of vaccine administration to the surrounding population and chemotherapy. Mass vaccination is the only practical option in developing countries in areas such as the sub-Saharan "meningitis belt", although the vaccines are not very effective in the first two years of life (WHO, 1996a).

5.5 Malaria, other tropical vector-borne diseases, and newly-emerging diseases

5.5.1 Debilitating diseases related to climate and ecological conditions

Malaria is the only tropical vector-borne disease significant enough at the global level to feature in the DALY-estimated burden of diseases (**Table 5.2**). However, other vector-borne diseases are important in specific situations and share similar environmental predispositions with malaria. They are accordingly included in this discussion. Newly-emerging diseases are also addressed since many of them are of animal origin, and their epidemiology resembles that of some of the older vector-borne diseases, particularly yellow fever and dengue haemorrhagic fever.

While about two-thirds of the malaria-associated global disease bur-

den occurs in the 0–4 age group, 95% of the burden of the other tropical vector-borne diseases occurs in the 5 years and over age group. The geographical distribution of their burden is another distinguishing feature of this group of diseases (**Table 5.4**). The African form of trypanosomiasis (sleeping sickness) is only found in sub-Saharan Africa. Its South American form (Chagas disease) is found only in South America. Onchocerciasis (river blindness) is an almost exclusively African disease, while malaria and schistosomiasis occur mostly in sub-Saharan Africa. Leishmaniasis and dengue are mostly diseases of the Indian sub-continent (Murray & Lopez, 1996b).

The environment plays a particularly important role in determining the distribution of vector-borne diseases (WHO, 1997h) (see Sections 3.3 and 4.4). In addition to water and temperature, other factors such as humidity, vegetation density, patterns of crop cultivation and housing may be critical to the survival of the different species of disease-carrying vector. All of these diseases are most serious in the poorest countries, and among those living in the most difficult and impoverished conditions. They contribute to a vicious circle of disease–poverty–disease and to the continued marginalization of peoples living in disease-ridden areas.

Increased risk for any of the tropical vector-borne diseases is directly linked to increased exposure to disease-carrying vectors which may, in turn, be due to a variety of economic, environmental and sociocultural factors. Several of these factors may act in concert. For example, activities associated with exploitation of natural resources and changed land use often bring human populations into more direct contact with vectors, and may also render environmental conditions more favourable for vector-breeding and survival. Urban slums are also associated with environmental changes that contribute to the spread of vector-borne disease. But there are many vector-borne diseases, and for each one, several vectors may be involved, each with different behavioural characteristics. Precise identification of the relevant enviromental changes is therefore extremely difficult. It is thus particularly important that disease surveillance systems monitor those environmental factors that determine where risks are greatest, so that timely, preventive and cost-effective control measures can be carried out.

5.5.2 Malaria

Globally, the malaria situation is serious and worsening. Global malaria mortality is estimated at 1.5–2.7 million and global malaria morbidity at 300–500 million; slightly more than 2000 million people are at risk (WHO, 1997h). The estimate used in the DALY calculations (856 000 deaths, Murray & Lopez, 1996b) is lower as efforts were

made to adjust the numbers of deaths in children for other common causes (see Section 5.1). The difference between the two sets of figures highlights the uncertainty of the global numbers in **Table 5.1**.

There are several epidemiological "types" of malaria: dry savanna and desert fringe malaria, forest malaria, urban and peri-urban malaria, (**Fig. 5.7**). These types differ sufficiently to call for different disease management and prevention measures (Najera, Liese & Hammer, 1992).

Around 90% of the malaria burden is estimated to occur in Africa, south of the Sahara, almost all due to *Plasmodium falciparum*, the parasite species associated with the most severe and fatal malaria (Najera & Hempel, 1996). Malaria is one of the most serious health problems facing African countries and a major obstacle to their social and eco-

Fig. 5.7

Main areas of malaria transmission worldwide

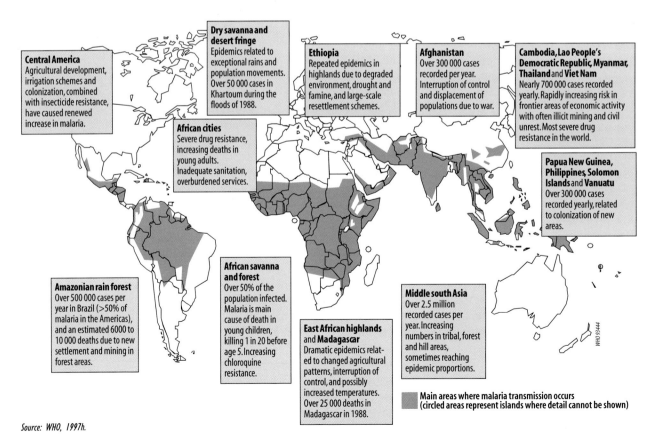

Central America
Agricultural development, irrigation schemes and colonization, combined with insecticide resistance, have caused renewed increase in malaria.

Dry savanna and desert fringe
Epidemics related to exceptional rains and population movements. Over 50 000 cases in Khartoum during the floods of 1988.

Ethiopia
Repeated epidemics in highlands due to degraded environment, drought and famine, and large-scale resettlement schemes.

Afghanistan
Over 300 000 cases recorded per year. Interruption of control and displacement of populations due to war.

Cambodia, Lao People's Democratic Republic, Myanmar, Thailand and **Viet Nam**
Nearly 700 000 cases recorded yearly. Rapidly increasing risk in frontier areas of economic activity with often illicit mining and civil unrest. Most severe drug resistance in the world.

African cities
Severe drug resistance, increasing deaths in young adults. Inadequate sanitation, overburdened services.

Papua New Guinea, Philippines, Solomon Islands and **Vanuatu**
Over 300 000 cases recorded yearly, related to colonization of new areas.

Amazonian rain forest
Over 500 000 cases per year in Brazil (>50% of malaria in the Americas), and an estimated 6000 to 10 000 deaths due to new settlement and mining in forest areas.

African savanna and forest
Over 50% of the population infected. Malaria is main cause of death in young children, killing 1 in 20 before age 5. Increasing chloroquine resistance.

East African highlands and **Madagascar**
Dramatic epidemics related to changed agricultural patterns, interruption of control, and possibly increased temperatures. Over 25 000 deaths in Madagascar in 1988.

Middle south Asia
Over 2.5 million recorded cases per year. Increasing numbers in tribal, forest and hill areas, sometimes reaching epidemic proportions.

Main areas where malaria transmission occurs (circled areas represent islands where detail cannot be shown)

WHO 93444

Source: WHO, 1997h.

nomic development. Children under the age of five years and women in their first pregnancy are the most vulnerable. Approximately 1 million deaths among children under 5 years of age can be attributed to malaria alone or in combination with other diseases.

Deaths from malaria in other areas of the world occur principally among non-immune people who become infected with *P. falciparum* malaria in areas where appropriate diagnosis and treatment are not available (**Fig. 5.7**). This includes agricultural workers, labourers, gold and gem miners, and refugees and displaced populations from non-endemic regions who settle in malarious areas (Najera & Hempel, 1996). Military conflicts and civil unrest have contributed substantially to the burden of malaria since they have resulted in the movement into malarious areas of large numbers of unprotected and non-immune people. Young adults are most severely affected, although in the case of refugees and settlers, whole families can be exposed.

In new agricultural colonies in forest areas in the Amazon basin and in South-East Asia, malaria has contributed to economic failure (UNEP, 1993). This is because it diminishes the working capacity of those who are not killed by the disease. Additionally, high transportation costs render treatment very expensive, effectively depriving colonists of much needed cash for basic needs (Najera, 1992).

Another disquieting problem is the re-emergence of malaria in areas from which it had been practically eradicated, namely Azerbaijan and Tajikistan. Malaria epidemics have also occurred in areas where malaria was previously well under control, namely Iraq and Turkey. The current malaria epidemics in these countries are the result of a rapid deterioration in malaria prevention and control operations due to military conflicts followed by economic crisis.

The malaria picture is not promising. Over the last 25 years malaria prevention efforts have stagnated in many malarious areas and the number of "hot spots" (**Fig. 5.7**) has grown. A Global Malaria Control Strategy was adopted in 1992 to remedy this situation. It emphasizes the strengthening of local and national capacity to analyse distribution and incidence of malaria, to plan, implement and evaluate environmental and other control interventions, and to contribute to the development of local health services (Litsios, 1996).

As nearly all malaria is associated with environmental conditions, including land and water management, we estimate that 90% of the global burden of this disease is attributable to environmental factors.

5.5.3 Other vector-borne diseases

Of all the insects that transmit disease, the mosquito represents by far the greatest human health threat. It transmits not only malaria, but also dengue and dengue haemorrhagic fever, and lymphatic filariasis (**Table 5.4**). Diseases transmitted by other insects include leishmaniasis (sandfly), African trypanosomiasis (tsetse fly), onchocerciasis (blackfly), and Chagas disease (triatomine bug). Schistosomiasis is caused by infection with blood flukes, whose larval stage develops in aquatic snails; the parasite penetrates the skin of anyone who comes into contact with infested water. Among the driving forces and pressures considered in earlier chapters, those of greatest relevance to these diseases are rapid and uncontrolled urbanization, poor housing and hygiene, water development schemes (including irrigation for agriculture), and road construction and mining activities.

Rapid urbanization inevitably creates ideal vector-breeding conditions for a wide range of insects, particularly those carrying dengue and yellow fever virus. Should the yellow fever virus be introduced into a human population and transmission initiated, thousands of cases and deaths can occur, even if a protective vaccine is available (WHO, 1996a). The huge increase that has occurred during the past 15 years in the incidence of dengue haemorrhagic fever, and in the frequency of dengue epidemics, is particularly noteworthy. Lack of effective mosquito control, changing lifestyles and adverse water-storage practices have allowed the dengue vectors to expand their distribution. Dengue vectors are also found in countries from which they had previously been eradicated or in which they were previously effectively controlled. Furthermore, increased movement of people and mosquito vectors due to air travel has led to increased movement of dengue viruses and vectors between countries (Gratz & Knudsen, 1996). For example, *Ae. albopictus*, a known secondary dengue vector, "hitchhiked" to the USA in 1985 from Japan in a shipment of used tyres. It is now firmly established in much of south-eastern USa (Lederberg, Shope & Oaks).

Populations of *Culex quinquefasciatus* have also increased enormously in many towns and become established in others where this species was previously unknown. The cities of Bangalore and Hyderabad in India, for example, were free of filariasis transmission until the early 1960s, at which date sanitation and sewerage facilities ceased to keep pace with the rapidly increasing number of people, resulting in an invasion of *C. quinquefasciatus* and the introduction of filariasis. Urbanization has also caused this vector to become the dominant human-biting mosquito in many towns in both East and West Africa. As a result, bancroftian filariasis — transmitted by the *Anopheles gambiae* complex and previously a mainly rural disease — has become a major urban disease (Service, 1989).

Poor housing and hygiene can also enhance vector-breeding potential (see Section 4.7), which can play a direct role in the risk of infection. For example, triatomine bugs, which are vectors for Chagas disease, favour crevices in the walls of poor-quality houses in rural areas and peri-urban slums as habitat (WHO, 1997m).

Water development projects, especially those associated with irrigation of large areas, have often been associated with increased incidence of schistosomiasis, malaria, and to a lesser degree, the leishmaniasis and filarial diseases (see Section 4.4). Intestinal schistosomiasis was unknown or infrequent in the Nile, Senegal and Volta Deltas before the construction of the Aswan, Diama and Alosombo upstream dams. Within 10 years of the dams' construction, however, prevalence of intestinal schistosomiasis had reached up to 75% in villages in these deltas, with high morbidity rates in heavily infected children.

The opening up of new areas and road construction also frequently create highly suitable aquatic habitats for various mosquito species and snail intermediate hosts of schistosomiasis. Roads that cut through disease-endemic areas place non-endemic workers at high risk. Similarly, the exploitation of mineral deposits may expose workers to vector-borne infections. In South America, leishmaniasis is regarded as an occupational disease of forest workers engaged in clearing forests for road building, timber, agricultural or mining purposes. Records show that a new case of leishmaniasis occurs for every kilometre of road constructed to extract iron ore from Brazilian tropical forest (Service, 1989).

5.5.4 Emerging infectious diseases: surveillance needed

The appearance of previously unknown infectious diseases (such as AIDS, Ebola, and Creutzfeldt-Jakob disease in humans) has focused attention on emerging diseases and led to a call for drastically improved international epidemic surveillance and control programmes. With the exception of AIDS, none of the newly-emerging diseases currently contributes significantly to the global disease burden. Nevertheless, the potential for these diseases to do so exists and since they are very closely linked to changing environmental conditions of one kind or another, their inclusion in this discussion was felt to be necessary.

During the past 20 years, at least 30 new diseases have emerged to threaten the health of hundreds of millions of people (WHO, 1996a). Environmental changes have contributed in one way or another to the appearance of most if not all of these. Human activity, such as the cutting down of forests or conversion of grasslands to agricultural lands, has contributed to such change. In other instances, simple behavioural changes have favoured the emergence of a disease pathogen: for example, new and widespread vector-breeding sites in urban environments have been created through careless disposal of food and beverage containers, and motor vehicle tyres.

Outbreaks of haemorrhagic fever bear witness to the fact that more and more local disease outbreaks are occurring. Individually, the latter do not involve great numbers of people. But in totality they are gaining steadily in recognized importance (WHO, 1996a). The outbreak of a severe haemorrhagic illness in Venezuela in late 1989 was first thought to be an outbreak of dengue haemorrhagic fever. The etiologic agent was named "Guanarito virus" after the municipality where the outbreak first occurred. Chronically infected cotton rats are believed to serve as the source of infection for humans. In this instance, land-use changes, including clearance of forest for agriculture, which provided more favourable habitats and food sources for rats, and influxes of seasonal workers, combined to create the ideal conditions for an outbreak (Tesh, 1994).

Previous outbreaks of other forms of haemorrhagic fever in Latin America provide further evidence of how land-use changes can cause an increase in the local rodent population and in human disease incidence. For example, after World War II, farmers in Argentina, having long experienced

great difficulty in growing profitable corn crops, used herbicides to eliminate weeds. However, taller grasses whose seeds serve as a food source for a native mouse species also profited. Mouse populations grew and were the source of an outbreak of Argentine haemorrhagic fever near the Junin river in 1955. The "Junin virus" is transmitted via the mouse's urine. Airborne transmission may also occur via dust contaminated with infected rodent excreta (Garrett, 1994).

In the past 35 years the area infected with Argentine haemorrhagic fever has expanded from 15 000 km^2 to around 102 000 km^2, commensurate with the regions undergoing agricultural development. More than 20 000 people have suffered acute Junin fever since its discovery. Between 3 and 600 cases occur annually, with a case-fatality rate as high as 30% of all infected people. Recently, however, a live, attenuated vaccine has been developed and shown to be efficacious (Garrett, 1994).

Another virus group consisting of hantaviruses is also found in a number of different rodents. In addition to causing acute illness, exposure to rodent-transmitted hantaviruses has been shown to be associated with the subsequent development of chronic renal disease, specifically hypertensive renal disease (LeDuc, Childs & Glass, 1992; Weiss, 1993).

5.6 Injuries and poisonings

5.6.1 Major causes of ill health in both children and adults

Injuries are one of the largest contributors to YLL and disability at the global level (**Table 5.2**). They are of great importance in developed and developing countries alike, but the categories of injury shift with development. Agricultural injuries, fires, drownings and war-related violence dominate at early stages of economic development, while road-traffic accidents and industrial injuries appear to increase with economic development.

The impact of injuries on communities and economies is profound. Since they tend to be concentrated among people between the ages of 1 and 45, and can result in long-term disability, they affect productivity severely, particularly among the lowest income groups, whose exposure to risk is greatest and whose earning capacity is most likely to rely on physical activity.

Two broad categories of injury can be described:

- **unintentional injuries** such as those caused by road-traffic accidents, poisoning, fires, falls, drowning, natural disasters and those sustained in the workplace

- **intentional injuries** such as suicide, homicide, rape, battering, child abuse and war-related violence.

As shown in **Table 5.3**, injuries were by far the leading contributor to global DALYs in 1990, accounting for around 19% of the global DALY burden for males and 11% for females (Murray & Lopez, 1996b). **Table 5.5** indicates the types of injury that appear to be increasing in importance. "Intentional injuries" are markedly on the rise,

whereas among "unintentional injuries", road-traffic accidents are the sole category projected to increase by the year 2020.

Many people consider accidents that cause injuries to be chance occurrences that can neither be predicted nor prevented. In fact, most injuries are associated with environmental factors or "accident hazards" that are either necessary for the injury to occur or contribute significantly to the risk of injury. In other words, most injuries could be prevented. For instance, injuries due to the collapse of poorly constructed housing in slum areas could be prevented by improving town planning and housing quality (see Section 4.7). Similarly, many slum areas are located on land that is very steep or that is prone to flooding and landslides. Such environmental conditions increase the likelihood of injury substantially yet could be avoided. Other environmental factors responsible for injury include poorly designed domestic stoves that enormously increase the risk of burns, particularly in children. Environmental factors that play a role in the risk of road-traffic accidents, occupational accidents and poisonings can also be identified. Overall it is estimated that about 30% of the global burden of unintentional injuries is associated with environmental factors (see Section 5.13).

5.6.2 Road-traffic accidents: a major health problem

Transport is an important part of the economy in many countries. But it exacts a high price from society and the environment. Road-traffic accidents, for instance, are the most important cause of unintentional injury (**Table 5.5**) and a major health problem worldwide: in 1990 they accounted for almost as much loss of healthy life as tuberculosis, and ranked ninth among all causes of disease and injury burden (Murray & Lopez, 1996b). In 1993 they caused an estimated 885 000 deaths (WHO, 1995a).

Table 5.5

Injuries as percentage of global burden of disease — 1990 and 2020

	1990 All	Male	Female	2020 All	Male	Female
Global burden of disease (DALYs)	1 379 238	722 032	657 206	1 388 836	592 692	796 144
All injuries (DALYs)	208 647	135 231	73 415	279 559	183 673	95 886
All injuries (% of global DALYs)	15.1	18.7	11.2	20.1	23	16.2
Unintentional injuries	11	13.8	8	13	15.1	10.3
Road-traffic accidents	2.5	3.5	1.4	5.1	6.2	3.6
Poisoning	0.5	0.5	0.4	0.5	0.5	0.5
Falls	1.9	2.3	1.5	1.5	1.6	1.5
Fires	0.9	0.7	1.1	0.8	0.6	1.1
Drowning	1.1	1.4	0.8	0.9	1.1	0.7
Other unintentional injuries	4.1	5.4	2.8	4.2	5.1	2.9
Intentional injuries	4.1	4.9	3.2	7.1	8	5.9
Self-inflicted injuries	1.4	1.4	1.3	1.9	1.8	2
Violence	1.3	1.9	0.6	2.3	3.2	1
War	1.5	1.6	1.3	3	3	2.9

Sources: Murray & Lopez, 1996b; WHO, 1996d.

Mortality rates per vehicle are highest at periods of rapidly increasing use and then typically decline as investments are made in better roads, and safety promotion leads to increased safety consciousness, better traffic awareness and use of more roadworthy vehicles (**Fig. 5.8**). In developing countries as a whole, there are on average about 3 motor vehicles for every 100 people; in the industrialized countries there are about 50 motor vehicles for every 100 people. But in 1990, the burden of disease from road-traffic accidents in sub-Saharan Africa was fully half as much as that in the established market economies (Murray & Lopez, 1996b), even though Africa would have to increase its vehicle numbers 17-fold to reach developed-country levels of ownership. The most vulnerable countries are therefore those low- and middle-income countries whose road networks and levels of vehicle ownership are growing fast (WHO, 1989c).

Box 5.2 describes the increased vulnerability of pedestrians and cyclists in countries where the number of motor vehicles (cars, buses, lorries) is increasing rapidly (**Box 5.2**). Greater consideration of traffic safety in the development of roads in both rural and urban areas is clearly needed. Traffic accident injuries could otherwise become a major burden on hospitals and health services in these countries.

5.6.3 Occupational accidents: considerable under-reporting

Mechanical hazards and other exposures that can lead to injuries are common in many workplaces, in developed and developing countries (see Section 4.8). Occupational injuries are major contributors to the global burden of unintentional injuries. ILO estimates that at least 220 000 fatalities due to occupational injuries occur each year (ILO, 1997), but this estimate is based

Fig. 5.8

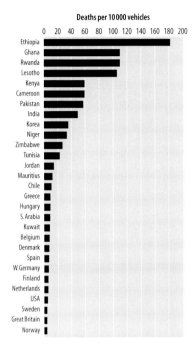

Road-traffic accident fatalities (deaths per 10 000 vehicles) in selected countries — 1990

Source: Jacobs, 1997.

Table 5.6

Occupational injury fatality rates (per 100 000 workers) for all industries

	United Kingdom	Slovenia	Zimbabwe	Thailand
1986	1.7	6.1	26	31
1990	1.6	1.6	6.4	21
1994	1.0	1.0	3.2	19

Source: ILO, 1996.

on official reports which often exclude injuries in the informal sector and injuries in people without insurance cover. The under-reporting is likely to be greatest in developing countries. For those developing countries who do report data to ILO, the occupational injury mortality rates are often 10 times higher than in developed countries (**Table 5.7**). And for each death at work, there may be as many as 600 non-fatal injury and disease cases, giving a global total of more than 125 million per year (see Section 4.8).

The industries with the highest known rates of reported injury are mining, forestry, agriculture, construction and transportation (Kjellström, Koplan & Rothenberg, 1992). Types of injury occurring at work include poisoning, falls, drowning, and other specific categories listed as unintentional injuries in **Table 5.5.** Most of them are likely to be classified in the "other" category, however.

5.6.4 Poisonings: few reliable data

Tens of thousands of human-made chemicals are in common use throughout the world, and each year between 1000 and 2000 new chemicals are introduced into the market. Assessing the contribution of toxic exposures to poisonings in a global context is difficult, but it is known that acute toxic exposures are a primary cause of hospitalization of children in some developed countries (Wiseman et al., 1987). Chronic toxic exposures represent a more serious health threat and may result from the release of toxic chemicals into the environment. These expo-

sures have been linked not only to poisoning, but also to congenital anomalies, cancer, fertility problems, and behavioural and immunological disorders. The global burden of disease due to poisoning was calculated at 0.5% of all DALYs in 1990 (**Table 5.5**), but this is likely to be a significant underestimate since many chronic poisonings are not recorded as such.

Exposure to pesticides is a major cause of poisonings. The use of pesticides has grown considerably during the last 40 years, and with it the number and types of exposure to pesticides (WHO, 1990a). Pesticide poisoning can occur via oral, respiratory or cutaneous routes of exposure, at work or in the home, through accidental or intentional exposure. High morbidity and mortality rates, often exacerbated by inappropriate diagnosis and lack of treatment, have been reported, especially for developing countries.

It is estimated that about 50 million people work on plantations in these countries and are in direct contact with pesticides, while over 500 million more are exposed through other forms of agriculture (WHO, 1990a). Even the "non-exposed" population may suffer toxic effects through exposure to food or water contaminated with pesticides.

Pesticide residues in food can become a serious problem when regulatory controls are not in place. For example, regulations should specify an adequate waiting time after pesticide spraying, otherwise farmers may harvest their crops and take them to market immediately. The pesticide residue levels of such crops are potentially unsafe (WHO, 1990a). Monitoring programmes can guard against such abuse.

Mass poisonings are undoubtedly the most dramatic pesticide-related incidents. Examples include the methyl mercury contamination of grain in Iraq which affected over 6000 people, resulting in 400 deaths (Bakir et al., 1973) and the contamination of food with parathion in Mexico and India which also caused hundreds of deaths (Ferrer &

Cabral, 1989). But even though epidemic and mass pesticide poisonings are reported, few reliable data exist on the epidemiology and real importance of human exposure to pesticides. One report estimated that in small Latin American countries 1000 to 2000 poisoning cases occur every year, with fatality rates varying from 1.5 to 12% (PAHO, 1994). However, it was demonstrated that more than half of pesticide poisonings were intentional (mainly suicidal), and only 25% occupational or accidental. The ready availability of pesticides and lack of restrictions governing their application contributed to their frequent use in suicide attempts.

Controversy thus continues about the real extent and severity of the adverse effects of pesticides on human health. Part of the problem lies in the fact that most of the epidemiological data on pesticide poisoning is limited to precise geographical areas and cannot be considered as representative of other regions. To date, global estimates of the annual number of acute pesticide poisonings (e.g. 3 million acute poisonings, WHO, 1990a) have been based on numbers of limited comparability, yet they have been cited repeatedly as no alternative updated information is available. An IPCS working group on harmonized collection of pesticide poisoning data is developing new approaches to fill this information gap.

It should be pointed out that natural toxins occur in foodstuffs under certain conditions and can cause serious poisoning outbreaks. For example weeds growing among staple foods can cause contamination with alkaloids (**Box 5.3**). Other examples relate to algae toxins that accumulate in shellfish, fish and seaweed (CDC, 1995a).

5.6.5 Intentional injuries: violence

Of all the changes in environmental conditions that have taken place in health during the 20th Century, the growth in violence is one of the most complex and far-reaching. From both an individual and a public health perspective its burden has increased dramatically, affecting not only the well-being of those involved, but also the health services called on to provide care and treatment. The growing problem of violence now also threatens family welfare, community cohesion and the capacity of societies to move towards better health and sustainable social development.

> **Box 5.3**
> ### Mass poisoning due to contaminated staple food
>
> In March 1993, 4000 cases of liver toxicity were reported in the south of Tajikistan and traced to consumption of bread made with contaminated flour. The wheat harvest that year had been delayed by two months. During this time a weed rich in pyrrolizidine alkaloids (*Heliotropium lasiocarpum*) had grown up among wheat crops. Its seeds were then harvested together with wheat. Contaminated wheat was then used to make bread and about six weeks later, the first case of liver toxicity occurred. Fortunately, most of those affected (55%) recovered rapidly. However, hepatomegaly developed in 30% of cases and ascites in a further 14%. The extent of the outbreak meant that health facilities, which were already barely adequate, became severely strained.
>
> Plant pyrrolizidine alkaloids are found in most environments in all parts of the world and have been known since the turn of the century to represent a health hazard for livestock. In the 1930s, pyrrolizidine alkaloid toxicity in humans was identified as endemic in the central Asian republics. Recent studies undertaken in Afghanistan and India have shown that poisoning caused by pyrrolizidine alkaloids has affected significant numbers of people and resulted in high mortality. Accidental contamination of staple food crops — especially following periods of drought — combined with periods when civil unrest precluded normal grain inspections and application of regulations, appear to have been the major factors in such poisoning. More generally, contamination of food crops is likely to occur in parts of the world with arid climates and low rainfall, and irrigated agriculture. Health services are often poorly developed in the areas affected and many individual cases or even outbreaks may go unnoticed or unrecorded, or be mistakenly ascribed to malnutrition.
>
> Prevention of foodborne pyrrolizidine poisoning depends on reducing or eliminating ingestion of the alkaloids. Effective procedures include control of the pyrrolizidine alkaloid-containing plants in agricultural areas, and educational programmes targeted at the populations at risk. In Uzbekistan, a state standard has been set for wheat grain quality and wheat grain must be certified by the state seed inspectorate. In addition, the sowing of wheat, rye, barley or oats contaminated by *Heliotropium* seeds or *Trichodesma* plants has been prohibited. State standards have also been set pertaining to the quality of grain stored for food; the pyrrolyzidine alkaloid level must not exceed 0.2%.
>
> *Sources: IPCS, 1988; WHO Programme on Chemical Safety, 1993 (unpublished information).*

Box 5.4

Landmines: economic, social and humanitarian costs

Currently more than 100 million land mines have been laid in around 60 countries. In 20 of these — most of them in the developing world — the level of mine infestation is such that it hinders development, farming, commerce, transport and recreation. Estimates indicate that up to 30 million land mines have been laid in Africa, and that at least 3 million have been laid since 1989 in former Yugoslavia. More than 250 million land mines have been manufactured during the past 25 years; anti-personnel mines continue to be made at an average rate of 5–10 million per year.

The UN estimates that 80 000 mines were cleared in 1993, but that many more are laid each year. A basic anti-personnel mine may cost a mere US$ 3, but clearing it may cost as much as US$ 200–1000. Work is under way on new detection and clearing methods, but so far none have come close to a 100% detection rate when used in the field.

Landmines cause around 26 000 deaths or injuries per year. The victims are usually civilian and often children. Many are disabled, representing a huge need for rehabilitation services. In Cambodia, 1 out of every 236 people is a mine amputee; the number is 1 in 470 in Angola and 1 in 1000 in northern Somalia. Aside from the humanitarian cost, land mines cause scarce public health resources to be diverted from primary medical care and preventive programmes to expensive, time-consuming surgical care.

Landmines also result in loss of productive human labour, and create an intolerable environment; in some areas parents find it necessary to tie their children to trees. There are other social and economic costs. For instance, the presence or fear of landmines means that almost half the land area of Cambodia is unsafe for farming or any other human use. Angola has also suffered a massive loss of arable land. In Afghanistan, about 3.5 million refugees are unable to return home because mountain roads and fields are infested with mines. In southern Sudan agricultural production is similarly paralysed. In all mined countries, power plants, transportation centres, water supplies, and other essential services are primary mining targets, leading to the weakening and potential collapse of the basic infrastructure of society, and making economic independence even more difficult to attain.

Sources: Cahill, 1995; Kakar, 1995; Anon, 1996b; Sivard, 1996.

Violence is influenced largely by social and economic conditions. Periods of social and economic transition are therefore often witness to increases in levels of violence, particularly levels of violent crime. In the USA, rates of violent death peaked in the 1930s, dipped dramatically in the early 1900s and the 1960s, and have once again risen to high levels (WHO, 1996d). Increasing violence has also been a feature of recent social and economic upheaval in the former socialist economies.

Violent crime is often linked to other types of crime. When drug trafficking became a serious problem in Colombia, the homicide rate rose considerably — from around 20 to more than 50 per 100 000 inhabitants in 1987. In South Africa, the national rate of homicide peaked in 1993 at around 90 per 100 000, but nevertheless was still as high as 85 per 100 000 in 1994. These rates are among the highest in the world (WHO, 1996d). More than half the world's population living in cities with 100 000 or more inhabitants are victims of a crime of some kind at least once every five years. Crime rates are particularly high in the cities of Africa and North and South America. Violent crime has increased in most cities in recent years and usually accounts for between 25% and 30% of all urban crimes (Zvekic & Alvazzi del Frate, 1995). It includes murder (or homicide), infanticide, assault, rape and sexual abuse and domestic violence.

However, much violent crime is under-reported, in contrast to road-traffic accidents, which, since they are highly visible, are usually reported to police and health services. The bulk of violent crime probably occurs in the home or its immediate surroundings, with children, women and the elderly its principal victims. Domestic violence against women is a particularly serious public health issue to which the health system has been slow to respond. Evidence is increasing that millions of women around the world are subjected to systematic and devastating violence by their partners (WHO 1994h). Worldwide, studies indicate that 20% to over 50% of women have been beaten by an intimate male partner. In the USA, up to one-third of women patients attending hospital emergency departments have injuries sustained during the course of domestic violence. A study in Alexandria, Egypt, showed domestic violence to be the leading cause of injury to women, accounting for 25% of all visits by women to trauma units (WHO 1995v). In developed countries, assaults have been reported to cause more injuries to women than motor vehicle accidents, rape and muggings combined (WHO 1993k).

War-related injuries are another area of increasing concern. They represent not only a direct and avoidable injury burden, but also divert valuable resources from other healthcare needs and from investment in health services. Since the end of the Second World War, at least 25 million people, two-thirds of them civilians, have been killed as a result of more than 400, mostly civil, armed conflicts. In 1990 in sub-Saharan Africa and the Middle Eastern Crescent, more years of healthy life were lost through war than through HIV/AIDS (WHO, 1996d). War is also affecting civilian populations increasingly, for example as a result of injuries caused by landmines (**Box 5.4**). Millions of landmines have been laid in recent wars, principally in Afghanistan, Cambodia, Iraq, Mozambique, Somalia and former Yugoslavia. Removing them could take 40 to 50 years. The indirect effects of war on civilian populations are also serious and include disruption of water supply systems and other environmental services, leading to increased rates of disease.

5.7 Mental health conditions

5.7.1 A growing health concern

Mental disorders comprise a large variety of conditions ranging from mild anxiety and depressive states to severe schizophrenia and dementia. The estimated global prevalence of the main categories of mental disorder is several hundred million cases (**Table 5.7**). Because patients with mental disorders often live with their illness for many years, and because many new cases occur among adults and the elderly, the mental health disease burden is one of disease rather than of death. This is why a very large difference is observable between the YLL

due to death and DALYs shown in **Table 5.2**. Nevertheless, suicide, with about 800 000 cases reported each year, is a major impact of mental illness (WHO, 1995a).

Mental disorders and other psychological problems account for around 11% of the total burden of disease (**Table 5.2**). Those affected are usually more disabled in everyday life than persons with other common chronic conditions such as arthritis, back pain and diabetes. The estimated DALYs per person does not seem to change with economic development (Murray & Lopez, 1996b), but due to the growing proportion of adults and elderly people in developing countries, these countries can be expected to experience a major increase in their total mental health burden. Of this burden, more than one-third is accounted for by unipolar major depression. Projections suggests that by 2020 unipolar major depression will have become the number two contributor to DALYs after ischaemic heart disease (Murray & Lopez, 1996b).

In considering the effects of environment on mental health, chemical and physical factors that influence the body's nervous system, and psychosocial factors that influence mental well-being, must be taken into account. It should be noted, however, that people's perceptions of their environment — as much as or even more than the actual environment itself — can influence mental health. That is, if people perceive their environment to be safe and secure, they are likely to have a better sense of well-being and a higher quality of life.

Overall, it is estimated that only a small component (10%) of the global burden of mental health conditions is associated with environmental factors (see Section 5.13).

5.7.2 Effects of chemical and physical factors

Many commonly occurring substances are known to be neurotoxic and to

Table 5.7

Global prevalence of mental health disorders

480 million cases of anxiety disorders
360 million cases of mood disorders (depression and mania)
250 million cases of personality disorders
60 million cases of mental retardation
45 million cases of epilepsy
29 million cases of dementia
22 million cases of schizophrenia

In relation to substance abuse, there are:
1100 million cases of tobacco dependence
250 million cases of alcohol dependence

Source: WHO Programme on Mental Health, 1996 (unpublished information).

affect both the central and peripheral nervous system. The most relevant of these are listed in **Table 5.8.** These substances can have a variety of health effects, ranging from peripheral neuropathy to dementia. Many of these chemicals occur in the workplace environment, and some, like lead, are found in a variety of exposure situations (see Section 4.10).

Head injury can also lead to mental health problems. Of particular note in this respect are traffic accidents. Despite the mandatory wearing of seat belts and crash-helmets in many countries, this form of injury remains prevalent and the cause of a significant amount of brain damage.

In addition to the effects of chemicals and trauma on the nervous system, attention has been paid to those arising from radiation exposure. These have been studied most recently by WHO (1996j), following the Chernobyl accident. A follow-up study was undertaken of children who were exposed to radiation in utero (in Belarus, Russia and Ukraine) to ascertain whether this exposure has led to any detectable brain damage. The investigation showed that the incidence of mild mental retardation in the group of exposed children was higher than that of the control group, and that an upward trend in behavioural disorders and emotional problems was detectable among children of the exposed group. However, some of these problems may be due to the psychosocial effects of the disaster

rather than to radiation exposure (see below).

5.7.3 Effects of psychosocial factors

Housing and the community environment influence human behaviour and mental health. For example, crime and violence (including arson and littering) and social problems, such as social breakdown, are more frequent in buildings with long internal corridors than in buildings with short external corridors (Newman & Franck, 1981). Additionally, the existence of many intersections, alleys and passageways in urban design is associated with vandalism, shop-lifting and hooliganism, with resulting increases in physical and mental stress-related illness. Such unfavourable design is commonly found in inner cities, but also in out-of-town housing estates and certain "new towns" (Coleman, 1985).

Schools play a particularly important role in children's mental health. The relationship between the psychosocial environment of a school and mental health in children has been studied in many countries, leading to guidance on "child-friendly" schools (WHO, 1997l). The focus is on elimination of violence and promotion of children's self-esteem and self-confidence.

Major technological accidents and natural disasters also constitute "environmental conditions" that can seriously affect the mental health of a population. The adverse effects of the Chernobyl nuclear power plant accident in 1986 were not limited to the direct effects of radiation (WHO, 1996j). It also had severe psychological impacts on the large population residing in the areas affected. Fear of the latent effects of exposure to radiation was exacerbated by the failure of the relevant authorities to provide health information immediately after the accident. Another psychological problem related to the evacuation of people from the most contaminated regions.

Table 5.8

Principal neurotoxic industrial chemicals

Metal	Inorganic chemicals	Organic chemicals	Pesticides	Other organic chemicals
Lead	Carbon monoxide	Toluene	Organophosphorous	Acylamide
Tetraalkyl lead	Hydrogen sulfide	Hexane	Organochlorine	Ethylene oxide
Mercury	Carbon disulfide	Methyl buthyl ketone	Carbamate	o-Phtalodinitrile
Alkyl mercury	Cyanide	Methyl alcohol		Methyl bromide
Arsenic		Methyl acetate		Nitroglycol
Manganese		Trichloroethylene		Triothocrecyl-
Alkyl tin		Styrene		phosphate
Thallium				Nicotine
Tellurium				

Source: WHO, 1997k.

Evacuees often suffer considerable stress because they not only experience disruption of their community infrastructure and social interaction, but must also face uncertainty regarding housing and employment. The immediate psychological impact of the Chernobyl accident on the people in the affected areas was similar to that witnessed following disasters such as earthquakes (WHO, 1996j).

5.8 Cardiovascular diseases

5.8.1 The most common cause of death

As shown in **Table 5.1**, cardiovascular disease (CVD) tops the list of global deaths, whichever estimate is used. Most of the people who die from CVD are elderly. In countries where every death is given an official "cause" in the form of a classification code, elderly people dying of unknown causes are most often classified as having died of heart disease (see Section 5.1).

CVD encompasses coronary heart disease (CHD), other diseases of the heart and heart valves, stroke, and diseases affecting the blood vessels. Its risk factors may be divided into four categories: non-modifiable risk factors (age, sex, race and family history); modifiable physiological risk factors (blood cholesterol, high blood pressure, diabetes and obesity); behavioural risk factors (smoking, diet, alcohol, sedentary lifestyle); and environmental risk factors (air pollution, temperature, heavy metal poisoning, infectious agents). Risk factors in the first three categories, especially diet and smoking, contribute most to the total burden of CVD. The estimated contribution by environmental factors to the global CVD burden is 10% (see Section 5.13).

Incidence, morbidity and mortality of CVD vary considerably. In many Western countries, CHD is the leading cause of mortality, but declining. Overall, however, it is increasing, particularly in Eastern Europe. The age-standardized mortality rates for Poland in

Fig. 5.9

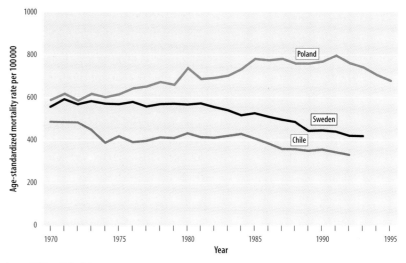

Fig. 5.9

CVD mortality in 3 countries

Source: WHO mortality data.

Fig. 5.9 illustrate this, as do the estimated DALYs per capita in the elderly age group in **Fig. 5.10**. The high burden CVD in the former socialist states of Europe (FSE) has been linked to poor diet and unhealthy lifestyles, as well as to high exposure to urban air pollution (WHO, 1995a). **Fig. 5.10** shows that, with the exception of the FSE countries, the DALYs per capita for this disease are expected to decrease with economic development. For women, the least developed countries have the highest DALY rates (**Fig. 5.10**), which may be partly explained by high exposures to indoor air pollution from biomass and coal combustion (see below).

5.8.2 Social and lifestyle risk factors

In developed countries those who are most deprived suffer most from CVD. Contributory factors include diet, behavioural and lifestyle factors, stress and lack of education. There is also a direct link with unemployment since this can cause considerable stress (Ferrie et al., 1995).

Increasing **urbanization** may be detrimental to cardiovascular health in many ways. In Nairobi, Kenya, people who had moved to the capital to work

Fig. 5.10

CVD among persons aged 60+, by region — DALYs per 1000 persons

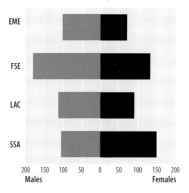

Source: calculated from data in Murray & Lopez, 1996b.

were shown to have developed higher blood pressure within two months of taking up employment (Hutt, 1991). Debate continues as to whether this type of effect is due to changes in diet, lifestyle factors, stress or some other unidentified factor associated with urban life. But all are probably implicated to some extent. A more sedentary lifestyle, which has a moderate association with CHD, may also result from changing job roles, mechanization and cultural change, each of which may accompany urban living.

Quantifying the effect of stress on CVD and separating its effect from other risk factors is difficult, but a study of civil servants in England suggested that a real effect does exist (Ferrie et al, 1995), as did a study undertaken in Taiwan which compared those in a stressful (military) situation with a group for whom other lifestyle and dietary factors were similar (Chen et al., 1995).

Strong evidence exists that **dietary factors** play a central role in CVD and account for much of the variation in disease rates between countries (WHO, 1990b). Thus the risks of CVD are known to be higher for populations whose diets are high in calories, saturated fats, refined sugars and salt, and low in fresh fruit and vegetables. Such diets result in overnourishment and obesity, increase the risk of high blood pressure and diabetes, and lead directly to increases in CVD (WHO, 1990b)

Those from more deprived socioeconomic groups tend to have poorer diets since they often cannot afford to buy nutritious food. Changes in types and quantities of food available and distribution can also play a role in poor diet. For instance, urban populations in developing countries have newly acquired access to heavily marketed "convenience" foods (Hutt, 1991). Similarly, in remote areas such as the Australian outback or the New Guinea Highlands, the few shops in existence often carry cheap staples such as white bread and sugar, which is consumed in

preference to home-grown produce. And in Eastern Europe, recent changes in the economic system have led to the withdrawal of subsidies that supported farming and food production. As a result, supply has diminished, prices have increased, and the consumption of total kilocalories, protein and micronutrients has declined (UNICEF, 1994). These increases in consumption of unhealthy foods have important implications for overall health as well as for CVD.

Tobacco smoking is also strongly associated with CVD. About 12% of CVD mortality in developed countries and 42% in the former socialist countries of Europe is attributable to smoking (Peto et al., 1994). Between 0.5 and 1.5 million of the estimated 3 million deaths a year from tobacco might be CVD deaths (Peto et al., 1994). In Africa, cigarette consumption has increased by over 40% in 20 years as a result of urbanization, acculturation, lifestyle changes and intensive marketing of tobacco products. It is increasing rapidly in other developing regions too (WHO, 1996s). If these trends continue and the prevalence of smoking in developing countries approaches that seen in developed countries, about 500 million of the world's current population may die of a smoking-related illness. Cardiovascular mortality will be a major contributor to this health burden. Other risk factors such as hypertension and high cholesterol enhance the effect of smoking on CVD, and may be exacerbated by air pollution — a particular problem in certain developing countries and eastern Europe.

5.8.3 Physical environmental risk factors

Indoor air pollution

The very high indoor air pollution levels caused by the use of biomass and coal for cooking and heating in hundreds of millions of households in developing countries (see Sections 3.6 and 4.2) have been linked to increased heart and lung disease mortality in exposed people (WHO, 1992c). Studies in India and Nepal have shown that cor pulmonale and chronic obstructive lung disease are common among and develop at an early age in women exposed to high levels of indoor smoke. This may be one explanation for the estimated high CVD mortality risk for older women in the least developed countries (**Fig 5.10**) and the decreasing trend in CVD mortality observed as development level increases.

The chemical components of indoor air pollution caused by cooking and heating with biomass fuels and coal are similar to those that characterize outdoor air pollution caused by energy production using the same fuels (see Section 4.2) and those found in indoor air pollution caused by tobacco smoking. In particular, CO can increase CVD through its reduction of blood oxygen transport (IPCS, 1979). Other components of indoor smoke influence CVD indirectly via their effects on the lungs.

The impact on CVD mortality of inhaling other people's tobacco smoke (passive smoking) may be substantial (see Section 4.2.5). One study suggests that in the USA, 37 000 CHD deaths a year may be linked to passive smoking (Kritz, Schmid & Sinzinger, 1995). This is equivalent to around 70% of the deaths associated with ETS in that country.

Outdoor air pollution

During extreme outdoor air pollution episodes — such as the "London Fog" of December 1953, when particulate air pollution levels reached more than 1000 $\mu g/m^3$ (Ministry of Health, United Kingdom, 1954) — overall mortality increases and many of the associated deaths will be attributed to CVD. During the London Fog episode and in subsequent weeks, about 4000 more deaths than usual occurred. Many of these were due to CVD and lung disease.

Deaths from other causes also rose, testifying to the general impact of the London Fog on mortality. Although most of the additional deaths occurred among elderly people (Ministry of Health, United Kingdom, 1954), the same relative increase (i.e. a doubling) in mortality was observed among infants and the elderly. In the infants, the stated cause of death was usually ARI, while in the elderly it was mainly CVD and pneumonia. During periods of severe air pollution in developing country cities (see Section 4.2), exposures can be as high as those in London in 1953. It is possible that the health effects are as serious as they were in London, but systematic studies have not yet been undertaken.

Increasing evidence, much of it from North America and Europe, suggests that CVD morbidity and mortality are associated with outdoor air pollution at relatively low levels (less than 100 $\mu g/m^3$), especially airborne particles (PM_{10}). A 10 $\mu g/m^3$ increase in PM_{10} levels has been estimated to be associated with a 1% increase in cardiovascular mortality (Pope, Bates & Raizenne, 1995). A recent and influential study of mortality in six US cities, which took account of cigarette smoking and other recognized risk factors, reported that mortality from heart and lung disease was 37% higher in the most polluted city than in the least polluted city (Dockery et al., 1993). The association between cardiovascular mortality and particulate pollution is most likely to be due to effects on the lungs leading to heart failure. Heart failure hospital admissions have been linked to PM_{10}, CO, and sulphur dioxide (SO_2) levels (Dockery et al., 1993; Pope et al., 1995; Schwartz & Morris, 1995). Air pollution effects on cardiovascular (and other) diseases are important because, although the risks may be relatively small for individuals, the effect on whole populations is large, and may be particularly significant for occupationally-exposed groups such as street vendors, traffic police and commercial drivers (Hertzman et al., 1995).

Temperature

Winter peaks in cardiovascular mortality and morbidity are well documented. It has been suggested that extremely cold spells may be a risk for those with existing CHD (Houdas, Deklunder & Lecroart, 1992). Increases in cardiovascular mortality have also been associated with summer peaks in temperature (Lee-Chiong & Stitt; 1995, Kalkstein & Greene, 1997) (see Section 4.9).

People with pre-existing CVD are particularly vulnerable to heat waves. Access to air conditioning, even for only part of each hot day, reduces mortality significantly (Kalkstein & Greene, 1997). The combination of heat and high levels of air pollution is a particular risk (McMichael et al., 1996). Increased CVD mortality in conjunction with heat waves could be a major health impact of climate change (McMichael et al., 1996).

Lead and arsenic

An elevated blood-lead level has been reported to be associated with hypertension, and animal studies have suggested a plausible mechanism. An overall assessment of the effect of lead on blood pressure concluded, however, that the public health importance of lead exposure as regards hypertension and CVD is uncertain (IPCS, 1995b).

Arsenic is another toxic metal that has been reported to affect the cardiovascular system. In Chile, high arsenic exposure via drinking-water was linked to increased ischaemic heart disease mortality, and in parts of China similar exposures have caused peripheral vascular disease ("blackfoot disease") (IPCS, 1981). Very large populations in India, Bangladesh, China and parts of Latin America are exposed to high levels of arsenic in drinking-water (see Section 4.4.4), the reported health effects of which are principally skin cancer and liver damage. Detailed investigations of the impact of arsenic exposure on CVD are not yet available.

Infections

In the least developed countries infections have the most impact on CVD. This effect diminishes as levels of hygiene increase. The following three infectious CVD disease categories are most closely linked to environmental conditions.

Rheumatic heart disease: This is caused by Group A Streptococcal infection and is connected with poverty, poor housing and overcrowding (Brundtland, 1994). It accounts for 30% of CVD hospital admissions and 6.9% of deaths in sub-Saharan Africa (Muna, 1993). Its impact is decreasing worldwide; for instance in the Middle Eastern Crescent, the total number of deaths from rheumatic fever declined by 70% during 1979–1984 (Alwan, 1993).

Endomyocardial fibrosis: Predominately a tropical disease found south of the Sahara, and rarely below the Zambezi river, it is also occasionally seen in India and Sri Lanka. In East Africa it accounts for 10% of hospital admissions. It is thought to be associated with parasitic diseases such as filariasis (Hutt, 1991) or possibly an abnormal immune response to malaria. As the disease's etiology is poorly understood, there are no known preventive measures.

Pericardial disease: Comprising 15% of CVD admissions in some countries, this disease is a secondary response to diseases such as malaria and tuberculosis (Muna, 1993), which are indirectly linked to environmental conditions.

5.9 Cancer

5.9.1 Diseases of concern at all levels of development

Of the estimated 51 million deaths which occurred in 1993, WHO (1995a) estimates that cancer was responsible for more than 6 million (12%) (**Table 5.1**). In terms of DALYs, cancer's percentage of the global total falls to slightly more than

5% (**Table 5.2**). Cancer incidence and mortality increase with age. Above 30 year of age, cancer is similar in importance to CVD in both developed and developing countries (Murray & Lopez, 1996b). The calculated number of DALYs per capita in the 45–59 years age group in sub-Saharan Africa is greater than in other developing countries and in developed countries (**Fig. 5.11**), the only exception being the high DALY rate for cancer in the former socialist countries of Europe.

Among the different cancer sites, cancer of the trachea, bronchia or lungs is the leading cause of death, accounting for more than 17.2 % of deaths in 1993, followed by stomach cancer, colon and rectum cancer, lip, oral cavity and pharynx cancer, liver cancer, and female breast cancer. Collectively, cancer in these sites accounted for 57% of all cancers in 1993 (WHO, 1995a). In developed countries, time trends for cancers have been dominated by the dramatic increase in lung cancer and the concurrent decrease in stomach cancer.

Environmental and lifestyle factors, as well as common medical practices such as use of diagnostic radiographic procedures, are generally believed to be major causes of cancer (WHO, 1996a), but several factors are often present simultaneously. For example, it is usually not possible to tell whether a particular case of lung cancer was caused by smoking, air pollution, inherited genes, or some other specific risk factor. Nevertheless, using a combination of laboratory investigations, studies of the exposures and health of large human populations, and studies of particular groups (often occupational) who are exposed to relatively high amounts of particular chemicals or other risk factors, scientists have been able to estimate the potential importance of various risk factors for different cancers for some populations. The most telling evidence that controllable (non-genetic) factors play an important role is that cancer rates are quite different in different parts of the world, and that when

people move from one region to another they gradually take on the cancer pattern of the new location.

From these investigations, it is clear that two non-genetic factors play by far the most important role in cancer production: smoking and diet. Trichopoulos, Li & Hunter (1996) have estimated that nearly two-thirds of cancer in developed countries could potentially be avoided by complete cessation of smoking and adherence to the healthiest diet (moderate total intake; increased amounts of fruits, vegetables, and high-fibre foods, and less consumption of saturated fat and alcohol). Such dramatic changes in behaviour are not likely to take place in the near future. Yet any movement in these directions would lower not only cancer rates but also the rates of heart disease and other important diseases. But in this book we have chosen not to discuss diet, active smoking, and other "non-environmental" risk factors in detail.

Trichopoulos, Li & Hunter (1996) concluded that about 5% of cancers could be due to occupational exposures, 5% to viruses and other infectious agents (many of which are due to environmental exposures), and 2% to air pollution. Solar UV radiation (UVR), radon gas, other types of radiation, food additives and other chemical exposures are additional contributory factors. Furthermore, tobacco smoking, diet and alcohol consumption interact with each other and with environmental exposure, producing a higher total combined risk than that produced by simply adding together the risks of each single factor (Willet, Colditz & Mueller, 1996).

The varied sets of cancer sites and causes, and the multiple exposures to risk factors that many people experience, make estimation of the environmental contribution particularly difficult. However, based on: the percentages given above (which were calculated mainly from developed country information); the higher exposures to occupational hazards reported for develop-

Fig. 5.11

Cancer DALYs per 1000 persons

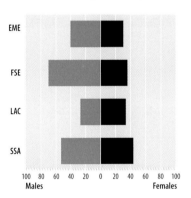

Source: Murray & Lopez, 1996b.

ing countries (see Section 4.8), and epidemiological information about infectious agents (see Sections 4.3, 4.4 and 4.5) and air pollutants (see Section 4.2), it can be assumed that the environmental contribution to cancer causation is greater in developing countries than in developed countries. The DALYs per capita figures (**Fig. 5.11**) support this. Taking into account the contribution from solar UVR, radon, ETS and other chemical exposures, it appears that as much as 25% of global cancer DALYs could be associated with environmental exposures (see Section 5.13).

5.9.2 Occupational cancer

A number of hazardous substances have been linked to cancer. In some workplaces, continual and close contact with such substances occurs, making it possible to evaluate whether they have the potential to induce a carcinogenic effect in humans. For example, as early as 1775, Percival Pott demonstrated the relationship between scrotal cancer in chimney sweeps and soot exposure. Evidence for this relationship could be found in Sweden as late as the 1960s (Hogstedt et al. 1982; Evanoff, Gustavsson & Hogstedt, 1993) since protective measures for chimney sweeps remained inadequate until this time.

Strong relationships between specific occupational exposures and certain cancers have also been found for asbestos, nickel, arsenic, benzene and ionizing radiation, to name a few. Polychlorinated dibenzo-p-dioxins (PCDDs) and polychlorinated dibenzo-p-furans (PCDFs) are recent additions to this list. Studies undertaken in Germany and the USA have demonstrated a strong dose-dependent relationship between mortality due to cancer and workplace exposure to PCDDs and PCDFs (Fingerhut et al., 1991; Flesch-Janys et al., 1995). Elevated cancer mortality in workers exposed to these chemicals become apparent after a latency period of about 20 years.

Between 300 and 350 different substances have been identified as occupational carcinogens (WHO, 1995i). Estimates for occupation-determined cancer morbidity vary between 2% and 38% of total cancer cases (Trichopoulos, Li & Hunter, 1996) (see also Section 4.8.2).

Cancer of the lung and mesothelioma continue to be major causes of mortality from occupational lung disease. In the past decade, at least a dozen case–control studies of lung cancer and occupation have been completed in several European countries and the USA (Benhamou, Benhamou & Flamat 1988; Vineis et al., 1988). After controlling for cigarette smoking, they show that 10–33% of all types of lung cancer in males is attributable to occupational exposure.

The epidemic of mesothelioma caused by the occupational use of asbestos will be sustained into the next century. In Britain, it is not expected to peak until around 2020, when it is anticipated that between 2700 and 3300 deaths from mesothelioma will occur annually, assuming current trends continue (Peto et al., 1995). These projections also suggest that the lifetime risk of dying from mesothelioma for British men born in the 1940s is approximately 1% (Peto et al., 1995). Mesothelioma was not identified as a separate pathological entity until 1930 because it had rarely, if ever, occurred previously. The current epidemic, which will last a minimum of 100 years, was entirely due to the use of asbestos.

Asbestos-related and other occupational cancers are now being reported from developing countries (Pearce et al., 1994). Three recent studies from China found elevated relative risks of 2.8 to 9.4 for lung cancer among workers in the asbestos, textile, mining and manufacturing industries (Wu, 1988; Cheng & Kong, 1992). Recent studies of miners exposed to silica, radon, and arsenic in South Africa and China have demonstrated excess lung cancer rates (Wyndham et al., 1986; Chen et al., 1990; Xuan et al., 1993; Pearce et al., 1994).

An important source of information on the carcinogenic potential of chemicals and other environmental factors is the monograph series entitled *Evaluation of carcinogenic risks to humans*, published by IARC. The monographs summarize and evaluate published data on the carcinogenic impact of different exposures in animals and humans, including specific occupational exposures. **Table 5.9** gives examples of monographs dealing with identified industries or occupations. Many of the other monographs dealing with specific chemicals also refer to workplace exposures.

5.9.3 Infectious agents

Studies conducted during the past 20 years show that many different types of cancer are triggered by viruses, bacteria and parasites. WHO (1996a) estimated that over 1.5 million (15%) of the new cancer cases occurring each year could be avoided by preventing infectious diseases associated with them.

Helicobacter pylori is one example of an infectious agent which can act as an environmental link with cancer. IARC (1994) has classified *H. pylori* as a class-1 carcinogen — the rank assigned to the most dangerous cancer-causing agents. Virtually all people infected with *H. pylori* contract chronic superficial gastritis, which, if left untreated, can persist for decades, even a lifetime, leading to ulcers and ultimately to one of several forms of stomach cancer (Blaser, 1996).

Stomach cancer is the most common type of cancer in many developing countries. About one million cases occur each year (WHO, 1996a). It is the only cancer that generally decreases in incidence with economic development (WHO, 1992b). In developing countries infection with *H. pylori* is common in all age groups, but in developed countries it is rare (IARC, 1994). It is not clear how the organisms pass from one person to another but poor sanita-

Table 5.9

Selected IARC evaluations of carcinogenic risks in specific industries

Industry	IARC monograph
Wood, leather and some associated industries	Vol. 25, 1981
Rubber industry	Vol. 28, 1982
Aluminium production, coal gasification, coke production, and iron and steel founding	Vol. 34, 1984
Petroleum refining	Vol. 45, 1989
Paint manufacture and painting	Vol. 47, 1989
Textile manufacturing	Vol. 48, 1990
Welding	Vol. 49, 1990
Insecticide applications	Vol. 53, 1991
Hairdressing and hair dyes	Vol. 57, 1993
Glass manufacturing industry	Vol. 58, 1994
Dry cleaning	Vol. 63, 1995
Printing processes	Vol. 65, 1996

tion and crowding clearly facilitate the process. In areas where living conditions have improved, the rate of *H. pylori* infection has decreased and the average age at which the infection is acquired has risen. At the turn of the century stomach cancer was the leading cause of death from cancer in the USA and many other developed countries. But incidence of many other cancers is now far higher in these countries (IARC, 1994).

About 12 600 (4%) of the 300 000 new cases a year of bladder cancer are attributed to the parasitic disease schistosomiasis, which occurs exclusively in developing countries (WHO, 1996a). People who contract this disease generally do so because their water supplies for bathing and washing are contaminated (see Section 4.4).

5.9.4 Air pollution

Shy & Struba (1982) pointed out that an association between air pollution and cancer incidence is suggested by:

- data showing that lung cancer incidence is higher in polluted urban areas

- observation of significant lung cancer excess incidence among groups occupationally exposed to chemical carcinogens

• indirect evidence of a quantitative relationship between atmospheric carcinogenic levels and lung cancer

• direct demonstrations of a link between exposure to ambient carcinogens and cancer in experimental animals.

An assessment of all the health effects of air pollution (WHO, 1997f) and some recent studies have provided further indications of such an association. For instance, a relationship — independent of smoking habits — between the risk of lung cancer and particulate air pollution was shown in several countries (Dockery et al., 1993; Pershagen & Simonato, 1993). And in a study conducted in Cracow, Poland, about 4% of lung cancer cases in males and 10% of lung cancer cases in females were attributed to residence in

an area where levels of black smoke had reached an annual average concentration of over 150 $\mu g/m^3$, several years before the cancer cases were registered (Jedrychowski et al., 1990). Other studies concerning populations living near certain types of industry have suggested an elevated risk of lung cancer as a result of exposure to ambient air pollution (Pershagen, 1985).

Aliphatic and aromatic hydrocarbons that have long been classified as carcinogens (e.g. IARC, 1973), make up a considerable portion of the many organic particulates found in polluted air. The principal source of these hydrocarbons is combustion of petroleum, gasoline and diesel fuel. Polynuclear aromatic hydrocarbons have been subject to much investigation because of their carcinogenic potency in animals. The relative carcinogenicity of different chemicals found in urban air is shown in **Table 5.10**. Benzo(a)pyrene is the strongest carcinogen.

5.9.5 Water pollution and contaminated food

As mentioned in Section 5.9.3, exposure to *H. pylori* can lead to stomach cancer and infection with this bacterium is associated with poor sanitation and potentially with contaminated water and food. The exact infection route has not been ascertained. Since stomach cancer is so common in developing countries, infection with *H. pylori* may represent the most important association between water pollution and cancer.

Water pollution from industrial activities, agricultural practices, the processing, packaging and preparation of food, and water treatment, can all contaminate food and water with chemical carcinogens. Concern about the possible carcinogenic risks arising from exposure to chemical contaminants in drinking-water focuses mainly on certain pesticides, halogenated organic compounds (such as tri- and terachloroethylene) and inorganic

Table 5.10

Carcinogenic polycyclic organic matter identified in urban air

Polycyclic aromatic hydrocarbons

Compound	Formula	Carcinogenicity
Chrysene	$C_{18}H_{12}$	+
Benz[a]anthracene	$C_{18}H_{12}$	+
Dibenzo[a.g]fluorine	$C_{21}H_{14}$	+
Dibenz[a.c]anthracene	$C_{22}H_{14}$	+
Indeno[1,2,3-cd]pyrene	$C_{22}H_{12}$	+
Benzo[b]fluoranthene	$C_{20}H_{12}$	+ +
Benzo[j]fluoranthene	$C_{20}H_{12}$	+ +
Benzo[j]aceanthrylene	$C_{20}H_{14}$	+ +
Dibenzo[a,e]pyrene	$C_{22}H_{14}$	+ +
Benzo[c]phenanthrene	$C_{18}H_{12}$	+ + +
Dibenzo[a,i]pyrene	$C_{22}H_{14}$	+ + +
Dibenzo[a,h]pyrene	$C_{22}H_{14}$	+ + +
Dibenz[a,h]anthracene	$C_{22}H_{14}$	+ + +
Benzo[a]pyrene	$C_{20}H_{12}$	+ + + +

Aza and imino arenes

Quinoline	C_9H_8N	+
Dibenz[a,h]acridine	$C_{21}H_{13}N$	+ +
Dibenz[a,j]acridine	$C_{21}H_{13}$	+ +
Dibenzo[c,g]carbazole	$C_{20}H_{13}N$	+ + +

Source: adapted from USEPA, 1978.

compounds, such as nitrate and arsenic. In certain European countries nitrate concentrations in drinking-water are sufficiently high to cause methaemoglobinaemia and may also be associated with gastrointestinal cancer. Nitrate can be converted to various nitrosamines, which are powerful carcinogens in animals (IARC, 1984, 1991a). The causal association between high arsenic concentrations in drinking-water and skin cancer is now well established on the basis of epidemiological studies conducted in areas with extremely high exposures (Tseng, 1968) (see Section 4.4.4).

It has been suggested that chlorination of water gives rise to complex mixtures of halogenated compounds with potential carcinogenic effects for populations that experience lifelong exposure to such compounds. Such risks should be kept in perspective. The risk of illness and death posed by microbiological pathogens in drinking-water is 100 to 1000 times (up to 1 million times for any specific illness) higher than the risk of cancer associated with chlorination and fluoridation by-products found in drinking-water (IARC, 1991b).

Procedures for the collection, disposal and treatment of wastes can be sources of carcinogenic hazard (Batstone, Smith & Wilson, 1989). For example, chemical agents may be present in the gases and particulates emitted during waste incineration, or in the contaminants leached from landfill sites into surface water and groundwater (see Section 4.3.2). Several epidemiological studies have explored the purported association between residence near waste sites and various types of cancer. IARC is coordinating a project to assess this problem in Europe. To date, however, no convincing evidence of cancer risks from hazardous waste disposal has been found. However, past uncontrolled exposures and the low biodegradability of carcinogenic components mean that such a possibility cannot be excluded.

Possible cancer hazards related to chemical contamination of food encompass a number of pesticides, organic compounds (such as PCDDs and PCDFs), inorganic compounds (such as nitrate and some heavy metals) and natural toxins (such as mycotoxins of the aflatoxin type) (IPCS, 1990b; IARC, 1997, in preparation). Generally, assessing the contribution of these factors to the actual cancer risk of the population is difficult, particularly since the available data are limited. The largest problem in developing countries may be exposures to mycotoxins in foods and arsenic in drinking-water (see Sections 4.4.4 and 4.5.2). In developed countries concern has focused on PCDDs. The results of a recent WHO multicentre evaluation of PCDDs and PCDFs in human milk indicated that exposure to these chemicals had on average decreased in several European countries between 1987 and 1993 (WHO, 1995a).

5.9.6 Ionizing radiation

Ionizing radiation exposures can cause cancer of different types depending on the type of radiation and the tissue receiving the highest dose (IAEA, 1996b). Following a nuclear accident and resultant increased exposure to radiation, cancer rates in the exposed population may rise, as was the case after the atomic bomb explosions in Hiroshima and Nagasaki (HICARE, 1993). The latency period will vary depending on the type of cancer (**Fig. 5.12**).

The most serious nuclear accident to date occurred at Chernobyl on 26 April 1986, releasing large amounts of radioactive material over vast areas of Belarus, Ukraine and the Russian Federation (WHO, 1996j). One of the main constituents of this release was a radioactive isotope of iodine-131. Four years after the Chernobyl accident, increased incidence of thyroid cancer was observed in children in the most highly exposed areas. This was much sooner than would have been predicted

Fig. 5.12

Latency period for development of malignant tumours

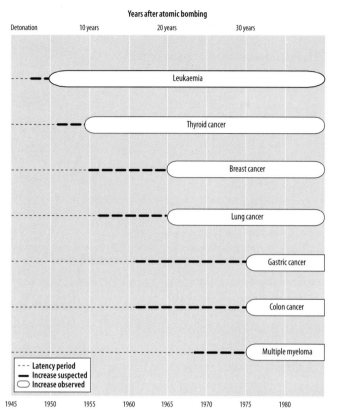

Source: HICARE, 1993.

Table 5.11

Thyroid cancers in children (under 15 years of age) in Belarus, Ukraine and the Russian Federation after the Chernobyl accident

Year	Belarus	Ukraine	Russian Federation (Bryansk and Kaluga regions)
1986	2	8	0
1987	4	7	1
1988	5	8	0
1989	7	11	0
1990	29	26	4
1991	59	22	3
1992	66	47	5
1993	79	43	11
1994	82	39	19
1995	91	44	9
Total	424	255	52

Sources: Nagataki & Yamashita, 1996; Tsyb et al., 1996; WHO, 1996k; Williams et al., 1996; Tronko, 1997.

from the studies of Japan's atomic bomb survivors (**Fig. 5.12**). Thyroid cancer is normally rare in children, but more than 700 cases of thyroid cancer in children under 15 years of age were reported between 1986 and 1996 (**Table 5.11**). Thyroid cancer incidence among children in an area of Belarus, with the highest radiation deposition, was about 200 times greater than that observed in England and Wales during the same time period (see also Sections 4.5.2, 5.7.3 and 5.7.4).

An increase in leukaemia incidence among children has not yet been observed in the contaminated areas around Chernobyl, or in any other European country modestly exposed to radiation fallout from the Chernobyl accident. Nevertheless, if patterns observed following the dropping of atomic bombs on Hiroshima and Nagasaki offer any indication (**Fig.**

5.12), a higher incidence of leukaemia, colon cancer, breast cancer and lung cancer may eventually occur.

In recent years, possible cancer risks associated with exposure to radon in houses have received attention. It is estimated that in the USA about 20 000 cases per year of lung cancer occur as a result of radon exposure (US Department of Health and Human Services, 1991). Smoking considerably increases the risk of lung cancer related to radon, and vice-versa (WHO, 1996j) (see also Section 4.2.6).

5.9.7 Non-ionizing radiation

The major sources of non-ionizing radiation are solar UVR and artificial light sources, and natural and human-made electromagnetic fields.

Ultraviolet radiation

The sun is the principal source of UV exposure for most people and known to be associated with various skin cancers (IARC, 1992). The excess cancer risk caused by UV exposure is difficult to estimate since most countries do not maintain skin cancer registries. It has been estimated that over 2 million cases of non-melanoma skin cancer and 200 000 malignant melanomas occur globally each year (WHO, 1994c). With stratospheric ozone depletion this number will rise (see Section 4.9). Stratospheric ozone filters out the more harmful components of solar UVR. In the event of a 10% decrease in stratospheric ozone, and if current trends and behavioural patterns continue, an additional 300 000 non-melanoma skin cancers can be anticipated worldwide (WHO, 1994c).

The main risk at present, however, arises from excessive UV exposure through individual choice, particularly as a result of sun-bathing. Changes in behaviour could therefore counter this hazard (WHO/UNEP, 1995). An annual two-week holiday in the sun can quintuple the life-time risk of non-melanoma skin cancer in northern

European indoor workers, because it multiplies their annual dose of biologically effective UVR. In the case of malignant melanoma, intermittent exposure and exposure sufficient to cause sunburn both increase risk, especially if such exposures occur during childhood. Malignant melanoma is a rare form of skin cancer with a high fatality rate (30–50%) with varying incidence in 1985 of 4.5–15.1 per 100 000 among males and 3.8–19.6 per 100 000 among females in western Europe (Coleman et al., 1993). Incidence has risen markedly in some countries during the last few decades.

Electromagnetic fields

The potential health effects of exposure to static and time-varying electric and magnetic fields are of great public and occupational health concern and need scientific clarification. Exposure to these fields is increasing in industry, research and medicine, and following developments in transport, telecommunications and power transmission, and among the general population as a whole (WHO, 1987c; WHO 1993e).

Major concern has also been expressed about the health effects of exposure to electromagnetic fields of extremely low frequency (ELF: <300 Hz) at power frequencies (50/60 Hz) and radiofrequencies (RF: 300 Hz–300 GHz) used in everyday life (for example, for radio and TV transmission, telecommunications, diagnosis and treatment of disease, and in industry for heating and sealing materials). There may be an association with an increased incidence of cancer in children and adults, and other adverse health outcomes (Repacholi, 1996).

However, the epidemiological studies undertaken to date lack consistency, since some suggest that cancer, especially leukaemia in children, or in people exposed to ELF fields at work, may be related to the exposure, while other studies show no effect (WHO, 1993e, NRC, 1996). However, a recent review by the US National Academy of Sciences concluded that children living in homes classified as "high wire code" (that is, near high voltage transmission lines, near pole transformers of local distribution lines and so on) are at 50% greater risk of developing leukaemia than children who do not live in such homes. Yet the association did not appear to be due to magnetic field exposure (NRC, 1996). From a public health point of view, the risk is likely to be very small: less than one extra case of childhood leukaemia per year associated with living near high voltage power lines, in a total population of 9 million (Feychting & Ahlbom, 1993).

Radiofrequency exposure has been reported to be associated with an increased cancer risk, but the evidence is very weak and much more research is needed (ICNIRP, 1996; Repacholi, 1997).

5.9.8 Environmental tobacco smoke: acute and chronic effects

Taking all diseases into account, tobacco products are estimated to have caused around 3 million deaths a year in the early 1990s, and the death toll is increasing steadily (WHO, 1996s). It is estimated that in developed countries the number of deaths caused each year by smoking rose from about three quarters of a million in 1955 to 2 million in 1995, with deaths among men accounting for three-quarters of these. It is also projected that by the 2020s or early 2030s smoking will be responsible for about 10 million deaths a year worldwide, 7 million of which will be in developing countries (WHO, 1996s). Tobacco smoking interacts with occupational and environmental exposures, such as asbestos and radon, to increase the cancer risk of these exposures up to 10 times.

Environmental tobacco smoke (ETS), to which non-smokers may be exposed, consists of sidestream smoke (SS) released from the burning tobacco product and mainstream smoke exhaled by smokers. As a rule, sidestream smoke contains the highest levels of carcinogenic compounds. In the USA, a significant proportion of the population is exposed to ETS in both the home and the workplace (Pirkle et al., 1996).

Exposure to ETS has been associated with acute and chronic health effects among nonsmokers: with increased risk for lung cancer and CVD among adults, and with impaired lung function and respiratory problems among children (Law & Hackshaw, 1996). Combined evidence from 25 epidemiological studies indicates a 20–30% increased risk of lung cancer in nonsmokers married to smokers (Pershagen, 1994). ETS exposure has been estimated to account for 9–13% of all lung cancer cases in adult smokers in Europe (USEPA, 1992). However, further careful studies are needed to clarify the relationship between other cancers and diseases and exposure to ETS, taking into account various sources of potential bias in the assessment of the epidemiological evidence concerning these relationships (see also Section 4.2.5).

5.10 Chronic respiratory diseases

5.10.1 The impacts of inhaling polluted air

Chronic respiratory diseases encompass a broad variety of human illness such as chronic obstructive lung disease due to particulate air pollution; interstitial fibrotic lung disease due to silica, beryllium, and asbestos exposure; upper airway irritation due to exposure to formaldehyde and other gases; asthma in workers exposed to organic substances; and chronic respiratory infections in people exposed to indoor smoke caused by combustion of biomass fuels (**Table 5.12**).

While most of the DALY burden of this group of diseases is to be found in the 45 years and older age group (75%), slightly more than 17% falls within the 0–4 age group (Murray & Lopez, 1996b). In sub-Saharan Africa and Latin American countries the DALY rate per capita is highest in the youngest and oldest age groups (**Fig. 5.13**).

Infants in urban areas appear to be at increased risk of mortality due to ambient (outdoor) air pollution (Bobak & Leon, 1992) and both rural and urban children develop asthma and ARI at excess rates as a result of exposure to indoor and outdoor air pollution (Smith, 1993). Additionally, hundreds of millions of adult women in developing countries are exposed to extremely high levels of airborne particulates when cooking on stoves using biomass fuels (Chen et al., 1990; Smith, 1993) (see also Section 4.2).

In the workplace — especially in manufacturing, construction, and farming — adult men, and to a lesser extent, women, are occupationally exposed to fibrogenic dusts, irritant gases and carcinogenic agents. The long-term effects of inhaling a lifetime of respiratory toxins are generally manifested in old age. Elderly people with underlying lung diseases are, moreover,

Table 5.12

Spectrum of environmental and occupational lung diseases

Exposure category	Settings	Populations at risk	Outcomes
Ambient air pollution	Urban areas Industrial settings	Infants, elderly People with pre-existing respiratory diseases	Respiratory mortality Cardiovascular mortality Chronic obstructive lung disease Asthma Infant respiratory mortality
Indoor air pollution	*Developed countries* Radon-exposed areas Office and commercial buildings Private residences	General population	Lung cancer Sick building syndrome Asthma Solvent-related symptoms Legionnaire's disease, other infectious diseases
	Developing countries Home biomass fuel use for cooking and heating Rural > urban	Women, children	Acute respiratory infection Chronic obstructive lung diseases Lung cancer
Occupational exposures	Workplaces	Men > women Young and middle-aged	Lung cancer Mesothelioma Asthma Chronic obstructive lung disease Pneumoconioses

highly vulnerable to the health effects that can result from exposure to ambient air pollution. Due to the importance of different exposures to air pollutants for the chronic respiratory diseases, it is estimated that 50% of the global burden of these diseases is associated with environmental factors (see Section 5.13).

It has long been known that the lung is a critical target organ for environmental agents, but its vulnerability is only now beginning to be fully understood. Epidemiological studies completed in the past ten years in the USA and Europe have consistently demonstrated that excess respiratory morbidity and mortality occurs at much lower levels of ambient urban air pollution than was previously realized (Bates, 1992; Dockery et al., 1993). Similarly, scientific documentation of the hazards associated with the use of biomass fuels for heat and food preparation in poorly ventilated indoor spaces in the developing world only began in the past decade (Smith, 1993). Nevertheless, the limited studies carried out to date suggest significant health risks that become greatly magnified if the large numbers of people exposed and the high intensity of exposures are taken into account.

A recent hospital-based case control study of elderly women with chronic obstructive pulmonary disease (COPD) in Colombia showed an odds ratio of 3.4 for women who had a history of using a wood cooking-stove in the home (Dennis et al., 1996). The risk of COPD increased with number of years of wood use. The authors estimated that as much as 50% of the COPD in the population studied, which consisted of older women of low socioeconomic status, might be attributable to use of wood cooking-stoves. Studies in India and Nepal have also reported COPD as well as CVD in women exposed to indoor smoke (WHO, 1992c) (see Section 5.8).

The problem of indoor air pollution due to use of biomass fuels in develop-

ing countries results from a complex web of economic, cultural and technical factors (WHO, 1992c) that are closely gender-based, and intimately tied to poverty (see Sections 3.6 and 4.2). The size of the exposed population, the intensity of exposures, and severity of associated health outcomes (Smith, 1993), indicate that multi-disciplinary research, especially of the intervention type, is urgently needed.

5.10.2 Occupational respiratory diseases

Occupational chronic respiratory diseases are generally believed to constitute one-third of all occupational illnesses. As many as 50 million cases may occur each year among the global labour force. These diseases are of great concern because they are widespread, debilitating, and affect people in the social and economic prime of their lives. They are also highly preventable. Indeed, the means by which hazardous exposures can be reduced or eliminated are well-known and generally available, at least in developed countries. **Table 5.13** provides a brief listing of selected occupational lung diseases and associated exposures.

Pneumoconioses, or dust diseases of the lungs, remain prominent among occupational lung diseases in many regions of the world. The prevalence of pneumoconiosis, including silicosis and asbestosis, in exposed populations in developing countries is between 20 and 35% (NIOSH, 1994) and may reach 50% in workers most heavily exposed to dusts containing silica or coal dust, or to asbestos fibres, all of which are also recognized carcinogens.

Silicosis takes the form of progressive parenchymal lung disease and is caused by inhalation of inorganic dust containing crystalline silica. It is not curable, usually leads to premature death, and is an occupational hazard for millions of workers. The Colombian Government, for instance, estimates that 1 800 000 Colombian workers are at risk. In India, the number is 1 689 000.

Fig. 5.13

Respiratory diseases by region, age group and gender — DALYs per 1000 persons

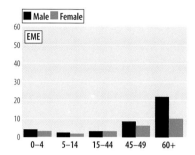

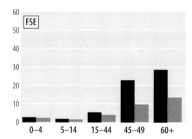

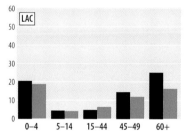

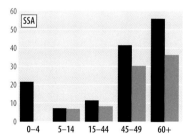

Source: Murray & Lopez, 1996b.

In the USA, 1 697 000 workers are potentially at risk and, according to existing estimates, about 60 000 exposed workers will suffer some degree of silicosis (NIOSH, 1994)

Asbestosis contributed to nearly 1000 deaths in the USA in 1990, compared to less than 100 in 1970 (NIOSH, 1994). The extent to which this increase is due to improved reporting or to an increase in underlying disease incidence is unclear. Although considerable amounts of asbestos have been used in developing countries for several decades, especially in Brazil, South Africa and Zimbabwe, epidemiological studies of the non-malignant effects of asbestos are lacking (Pearce et al., 1994). Conversely, silicosis continues to be well-documented in developing countries in relation to mines, quarries, foundries, and other selected workplaces (Pearce et al., 1994).

Acute and chronic occupational respiratory diseases can also be caused by exposure and over-exposure to industrial respiratory irritants such as chlorine, formaldehyde, nitrogen oxides and SO_2. Many of these possess an allergic effect, as evidenced by the increasing prevalence of asthma — from 10% to 50% depending on occupation. Byssinosis of textile workers,

"black-lung disease" of farmers, mesothelioma and lung cancer of asbestos-exposed workers, lung cancer due to exposure to some metals (nickel, cadmium and chromium compounds and beryllium), pesticides and other chemicals, are further examples of occupational respiratory diseases (see also Section 4.8.2).

5.11 Other diseases

A number of other diseases and health problems are associated with exposures to environmental factors. Two specific examples have been of concern in recent years: allergies and reproductive health problems. Other health conditions, such as endocrine system disruption by persistent organic pollutants (POPs) (see **Box 2.8**) have also been receiving much attention. Estimating the quantitative contribution of environmental exposures to the global burden of these varied diseases is not possible, however. Yet as these "other" diseases make up about 30% of the total global DALYs (see Section 5.1), even a relatively small contribution by environmental factors to their causation would mean that they add significantly to the environmental burden of disease (see Section 5.13).

5.11.1 Allergies

The effects of environmental hazards such as air pollution, food additives and occupational chemical exposures on the immune system are of increasing concern (IPCS, 1997). However, many allergens occur naturally in the environment, for example, proteins in pollen, dust from animals, insect toxins and foodstuffs (King et al., 1995). These may cause a greater proportion of the global burden of disease than do chemical exposures, but it is chemically-induced allergies that are on the increase (IPCS, 1997).

Allergic diseases mainly affect the respiratory system (asthma, hay fever,

Table 5.13

Occupational diseases of the respiratory tract

Part of respiratory system	Disease	Examples of causal occupational agents
Upper respiratory tract	Nasal perforation	Chromium
	Nasal cancer	Wood dust, chromium, nickel
	Oropharyngeal cancer	Asbestos
	Laryngeal spasm/oedema	Ammonia
	Cancer of the larynx	Asbestos
	Upper respiratory irritation	Formaldehyde, ammonia
Airways	Chronic obstructive lung disease	Cotton dust, grain
	Chronic bronchitis	Many dusts
	Asthma	Isocyanates, wood dusts, animal proteins
	Pneumonitis/pulmonary oedema	Cadmium, chlorine, nitrogen oxide
	Pneumoconiosis	Silica, asbestos, beryllium
Parenchyma	Allergic alveolitis	Animal proteins, nitrogen oxide
	Cancer	Asbestos, nickel, arsenic, uranium, chromium
	Infectious disease	Legionella, TB
Pleura	Fibrosis	Asbestos
	Cancer	Asbestos
	Effusion	Asbestos

Source: adapted from Markowitz, 1992.

allergic rhinitis), the skin (eczema) and the digestive system, and other parts of the body in the form of autoimmune diseases (IPCS, 1997). Asthma and eczema can also occur in non-allergic forms. Available data indicate that asthma is increasing in the USA (CDC, 1995b) and other developed countries (Buist & Vollmer, 1990). Air pollution from motor vehicles is known to be contributing to this increase (Bascom, 1996; Keil et al., 1996). The role of air pollution from power stations and industry is uncertain, however, as studies comparing areas of eastern Europe (with high levels of industrial air pollution) and western Europe (with lower levels of industrial pollution) show that asthma incidence is actually greater in the latter (Løvik, Dybing & Smith, 1996). Growing motor vehicle air pollution (see Section 4.2) makes it likely that asthma incidence will rise. Other environmental exposures contributing to increased asthma include chemicals in the workplace, indoor air pollutants and certain food additives (IPCS, 1997). The estimated global burden of disease for asthma is currently 10 775 DALYs (Murray & Lopez, 1996b), which is less than 1% of the total global burden of disease.

Hand eczemas are common in the general population, one estimate showing a prevalence of 10% (Meding, 1990). Many are caused by contact allergies, specifically, nickel, chromate and rubber additives, preservatives in food and fragrances (Menne & Maibach, 1993). Some of the exposures can be considered attributable to lifestyle rather than to the environment, but workplace exposures are likely to be a major contributor (Raffle et al., 1994).

5.11.2 Reproductive health problems

Other health conditions that have been linked to environmental hazard exposures relate to reproduction, childbirth and the first days after a child is born. Perinatal conditions contribute be-tween 2.4 and 3.2 million deaths to the global burden of disease each year (**Table 5.1**), of which about 1 million are due to low birth weight. Other reproductive health conditions that have major impacts on health status include congenital anomalies (589 000 deaths annually) and maternal deaths during childbirth (454 000 deaths annually) (Murray & Lopez, 1996b). In terms of priorities for reproductive health programmes (WHO, 1996t), the focus for future action should be on improved antenatal care, management of childbirth, and healthcare for the newborn. However, living conditions and exposures to environmental hazards play important roles with respect to the health of the mother and the newborn child, and other aspects of reproductive health.

Genetic damage has possibly the most adverse basic effect on reproduction since it may interfere with cell division and early development of the embryo and fetus. Experimental studies have shown that ionizing radiation and certain chemical compounds can cause such damage (IPCS, 1984b). In humans, the effects of genetic damage at early stages of development may lead to early fetal death. But they are difficult to study because such deaths can be caused by a number of factors.

Other effects of environmental hazards on the fetus include slow growth and low birth weight. CO exposure, in particular, is associated with low birth weight (WHO, 1997f). This chemical occurs in outdoor and indoor air pollution (see Section 4.2) as well as in tobacco smoke. In developing countries, though, poor nutrition of the mother may be the primary cause of low birth weight (WHO, 1996t). Congenital anomalies are yet another environmental health concern since laboratory experiments have shown that a number of chemicals cause abnormal growth in the fetus (IPCS, 1984a). Ionizing radiation and infections such as rubella have also been shown to cause congenital anomalies in humans (IAEA, 1996b).

Infertility in both women and men has been associated with exposure to environmental hazards (Olsen, 1994). POPs and subsequent disruption of endocrine functions have received much attention in this respect (see **Box 2.8**), and in relation to the causation of breast cancer (Safe, 1994). As these chemicals accumulate in the environment, more and more people may be increasingly exposed. A major international effort, spearheaded by the International Forum on Chemical Safety, is under way to bring these chemicals under control.

5.12 Special features of occupational diseases and injuries

As pointed out in Section 4.8, among others, a variety of hazards occur in workplaces and can cause injuries, nervous system damage, respiratory diseases and cancer. (These major categories of occupational health problem have been described in Sections 5.6, 5.7, 5.9 and 5.10). Many other types of health problem can be related to workplace exposures, including noise-induced hearing loss, skin disease, reproductive disorders, CVD and musculoskeletal illnesses (WHO, 1995i).

The burden of occupational diseases and injuries is increasing in many countries. Exposure to chemicals, many of which affect the nervous system or the lungs, afflict workers in most countries. Pesticides, organic solvents, lead, and other metals, also cause major occupational health problems worldwide (see also Sections 4.8, 5.7 and 5.10). In some developed countries the growth of musculoskeletal illnesses of the "repeated trauma" type has become apparent (NIOSH, 1996). This type of illness is also called "overuse syndrome" and is usually caused by work that involves repetitive movements of the arms and hands for several hours each day. It affects assembly workers in the manufacturing industry, check-out counter operators in shops, typists and keyboard operators.

In developing countries the more fatal occupational health problems, such as injuries, occur at a higher rate than in developed countries (see Section 5.6). Since industries such as mining, construction and transport, can be expected to grow with economic development (see Section 2.7), severe occupational health problems pertaining to injury hazard will doubtless remain or increase in these countries, unless major efforts to introduce effective prevention are made now (WHO, 1995i).

It should be pointed out that in developing countries workers suffer not only from occupational diseases and injuries, but often simultaneously from infectious diseases, poor nutrition, unhealthy housing and other conditions related to poverty, as described in Section 4.8.

5.13 Environmental factors and the global burden of disease

In different ways and to different degrees, each of the disease and disability categories discussed above owe their presence to one environmental factor or another. A summary portrayal of the environmental portion of the global burden of disease is given in **Table 5.14**. Applying these percentages across the diseases and conditions indicated leads to an estimate of the total DALY burden that is associated with environmental factors. This is 320 470 or 23% of the world's total DALY burden.

The percentages shown reflect how important these factors are in causing the burden and indicate how much their control would contribute to its reduction. Thus, even though many diseases (diarrhoeal diseases, malaria, measles, polio and tetanus) might be arguably 100% environmental, a lesser percentage is indicated because of the availability of effective preventive and curative care, including vaccines in some instances. On the other hand, no one would deny that it would be preferable, even for diseases for which effective vaccines are available, to improve the environment in order to reduce their transmission. However, for environmentally-mediated infectious diseases for which effective vaccines are not available, we attribute a high proportion to environment (e.g. ARI and malaria).

In our analysis of the approximate environmental contribution of the health conditions described in this chapter, we emphasize long-term sustainable prevention rather than curative measures. We also assume that environmental preventive actions are taken first. The environmental fraction is considered as the fraction of disease occurrence that could be averted through feasible environmental interventions, before application of other interventions. Using this approach, it was estimated that approximately 60% of the current global ARI disease burden could be avoided in a sustainable manner if environmental improvements

were made to eliminate exposures to severe indoor air pollution in developing countries (see Section 5.2). Less crowding and improved housing conditions would also contribute to ARI reduction. The estimate is based on the very large potential for prevention shown in **Fig. 5.1**, the high level of air pollution exposures in populations in developing countries, the major ARI health risks calculated in Section 4.2 and the historical trends of these diseases (see Section 5.2). To achieve maximum impact, improvement of environmental conditions should be combined with improved nutrition and effective treatment of childhood pneumonia.

In the case of diarrhoeal diseases, our estimate of a 90% environmental contribution (**Table 5.14**) is based on the remarkable variation between different regions in DALYs per capita in (see Section 5.3), and the known environmental transmission pathways for these diseases. Although diarrhoeal deaths are averted effectively through ORT in the immediate term, the longer-term solution is to improve basic sanitation, water supply and food safety.

Table 5.14

Proportion of global DALYs associated with environmental exposures — 1990

	Global DALYs (thousands)	Environmental fraction (%)	Environmental DALYs (thousands)	% of all DALYs (all age groups)	(age 0–14 years)
Acute respiratory infections	116 696	60	70 017	5	4.5
Diarrhoeal diseases	99 633	90	89 670	6.5	6.1
Vaccine-preventable infections	71 173	10	7 117	0.5	0.49
Tuberculosis	38 426	10	3 843	0.3	0.04
Malaria	31 706	90	28 535	2.1	1.8
Injuries					
unintentional	152 188	30	45 656	3.3	1.6
intentional	56 459	N.E.	N.E.		
Mental health	144 950	10	14 495	1.1	0.08
Cardiovascular diseases	133 236	10	13 324	1	0.12
Cancer	70 513	25	17 628	1.3	0.11
Chronic respiratory diseases	60 370	50	30 185	2.2	0.57
Total these diseases	975 350	33	320 470	23	15.4
Other diseases	403 888	N.E.	N.E		
Total all diseases	1 379 238	(23)	(320 470)		

N.E.: not estimated

Source: DALY data from Murray & Lopez, 1996b.

The vaccine-preventable infectious diseases and tuberculosis are all transmitted more rapidly in conditions of crowding and poor housing (see **Section 5.4**). Environmental improvements are of value, but are not as effective as vaccines. The environmental fraction was set at 10% (**Table 5.14**). Using similar considerations approximate environmental fractions were assigned to most of the disease groups described in this chapter.

When combined, these estimated environmental contributions add up to 23% of the global burden of disease (**Table 5.14**), but this figure does not take into account that "other diseases" and "intentional injuries" have some environmental associations. The proportion of all DALYs contributed by environmental DALYs to each disease (**Table 5.14**) creates numbers that can be compared with a previous estimate of the importance of different risk factors for the global burden of disease (WHO, 1996d). Few environmental "risk factors" were assessed, but estimates were made for "water and sanitation" (6.8%), "occupation" (2.7%) and "outdoor air pollution" (0.5%), among other "risk factors" such as "tobacco smoking" (2.6%). Only 40% of all DALYs were associated with the risk factors analysed, and several of the major disease problems listed in **Table 5.14** (e.g. malaria and injuries) were not referred to at all. It is reassuring to note that the approach taken by WHO (1996d) resulted in very similar estimates to our own for diarrhoeal diseases (6.8% for "water and sanitation" in WHO, 1996d, versus 6.5% for diarrhoeal diseases in **Table 5.14**).

The diseases which contribute the most environmental DALYs (ARI, diarrhoeal diseases, malaria and unintentional injury) are also the diseases which particularly affect children. Using the percentage of all DALYs contributed by children under age 15 (**Table 5.3**), estimates of the "child component" of environmental DALYs can be made (**Table 5.14**). As seen in **Table 5.14**, this child component adds up to 15% of all DALYs or about two-thirds of environmental DALYs. Taking action to reduce environmental DALYs could thus make a major contribution to child health.

Ideally at this point in our analysis we would explore alternative future scenarios to better understand the importance of controlling the various environmental factors discussed. Unfortunately, we are too handicapped by the lack of suitable comparative data to be able to generate convincing scenarios. Instead, we turn to recently developed scenarios which project the global DALY burden to the year 2020 to see to what degree environmental factors have been taken into account.

As noted in Section 2.2, the world's population grew from 5300 million in 1990, and is expected to reach 6100 million by the year 2000, and 7700 million by 2020. In 2020, nearly 10% of the population will be over the age of 65. Cities are developing and growing fast. At present about half of humanity lives in urban areas; this is expected to rise to almost two-thirds by 2020.

The impact of these changes alone on the relative importance of different diseases and disabilities upon the total disease burden is expected to be profound. These changes are expected to contribute to new disease patterns, whereby non-communicable diseases come to the forefront in developing countries. The decline of infectious diseases is "implicitly based on the presumption that socioeconomic development will decrease disease incidence and severity, and/or that research and development will guarantee the availability of antibiotics effective against resistant strains of major pathogens" (Murray & Lopez, 1996b). This assumption may be considered very optimistic in light of the severe constraints outlined in earlier chapters; e.g. increased waste production and pollution (Section 3.2), water scarcity (Section 3.3), land limitation (Section 3.4), and global environmental change

(Section 4.9). A major commitment to socioeconomic development for the poor, incorporating environmental improvements and major investments in water, sanitation and other infrastructure is needed to achieve the assumed improvements in health.

In projecting DALYs for the year 2020, Murray and Lopez 1996b developed base-line, optimistic and pessimistic scenarios. Underlying mortality rates were derived from regression equations relating age-, sex- and cause-specific mortality rates to four determinants of mortality: income per capita, human capital (average number of years of schooling of the population), smoking intensity and time. There is a wide range of difference between the optimistic future and the pessimistic future for the infectious disease groups. Road traffic accidents (a sub-group of the injuries groups) are higher in number in the "optimistic" scenario than they are in the "pessimistic" scenario. The underlying statistical approach used in the making of these projections

forces this outcome; wealth means more cars and more cars means more accidents. Similarly, where development and technology lag, incidence of infectious diseases will increase proportionately. None of these projections takes into account the nature of specific interventions that might be undertaken to reduce risks or hazards (with the exception of smoking which is built into the model directly).

While specific environmental interventions have not been factored into these scenarios, the DALY projections nevertheless provide an interesting starting point for generating alternative scenarios which do incorporate environmental factors, both in terms of the prevalence and incidence of various conditions as well as in terms of the potential for interventions to modify these factors. The potential detrimental consequences of global environmental change on human health worldwide makes it even more imperative that future scenarios take these consequences explicitly into account. ❏

Chapter 6

Integrated Policies, Strategies and Actions: Progress Since The Earth Summit

Driving Force
Pressure
State
Exposure
Effect
Action

6.1 The need for an integrated framework

6.1.1 Changing perspectives in health

Recent international meetings — from the Earth Summit held in Rio de Janeiro in 1992, to HABITAT II held in Istanbul in 1996 — have made it evident that health-and-environment concerns rise ever higher on the broad environment and development agenda, and that environmental issues are growing in prominence on the public health agenda (see Section 1.2). The health movement has especially emphasized the issues of social justice, equity and human development, while the environment movement has highlighted sustainability in particular. But there is no doubt that health, environment and sustainable development are anything other than inextricably linked together (WHO, 1997e).

The problems facing the health sector today are increasingly complex, multidisciplinary in nature, often ill-defined, and solutions to them uncertain. The health sector cannot address these problems on its own. New and innovative approaches are needed to integrate and operationalize concepts of environmental sustainability, economic development and community development, if human development is to be achieved. Wide-ranging reforms are also needed to more adequately deal with assessment and management of environmental health risks within a framework of sustainable development.

This book has shown how environmental quality is determined by soci-etal driving forces linked to the basic foundations of development. It has shown too how poor environmental quality can lead to severe public health problems. The different elements in the health-and-environment cause–effect framework (**Fig.1.3**) have all been described. Effective action to protect health needs to consider each of these and might, for example, incorporate:

* action on the driving forces through policy development and implementation

* action on the pressures through cleaner production and emissions reduction

* action on the state of the environment through pollution control devices

* action on human exposures through education and personal protection

* action on the resultant health effects through medical care of those who become ill.

Action on exposure and on health effects may be seen as a reactive approach, whereas action on driving forces and pressures may be seen as proactive since it will deal with root

> "The environment-and-health problems faced by many people throughout the world pose a challenge of near herculean dimensions. It is clear that new approaches are urgently needed to tackle such problems in the future"
>
> *WHO, 1997e.*

> ### Box 6.1
>
> #### Role of local authorities
>
> Local authorities have a critical role to play in ensuring that development is sustainable and health–promoting.
>
> Local authorities:
> * operate the economic, social and environmental infrastructure
> * oversee planning processes
> * establish local policies and regulations
> * determine parameters for economic development
> * serve as important vehicles in the development and implementation of local, regional and national policies
> * facilitate community involvement.
>
> *Source: UN, 1993.*

causes. However, one does not exclude the other. Specific health hazards need to be dealt with as soon as they become known or suspected, and the victims of environmental hazards need treatment and care.

6.1.2 New planning frameworks

Agenda 21 calls for the integration of environmental and developmental concerns in decision-making. It also calls for the integration of the social sector, including health, into the process of development planning. It further specifies that countries develop plans for priority actions, based on cooperative planning between the various government levels, nongovernmental organizations (NGOs) and local communities. Only by integrating local and national health concerns into environment and development planning can the most relevant policies and solutions to health-and-environment problems be found.

Agenda 21 also emphasizes the role that local governments can play in fostering sustainability (**Box 6.1**). It calls on local governments to enter into a dialogue with citizens, local organizations and private enterprises, and to adopt a *Local Agenda* 21.

Endorsement for new planning approaches involving four elements is provided by *Agenda* 21:

* identification and assessment of health hazards associated with environment and development

* development of an environmental health policy incorporating principles and strategies for all sectors responsible for development

* communication and advocacy of this policy to all levels of society

* a participatory approach to implementing health-and-environment programmes.

Regarding public participation, *Agenda* 21 explicitly requests the involvement of citizens, the health sector, the health-related sectors, and relevant non-health sectors (such as businesses and social, educational and religious institutions) in finding solutions to health problems. It thus stresses the need for improved coordination between health and related sectors at all appropriate levels of government, and within communities and relevant organizations. It also underscores the need for intersectoral approaches to the reform of health sector personnel development.

A broad array of activities is clearly needed to solve the health–environment–development problems facing us today. To be effective they must form part of integrated and balanced strategies that are holistic in their approach to improving health. Although there are shared global and transnational problems, the specific health-and-environment problems confronting each country, region and community are unique. Solutions to them must therefore be based on consideration of local resources, customs, institutions and values (WHO, 1993f). This implies that a combination of global, national and local strategies needs to be developed, which must be harmonized, and which must integrate health, environment and development concerns (see Sections 6.2, 6.3 and 6.4).

6.1.3 New health information systems

One of the key elements emphasized throughout this book is the need for information on the ways in which human health is influenced by factors such as driving forces and pressures operating at different levels. Efficient, intersectoral health-and-environment programmes depend on convenient access to information about a large variety of hazards, ranging from biological hazards in food and water, to chemical hazards such as pesticides, to the different physical hazards. Information on health risks helps a health authority discharge its responsibility to protect public health. But it also serves to clarify the extent to which health hazards are attributable to environmental conditions and/or to the activities of sectors other than the health sector.

The Commission on Sustainable Development (CSD, 1997a) identified several issues that warrant special attention:

- the need to integrate health into environmental impact assessment procedures

- the need for effective and efficient environmental health information systems

- the need to improve knowledge of environment–health linkages.

In respect of risk assessment and management, information on exposures must be linked to information on health outcomes, so that risks can be better understood and managed. Environmental monitoring systems should therefore be designed to ensure that the exposure information they contain is relevant to health concerns and not merely to environmental control. Currently, few monitoring systems are set up with the aim of comprehensively assessing the various exposure routes (such as air and water) of poten-

tial contaminants. Moreover, integrated pollution control mechanisms are usually lacking.

In general, knowledge of environmental health risks is segmented and information on them incomplete. Commonly, no mechanism exists to ensure coordination at the national, regional and local levels of the evaluation of environmental health effects of hazards, or the development of adequate national reporting systems. Equally, mechanisms are frequently not in place to ensure that such information once obtained is transmitted to the various relevant sectors for action.

Need for integrated health–environment databases

Integrated databases on environmental exposures and health are urgently required. Creation of these will necessitate identification of minimum data sets. Unfortunately, available information is often too specialized for intersectoral use (de Kadt, 1989), and so is frequently not used. Also, highly aggregated national data tend to mask inequities in local health-and-environment conditions, and usually do not address linkages between sectors. Well-developed health-and-environment information systems, based on relevant data sets, are essential if scientific monitoring information is to be provided in support of policy- and decision-making, planning and evaluation.

This is the focus of WHO's work to develop indicators for decision-making in environmental health (see Section 1.5). It is addressing the links between key driving forces, the pressures which they exert on the environment, the resulting state (quality) of the environment, human exposures and health effects (Briggs, Corvalán & Nurminen, 1996; WHO, 1996m; WHO, 1997d). Analysis of these linkages can help authorities and communities plan more effective action.

6.2 International initiatives

6.2.1 Involvement of the UN system: institutional arrangements

UNCED asked the UN organizations to play an active role in supporting countries in sustainable development planning and implementation of *Agenda* 21 (UN, 1993). Many agencies are active in health and environment, including WHO, UNDP and UNEP. Some of the institutional arrangements and initiatives undertaken by selected UN agencies and other bodies since UNCED, which are contributing to integrated approaches to health, environment and development issues, are discussed below. These, and many other related initiatives have been documented in a draft (unpublished) report compiled by CSD (CSD, 1997f).

The Commission on Sustainable Development (CSD) (see Section 1.2) was established as a functional commission of the Economic and Social Council, and has been reviewing progress made in implementing *Agenda* 21. Health-and-environment issues are regularly on the agenda.

The Inter-Agency Committee on Sustainable Development was established in October 1992. It provides a mechanism for system-wide coordination of the follow-up to UNCED, implementation of *Agenda* 21, and sustainable development work in general.

UNEP has established the **Inter Agency Environment Coordination Group**, which is an advisory and consultative body set up to help UNEP discharge its coordination mandate. Areas of cooperation between UNEP and **UNDP** have also been intensified, particularly for development of national frameworks for sustainable development, provision of assistance to governments concerning the servicing and implementation of the Rio and Post-Rio conventions, and mobilization of UNDP's country-based capacity for dissemination of environmental information. Collaboration between UNEP,

UNDP and other agencies also takes place with respect to the Montreal Protocol and the Global Environment Facility.

UNDP created a new Sustainable Energy and Environment Division in 1995, which consists of *Capacity 21* and the Sustainable Development Networking Programme, the Natural Resources Management Programme, the Energy and Atmosphere Programme, the Office to Combat Desertification and Drought, and the Global Environment Facility. The creation of this consolidated division has resulted in a stronger focus on sustainable development in the organization, and facilitates better coordination among its various entities, which in turn means better support to UNDP country offices, regional bureaux and partner countries regarding natural resource management and integration of environment and development.

The *Capacity 21* unit was established in UNDP as a direct response to UNCED and the mandate given to UNDP to undertake capacity-building in support of *Agenda* 21. Its role is to assist the integration of sustainable development issues into development policies, to help involve stakeholders in development planning and environmental management, and to create a body of expertise in capacity-building for sustainable development. *Capacity 21* focal points have been established in each of the five regional bureaux at UNDP headquarters, as well as in each country where a *Capacity 21* programme is being implemented. In addition, at field level, national sustainable development advisors have been assigned, whose role it is to assist in development of national programmes. The Sustainable Development Network Programme aims to facilitate access to information and as of 1995 was operational in 30 countries where *Capacity 21* programmes are under way.

Since UNCED, the **Trade and Development Board** of **UNCTAD** has placed increasing emphasis on issues

"Agenda 21, as the basis for action by the international community to integrate environment and development should provide the principal framework for the coordination of relevant activities within the United Nations system"

UN, 1993.

relating to sustainable development. An ad hoc working group on trade, environment and development was established in 1994 which has dealt *inter alia* with issues such as environmental legislation, environmentally friendly products, and emerging environmental policy instruments which have a trade impact.

At the intergovernmental level, a policy was adopted by the Executive Board of **UNICEF** in 1993 to integrate primary environmental care in all UNICEF-assisted programmes. The aim is to help meet people's basic livelihood and health needs, ensure optimal use and sustainable management of natural resources, and empower local groups or communities to undertake self-directed sustainable development. Additionally, a new water, environment and sanitation group has been formed to help incorporate primary environmental care in UNICEF-supported country programmes. At regional and country levels, programme officers for water and sanitation have been assigned responsibility for coordinating and promoting activities relating to primary environmental care.

Following on from the HABITAT II Conference held in Istanbul in 1996 (UNCHS, 1996a), efforts are being made by **UNCHS** to establish an open-ended "Urban Forum" to stimulate a broad-based dialogue among all key urban stakeholders. This followed from the recognition that issues relating to human settlements were cross-sectoral. UNCHS has also committed itself to strategically addressing *Agenda* 21 priorities related to human settlements. Specific areas that are being focused on include financing of sustainable human settlements development, improved global-to-local financial instruments, sustainable land resource management, changing consumption patterns in human settlements, and promotion of best practices regarding human settlements delivery mechanisms.

WHO has a long history of technical cooperation in environmental health with countries, and in collaboration with other international and bilateral development assistance organizations. It is the only agency whose specific role is to protect and promote health. In response to UNCED, a new Global Strategy on Health and Environment was adopted by the World Health Assembly in 1993. Reorganization at headquarters has taken place in order to promote health-and-environment initiatives, while in the regional offices, new directorates for environmental health have been established.

In 1992, the Director General's Council on the Earth Summit Action Programme for Health and Environment was established to advise on organizational, institutional and financial issues related to the implementation of *Agenda* 21, and the WHO Global Strategy for Health and Environment. The Council highlighted the importance of helping countries to develop and implement national action plans for health and environment, in support of national planning for sustainable development.

ILO has integrated environment and sustainable development issues into its mainstream programmes, into the design and implementation of its technical cooperation activities, into its collaborative activities with UN and other institutional and regional institutions, and in its support to tripartite constituents (for example ministries of employment and labour, and employers and workers organizations). In particular, an environment and "world of work" interdepartmental project has been initiated to implement work-related initiatives emanating from *Agenda* 21.

Following UNCED, it was decided that **FAO** should integrate sustainability criteria into its programmes and activities. The objectives and activities of *Agenda* 21 are now important components of FAO programmes in agriculture, fisheries and forestry. At FAO headquarters, a sustainable development department has been set up to

"If sustainable development is about leaving future generations more capital per capita than we have had, then the rate of genuine saving becomes a good measure of whether our aggregate activities are on a sustainable path"

Mr I. Serageldin,
World Bank.

catalyse and integrate cross-sectoral action in agriculture, forestry, fisheries, rural development and nutrition, and to promote general concepts, strategies and methods relating to sustainable development. Sustainable development multidisciplinary teams have been established at the regional and sub-regional level. An integrated pest management facility has also been established, under the co-sponsorship of FAO and the World Bank.

Both the environmental sciences programme, as well as the environmental education programmes at **UNESCO** have been re-oriented since UNCED, to focus on interlinkages between development and environment. Activities focus on human resources development and capacity-building in developing countries. The Bureau for Coordination of Environmental Programmes is responsible for ensuring cross-sectoral and inter-programme policy development. In addition, an integrated management unit was created outside the structure of the organization's programme sectors for a new project on environment and population education and information for development.

Activities related to UNCED follow-up at **WMO** are being undertaken by existing departments and programmes, and a resource mobilization unit has been formed to secure resources for projects related to the monitoring of atmosphere and related activities. WMO has a particularly important role to play in providing scientific information and advice on climate and climate-related activities. A nongovernmental, non-profit foundation (in effect an alliance for air, water and environment) linked with WMO has been formed, and will work to obtain resources from the private sector for carrying out environmental projects.

UNIDO has established new organizational priorities. The environment and energy priority concerns support for the formulation and implementation of national strategies for environmentally sustainable industrial development, the transfer of technology for

clean and safe industrial production, and support for developing countries in implementing international protocols, conventions and agreements, and industry-related norms and standards. Additionally, an Industrial Sectors and Environment Division has been created to integrate UNIDO's technical expertise with development and implementation of its environment programme, and to foster closer coordination between its policy and operational activities.

At **IAEA,** an Inter-departmental Coordination Group on *Agenda* 21 has been set up to review and coordinate activities relating to *Agenda* 21. IAEA is currently involved in a wide range of activities of relevance to *Agenda* 21, in the areas of: energy; nuclear safety and radiation protection; radioactive waste; food and agriculture; land, forestry and water; human health; biotechnology, and environmental monitoring.

Since UNCED, the **World Bank** has encouraged its borrowing countries to promote environmental stewardship. This has been done by targeting loans to reduce pollution, protect soils and forests, and strengthen environmental policies and institutions. The Bank has environmental programmes in 68 countries. Each operation is now reviewed to ensure that the environmental dimensions of projects are addressed; the technical quality and impact of these assessments has improved markedly. The Bank has also been encouraging a partnership approach with respect to environment programmes, which involves working with NGOs and community groups. Joint programmes with the private sector and other international agencies have also been expanded. The World Bank coordinates external assistance and financing for several regional sea and river programmes, and is one of the implementing agencies for the Global Environment Facility and the Montreal Protocol Fund.

The World Bank has also promoted "win-win" strategies by recognizing the need to encourage the growth of natural capital through reduction of exploitation levels, investment in projects to relieve pressure on natural capital stocks, and increasing investment in human resources, particularly those of the poor (Serageldin, 1996).

6.2.2 Selected cooperative initiatives

Cooperation among the agencies of the UN system and with other intergovernmental and nongovernmental bodies in the health-and-environment area is very important because of its intersectoral nature. Examples of cooperative initiatives in the areas of water and sanitation, environmental management of vector-borne diseases, chemical safety and occupational health, are discussed below.

Water and sanitation
The Water Supply and Sanitation Collaborative Council (WSSCC, 1996) was formed at the end of the UN International Drinking Water Supply and Sanitation Decade (1981–1990). An alliance of professionals working in water supply, sanitation and waste management, its mission is to enhance collaboration among developing countries and external support agencies, so as to accelerate provision of sustainable water supplies, and sanitation and waste management services, particularly to the poor. The Council focuses on improving country-level collaboration, on addressing the service needs of the urban poor, on operation and maintenance activities, and on water demand management and conservation, applied research, and development advocacy and dissemination strategies. Institutional and management options for service delivery are also addressed, with a focus on community-based management and partnerships with civil societies.

Water-related vector-borne diseases
Since 1981, WHO, FAO and UNEP have undertaken collaboration in the form of joint Panel of Experts on Environmental Management for Vector Control (PEEM),

to address the vector-borne disease problems that can result from water resources development projects. In 1991 this interagency collaboration was extended to include UNCHS (HABITAT). At the same time, the scope of PEEM's mandate was extended to include urban management and wastewater use, as well as a shift in focus from mainly promotional to field-oriented activities. Development policy adjustment, health impact assessment, field research to classify specific health risk factors in water resources development and to test the effectiveness of environmental management interventions, are also important aspects of PEEM's work. Capacity-building to strengthen health sector input into the national development dialogue is another main activity (WHO, 1991c).

Essentially, though, PEEM has maintained its intersectoral focus on preventing diseases such as malaria and schistosomiasis from becoming major public health problems in the wake of water resources development. In so doing, it is helping to minimize the burden of these diseases on the health sector and to reduce the need for less environmentally sound interventions such as use of insecticides for vector control.

In the past five years PEEM has been able to launch various initiatives. For example, in the traditional area of promotion, it continued to produce technical guidelines and organized national seminars for policy- and decision-makers on water resources development and vector-borne diseases (WHO, 1994e; WHO, 1995t).

Safe management of chemicals
The International Programme on Chemical Safety (IPCS) dates back to 1980, and is a joint initiative of WHO, ILO and UNEP. IPCS was instrumental in preparing for chemical safety initiatives at the Earth Summit, and laid the groundwork for the development of cooperative initiatives in this area. Then in 1994, in response to an UNCED rec-

> "The full recognition of the role of all sectors of society — governments, social partners, industry, scientific organizations and environmental, public interest and worker groups — in promoting the sound management of chemical risks is an essential element in the Forum's working mechanism"
>
> President's progress report 1994–1997, IFCS.

ommendation, the Intergovernmental Forum on Chemical Safety (IFCS) was established. The Forum is a non-institutional arrangement in which national governments, intergovernmental organizations and NGOs can meet to consider issues associated with the assessment and management of chemical risks. The principal aims of IFCS include:

- identification of priorities for cooperative action on chemical safety
- recommendation of international strategies for hazard identification and risk assessment
- collaboration between national, regional and international bodies in the area of chemical safety
- provision of support for the strengthening of national coordinating mechanisms and capabilities for chemical management
- information exchange
- strengthening of national programmes
- promotion of international cooperation for prevention of and preparedness for chemical accidents.

Achievements have been considerable. For example, the international assessment of chemicals has been accelerated; it is projected that by the end of 1997 over 200 additional assessments will have been completed. And in developing recommendations for international action on a list of identified persistent organic pollutants (POPs) (see **Box 2.8**), the Forum was able to substantially and quickly advance the groundwork required for international action on POPs.

Chemical safety is also being increased through the activities of the Inter-Organization Programme for the Sound Management of Chemicals

(IOMC). This is a cooperative agreement between UNEP, ILO, FAO, WHO, UNIDO and OECD, which was established in 1995, following recommendations made by UNCED to strengthen cooperation and increase international coordination in the field of chemical safety. It promotes coordination of the policies and activities pursued by the participating organizations, jointly or separately, to provide sound management of chemicals in relation to human health and the environment. IOMC's scientific and technical work is carried out through the existing structures of the participating organizations. Activities undertaken within its framework correspond to *Agenda 21* priority programme areas in chemical safety, and include chemical risk assessment, harmonization of classification and labelling of chemicals, risk reduction programmes, strengthening of national capabilities and capacities for management of chemicals, prevention of illegal international traffic in toxic and dangerous products, and information exchange on chemicals and chemical risks (IOMC, 1996).

Since the recognition by all governments at the Earth Summit of the need for sound use of chemicals, and as a result of growing public awareness of chemical risks, a greater number of governments are now taking action to develop chemical safety programmes and to establish national coordinating mechanisms. Coordination is a key element of national programmes for sound management of chemicals. This is because many different parts of the community, in addition to various government departments, should be involved in development and implementation of chemical safety measures.

Occupational health
Both WHO and ILO have been involved in developing cooperative occupational health policies and programmes. For example, ILO has participated in IPCS and is a partner of both IOMC and IFCS. It has also been assigned lead responsi-

bility for coordinating the global harmonization by the year 2000 of existing systems for the classification and labelling of chemicals, including material safety data sheets and easily understandable symbols.

ILO continues also to play an active role in coordinating action on safety and health among international organizations. This involves participation in the joint ILO/WHO Committee on Occupational Health, as well as collaboration with other international bodies. Emphasis continues to be placed on the prevention and detection of occupational lung diseases, which are one of the largest categories of work-related diseases in the world. ILO's labour standards on occupational safety and health form the basis for work in assisting member states to develop and implement national policies for the prevention of work-related injuries and diseases.

At the World Health Assembly in 1996 (see Section 4.8.2) a Global Strategy on Occupational Health was adopted by Member States. It identifies ten priorities for occupational health action at the national and international levels:

- strengthening of international and national policies for health at work, and development of the necessary policy tools

- development of healthy work environments

- development of healthy work practices and promotion of health at work

- strengthening of occupational healthcare services

- establishment of appropriate support services for occupational health

- development of occupational health standards based on scientific risk assessment

- development of human resources for occupational health

- establishment of registration and data systems, development of information services for experts, effective transmission of data, and raising of public awareness through public information distribution

- strengthening of research

- development of collaboration in occupational health with other organizations.

Cooperative legal initiatives

The development of international conventions has proved to be an important tool for securing international cooperation on health-and-environment issues. At the Earth Summit, such conventions were considered on biodiversity, desertification and climate change. These have subsequently been ratified by many countries throughout the world, with other conventions such as the Basel Convention, which deals with the control of transboundary movement of hazardous wastes and their disposal, having been strengthened by several amendments. In the case of the UN Framework Convention on Climate Change, which entered into force in 1994, it has been decided to negotiate a protocol or other legal instrument for adoption, in order to strengthen the commitments of developed countries and those with economies in transition, beyond the year 2000 (CSD, 1997f).

6.3 A stronger health focus in national planning for sustainable development

*A*genda 21 has presented a golden opportunity for health authorities to increase their influence on national planning and to reverse the trend of environmentally damaging and health-threatening development. Many

> "Industrial development with workplace health programmes provides the opportunity to address a great many health issues of relevance to workers, such as accidents or poisonings"
> WHO 1995l.

countries have instituted new policy and planning tools since the Earth Summit to make environmental concerns a part of the planning process, for instance, via national environmental action plans (NEAPs) (World Bank, 1995b).

However, although much progress has been made in recent years concerning development of more comprehensive environmental health policies and strategies, many countries have been relatively slow to adopt them. This has been due in part to gaps in knowledge, the perception that evidence on which to act is insufficient (Anon, 1996c), and the very real challenges facing the health sector in addressing policy needs with respect to energy, industrialization and advanced technology. Nevertheless, appreciation is growing that the health sector has a key role to play in helping ensure that the policies and strategies of various sectors and organizations contribute positively to health protection and promotion.

6.3.1 Regional and country initiatives

The first regionally coordinated health-and-environment activity took place in Europe in 1989, when a meeting was held in Frankfurt to bring together ministers of health and environment. The **European Charter on Health and Environment** was adopted at the meeting and it was also decided that a review of the key environmental health threats in Europe should be the foundation for future national and regional preventive action (WHO, 1989b). This review was produced in 1995 as *Concern for Europe's tomorrow* (WHO, 1995p). It presents detailed analysis of Europe's current and potential environmental health problems.

A follow-up meeting of the same ministers was held in Helsinki in 1994, when it was decided that each WHO Member State in Europe should prepare a national environmental health action plan (NEHAP) before the end of 1997. In addition, a declaration entitled **Action for Environment and Health**

(WHO, 1994d) was adopted.

Subsequent to this, a meeting of representatives of the ministries of environment and health of the Central Asian Republics was held at Lake Issyk-Kul, in order to determine practical actions which could be implemented in respect of environment and health in this sub-region. The resulting **Issyk-Kul Resolution on Action for Environment and Health Protection in Central Asian Republics** stressed the need to ensure that NEHAPs are integrated into, or closely linked to NEAPs (WHO, 1996w).

In 1995, the Pan American Conference on Health and Environment in Sustainable Development was held in Washington which resulted in the **Pan American Charter on Health and Environment in Sustainable Human Development** (PAHO, 1996a). The conference's most important outcome was its political contribution to the reaffirmation, facilitation and consolidation of those national processes which seek to incorporate health-and-environment considerations into national development plans and policies, and to ensure that national development processes are sustainable. The recommendations of the Pan American Conference were also adopted by the Summit of the Americas, recently held in Bolivia. A Regional Plan of Action has been developed to guide implementation of the charter at national level (PAHO, 1996b).

Several countries in the Pan American Region have demonstrated additional commitment to coordination of health-and-environment policies. For example, Central American countries have collaboratively drafted a **Declaration on Ecology and Health**, referring to the Central American Isthmus. The declaration is aimed at securing the consensus of various national sectors regarding health, the environment and development.

In the Eastern Mediterranean Region, a conference was held on health, environment and development in 1995. Attended by ministers of health and ministers of environment of the Member States of this region, it led to the **Beirut Declaration on Action for a Healthy Environment** (WHO, 1996n).

Measures to incorporate health-and-environment initiatives into national programmes have varied from country to country, depending on planning mechanisms, the current status of a country's sustainable development programme, and the division of planning responsibilities. Thus different approaches are being used for promoting health sector involvement in addressing health-and-environment issues. In some countries, health-and-environment plans have been prepared for inclusion in national plans for sustainable development. In others, sectoral plans have been reviewed and modified to include health-and-environment concerns. In many cases, the inclusion of health-and-environment activities in the plans of other sector ministries may actually be more important than the existence of a separate plan (WHO, 1995l).

Many countries have established intersectoral committees for follow-up on *Agenda* 21. The health sector has been able to exert significant influence through these fora — which often include task forces and working groups set up to address specific issues.

In 1993, in cooperation with UNDP, WHO launched an initiative to help governments incorporate health-and-environment considerations into their national planning. This work has included evaluation of existing mechanisms for interministerial coordination, assessment of options for establishing formal relationships between ministries and agencies, ensuring that health-and-environment sectors are represented on interministerial committees for sustainable development, and sensitization of planning and sectoral ministries to health-and-environment issues. Awareness-raising in the different sectors of the importance of health-and-environment issues, promotion of intersectoral action, and strengthening of the role of

the health sector in planning for sustainable development, have been important components of this work. Examples of country initiatives are given in **Box 6.2**.

Similar initiatives are under way in, for example, Barbados (which has developed a broadly endorsed health-and-environment plan), the Maldives, Mexico, Bolivia and Kyrgyzstan, while in Ghana, decentralization of authority to the district and local level has provided an opportunity to facilitate intersectoral action.

In Europe, some countries have

Box 6.2

Country initiatives

In Jordan, an intersectoral working group was set up by the Ministry of Health and a national health-and-environment action plan prepared.

In Guatemala, a working team was established with representation from the Health Ministry, planning and environment sectors, and a national plan for environmental health and sustainable development produced, accompanied by an institutional analysis of national sectors associated with health and the environment.

In Guinea-Bissau, a national inter-ministerial committee on health and the environment was constituted to foster a national process of coordination among agencies, government, and civil society, conducive to the integration of health-and-environment concerns into overall national sustainable development planning. A national plan of action on health and environment for sustainable development was produced.

In Iran, a draft strategy document on health and environment was developed, to be incorporated ultimately into a national strategy on sustainable development. The draft strategy included a situation analysis, and proposals for structural and institutional reform.

In Nepal, a health perspective was added to the draft Nepal Environmental Policy and Action Plan. Initially, it did not incorporate a public health component. Through the Nepal Environmental Health Initiative, a comprehensive health-and-environment strategy was developed, and most of the resultant recommendations incorporated into the final Environmental Policy and Action Plan.

In the Philippines, collaboration was strengthened between health agencies and the Philippine Council for Sustainable Development. The latter oversees implementation of activities in support of commitments to sustainable development principles made at the Earth Summit. An Interagency Committee on Environmental Health organized by the Ministry of Health and the Council jointly sponsored a detailed analysis with case studies of the best way of integrating health-and-environment issues into the development and implementation of national plans for sustainable development.

Source: WHO, 1995l.

Fig. 6.1

Selected environmental health objectives of the US department of health and human services

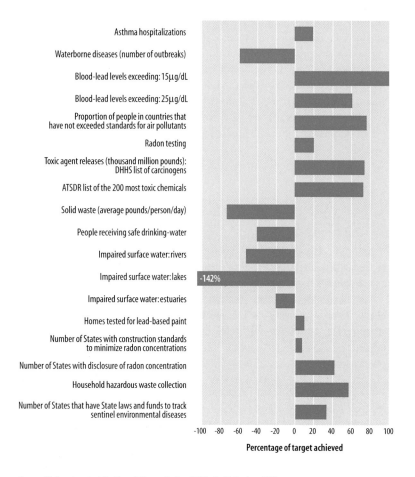

Source: US Department of Health and Human Services, Public Health Service, 1995.

health could be made, indicating who would be responsible for implementing them. It contains more than 160 actions for improving national environmental health, taking into account the opinions of various stakeholders. Areas covered by the plan include institutional frameworks, environmental health management tools, specific environmental hazards, living and work environments, and economic (development) sectors.

Hungary has submitted a draft NEHAP to the Hungarian Parliament for consideration (Ministry of Welfare, 1996). A joint effort between the Ministry of Welfare and the Ministry of Environment and Regional Policy, working under the auspices of the national public health committee, it will form the basis for securing environmental protection from an environmental health perspective.

Sweden's NEHAP was prepared by a special Commission on Environmental Health. Its report was called *Environment for sustainable health development* (Ministry of Health and Social Affairs, 1996), to highlight the fact that Sweden has a high level of health, but aims to create an environment that will maintain and sustain health in the future. One of the Commission's tasks was to determine what more could be done without recourse to new financial resources.

In the USA a wide range of environmental health objectives has been incorporated into the National Health Promotion and Disease Prevention Objectives of the US Department of Health and Human Services (US Department of Health and Human Services, 1995). The status of these is given in **Fig. 6.1**.

These country experiences with regard to integrated planning initiatives are important, since they show how new impetus for health-and-environment protection can be created within different government agencies. Within countries, considerable action has also been undertaken at the local level.

already developed NEHAPs (for example UK, Hungary and Sweden), and many others are in the process of doing so. Those NEHAPs which have been developed are important as "blueprints" for priority action. But their greatest importance may lie in the process of intersectoral consultation and collaboration which they have encouraged. This process has led to a greater understanding of the importance of environmental issues within health ministries and a greater understanding of the importance of health issues within environment ministries.

The UK NEHAP sets out ways in which improvements to environmental

6.4 A stronger health focus in local planning for sustainable development

6.4.1 Relevance at local level

While we may not fully understand how, or even if, sustainable development can truly be achieved, there is consensus that it can only occur at global level if it first occurs at local level (ICLEI, 1996).

Accordingly, while it is recognized that local governments frequently have the main responsibility for ensuring healthy living environments, they fulfil this task by working in collaboration and partnership with other tiers of government, NGOs, community-based organizations, and the private sector. The traditional service roles of government, the private sector, community organizations and trade unions have all changed rapidly in recent years due to fiscal constraints, constitutional and legal reforms, resource scarcity, globalization of economies, liberalization of markets, ecological concerns, changing social norms and values, and demographic pressures (ICLEI, 1996). As a result, local government bodies have understood the need to adopt a partnership approach to service provision and planning.

One of UNCED's most notable results has been the creation of a large number of local *Agenda* 21 initiatives, especially in cities, but also in villages, and even on islands. Since 1992, more than 1300 local authorities from 31 countries have responded to the *Local Agenda* 21 mandate by developing their own action plans (ICLEI, 1996). Many of these feature health and health-related objectives and activities. In Europe, in 1994, the European Sustainable Cities and Towns Campaign was created to assist local governments to establish *Local Agenda* 21 processes in their cities.

Local Agenda 21 and related activities include, among others, the **WHO Healthy Cities Movement**, the **Sustainable Cities Movement** (of UNCHS) and the **Model Communities Programme** of the International Council for Local Environmental Initiatives (ICLEI). They all recognize the fundamental importance and central role that communities must play in bringing about change. This implies decentralization. Indeed, a global trend towards decentralized government services, and greater emphasis on health-and-environment actions on the part of NGOs and the community itself, can now be observed. All these initiatives focus on the development of participatory planning models.

Many of the approaches and the ultimate goals of the various participatory planning initiatives referred to above are similar. An attempt is now being made to bring these various movements together — this is reflected in the growing trend whereby international meetings focus on issues relating to healthy and sustainable cities, environmentally sound and healthy cities, and so on. The idea is to better integrate environmental, social, economic, health and land-use planning considerations at the local level.

In Europe, an initiative is under way to provide guidance on incorporating health and sustainable development concerns in long-term strategic plans for European cities. A multi-city action plan has been established within the framework of the WHO Healthy Cities Project, and the European Sustainable Cities and Towns Campaign. It is hoped that practical steps will be developed to ensure that health concerns are incorporated into the *Local Agenda* 21 process. So far, twelve local authorities have committed themselves to participating in the plan over a two-year period (WHO, 1996u).

6.4.2 Focus on urban areas

Urban human settlements were the main item on the agenda at the HABITAT II meeting held in Istanbul, Turkey, in 1996 (UNCHS, 1996a). It drew

"We all must move down from the Summit and into the trenches where the real world actions and decisions are taken that will, in the final analysis, determine whether the vision of Rio will be fulfilled and the agreements reached there implemented"

Maurice Strong
Secretary-General, UNCED.

attention to cities, in the light of rapid urbanization trends occurring throughout the world. Several international conferences have now taken place that emphasized the importance of urban environments and sustainable development, including the 1994 Global Forum meeting held in Manchester in the UK.

Healthy Cities

WHO's Healthy Cities Programme is a long-term urban health and development initiative which aims to improve the health and well-being of people living and working in cities (Tsouros, 1992). It is based on a number of key principles: that health should be an integral part of settlements management and development; that health can be improved by modifying the physical, social and economic environment; that conditions in settings such as the home, school, village, workplace and city, profoundly influence health status, and that intersectoral coordination for health is necessary at the local level. Health challenges currently facing cities in the quest for sustainable development are briefly outlined in **Box 6.3**.

The project is purposefully political and process-oriented, promoting political commitment and advocating for fundamental change in local government and its relationships with cities. It supports two aspects of local gover-

nance in particular to address health-and-environment issues. Firstly, it supports local-level technical activities such as resource mobilization and allocation, plan formulation and technology application. Secondly, it supports representational and participatory activities, channels for popular representation, and increased transparency and accountability in the workings of local authorities.

When the programme was initiated in 1985, little experience had been gained of collaborative work between sectors and communities to improve health. Very little was also known about health inequities at local and district levels, and appreciation of the social and environmental determinants of health was limited. The Healthy Cities approach seeks to ensure that health does not remain the exclusive affair of health departments and professionals, but that all development sectors and agencies, including those dealing with housing, local government, agriculture, industry, transport and planning, address health issues in their work.

Developing solutions to problems on a community-wide basis not only requires partnerships between municipal government agencies (health, water, sanitation, housing, social welfare, etc.), but also with universities, NGOs, private companies, community organizations and groups. **Mayors/ municipalities** may commit themselves to a Healthy City process, that involves formulation and adoption of a **municipal health plan,** involving the collaboration of many different agencies.

Healthy Cities projects have generated a large amount of practical knowledge concerning strategies and structures for more integrated approaches to health and development at the local level (**Box 6.4** describes Healthy City activities in Tunisia). Examples from all continents were reviewed during the HABITAT II Dialogue entitled "Creating Healthy Cities in the 21st Century" (WHO, 1996o). Much has been learnt

---

Box 6.3

Health challenges for cities

Cities are challenged to:

- reduce inequalities in health status and in the determinants of health
- develop healthy public policies at the local level to create physical and social environments that support health
- strengthen community action for health
- help people develop new skills for health compatible with these approaches
- reorient health services in accordance with policy.

about how to promote health in cities, by building on local resources and capacities and linking such actions to local *Agenda* 21 initiatives (WHO, 1997e).

Networks of cities in all regions of the world have been formed, to make health an integral component of settlements management (Goldstein, 1996). They include:

* a network of Healthy Cities in French-speaking African countries, as well as projects in other cities such as Accra (Ghana), Dar es Salaam (Tanzania) and Johannesburg (South Africa)

* individual projects as well as national or state Healthy Cities networks in Latin America

* projects in many cities and several national and state networks in Canada and the USA

* projects and networks in the Eastern Mediterranean Region, the South-East Asian Region, and the Western Pacific Region

* over 600 projects in Europe.

City "**twinning**" initiatives have also become popular, and are based on relationships between cities that have particular ties with respect to language, culture, level of development, political history and so forth. They share agendas to improve health-and-environment conditions in cities. **Multi-city action plans** are another approach to the planning of healthy cities. For these, networks of cities simultaneously address a particular issue such as tobacco use, transport, or a health problem such as asthma. The Healthy Cities Programme and approach has also been applied to a number of rural areas as "Healthy Villages" projects (see Section 6.4.3).

Box 6.4
Tunisia Healthy City Project

Tunisia, like many other countries, is undergoing rapid urbanization, resulting in increased urban health risks. The Healthy Cities concept has consequently won the support and commitment of leading politicians in the country. In 1990, following a successful symposium on Healthy Cities held in the Maghreb, which brought together representatives from four neighbouring countries, a Healthy Cities network was established. This has expanded steadily, and includes the participation of the ministries of the interior, housing, environment, land use and planning, social affairs, youth and children, and education and science, of each country. Special efforts are made to raise awareness of the project through television, radio and the press.

Each city in Tunisia has its own network of neighbourhood committees. These contribute to local development and support municipal activities. Funded by the residents themselves, each committee encourages positive community participation in all matters relating to the environment and health, and seeks improvements in community-based hygiene, particularly in its poorer areas. School competitions are held, festivals and clean-up campaigns are run, and tree-planting activities and greening programmes initiated. Today, Tunisia has over 5000 neighbourhood committees.

These activities have made tangible improvements to Tunisian cities, and the experience has made the neighbourhood committees increasingly self-confident.

Successes include the following:

* urban areas now have safe drinking-water, and general sanitation in the cities is improving

* development projects frequently include a health component

* coordination between the different sectors concerned with health and the environment is good

* primary health care services are being strengthened

* the physical appearance of clean cities has improved — cities now contain well cared for trees and green open spaces

* improved coastal water quality

* decline in the incidence of common communicable diseases due to improvements in social conditions.

Source: WHO Regional Office for the Eastern Mediterranean.

Local Agenda 21 and Sustainable Cities

The UN Centre for Human Settlements (UNCHS or HABITAT) has been administering its Sustainable Cities programme since 1989, in collaboration with UNDP and UNEP. The project is working towards implementation of *Agenda* 21 at local level, with the ultimate aim of developing participatory environmental management and planning practices, to encourage sound natural resource management and reduce environmental hazards that threaten the sustainability of urban growth and development. The programme is currently working with local governments in Asia, Latin America and Eastern Europe.

In fact, a wide range of initiatives in urban environmental management is ongoing worldwide. Strategies for improvement of environmental information and technical expertise, better implementation of policies and strategies, enhanced institutional and participatory capacities, and more effective use of scarce resources for effecting change, have been recommended. At a meeting of participating cities held immediately prior to HABITAT II, the **Istanbul Manifesto** was adopted, which will help cities and programmes in the follow-up and implementation of global and national plans of action. This activity is an important step in a process of city-driven global support activities which will define local efforts and international cooperation in urban environment matters (UNCHS/UNEP, 1996).

ICLEI has created a *Local Agenda 21* initiative which includes a research programme (involving selected cities) to develop tools and models of sustainable development training, as well as a larger network of local governments and their partners who undertake sustainable development planning processes (ICLEI, 1996).

6.4.3 Focus on rural areas

The Healthy Villages concept is an emerging approach to public health and health promotion at the village level. Many of its components are similar to those described above for Healthy Cities. Healthy Cities projects in a number of countries have extended to include neighbouring villages and rural areas, enabling adoption of a comprehensive and integrated approach to dealing with health in urban and rural development. Basic human needs are often similar for urban and rural dwellers, and the Healthy Cities approach provides a mechanism for communities to organize themselves and form partnerships with local and district government agencies, to address local health-and-environment issues (WHO, 1996p).

In 1995, the first Healthy Village conference was held in Isfahhan, in the Islamic Republic of Iran. In Iran, the Healthy Village concept and programme operates within the primary health care system. There is also a Healthy Village project in Egypt, which is concerned with issues such as water and sanitation, health and hygiene education, housing, income generation

---

Box 6.5

Egypt Healthy Villages Project

A large-scale Healthy Village project run by WHO/UNDP and the Egyptian Government has been in operation since 1993. The project is currently operating in 13 governorates and will expand to 26 soon. It is concentrating on improvement of low-cost sanitation options, hygiene education and housing, as well as income-generation in the villages. Community participation and consultation are fundamental to the project's approaches and activities. The government implementing agency is the Organization for the Development of Egyptian Villages, within the Ministry of Local Administration.

The project has successfully developed an information and communication system which has been an effective vehicle for health promotion, produced low-cost sanitation technologies and methodologies, and mobilized the local government and community resources necessary for project implementation. The project has demonstrated that using the resources of local government, universities and individuals reduces development costs and saves time and money; that problem-oriented and issue-specific health action attracts more public attention and involvement than generic, vertical, health programmes (thereby facilitating health promotion processes) and that poverty alleviation is the first step in health promotion.

Source: WHO Regional Office for the Eastern Mediterranean.

and employment (see **Box 6.5**). Healthy Village projects exist also in Syria, Oman, Nepal and Sri Lanka, to name a few.

Relevant rural environmental health issues include safe water supplies, basic sanitation, vector-borne diseases, risks arising from misuse of agrochemicals, poor indoor air quality, transport- and workplace-related accidents, and school health issues (see Sections 3.3.6, 3.4.2, 4.2, 4.4.4, 5.6.2, 5.6.3 and 5.7.3).

6.4.4 Focus on islands

The Healthy Cities approach has also been adopted to address health-and-environment issues on islands, in line with WHO's regional New Horizons in Health Policy for island settings (WHO, 1955n). In March 1995, for example, on Yanuca Island, Fiji, a conference of Ministers of Health of the Pacific Islands adopted the Healthy Islands concept as their unifying theme for health promotion and health protection, and issued the **Yanuca Island Declaration on Health in the Pacific in the 21st Century** (WHO, 1996v).

By applying the Healthy Island concept, islands can improve their health system, create stronger links between island nations through networking, and ensure that greater attention is paid to health promotion and protection, environmental health, and to intersectoral initiatives to secure these.

Since the **Yanuca Island Declaration**, many Healthy Island projects have been initiated in a number of island nations (see **Box 6.6** for an example).

6.5 Integrated planning initiatives: successes and achievements

It is probably true to say that during the 1980s many of the concepts concerning intersectoral collaboration and integrated development looked very promising in theory, but that prac-

---

Box 6.6

Solomon Islands Healthy Islands Project

Honiara, the small quiet capital of the Solomon Islands has been christened the "Malaria Capital of the Pacific". During 1992, the number of reported malaria cases exceeded the total population number. In 1995, the community joined forces with WHO's Malaria Control Programme to mount an intensive effort to reduce malaria to a point where it would no longer be a public health burden. With input from international donor partners, WHO created a package of targeted control measures that covered the entire population. Diagnosis and treatment control facilities were upgraded, insecticide-treated bednets were distributed to households (particularly for pregnant women and infants), and measures to eliminate breeding sites put into place. The construction of a special pipeline at the mouth of the river that flows through the centre of Honiara enabled water to flow constantly between the river and the sea. Together with regular cleaning of the river banks, this resulted in virtual elimination of the mosquito problem.

This activity also stimulated interest in cleaning up the river. Improvement of sanitation and solid waste disposal in settlement areas along the river has now occurred; in areas where latrines once overhung the river, pour-flush toilets have been installed, collection of household waste has been improved, and a project designed to drain a major swamp along the river.

Malaria control efforts have been accompanied by an intensive community education programme that increased community awareness about malaria and what could be done to control the disease. These efforts succeeded in reducing malaria incidence in the most malarious parts of Honiara by 78%. Moreover, for the first time, the residents of the settlement areas and the capital have seen that, together, they can act to improve their health status. This is just one example of how the concepts of the Yanuca Declaration on Healthy Islands can be put into practice.

Source: WHO Regional Office for the Western Pacific.

---

tice proved disappointing. However, many important lessons have been learned in recent years from the successes and failures of various initiatives (WHO, 1997e). It is now possible to better identify what does and doesn't work, and pinpoint the constraints to creation and development of integrated, intersectoral initiatives.

In the past, complexity, and the interrelatedness of issues has tended to be ignored. But it has now been shown that the "one problem, one solution" approach is no longer valid. Ad-hoc, piecemeal approaches that serve narrowly defined, short-term interests cannot achieve policy goals. Environment, health and development issues cannot be dealt with as if they were discrete, independent entities, unconnected to one other. Furthermore, individual sectors working in isolation cannot respond adequately to people's needs. Instead, the efforts of all sectors and departments whose work impinges on health and environment must be combined and focused (Lawrence, 1996).

Initiatives have been successful in the following ways (UNCHS 1996a; WHO, 1997e):

- We know more about the consequences for health of factors such as poor housing, food, education and unemployment.

- A broader approach to health is being adopted, and the need to incorporate health-and-environment planning into sustainable development planning has been recognized.

- A reorientation of thinking away from purely curative medicine has occurred.

- Better policies, plans and practices have been implemented that contribute to health.

- Health is more visible on the political agenda. The importance of increasing the visibility of and gaining political support for health has been recognized, and means of achieving this have been documented.

- Knowledge of effective organizational structures and management strategies has been obtained.

- Examples now exist of how the stakeholders in a community can be brought together to develop a shared vision and understanding of actions that can be taken to improve health and environment.

- We have gained a deeper understanding of the practical issues that must be addressed if plans for improving health and environment are to succeed.

- Tools such as indicators have been developed to measure performance in achieving goals and targets.

- We have many examples of initiatives that have promoted equity, sustainability, supportive environments, active community participation, and, ultimately, better health.

6.6 Renewing "Health for All"

In 1977, the World Health Assembly decided that the main social target of governments and of WHO should be attainment by all the people of the world by the year 2000 of a level of health that will permit them to lead a socially and economically productive life — popularly known as Health for All by the Year 2000. The following year an international conference on primary health care, held in Alma-Ata, USSR, identified primary health care as the key to meeting this target. Then in 1979 the World Health Assembly launched the Global Strategy for Health for All, by endorsing the Alma-Ata Declaration, and inviting Member States to act individually in formulating national strategies, and collectively in formulating regional and global strategies (WHO, 1981).

But beneath encouraging facts about decreasing mortality and increasing life expectancy, and many other unquestionable advances, lie unacceptable disparities in health between rich and poor, between one population group and another, between age groups, and between the sexes (see Section 2.4). In particular, obstacles to the attainment of health — such as rapid unplanned urbanization and environmental degradation — have increased in magnitude and are exacting a heavy toll in terms of disease and mortality.

Therefore, in 1995 the World

"Whilst some of the necessary reforms for meaningful improvements to health may take 20 to 30 years to achieve, nevertheless many successes have indeed already been achieved"

WHO, 1997e.

Health Assembly called for a reassessment of the Health-for-All Strategy, to culminate in a Renewal Strategy (see Section 1.10). Various trends have made renewal necessary, including globalization of trade, travel and technology, urbanization and the growth of megacities, widening gaps between rich and poor, changing concepts of health, the rise in non-communicable diseases, and growth in environmental threats.

Renewal has three dimensions:

- reaffirming the Health-for-All principle

- applying what has been learned from experience and research in the last 20 years, particularly with regard to making health services more effective, efficient and equitable

- adapting existing approaches or introducing new ones to face new realities.

Advancing intersectoral action involves better defining the sectoral burden of disease, so that a balance sheet can be developed for each sector, which shows its impacts — both positive and negative — on health. The new strategy will therefore work on incorporating forecasts of future trends in disease burden in policy-making and forward planning. More accurate estimation of future disease burdens will thus be needed. This in turn will demand a more comprehensive understanding of health determinants, including the complex interactions between socioeconomic, environmental, demographic, macropolitical and health sector determinants.

The draft Health-for-All Policy (HFA) (WHO, 1997b) affirms that health has to be placed firmly at the top of the development agenda. The extreme ill health and environmental degradation associated with poverty makes it essential that combating poverty becomes the highest develop-

ment priority. Integrated long-term development strategies and approaches that include debt reduction and provision of credit are needed, as are strategies to reduce unemployment and create sustainable livelihoods. Economic policies that enhance equity will reduce poverty and contribute to improved health and environmental sustainability. The need to adopt a gender perspective is seen as critical, in particular the need to enhance the dignity, self-worth, capacity and contributions of women.

HFA also stresses the need for stronger collaboration between health and other sectors, and the need to promote health in all settings. HFA emphasizes that the policies of all sectors that have major direct or indirect effects on health should be aligned to promote and protect health. Fiscal policies, such as those that discourage production and consumption of products harmful to health and the environment, when combined with appropriate legislation and education programmes, will help to delay and reverse negative trends, particularly the increases in non-communicable diseases and trauma.

The health sector has a major responsibility to ensure that appropriate policies are developed and actions taken to support HFA, which are based on knowledge of the broader determinants of health, and on workable strategies to address these, involving all relevant sectors and civil society. Capacity-building based on multidisciplinary, intersectoral approaches is fundamental in this regard, as is the need to overcome the fragmentation and lack of coordination between different sectors, and within the health sector itself, at all tiers of government, through institutional restructuring. The creation of sustainable health systems is seen as a vital component of the renewed HFA Strategy (WHO, 1997b). Equally important is the need for sustainable environmental management systems. Fundamental in this regard is

> *"Health for All is not an achievable goal until millions more women are empowered to promote and safeguard their own health, and consequently their own development"*
> WHO, 1995v.

that stronger local governance of health-and-environment systems be encouraged and facilitated, supported by national and global governance systems.

Health for All thus remains the overriding vision for health in the 21st Century. It provides support for many of the key concepts, policies and strate-gies recommended in *Agenda* 21 (WHO, 1997b). The policy's operational principles are compatible with human-centred sustainable development and give priority to intersectoral action and partnerships. Governments implementing policies with a strong equity orientation are more likely to follow a path to sustainable development. ❑

Chapter 7
Conclusions

Driving Force
Pressure
State
Exposure
Effect
Action

At the time of the Earth Summit in 1992, the WHO Commission on Health and Environment presented an assessment of the relationship between health and environment, in the context of development. The Commission's report was a major contribution to UNCED and brought health towards the top of the environment and development agenda. The Rio Declaration's first principle affirms that human beings are entitled to a healthy life.

Five years is a short time to report on progress in such a complex field as health and environment, but the Special Session of the UN General Assembly presented an opportunity for reassessing the available information on health-and-environment linkages and analysing this information from the point of view of sustainable development.

The major health problems due to environmental hazards remain, but progress can be seen in awareness raising, policy and planning at various levels, and concrete action, particularly action at the local level. Health indicators in some countries have improved, mainly due to economic development. However, the benefits of development are not equitably distributed; absolute poverty is still on the increase globally, and it is the poor who are most vulnerable to health-and-environment hazards.

This reassessment includes recent quantitative information on the global and regional burdens of disease and gives estimates of the impacts of major environmental hazards on specific health conditions.

It is becoming increasingly clear that the environmental factors that most affect health are in turn linked to underlying pressures on the environment. These pressures are determined by driving forces such as population growth, inequitable resource distribution, consumption patterns, technological development and components of economic development. Since these pressures and subsequent health hazards are associated with the activities of several sectors, effective action to protect health will require coordination and collaboration between these sectors.

In brief, a new perspective on health has emerged whereby health is seen as an essential component of sustainable development, which in turn depends on concerted action by all sectors of society. The 21st Century calls for a new health system which is partnership-oriented, population health-based, and proactive rather than reactive. The health sector must be a guide and partner in these actions so that health concerns are represented appropriately at all stages of implementation.

A number of major conclusions emerge from the assessments made in this book. They are not listed here in order of priority because each of them is of major importance at global level, and the specific concerns at the local and national levels vary.

• Environmental quality is an important direct and indirect determinant of human health. Deteriorating environmental conditions are a major contributory factor to poor health and poor quality of life, and hinder sustainable development.

- •• Most detrimental environmental impacts on health are related to poverty which itself stems from lack of economic development and inequitable distribution of economic benefits. However, economic development without due concern for health and environment often creates major health risks.

- •• Populations in the least developed countries are most at risk from "traditional" environmental health hazards, which constitute the largest environmental proportion of the global disease burden. They include lack of water supply and sanitation, poor housing and shelter, unsafe food and high prevalence of disease vectors.

- •• The populations of developing countries that are undergoing rapid industrialization tend to be at risk both from the "traditional" environmental health hazards and from "modern" hazards such as air and water pollution, hazardous waste, unsafe use of chemicals including pesticides, workplace hazards and traffic accidents.

- • Major challenges to sustainable development are posed by mismanagement of natural resources, excessive waste production and associated environmental conditions that affect health.

  - •• Wasteful consumption and production patterns in the more affluent countries result in environmental disruption, and counteract efforts to ensure more equitable access to and sustainable use of natural resources.

- •• Growing populations in many countries, combined with the unmet basic needs of the poor, create major challenges with respect to the attainment of sustainable development.

- •• A disproportionate number of the poor are women. Their poverty, in combination with their traditional social roles, puts them at increased risk for certain environmental hazards.

- • Impoverished populations living in rural and peri-urban areas are at greatest risk from degraded environmental conditions. The cumulative effects of inadequate and hazardous shelter, overcrowding, lack of water supply and sanitation, unsafe food, air and water pollution, and high accident rates, impact heavily on the health of these vulnerable groups.

  - •• The number of urban poor is growing rapidly; estimates suggest that in the year 2000 it will have risen to at least 1000 million. On average, 50% of the urban population in developing countries lives in conditions of extreme deprivation. In some cities, the figure may be even higher .

  - •• Within cities, mortality and morbidity rates are higher among people in low-income settlements — due to poor housing, high population density, pollution, lack of basic services and inadequate social amenities — than among people in more affluent areas.

  - •• In rural areas, the main environmental health problems consist of the traditional hazards caused by water and sanitation deficiencies, poor indoor air quality and disease vectors. To these may be added the increasing risk of exposure to modern hazards such as those created by unsafe use of chemicals in agriculture.

** Lack of economic development in rural areas, and out-migration of males, frequently leave women in difficult economic and environmental conditions.

• Poor environmental quality is directly responsible for around 25% of all preventable ill-health in the world today, with diarrhoeal diseases and acute respiratory infections (ARI) heading the list. Other diseases such as malaria, schistosomiasis, other vector-borne diseases, chronic respiratory diseases and childhood infections are also strongly influenced by adverse environmental conditions, as are injuries.

** On average, the individual burden of diarrhoeal diseases and ARI is about 100 times greater in the least developed countries than in developed countries. These diseases are particularly serious among children.

** Vector-borne diseases are closely linked to geographic and climatic conditions, and constitute the largest share of the disease burden of certain tropical countries.

** Unintentional injuries, chronic respiratory diseases and cancers are the most serious environmentally-related health problems affecting adults.

** The workplace is one of the most hazardous environments, with 125 million injured each year in the formal sector; workers in the informal sector may experience even greater health risks.

• In today's world, it is children's health that is most damaged by poor environmental quality. As much as two-thirds of all preventable ill health due to environmental conditions occurs among children.

** Deaths due to environmentally-related childhood diseases could be virtually eliminated by a combination of environmental improvements, immunization and proper health care.

** Environmental improvements are crucial to significant and long-term reduction in the morbidity of these diseases.

** In parallel with industrial development, particular problems for children's health have come to the fore, such as exposure to lead and other hazardous chemicals, which affect children's mental and physical development.

** Environmental improvements create health benefits for both adults and children, thus doubly benefiting children.

• Lack of basic sanitation, poor water supply and poor food safety contribute greatly to diarrhoeal disease mortality and morbidity. Curative measures have brought the number of deaths from diarrhoeal diseases down, but action that deals with the root causes of these diseases continues to be lacking.

** From 1990 to 1994 the number of people without sanitation increased by nearly 300 million, and in 1994 totalled 2900 million for developing countries; this figure is projected to increase to 3300 million by the year 2000.

•• From 1990 to 1994 nearly 800 million people gained access to safe water supplies. Due to population growth, however, the number of unserved decreased only from 1600 million in 1990 to 1100 million in 1994.

•• In both cases, it is rural populations who are worse off. In 1994 sanitation coverage in rural areas was a mere 18%, whereas it was 63% in urban areas. Likewise, access to water amounted to 70% coverage in rural areas, but to 82% in urban areas.

•• The reported incidence of foodborne diarrhoeal diseases is increasing in both developed and developing countries.

•• Programmes to improve sanitation and related hygiene behaviours continue to receive very low priority and to be allocated few resources. A major change in the understanding of the importance of these issues is urgently required.

• Air pollution figures prominently as a contributor to a number of diseases (ARI, chronic respiratory diseases, cardiovascular diseases and cancer) and to a lowering of the quality of life in general.

•• By far the highest exposures to air pollution occur indoors in developing countries, where biomass and coal are used for cooking and heating, causing millions of cases of ARI and chronic respiratory disease. As many as 1000 million people, mostly women and children, are severely exposed.

•• Urban air pollution, while declining somewhat in most developed countries, is increasing in many developing country cities, particularly with respect to suspended particulate matter, sulfur dioxide, nitrogen dioxide, hydrocarbons and ozone.

•• An estimated 3 million premature deaths, mainly from acute and chronic respiratory infections, are attributed to exposure to air pollution on a global basis. Of these deaths, 2.8 million are due to indoor air pollution exposures, primarily in developing countries.

•• There is every indication that urban air pollution will continue to increase in developing countries due to population growth, urbanization, and increases in motor vehicle traffic, and in industrial and energy production.

• The occurrence of the major vector-borne diseases is closely related to naturally existing environmental conditions. In addition, the incidence, severity and distribution of vector-borne diseases are affected substantially by human activities such as water and agricultural developments, and by urbanization.

•• Malaria is a major disease transmitted by mosquitos, the habitat of which is closely linked to climatic and environmental conditions. Over 500 million people are affected by malaria, in over 90 countries. The problem is increasing, due at least in part, to land degradation, deforestation, the expansion of agriculture and mining into new areas, and urbanization. The high rate of malaria in the countries affected is in itself a major impediment to economic development.

•• Schistosomiasis is another tropical disease which is strongly related to environmental conditions. Spread via a parasite in freshwater snails, it infects more than 200 million people.

•• Other major vector-borne diseases, each affecting more than 10 million people and particularly influenced by environmental conditions, such as water, sanitation and housing, include lymphatic filariasis, dengue fever, leishmaniasis and Chagas disease.

• Hazardous chemicals and various forms of hazardous waste, including healthcare wastes, are growing health-and-environment concerns. Lack of detailed quantitative information on the production and disposal of such waste, and on the resulting health risks, severely hampers efforts to control this problem.

•• Hundreds of new chemicals are developed each year, but assessment of their possible long-term risks to health is not keeping pace with this rate of development.

•• Evidence is mounting that in developed countries the human exposures and health risks arising from existing hazardous chemicals (such as lead, cadmium, mercury, DDT and polychlorinated biphenyls) have been brought under control, but that this is not the case in developing countries. Of particular concern are exposures to lead and persistent organic pollutants.

•• The degree to which healthcare waste is safely handled is not known, but there is reason to believe that it is frequently inadequately treated.

• Global environmental change has great implications for health, particularly that of the poor. Marginalized population groups are again at greatest risk, as their ability to adapt is limited due to lack of resources.

•• The potential future health impact of global climate change includes changes in the distribution of infectious and vector-borne diseases, increased heat-related illness, and injuries and diseases due to sea level rise and extreme weather disasters. In addition, dislocation and loss of livelihood may indirectly cause major health problems.

•• The increase in the amount of solar ultraviolet radiation reaching Earth's surface is the result of damage to the stratospheric ozone layer caused by the atmospheric release of chlorofluorocarbons and other chemicals. Anticipated health impacts include increased risk of cataracts and skin cancer, and, potentially, damage to the immune system.

•• The major pollutants that damage the ozone layer appear to be under control, but it appears unlikely that developed countries will in the near future be able to reduce greenhouse gas emissions to levels considerably below current levels.

•• Although not yet causing a significant portion of global ill health, apparent environmental links with the deadly emerging/re-emerging infectious diseases have created an urgent need to monitor and improve environmental conditions.

• There are some promising signs — not yet in terms of environmental improvement, but rather in the national development of policies and infrastructure to address the problems described here. However, the lack of financial and human resources is a major deterrent to progress.

•• Health-and-environment concerns are being incorporated in sustainable development planning in numerous countries. Many countries on all continents have now developed intersectoral health-and-environment plans or are in the process of doing so.

•• Community-driven *Local Agenda* 21 and Healthy Cities/Villages/ Islands initiatives are growing in number worldwide.

•• Local government and nongovernmental organizations are emerging as major development forces and key players in health and environment.

•• New effective international mechanisms for collaboration to ensure protection from hazardous chemicals have been developed.

•• The development and application of cleaner technologies in industry are being given increased priority.

• The health sector has an essential advocacy role to play in highlighting the links between health, environment and sustainable development when future policies are developed and actions planned. A much stronger partnership between the health sector and other sectors is required for successful reduction of health threats arising from poor environmental conditions. Renewal of the WHO Health-for-All Policy for the 21st Century, which is currently in progress, provides guidance for the way ahead.

•• Intersectoral action needs to be facilitated through new approaches to legislation, budgeting and human resources development.

•• Improved information on health-and-environment linkages is required at all levels to support policy development, priority-setting and decision-making for action.

•• Actions for health are required at all levels: local, provincial, national and global. ❑

Glossary

This glossary has been produced to be of help to readers of this particular text. It has been compiled with the aid of a number of glossaries and dictionaries, and as such should not be considered to be an approved glossary of WHO.

algal bloom: abnormally increased biomass of algae in a lake, river or ocean.

aliphatic hydrocarbons: chemical compounds including carbon and hydrogen with a straight structure.

aromatic hydrocarbons: chemical compounds including carbon and hydrogen with a structure including at least one benzene ring.

ascariasis: disease caused by infection with *Ascaris* or related ascarid nematodes.

ascites: accumulation of serous fluid in the abdominal cavity.

atherosclerosis: a disease in which fat compounds build up on the inside of arteries, potentially blocking blood flow.

atmosphere: gaseous envelope that surrounds Earth and which is subdivided into the troposphere, stratosphere and mesosphere.

attenuated vaccine: vaccine based on live infectious material that has been treated in such a way that it creates an antibody response but does not cause the disease.

attributable risk: the proportion of a disease or other outcome in exposed individuals that can be attributed to the exposure of interest.

biofuel: renewable hydrocarbon fuel, usually alcohol, e.g. methanol, ethanol, derived from corn (maize) and other grains.

"blackfoot disease": disease reported in China of the peripheral blood vessels which is caused by arsenic exposure. The disease constricts the arteries, the blood flow is diminished and the feet look black.

chlorofluorocarbons (CFCs): halocarbons that are major greenhouse gases. CFCs are of human origin and have long atmospheric lifetimes (more than 100 years). They are destroyed only by photolytic destruction in the stratosphere where they cause ozone depletion.

coliform: general, ill-defined term used to denote gram-negative, fermentative rods that inhabit the intestinal tract of man and other animals.

copepod: any member of the subclass Copepoda. (Copepoda are abundant, free-living, freshwater and marine crustaceans of fundamental importance to the aquatic food-chain in both marine and freshwater environments.)

cor pulmonale: in chronic cases characterized by hypertrophy of the right ventricle, resulting from disease of the lungs; in acute cases, characterized by dilation and failure of the right side of the heart due to pulmonary embolism.

Cryptosporidium: genus of coccidian sporozoans that are important pathogens of calves and other domestic animals, and common opportunistic parasites of humans that flourish under conditions of compromised immune function.

cutaneous melanoma: type of skin cancer. A melanoma is a malignant neoplasm, derived from cells that are capable of forming melanin.

cyanobacterial poisoning: reaction to the toxins produced by cyanobacteria.

dengue fever: disease of tropical and sub-tropical regions, caused by mosquito-transmitted dengue viruses.

dracunculiasis: also called guinea-worm disease, caused by a parasite whose larvae can grow under the skin, reaching up to one metre in length.

El Niño: name originally given by local inhabitants to a weak warm ocean current flowing along the coast of Ecuador and Peru. El Niño occurs irregularly, but approximately every four years on average.

endemic disease: the constant presence of a disease or infectious agent within a given geographic area or population group; may also refer to the usual prevalence of a given disease within such area or group.

epidemic: the occurrence in a community or region of cases of an illness, specific health-related behaviour or other health-related events clearly in excess of normal expectancy.

erethism: an abnormal state of excitement, irritation or sensitivity to stimulation, either general or local.

eutrophication: the occurrence of high nutrient levels in freshwater and marine ecosystems, usually resulting in excessive plant growth and the death of animal and some plant life due to oxygen deprivation

filariasis: presence of filariae in the body, occurring in tropical and sub-tropical regions.

fluorosis: condition caused by an excessive intake of fluorides, characterized mainly by mottling, staining, or hypoplasia of the enamel of the teeth.

food security: a situation in which all households have both physical and economic access to adequate food for all members and where households are not at risk of losing such access.

free radical: highly reactive chemical molecule that has at least one unpaired electron.

greenhouse gas: gas that absorbs radiation emitted by Earth's surface and clouds. The effect is a local trapping of part of the absorbed energy and a tendency to warm Earth's surface. Water vapour, carbon dioxide, nitrous oxide, methane, and ozone are the primary greenhouse gases in Earth's atmosphere.

half-life: period during which the radioactivity of a radioactive substance decreases to half of its original value; similarly applied to the decrease in activity of any unstable active substance with time.

halocarbons: generic term to describe a group of human-made chemicals that contains carbon and members of the halogen family. Halocarbons include chlorofluorocarbons and halons, substances that deplete stratospheric ozone.

halons: various gaseous compounds of carbon, bromine and other halogens, usually bromoflouromethanes, used to extinguish fires, that contribute to destruction of stratospheric ozone.

helminth: intestinal vermiform parasite; primarily nematodes, cestodes, trematodes, and acanthocephalans.

hepatomegaly: enlargement of the liver.

incidence: the number of cases of illness commencing, or of persons falling ill, during a given time period within a specified population.

Internet: global computer network providing access to and dissemination of a vast amount of information.

ionizing radiation: electromagnetic or particle radiation of a sufficient energy to cause ionization in biological cells.

isotope: one of two or more nuclides that are chemically identical yet differ in mass number.

Japanese encephalitis: encephalitis (inflammation of the brain) caused by a mosquito-transmitted Flavivirus, affecting large populations in rice-growing, suburban, and rural regions of South-East Asia.

keratosis: any lesion on the epidermis marked by the presence of circumscribed overgrowths of the horny layer.

leishmaniasis: infection with a species of *Leishmania*; transmission is by various sandfly species of the genus *Phlebotomus* or *Lutzomyia*.

leptospirosis: illnesses caused by infection with *Leptospira*; transmission is associated with contact with infected animals or water contaminated with rat urine.

manufacturing value added: the difference between the value of goods and the cost of materials or supplies that are used in producing them. Value added is derived by subtracting the cost of raw materials, parts, supplies, fuel, goods purchased for resale, electric energy, and contract work from the value of shipments. It is the best money gauge of the relative economic importance of a manufacturing industry because it measures that industry's contribution to the economy rather than its gross sales.

mesothelioma: a cancer in the mesothelial tissues, usually in the lining of the lung.

nuclide: particular (atomic) nuclear species with defined atomic mass and number.

oblast: Russian word for "region".

odds ratio: epidemiological term used to express the relative risk of disease when comparing groups. It is the ratio of the odds of exposure among the cases of disease to the odds of exposure in the controls.

oedema: swelling caused by the accumulation of fluid in body tissues.

onchocerciasis: tropical disease caused by a filarial parasite transmitted by blackflies.

ozone: form of the element oxygen with three atoms instead of the two that characterize normal oxygen molecules. Ozone (O_3) is an important greenhouse gas. The stratosphere contains 90% of all the O_3 present in the atmosphere that absorbs harmful ultraviolet radiation.

pH: measure of the acidity or alkalinity of a solution, ranging from 0 (acidic) to 7 (neutral) to 14 (alkaline).

parenchymal lung disease: disease of lung due to its disfunction.

peripheral neuropathy: disease involving the peripheral nerves.

peripheral vascular disease: disease of the peripheral blood vessels

pertussis: commonly called whooping cough, caused by *Bordetella pertussis*.

photovoltaic: term applied to devices that creates electricity when exposed to light.

"polluter pays" principle: a system of charges on the person or company that cause pollution.

primary health care: essential health care made accessible at a cost the country and community can afford, with methods that are practical, scientifically sound and socially acceptable.

prevalence: proportion of persons within a given population who are currently affected by a particular disease or risk factor.

radiative forcing: a simple measure of the importance of a potential climate change mechanism. The amount of perturbation of the energy balance of the Earth–atmosphere system following, for example, a change in carbon dioxide concentrations or a change in the output of the sun.

radionuclide: a nuclide of artificial or natural origin that exhibits radioactivity.

radon: radioactive element, resulting from the breakdown of radium.

relative risk: ratio of risk of occurrence of a disease in one group as compared to the risk of occurrence in another group.

residual house-spraying: spraying of the internal walls of houses with an insecticide in formulation and dose that ensures prolonged (i.e. residual) action.

rotavirus: wheel-shaped virus that causes infantile acute gastroenteritis and diarrhoea.

schistosomiasis: infection with species of *Schistosoma*. Manifestations of this disease vary with the infecting species.

secondary (photochemical) pollutants: air pollutants created by chemical reactions in the atmosphere from other pollutants that have been emitted from motor vehicles or industry.

serotype: group or category of bacteria or other microorganisms that have a certain set of antigens in common or against which common antibodies are produced; the combination of antigens by which such a group is categorized.

stomatitis: inflammation of the mucous membrane of the mouth.

stratosphere: highly stratified and stable region of the atmosphere above the troposphere extending from about 10 km to 50 km.

subclinical: without clinical manifestations; generally the early stage of an infection or other disease before symptoms and signs become clinically apparent.

trachoma: infectious inflammation of the eye, often associated with lack of water for personal hygiene.

teratogenesis: a process that damages the growth of the fetus *in utero*.

trematode: flat worm of the class *Trematoda*, including the parasitic worms called "flukes". Trematodes that cause disease in humans have intermediate stages in snails.

troposphere: lowest part of the atmosphere in which clouds and weather phenomena occur. The troposphere is defined as the region in which temperatures generally decrease with height.

trypanosomiasis: infection with protozoa, *Trypanosoma* including American trypanosomiasis (Chagas disease) or African trypanosomiasis.

vibrio: type of actively mobile bacteria. The species include the cholera vibrios, highly pathogenic for humans.

zoonosis: infectious disease of vertebrate animals, such as rabies, that can be transmitted to humans.

References

AAMA (1996) *World motor vehicle data 1996*. Detroit, Michigan, American Automobile Manufactures Association.

Aaby P et al. (1988) Further community studies on the role of overcrowding and intensive exposure on measles mortality. *Review of infectious diseases*, 10(2):474–477.

Adams MR & Moss MO (1995) *Food microbiology*. London, Royal Society of Chemistry.

Agaki H, Malm O & Branches FJP (1996) Human exposure to mercury due to gold mining in the Amazon, Brazil: a review. *Environmental sciences*, 4(3):199–211.

Agarwal B (1985) *Cold hearths, barren slopes*. New Delhi, Allied Publications.

Albonico M et al. (1994) A randomised controlled trial comparing Mebendazole 500 mg and Albendazole 400 mg against *Ascaris, Trichuris* and the hookworms. *Transactions of the Royal Society of Tropical Medicine and Hygiene*, 88:585–589.

Alexandratos N, ed. (1995) *World agriculture: towards 2010. An FAO study.* Rome/Chichester, UK, FAO/John Wiley and Sons.

Alwan AAS (1993) Cardiovascular diseases in the Eastern Mediterranean Region. *World health statistics quarterly*, 46:97–100.

Annest JL et al. (1983) Chronological trend in blood lead levels between 1976 and 1980. *New England journal of medicine*, 308:1373–1377.

Anon. (1995) The challenge of tuberculosis: statement on global control and prevention. *Lancet*, 346:809–819.

Anon. (1996a) Europe's bathing waters fail to meet quality standards. *World water and environmental engineering*, July 9.

Anon. (1996b) One false step ... and you're dead. *New scientist*, 4 May 1996:32–37.

Anon. (1996c) Greening our health (editorial). *Lancet*, 348(9021):139.

Armstrong BK (1994) Stratospheric ozone and health. *International journal of epidemiology*, 23(5):873–885.

Ashby J et al. (1997) The challenge posed by endocrine-disrupting chemicals. *Environmental health perspectives*, 105(2):164–169.

Asian Development Bank (1993) *Water utilities data book: Asian and Pacific region.* Bangkok, Asian Development Bank.

Avramov D (1995) *Homelessness in the European Union: social and legal context for housing exclusion in the 1990s.* Brussels, European Federation of National Organizations Working with the Homeless.

Aziz KMA et al. (1990) Reduction in diarrhoeal diseases in children in rural Bangladesh by environmental and behavioural modifications. *Transactions of the Royal Society of Tropical Medicine and Hygiene*, 84:433–438.

Baarse G (1995) *Development of an operational tool for global vulnerability assessment (GVA): update of the number of people at risk due to sea level rise and increased flooding probabilties.*

The Hague, Ministry of Transport, Public Works and Water Management (CZM Centre Publication No. 3).

Bagla P & Kaiser J (1996) India's spreading health crisis draws global arsenic experts. *Science,* 274:174–175.

Bakir F et al. (1973) Methylmercury poisoning in Iraq: an inter-university report. *Science,* 181:230–241.

Barbiroli G (1996) The role of technology and science in sustainable development. In: Nath B et al., eds. *Sustainable development.* Brussels, VUB University Press.

Bascom R (1996) Environmental factors and respiratory hypersensitivity: the Americas. *Toxicology letters,* 86:115–130.

Bates DV (1992) Health indices of the adverse effects of air pollution: the question of coherence. *Environmental resources* 59:336–349.

Batliwala (1987) Women's access to food. *Indian journal of social work,* 48(3):255–271.

Batstone R, Smith JE & Wilson D, eds. (1989) *The safe disposal of hazardous wastes.* Washington, World Bank (World Bank Technical Paper No. 93).

Benhamou S, Benhamou E & Flamant R (1988) Occupational risk factors of lung cancer in a French case–control study. *British journal of industrial medicine,* 45 (4):231–233.

Berman S (1991) Epidemiology of acute respiratory infections in developing countries. *Review of infectious diseases,* (Suppl 6):S454–462.

Bird CJ & Wright JLC (1988) The shellfish toxin domoic acid. *World aquaculture,* 20(1):40–41.

Birley MH et al. (1996) A multisectoral task-based course: health opportunities in water resources development. *Education for health,* 9(1):71–83.

Blaser MJ (1996) *Helicobacter pylori:* its role in disease. *Clinical infectious diseases,* 15(3):386–391.

Bobak M & Leon DA (1992) Air pollution and infant mortality in the Czech Republic, 1986–88. *Lancet,* 340:1010–1014.

Bojkov RD (1995) *The changing ozone layer.* Geneva, WMO.

Bojkov RD et al. (1997) *Proceedings of Ozone Symposium, Aquila, Italy, 1997.* Geneva, International Ozone Commission.

Bolger PM et al. (1991) Reductions in dietary lead exposure in the United States. *Chemical speciation and bioavailability,* 3(314):31.

Bradley DJ & Narayan R (1987) Epidemiological patterns associated with agricultural activities in the tropics with special reference to vector-borne diseases. In: *Effects of agricultural development on vector-borne diseases.* Rome, FAO (unpublished document AGL/MISC/12/87).

Briggs D, Corvalán C & Nurminen M, eds. (1996) *Linkage methods for environment and health analysis: general guidelines.* Geneva, WHO (unpublished document WHO/EHG/95.26).

British Petroleum Company (1996) *British Petroleum statistical review of world energy, 1996.* London, British Petroleum Co.

Brouwer ID (1994) *Food and fuel: a hidden dimension in human nutrition* [Thesis]. Netherlands, Wageningen University.

Brown LR et al. (1994) *State of the world 1994: a Worldwatch Institute report on progress toward a sustainable society.* New York/London, W.W. Norton & Company Inc.

Brown LR et al. (1996a) *Vital signs 1996: the trends that are shaping our future.* New York/London, W.W. Norton & Co.

Brown LR et al. (1996b) *State of the world 1996: a Worldwatch Institute report on progress toward a sustainable society.* New York/London, W.W. Norton & Company, Inc.

Brown LR et al. (1997) *State of the world 1997: a Worldwatch Institute report on progress toward a sustainable society.* New York/London, W.W. Norton & Company, Inc.

Brundtland GH (1994) Influencing environmental factors in cardiovascular disease prevention: global view. *Preventive medicine*, 23:531–534.

Buist AS & Vollmer WM (1990) Reflections on the rise in asthma morbidity and mortality. *JAMA*, 264:1719–1720.

Burridge R & Ormandy D (1993) The legal environment of housing conditions. In: Burridge R & Ormandy D, eds. (1993) *Unhealthy housing: research, remedies and reforms*. London, E & FN Spon.

Byass et al. (1995) Assessment and possible control of endemic measles in urban Nigeria. *Journal of public health medicine*, 17(2):140–145.

CDC (1994) Lead-contaminated drinking water in bulk water storage tanks: Arizona and California, 1993. *Morbidity and mortality weekly report*, 43:751, 757–758.

CDC (1995a) Outbreak of gastrointestinal illness associated with consumption of seaweed. *Morbidity and mortality weekly report*, 44(39):724–727.

CDC (1995b) Asthma-United States, 1982–1992. *Morbidity and mortality weekly report*, 43(51–52):952–955.

CSD (1997a) *Overall progress achieved since the United Nations Conference on Environment and Development: protecting and promoting human health. Report of the Secretary General*. New York, Commission on Sustainable Development (E/CN.17/ 1997/ 2/Add.5).

CSD (1997b) *Overall progress achieved since the United Nations Conference on Environment and Development: combating poverty. Report of the Secretary General*. New York, Commission on Sustainable Development (E/CN.17/1997/2/Add.2).

CSD (1997c) *Overall progress achieved since the United Nations Conference on Environment and Development: environmentally sound management of solid waste and sewerage-related issues. Report of the Secretary General*. New York, Commission on Sustainable Development (E/CN.17/1997/2/Add.20).

CSD (1997d) *Comprehensive assessment of freshwater resources of the world: report of the Secretary General*. New York, Commission on Sustainable Development (E/CN.17/ 1997/9).

CSD (1997e) *Overall progress achieved since the United Nations Conference on Environment and Development: changing consumption and production patterns. Report of the Secretary General*. New York, Commission on Sustainable Development (E/CN.17/ 1997/2/Add.3).

CSD (1997f) Unpublished data: post-UNCED institutional arrangements (UN System).

Cabelli VJ (1983) *Health effects criteria for marine recreational waters*. Research Triangle Park, NC, USEPA (R & D Report No. EPA-600/1-80-031).

Cahill KM, ed. (1995) *Clearing the fields: solutions to the global landmine crisis*. New York, Basic Books (A joint publication of Basic Books and the Council on Foreign Relations).

Cai S et al. (1995) Cadmium exposure among residents in an area contaminated by irrigation water in China. *Bulletin of the World Health Organization*, 73:359–367.

Caldeira T (1996) Building up walls: the new pattern of spatial segregation in Saõ Paulo. *International social science journal*, 147:55–66.

Calder M (1994) *Staffing, professional education and training in environmental health*. Copenhagen, WHO Regional Office for Europe (unpublished document EUR/ICP/CEH/123/D).

Carnevale P et al. (1991) L'impact des moustiquaires imprégnées sur la prévalence et la morbidité liée au paludisme en Afrique sub-Saharienne. *Annales de la Société belge de Médecine Tropicale*, 71(suppl):127–150.

Castegnaro M & Chernozemsky I (1987) Endemic nephropathy and urinary tract tumours in the Balkans, *Cancer research*, 47:3608–3609.

Chambers R (1983) *Rural development: putting the last first.* London, Longman Scientific & Technical.

Chao TC, Maxwell SM & Wong SY (1991) An outbreak of aflatoxicosis and boric acid poisoning in Malaysia: a clinicopathological study. *Journal of pathology*, 164:225–233.

Chandiwana SK & Snellen WB (1994) *Incorporating a human health component into the integrated development and management of the Zambesi basin.* Geneva, WHO (unpublished document WHO/EOS/94.53).

Chatterjee M & Lambert J (1989) Women and nutrition: reflections from India and Pakistan. *Food and nutrition bulletin*, 4:13–28.

Chen BH et al. (1990) Indoor air pollution in developing countries. *World health statistics quarterly*, 43:127–138.

Chen SY et al. (1990) Mortality experience of haematite mine workers in China. *British journal of industrial medicine*, 45:175–181.

Chen CH et al. (1995) A population based epidemiological study on cardiovascular risk factors in Kin-Chen, Kinmen. *International journal of cardiology*, 48(1):75–88.

Cheng WN & Kong J (1992) A retrospective mortality study of chrysotile asbestos products workers in Tianjin 1972–1987. *Environmental resources* 59:271–278.

Cheung WHS (1990) Epidemiological study of beach-water pollution and health-related bathing water standards in Hong Kong. *Water science technology*, 23:243-252.

Cobb C, Halstead T & Rowe J (1995) *The genuine progress indicator: summary of data and methodology.* San Francisco, CA, Refining Progress.

Coleman A (1985) *Utopia and trail.* 2nd edition. London, Hilary Shipman Ltd.

Coleman MP et al. (1993) *Trends in cancer incidence and mortality.* Lyon, IARC (IARC Scientific Publications No. 121).

Colwell RR (1996) Global climate and infectious disease: the cholera paradigm. *Science*, 274:2025–2031.

Coosemans M (1985) Comparaison de l'endémie malarienne dans une zone de riziculture et dans une zone de culture de coton dans la plaine de la Ruzizi (Burundi). *Annales de la Société belge de Médecine Tropicale*, 65(suppl.2):187–200.

Daley RM (1995) *Final report. Mayor's Commission on Extreme Weather Conditions.* City of Chicago.

Dalhammar G & Mehlmann M (1996) *Wastewater treatment problematique.* Enebyberg, Sweden, GAP International (Global Action Plan for the Earth).

Daniels DL et al. (1990) A case–control study of the impact on diarrhoea morbidity of improved sanitation in Lesotho. *Bulletin of the World Health Organization*, 68(4):455–463.

Das Gupta M (1987) Selective discrimination against female children in rural Punjab, India. *Population and development review*, 13(1):77–100.

De Kadt E (1989). Making health policy management intersectoral: issues of information analysis and use in less developed countries. *Social science and medicine*, 29(4), 503–514.

Dennis RJ et al. (1996) Woodsmoke exposure and risk of obstructive airways disease among women. *Chest*, 109(1):115–119.

Department of the Environment, United Kingdom (1996). *The United Kingdom national environmental health action plan.* London, Department of the Environment.

Dhatt PS et al. (1982) Aflatoxin and Indian childhood cirrhosis. *Indian pediatrics*, 19:407–408.

Diop M & Jobin WR (1994) *Senegal river basin health master plan study.* Arlington, VA, WASH (WASH field report No. 453).

Dockery DW et al. (1993) An association between air pollution and mortality in six US cities. *The New England journal of medicine,* 329(24):1753–1759.

Dockery DW & Pope III CA (1994) Acute respiratory effects of particulate air pollution. *Annual review of public health,* 15:107–132.

EC (1995a) *Health and safety at work: community programme 1996–2000.* Luxembourg, Office for Official Publications of the European Communities.

EC (1995b) *Indoor air quality: its impact on man. Report No. 15: radon in indoor air.* Luxembourg, European Commission (Report EUR 16123 EN).

ECETOC (1988) *Nitrate and drinking-water.* Brussels, ECETOC (Technical Report No. 27).

Economopoulos AP (1993) *Assessment of sources of air, water, and land pollution: a guide to rapid source inventory techniques and their use in formulating environmental control strategies. Part one: rapid inventory techniques in environmental pollution.* Geneva, WHO (unpublished document WHO/PEP/GETNET/93.1–A).

El–Hinnawi E (1985) *Environment refugees.* Nairobi, Kenya, UNEP.

Engelman R & LeRoy P (1995a) *Sustaining water: an update.* Washington, DC, Population Action International.

Engelman R & LeRoy P (1995b) *Conserving land: population and sustainable food production.* Washington DC, Population Action International.

Environment Agency of Japan (1996) *Our intensive efforts to overcome the tragic history of Minamata disease.* Tokyo, Environmental Health Department (unpublished document).

Environment Canada (1987) *Summary report: Canada–Manitoba agreement on the study and monitoring of mercury in the Churchill river diversion.* Winnipeg, Manitoba/Hull, Quebec, Environment and Workplace Safety and Health/Environment Canada.

Epstein PR, Ford TE & Colwell RR (1994) Marine ecosystems. *Lancet,* 342:1216–1219.

Erlam K & Plass L (1996) *Trade and environment: a business perspective.* Geneva, World Business Council for Sustainable Development (unpublished document).

Esrey SA (1990) Food contamination and diarrhoea. *World Health,* January–February:19–20.

Esrey SA (1996) Water, waste and well-being: a multi–country study. *American journal of epidemiology,* 143(6):608–623.

Esrey SA & Feachem RG (1989) *Interventions for the control of diarrhoeal diseases among young children: promotion of food hygiene.* Geneva, WHO (unpublished document WHO/CDD/89.30).

Esrey SA Feachem RG & Hughes JM (1985) Interventions for the control of diarrhoeal diseases among young children: improving water supplies and excreta disposal facilities. *Bulletin of the World Health Organization* 63(4):757–772.

Esrey SA et al. (1991) Effects of improved water supply and sanitation on ascariasis, diarrhoea, dracunculiasis, hookworm infection, schistosomiasis, and trachoma. *Bulletin of the World Health Organization,* 69(5):609–621.

Evanoff B, Gustavsson P & Hogstedt C (1993) Mortality and incidence of cancer in a cohort of Swedish chimney sweeps: an extended follow-up study. *British journal of industrial medicine,* 50:450–459.

FAO (1994a) Water policies and agriculture. In: *The state of food and agriculture 1993.* Rome, FAO.

FAO (1994b) *Compendium of food consumption,* Vols.1–2. Rome, FAO.

FAO (1995) *FAO production yearbook 1995,* Vol. 49. Rome, FAO.

FAO (1996a) *Rome declaration on world food security and world food summit plan of action.* World Food Summit, 13–17 November 1996. Rome, FAO (WFS/96/3).

FAO (1996b) *World Food Summit: technical background documents,* 3 vols. Rome, FAO.

FAO/WHO (1994) *This is Codex Alimentarius,* 2nd edition. Rome, FAO.

Falkenmark M et al. (1989) Macro-scale water scarcity requires micro-scale approaches: aspects of vulnerability in semi-arid development. *Natural resources forum,* 13(4):258–267.

Feachem RGA et al. (1983) *Sanitation and disease: health aspects of excreta and wastewater management.* New York, John Wiley & Sons.

Feachem RGA et al., eds. (1992) *The health of adults in the developing world.* New York, Oxford University Press.

Ferrer A & Cabral R (1989) Epidemics due to pesticide contamination in food. In: *World Conference on Chemical Accidents.* Edinburgh, CEP Consultants Ltd.

Ferrie JE et al. (1995) Job change and non-employment: longtitudinal data from the Whitehall II Study. *British medical journal,* 311(7015):1264–1269.

Feychting M & Ahlbom A (1993) Magnetic fields and cancer in children near Swedish high-voltage power lines. *American journal of epidemiology,* 138:467–481.

Fingerhut MA et al. (1991) Cancer mortality in workers exposed to 2, 3, 7, 8-tetra-chlorodibenzo-p-dioxin. *New England journal of medicine* 1991:212–218.

Flesch-Janys D et al. (1995) Exposure to polychlorinated dioxins and furans (PCDD/F) and mortality in a cohort of workers from a herbicide producing plant in Hamburg, Federal Republic of Germany. *American journal of epidemiology,* 142:1165–1175.

Fluss S (1997) International public health law: an overview. In: Detels R et al., eds. *Oxford textbook of public health,* Vol. 1: *The scope of public health,* 3rd edition. Oxford/New York, Oxford University Press.

Franceys R, Pickford J & Reed R (1992) *A guide to the development of on-site sanitation.* Geneva, WHO.

Freeman H (1993) Mental health and high-rise housing. In: Burridge R & Ormandy D, eds. *Unhealthy housing: research, remedies and reforms.* London, E & FN Spon.

Friberg L et al. (1985) *Cadmium and health: a toxicological and epidemiological appraisal,* Vol. 1. *Exposure, dose and metabolism.* Boca Raton, Florida, Chemical Rubber Co Press.

Friberg L et al. (1986) *Cadmium and health: a toxicological and epidemiological appraisal,* Vol. 2. *Effects and response.* Boca Raton, Florida, Chemical Rubber Co. Press.

Gabe J & Williams P (1993) Women, crowding and mental health. In: Burridge R & Ormandy D, eds. *Unhealthy housing: research, remedies and reforms.* London, E & FN Spon.

Gao QY et al. (1990) A review of botulism in China. *Biomedical and environmental sciences,* 3:326–336.

Garenne M, Ronsmans C & Campbell H (1992) The magnitude of mortality from acute respiratory infections in children under 5 years in developing countries. *World health statistics quarterly,* 45:180–191.

Garrett L (1994) *The coming plague: newly emerging diseases in a world out of balance.* New York, Farrar, Straus and Giroux.

Ginsburg NS, Koppel B & McGee TG, eds. (1990) *The dispersed metropolis: a phase of the settlement transition in Asia.* Honolulu, University of Hawaii Press.

Gittelsohn J (1991) Opening the box: intrahousehold food allocation in rural Nepal. *Social science and medicine,* 33(10):1141–1154.

Gitonga S (1997). The energy efficiency household programme in Kenya. Proceedings European Union (DG XVII) and O.Ö. Energiesparverband World Energy Efficiency Day, 6 March 1997. Wels, Austria.

Gleick PH ed. (1993) *Water in crisis: a guide to the world's fresh water resources.* New York/Oxford, Oxford University Press.

Gleick PH (1996) Basic water requirements for human activities: meeting basic needs. *Water international,* 21:83–92.

Goldstein G (1996). WHO Healthy Cities: towards an interregional programme framework. In: Price C & Tsouros A, eds. *Our cities our future: policies and action plans for health and sustainable development.* Copenhagen, WHO Regional Office for Europe.

Gorter AC et al. (1991) Water supply, sanitation and diarrhoeal disease in Nicaragua: results from a case–control study. *International journal of epidemiology,* 20(2):527–533.

Gotaas HB (1956) *Composting: sanitary disposal and reclamation of organic wastes.* Geneva, WHO (Monograph Series No. 31).

Gratz NG & Knudsen AB (1996) *The rise and spread of dengue, dengue haemorrhagic fever and its vectors: a historical review (up to 1995).* Geneva, WHO (unpublished document CTD/FIL (DEN) 96.7).

Greider W (1997) *One world, ready or not.* New York, Simon & Schuster.

Gribbin B & Crook DWN (1996) Infective endocarditis. In: Weatherall DJ, Ledingham JCG & Warrel DA, eds. *Oxford textbook of medicine,* 3rd ed. Oxford, Oxford University Press.

Grossklaus D, ed (1988) *Impact of the Chernobyl nuclear power plant accident in the Federal Republic of Germany.* Stuttgart, Sustav Fischer.

Gutiérrez G et al. (1996) Impact of oral rehydration and selected public health interventions on reduction of mortality from childhood diarrhoeal diseases in Mexico. *Bulletin of the World Health Organization,* 74(2):189–197.

Haglund BJA et al. (1992) *We can do it: the Sundsvall handbook.* Stockholm, Karolinska Institute, Department of Social Medicine.

Hall DO, Rosillo–Calle F & Woods J (1994) Biomass utilization in households and industry: energy use and development. *Chemosphere,* 29(5):1099–1133.

Health, Safety and Environmental Management Consultancy, Inc. (1994) *Report on the integration of health and environment issues in the development and implementation of national plans for sustainable development in the Philippines.* Manila, Philippines, Department of Health.

Hertzman C et al. (1995) *Environment and health in the Philippines.* Vancouver, The University of British Columbia, Centre for Health Services and Policy Research (Health Policy Research Unit Discussion Paper Series).

HICARE (1993) *A-bomb radiation effects digest.* Chur, Switzerland, Harwood Academic Publishers GmbH.

Hogstedt C et al. (1982) A cohort study on mortality among long-time employed Swedish chimney sweeps, *Scandinavian journal of work, environment and health,* 8(suppl. 1):72–78.

Holdren JP (1992) The transition to costlier energy. In: Schipper L & Meyers S, *Energy efficiency and human activity: past trends, future prospects.* Cambridge, UK, Cambridge University Press.

Holt LE (1913) Infant mortality, ancient and modern: an historical sketch. *Archives pediatrics,* 30:885–915.

Hong CJ, Corvalán C & Kjellström T (1997) Air pollution. In: Murray CJL & Lopez AD, eds. *Quantifying global health risks: the burden of disease attributable to selected factors.* Cambridge, MA, Harvard University Press (in press).

Hopenhayn-Rich C et al. (1996) Bladder cancer mortality associated with arsenic in drinking water in Argentina. *Epidemiology,* 7:117–124.

Houdas Y, Deklunder GT & Lecroart JL (1992) Cold exposure and ischemic heart disease. *International journal of sport medicine,* 13 (Suppl 1):S179–181.

Howard M (1993) The effects on human health of pest infestation in houses. In: Burridge R & Ormandy D, eds. *Unhealthy housing: research, remedies and reforms.* London, E & FN Spon.

Hsiao WCL & Yuanly Liu (1996) *Economic reform and health lessons from China* (editorial). *New England journal of medicine,* 335:430–432.

Hunt S (1993) Damp and mouldy housing: a holistic approach. In: Burridge R & Ormandy D, eds. *Unhealthy housing: research, remedies and reforms.* London, E & FN Spon.

Hunter JM et al. (1993) *Parasitic diseases in water resources development: the need for intersectoral negotiation.* Geneva, WHO.

Hutt MSR (1991) Cancer and cardiovascular diseases. In: Feachem RG & Jamison DT, eds. *Disease and mortality in sub-Saharan Africa.* Oxford, Oxford University Press (A World Bank Book).

Huttly SRA et al. (1990) The Imo State (Nigeria) drinking water supply and sanitation project II: impact on dracunculiasis, diarrhoea and nutritional status. *Transactions of the Royal Society of Tropical Medicine and Hygiene,* 84:316–321.

Huttly S (1996) Water, sanitation and personal hygiene. In: Murray CJL & Lopez AD, eds. *Quantifying global health risks: the burden of diseases attributable to selected risk factors.* Cambridge, Harvard University Press.

Iacob I & Tanase I (1996) *GIS for exposure of well water nitrate.* Bucharest, Institute of Hygiene and Public Health (unpublished report).

IAEA (1996a) Chernobyl: ten years after. *IAEA bulletin,* 38(3):2–64 (special issue).

IAEA (1996b) *International basic safety standards for protection against ionizing radiation and for the safety of radiation sources.* Vienna, IAEA (Safety Series No. 115).

IARC (1973) Certain polycyclic aromatic hydrocarbons and heterocyclic compounds. Lyon, IARC (Monographs on Evaluating Carcinogenic Risks to Humans No. 3).

IARC (1984) *N-nitroso compounds: occurrence, biological effects and relevance to cancer.* Lyon, IARC (IARC Scientific Publication No. 57).

IARC (1991a) *Relevance to human cancer of N-nitroso compounds, tobacco and mycotoxins.* Lyon, IARC (IARC Scientific Publications No. 105).

IARC (1991b) *Chlorinated drinking-water, chlorination by-products, some other halogenated compounds, cobalts and cobalt compounds.* Lyon, IARC (Monographs on Evaluating Carcinogenic Risks to Humans No. 52).

IARC (1992) *Solar and ultra-violet radiation.* Lyon, IARC (Monographs on Evaluating Carcinogenic Risks to Humans No. 55).

IARC (1993) *Some naturally occurring substances: food items and constituents, heterocyclic aromatic amines and mycotoxins,* Lyon, IARC (Monographs on the Evaluation of Carcinogenic Risks to Humans No. 56).

IARC (1994) *Schistosomes, liver flukes and Helicobacter pylori.* Lyon, IARC (IARC Monographs on the Evaluation of Carcinogenic Risks to Humans No. 61).

IARC (1997) *Natural toxins.* Lyon, IARC (IARC Monographs on the Evaluation of Carcinogenic Risks to Humans, in preparation).

IASC (1995) *Effects of increased ultraviolet radiation in the Arctic.* Oslo, Norway, International Arctic Science Committee (IASC report No. 2).

ICLEI (1996). *The local Agenda 21 planning guide: an introduction to sustainable development planning.* Toronto, Canada, ICLEI.

ICNIRP (1996) Health issues related to the use of hand-held radiotelephones and base transmitters. International Commission on Non-Ionizing Radiation Protection. *Health physics,* 70:587–593.

ICRP (1990) *1990 recommendations of the International Commission on Radiological Protection, adopted by the Commission in November 1990.* Oxford, Pergamon Press.

IFCS (1996) *Persistent organic pollutants: considerations for global action. IFCS Experts meeting on POPs: final report.* Geneva, IFCS (unpublished document IFCS/EXP. POPs/Report.1).

ILEC & Lake Biwa Research Institute, eds. (1998–1993) *Survey of the state of world lakes.* Vol. I–IV. Otsu/Nairobi, ILEC/UNEP.

ILO (1988) *Major hazard control: a practical manual.* Geneva, ILO.

ILO (1991) *Prevention of major industrial accidents: an ILO code of practice.* Geneva, ILO.

ILO (1996) *Yearbook of labour statistics.* 55th ed. Geneva, ILO.

ILO (1997) *The Director-General's programme and budget proposals for 1998–1999.* Geneva, ILO.

IMO (1995) *Global waste survey: final report.* London, IMO.

IOMC (1996) *IOMC inventory of activities.* Geneva, IOMC.

IPCC (1996) *Climate change 1995: the science of climate change.* Contribution of Working Group I to the *Second assessment report* of the Intergovernmental Panel on Climate Change. Houghton JT et al., eds. Cambridge, New York, Cambridge University Press.

IPCS (1979) *Environmental health criteria 13. Carbon monoxide.* Geneva, WHO.

IPCS (1981) *Environmental health criteria 18. Arsenic.* Geneva, WHO.

IPCS (1984a) *Environmental health criteria 30. Principles for evaluating health risks to progeny associated with exposure to chemicals during pregnancy.* Geneva, WHO.

IPCS (1984b) *Environmental health criteria 46. Guidelines for the study of genetic effects in human populations.* Geneva, WHO.

IPCS (1984c) *Environmental health criteria 37. Aquatic (marine and freshwater) biotoxins.* Geneva, WHO.

IPCS (1984d) *Environmental health criteria 36. Fluorine and fluorides.* Geneva, WHO.

IPCS (1988) *Environmental health criteria 80. Pyrrolizidine alkaloids.* Geneva, WHO.

IPCS (1989) *Environmental health criteria 86. Mercury: environmental aspects.* Geneva, WHO.

IPCS (1990a) *Environmental health criteria 113. Fully halogenated chlorofluorocarbons.* Geneva, WHO.

IPCS (1990b) *Environmental health criteria 101. Methylmercury.* Geneva, WHO.

IPCS (1990c) *Environmental health criteria 105. Mycotoxins.* Geneva, WHO. IPCS (1992a) *Environmental health criteria 134. Cadmium.* Geneva, WHO.

IPCS (1992 b) *Environmental health criteria 135. Cadmium: environmental aspects.* Geneva, WHO.

IPCS (1995a) *Persistant organic pollutants: an assessment report on DDT-Aldrin-Dieldrin-Endrin-Chlordane-Heptachlor-Hexachlorobenzene-Mirex-Toxaphene, Polychlorinated biphenyls, dioxins and furans.* Geneva, WHO (unpublished document PCS/95.38).

IPCS (1995b) *Environmental health criteria 165. Inorganic lead.* Geneva, WHO.

IPCS (1996a) *IPCS INCHEM CD-ROM.* Geneva, IPCS.

IPCS (1996c) *Environmental health criteria 171. Diesel fuel and exhaust emissions.* Geneva, WHO.

IPCS (1997) *Environmental health criteria: scientific principles and methods for assessing allergic hypersentization associated with exposure to chemicals.* First draft. Geneva, WHO (unpublished document PCS/EHC/97.5).

ISRIC/UNEP (1991) *World map of the status of human-induced soil degradation.* Nairobi, UNEP, Global Assessment of Soil Degradation (International Soil Reference and Information Centre).

Jacobs GD (1997) Road safety in the developing world. In: Hetcher T & McMichael AJ, eds. *Health at the crossroads: transport policy and urban health.* Chichester, UK, John Wiley & Sons.

Jacobson JL & Jacobson SW (1996) Intellectual impairment in children exposed to polychlorinated biphenyls in utero. *The New England journal of medicine,* 335:783–789.

Jamison DT et al. (1993) Poliomyelitis. In: Jamison DT et al., eds. *Disease control priorities in developing countries.* New York, Oxford University Press (A World Bank Book).

Jazairy I, Alamgir M & Panuccio T (1992) *The state of world rural poverty: an inquiry into its causes and consequences.* Rome, IFAD.

Jedrychowski W et al. (1990) Case–control study of lung cancer with special reference to the effect of air pollution in Poland. *Journal of epidemiology and community health,* 44:114–120.

Jelinek C (1992) *Assessment of dietary intake of chemical contaminants.* WHO, Geneva.

Johnston R et al. (1986) Soil acidification during more than 100 years at Rothamsted. *Soil use and management,* 2:3–10.

Kakar F (1995) *Direct and indirect consequences of landmines on public health.* Geneva, WHO (unpublished document).

Kalkstein LS & Greene JS (1997) An evaluation of climate/mortality relationships in large US cities and the possible impacts of climate change. *Environmental health perspectives,* 105(1):2–11.

Karl M (1995) *Women and empowerment: participation and decision–making.* London, UK, Zed Books.

Keil U et al. (1996) The International Study of Asthma and Allergies in Childhood (ISAAC): objectives and methods. Results from German ISAAC centres concerning traffic density and wheezing and allergic rhinitis. *Toxicology letters,* 86:99–103.

King M et al. (1995) Does demographic entrapment challenge the two-child paradigm? *Health policy and planning,* 10(4):376–383.

King TP et al. (1995) Allergen nomenclature. *Journal of allergy and clinical immunology,* 96:5.

Kjeller LO et al. (1991) Increases in the polychlorinated dibenzo-p-dioxin and -furan content of soils and vegetation since the 1840s. *Environmental science and technology,* 25(9):1619–1627.

Kjellström T, Koplan JP & Rothenberg RB (1992) Current and future determinants of adult ill-health. In: Feachem RGA et al., eds. *The health of adults in the developing world.* Oxford, Oxford University Press (A World Bank Book).

Kjellström T & Corvalán C (1995) Framework for the development of environmental health indicators. *World health statistics quarterly,* 48:144–154.

Krishnamachari KAVR et al. (1975) Hepatitis due to aflatoxicosis: an outbreak in Western India. *Lancet,* i1061–1062 .

Kritz H, Schmid P & Sinzinger H (1995) Passive smoking and cardiovascular risk. *Archives of internal medicine,* 155(18) 1942–1948.

Krzyzanowski M (1995) *Exposure to toxic materials and health risk in buildings. Proceedings of Healthy Buildings '95, an international conference on healthy buildings in mild climates.*

Kungskulniti NC et al. (1991) Solid-waste scavenger community: an investigation in Bangkok. *Asia-Pacific journal of public health,* 5(1):54–65.

Lai CKW et al. (1996) Asthma epidemiology in the Far East. *Clinical and experimental allergy,* 26:5–12.

Law MR & Hackshaw AK (1996) Environmental tobacco smoke. *British medical bulletin,* 52(1):22–34.

Lawrence R (1996) Urban environment, health and the economy: cues for conceptual clarification and more effective policy implementation. In: Price C & Tsouros A, eds. *Our cities our future: policies and action plans for health and sustainable development.* Copenhagen, WHO Healthy Cities Project Office.

Lean G (1992) *WWF atlas of the environment.* Oxford, Helicon.

Lederberg J, Shope RE & Oaks SC, eds. (1992) *Emerging infections: microbial threats to health in the United States.* Washington DC, National Academy Press.

LeDuc JW, Childs JE & Glass GE (1992) The hantaviruses, etiologic agents of haemorrhagic fever with renal syndrome: a possible cause of hypertension and chronic renal disease in the United States. *Annual review of public health*, 13:79–98.

Lee-Chiong TL & Stitt JT (1995) Heatstroke and other heat-related illnesses: the maladies of summer. *Postgraduate medicine*, 98(1):26–36.

Leigh JP et al. (1996) *Costs of occupational injuries and illnesses*. Final report to NIOSH (Cooperative Agreement U60/902886).

Lengeler C, Cattani J & de Savigny D, eds (1996) *Net gain: a new method for preventing malaria deaths*. Geneva, WHO (joint publication with IDRC).

Leonard HJ (1989) *Environment and the poor: development strategies for a common agenda*. New Brunswick/Oxford, Transaction Books.

Linder FE & Grove RD (1943) *Vital statistics rates in the United States 1900–1940*. Washington DC, United States Department of Commerce, Government Printing Office.

Litsios S (1996) *The tomorrow of malaria*. Wellington, Pacific Press.

Loomis DP et al. (1996) *Ozone exposure and daily mortality in Mexico City: a time-series analysis*. Cambridge, MA, Health Effects Institute (Research Report No. 75).

Løvik M, Dybing E & Smith E (1996) Environmental chemicals and respiratory hypersensitization: a synopsis. *Toxicology letters*, 86:211–222.

MARC (1996) *Air quality management and assessment capabilities in 20 major cities*. Nairobi/Geneva, UNEP/WHO (unpublished document UNEP/DEIA/AR.96.2, WHO/EOS/95.7).

MOHSPE, The Netherlands (1994) *Conference report: Ministerial Conference on Drinking Water and Environmental Sanitation, Noordwijk, The Netherlands, 22–23 March 1994, Vol 2*. The Hague, Ministry of Housing, Spatial Planning and the Environment.

MacKay KT (1993) Alternative methods for pest management in developing countries: impact of pesticide use on health in developing countries. In: Forget G, Goodman T & de Villiers A, eds. *Impact of pesticide use on health in developing countries: proceedings of a symposium, Ottawa, Canada, 17–20 September 1990*. Ottawa, Canada, IDRC.

MacKenzie WR et al. (1994) A massive outbreak in Milwaukee of Cryptosporidium infection transmitted through the public water supply. *New England journal of medicine*, 331:161–167.

Mage T & Zali O (1992) *Motor vehicle air pollution: public health impact and control measures*. Geneva, WHO (unpublished document WHO/PEP/92.4).

Malm O et al.(1990) Mercury pollution due to gold mining in the Madeira River Basin, Brazil. *Ambio, a journal of the human environment*, 19(10):11–15.

Mara DD & Cairncross S (1989) *Guidelines for the safe use of wastewater and excreta in agriculture and aquaculture*. Geneva, WHO.

Mara DD & Alabaster GP (1995) An environmental classification of housing-related diseases in developing countries. *Journal of tropical medicine and hygiene*, 98:41–51.

Markowitz S (1992) Primary prevention of occupational lung disease. *Israel journal of medical sciences*, 28:513–519.

Martin B (1993) *In the public interest? Privatization and public sector reform*. London, Zed Books.

Martines J, Phillips M & Feachem GA (1993) Diarrhoeal diseases. In: Jamison DT et al, eds. *Disease control priorities in developing countries*. New York, Oxford University Press.

Masuda Y (1985) Health status of Japanese and Taiwanese after exposure to contaminated rice oil. *Environmental health perspectives*, 60:321–325.

Mather TH, Sornmani S & Keola KA (1994) *Incorporating a human health component into the integrated development and management of the Lower Mekong Basin.* Geneva, WHO (unpublished document WHO/EOS/94.52).

McMichael AJ et al., eds (1996) *Climate change and human health: an assessment prepared by a task group on behalf of the World Health Organization, the World Meteorological Organization and the United Nations.* Geneva, WHO (unpublished document WHO/EHG/96.7).

Meadows DH et al. (1972) *The limits to growth: a report for the Club of Rome's project on the predicament of mankind.* New York, Universe Books.

Meding B (1990) Epidemiology of hand eczema in an industrial city. *Acta dermato-venereologica* (suppl.), 153:2–43.

Menné T & Maibach HI (1993) *Hand eczema.* Boca Raton, FL, CRC Press.

Metcalf & Eddy, Inc. (1972) *Wastewater engineering: collection, treatment, disposal.* New York, McGraw–Hill.

Mikheev M (1994) New epidemics: the challenge for international health work. In: *New epidemics in occupational health.* Helsinki, Finnish Institute of Occupational Health.

Ministry of Foreign Affairs, Denmark (1994) *Report of the Copenhagen CSD intersessional workshop on health, the environment and sustainable development, 23–25 February 1994, Copenhagen.* Copenhagen, Denmark, Ministry of Foreign Affairs (unpublished document).

Ministry of Health, UK (1954) *Mortality and morbidity during the London fog in December 1952.* London, Her Majesty's Stationery Office (Report No. 95).

Ministry of Health and Social Affairs, Sweden (1996). *Environment for sustainable health: an action plan for Sweden.* Commission on Environmental Health, Stockholm.

Ministry of Welfare, Hungary (1996) *Hungarian environmental health action programme.* Budapest, Hungary.

Mitchell JK et al. (1996) *The long road to recovery: community responses to industrial disasters.* Tokyo, United Nations University Press.

Mood EW (1993) Fundamentals of healthful housing: their application in the 21st century. In: Burridge R & Ormandy D, eds. (1993) *Unhealthy housing: research, remedies and reforms.* London, E & FN Spon.

Motarjemi Y et al. (1993) Contaminated weaning food: a major risk factor for diarrhoea and associated malnutrition. *Bulletin of the World Health Organization,* 71(1):79–92.

Mulholland EK et al. (in press) Haemophilus influenzae type b-tetanus protein conjugate vaccine prevents pneumonia and meningitis due to Haemophilus influenzae type b in Gambian infants. *Lancet.*

Muna WFT (1993) Cardiovascular disorders in Africa. *World health statistics quarterly,* 46:125–133.

Murray CJL & Lopez AD (1996a) *Global health statistics: incidence, prevalence, and mortality estimates for over 200 conditions.* Cambridge, Massachussets, Harvard University Press on behalf of WHO, the World Bank, and the Harvard School of Public Health.

Murray CJL & Lopez AD, eds. (1996b) *The global burden of disease: a comprehensive assessment of mortality and disability from diseases, injuries, and risk factors in 1990 and projected to 2020.* Published by Harvard School of Public Health on behalf of WHO and the World Bank. Cambridge, Massachussets, Harvard University Press.

Myers N (1994) Eco–refugees: a crisis in the making. *People and the planet,* 3(4):6–9.

Nagataki S & Yamashita S (1996) *Nagasaki Symposium Radiation and Human Health: proposal from Nagasaki. Proceedings of the Nagasaki Symposium '95.* Amsterdam, Elsevier.

NIOSH (1994) *Surveillance of occupational lung disease.* Atlanta, USA, CDC/DHHS.

NIOSH (1996) *National occupational research agenda.* Atlanta, USA, CDC/DHHS.

NRC (1996) *Possible effects of exposure to residential electric and magnetic fields.* Washington DC, National Academy Press.

Najera JA (1992) Tropical diseases, environment and development (with special reference to malaria and its control). X Giornata dell'Ambiente: Ambiente, Salute e Sviluppo. Rome, 5 giugno 1992. *Rend Acc Naz Lincei,* 102:65–83.

Najera JA, Liese B & Hammer JS (1992) *Malaria: new patterns and perspectives.* Washington DC, The World Bank (World Bank Technical Paper No. 183).

Najera JA & Hempel J (1996) *The burden of malaria.* Geneva, WHO (unpublished document CTD/MAL/96.10).

Nakicenovic N & Grubler A (1996) *Energy and the protection of the atmosphere.* Laxenburg, Austria, IIASA.

Naturvardsverket (1997) [*Environment taxes in Sweden*]. Stockholm, Swedish Environment Protection Board.

Newman O & Franck K (1981) *Housing design and children's antisocial behaviour.* New York, Institute of Community Design Analysis.

Nriagu JO (1996) A history of global metal pollution. *Science,* 272:223–224.

OECD (1992) *Environmental indicators of accidents involving hazardous substances.* Paris, OECD (unpublished document ENV/EPOC/ACC(92)1).

OECD (1993a) *OECD core set of indicators for environmental performance reviews.* Paris, OECD (Environmental Monograph No. 83).

OECD (1993b) *Lead background and national experience with reducing risk.* Paris, OECD (Series on Risk Reduction No. 1).

OECD (1997) *Geographical distribution of financial flows to aid recipients: Disbursements, commitments, country indicators 1991–1995.* Paris, OECD.

Oxfam (1995) *The Oxfam poverty report.* Oxford, UK, Oxfam.

PAHO (1994) *Health conditions in the Americas.* Washington DC, PAHO (Scientific Publication No. 549).

PAHO (1996a). *Americas in harmony: an opportunity for change and a call to action. Pan American Conference on Health and Environment, 1–3 October 1995. Washington, DC, PAHO.*

PAHO (1996b). *Americas in harmony: regional plan of action. Pan American Conference on Health and Environment in Sustainable Human Development, 1–3 October 1995, Washington, DC.* Washington, PAHO.

Pan American Sanitary Bureau/UN–ECLAC (1994) *Health, social equity and changing production patterns in Latin America and the Caribbean.* Document submitted to the Twenty–fourth Pan American Sanitary Conference, Washington, DC, 26–30 September 1994. Cartagena.

Pearce F (1996a) Trouble bubbles for hydropower. *New Scientist,* 4 May 1996:28–31.

Pearce F (1996b) A heavy responsibility. *New scientist,* 27 July:12–13.

Pearce N et al., eds. (1994) *Occupational cancer in developing countries.* Lyon, IARC (IARC Scientific Publications No. 129).

Pershagen G (1985) Lung cancer mortality among men living near an arsenic-emitting smelter. *American journal of epidemiology,* 122 (4):684–694.

Pershagen G (1994) Passive smoking and lung cancer. In: Samet JM, ed. *Epidemiology of lung cancer.* New York, Marcel Dekker.

Pershagen G & Simonato L (1993) Epidemiological evidence on outdoor air pollution and cancer. In: Tomatis L, ed. *Indoor and outdoor air pollution and human cancer.* Berlin, Springer-Verlag.

Peto R et al. (1994) *Mortality from smoking in developed countries 1950–2000: indirect estimates from national statistics.* Oxford, Oxford Medical Publications.

Peto J et al. (1995) Continuing increase in mesothelioma mortality in Britain. *Lancet,* 345:535–538.

Pimentel D et al. (1997) Water resources: agriculture, the environment, and society. An assessment of the status of water resources. *Bioscience,* 47(2):97–106.

Pirkle JL et al. (1996) Exposure of the US population to environmental tobacco smoke. The third national health and nutrition examinations survey, 1988 to 1991. *JAMA,* 275: 1233–1240.

Pope CA et al. (1995) Heath. Particulate air pollution as a predictor of mortality in a prospective study of US adults. *American journal of respiratory and critical care medicine,* 151(3 Pt 1):669–74.

Pope CA, Bates DV & Raizenne ME (1995) Health effects of particulate air pollution: time for reassessment? *Environmental health perspectives,* 103(5):472–480.

Postel S (1987) *Defusing the toxics threat: controlling pesticides and industrial waste.* Washington DC, Worldwatch Institute (Worldwatch Paper, No. 79).

Pretty JN & Guijt I (1992) Primary environmental care: an alternative paradigm for development assistance. *Environment and urbanization,* 4(1):22–36.

Pruess A (1996) *Background paper on health effects of exposure to recreational water: microbiological aspects of uncontrolled waters.* Copenhagen, WHO Regional Office for Europe (unpublished document ICP EUD 022 DL96/1 EHPM 07.2.4).

Psacharaopoulos G et al. (1993) *Poverty and income distribution in Latin America: the story of the 1980s.* Washington, DC, The World Bank, Latin America and the Caribbean Technical Department, Regional Studies Program (Report No. 27).

Raffle PAB et al., eds. (1994) *Hunter's diseases of occupations,* 8th edition. London, Hodder Headline Group.

Rantanen J, Lehtinen S & Mikheev M, eds. (1994) *Health protection and health promotion in small-scale enterprises: proceedings of the Joint ILO/WHO Task Group, Bangkok, 1–3 November 1993.* Helsinki, Finnish Institute of Occupational Health.

Razali I (1997) Presentation at Symposium "United Nations Conferences — From Promises to Performance", 3 March 1997. Washington, DC, American University.

Repacholi MH (1996) The International Electromagnetic Fields (EMF) Project. In: Matthes R, ed. *Non-ionizing radiation: proceedings of the third international non-ionizing radiation workshop, Baden, 1996.* Oberschleißheim, Germany, ICNIRP.

Repacholi MH (in press) Low-level exposure to radiofrequency fields: health effects and research needs. *Bioelectromagnetics.*

Rodrigues LC & Smith PG (1990) Tuberculosis in developing countries and methods for its control. *Transactions of the Royal Society of Tropical Medicine and Hygiene,* 84:739–744.

Rojas-Lopez M et al. (1994) Use of lead-glazed ceramics is the main factor associated to high lead in blood levels in two Mexican rural communities. *Journal of toxicology and environmental health,* 42:45–52.

Rossi-Espagnet A, Goldstein GB & Tabibzadeh I (1991) Urbanization and health in developing countries: a challenge for health for all. *World health statistics quarterly,* 44(4):186–244.

Rushbrook PE & Finnecy EE (1988) Planning for future waste management operations in developing countries. *Waste management & research,* 6:1–21.

Rylander R, Bonevik H & Rubenowitz E (1991) Magnesium and calcium in drinking water and cardiovascular mortality. *Scandinavian journal of work, environment and health,* 17(2):91–94.

SCOPE (1993) *Effects of increased ultraviolet radiation on global ecosystems.* Paris, SCOPE.

Safe SH (1994) Dietary and environmental estrogens and anti-estrogens and their possible role in human disease. *Environmental science and pollution research*, 1(1):29–33.

Sattherthwaite D et al. (1996) *The environment for children*. London, Earthscan Publications Ltd.

Savigny D & Wijeyaratne P, eds. (1995) *GIS for health and the environment: proceedings of an international workshop, Colombo, Sri Lanka, 5–10 September 1994*. Ottawa, Canada, IDRC.

Schwartz J & Morris R (1995) Air pollution and hospital admissions for cardiovascular disease in Detroit, Michigan. *American journal of epidemiology*, 142(1):23–25.

Schwela D (1996a) Health effects of and exposure to indoor air pollution in developed and developing countries. In Yoshizawa et al., eds. *Indoor air '96: proceedings of the 7th International Conference on Indoor Air Quality and Climate, Nagoya, Japan, 21–26 July 1996*. Tokyo, Institute of Public Health.

Schwela D (1996b) Exposure to environmental chemicals relevant for respiratory hypersensitivity: global aspects. *Toxicology letters*, 86:131–142.

Schwela DH & Köth–Jahr I (1994) *Leitfaden für die Aufstellung von Luftreinhalteplänen. [Guidelines for the implementation of clean air implementation plans]*. Landesumweltamt des Landes Nordrhein Westfalen (Report No. 4).

Serageldin I (1996) *Sustainability and the wealth of nations: first steps in an ongoing journey*. Washington DC, World Bank (Environmentally Sustainable Development Studies and Monograph Series No. 5).

Service MW, ed. (1989) *Demography and vector-borne diseases*. Boca Raton, Florida, CRC Press Inc.

Seymour J (1996) Trafficking in death. *New Scientist*, 14 September 1996:34–37.

Shahi GS et al., eds. (1997) *International perspectives on environment, development and health*. New York, Springer Publishing Co.

Shann F (1986) Etiology of severe pneumonia in children in developing countries. *Pediatric infectious diseases*, 5:247–251.

Shy CM (1990) Lead in petrol: the mistake of the XXth century. *World health statistics quarterly*, 43:168–176.

Shy CM & Struka RJ (1982) *Air and water pollution*. In: Schottenfeld D and Fraumen J, eds. Cancer epidemiology and prevention. Philadelphia/London, Saunders.

Sims J (1994) *Women, health and environment: an anthology*. Geneva, WHO (unpublished document WHO/EHG/94.11).

Sivard RL (1996) The plague of landmines. In: Sivard RL, ed. *World military and social expenditures 1996, 16th edition*. Washington DC, World Priorities.

Smith KR (1991) Managing the risk transition. *Toxicology and industrial health*, 7:319–327.

Smith KR (1993) Fuel combustion, air pollution, and health: the situation in developing countries. *Annual review of energy and environment*, 18:529–566.

Smith KR (1996) Indoor air pollution in developing countries: growing evidence of its role in the global disease burden. In Yoshizawa S et al., eds. (1996) *Indoor air '96: proceedings of the 7th International Conference on Indoor Air Quality and Climate, Nagoya, Japan, 21–26 July 1996*. Tokyo, Institute of Public Health.

Smith KR (1997) *Development, health and the environmental risk transition*. In Shahi GS et al., eds. International perspectives on environment, development, and health: toward a sustainable world. New York, Springer Publishing Co., pp. 51–62.

Smith KR & Figueroa M (1997) *Global household use of solid fuels: a rough estimation* (in preparation).

Snow J (1849) On the pathology and mode of communication of cholera. *London medical gazette*, 9:745–753; 923–949.

Solo-Gabriele H & Neumeister S (1996) US outbreaks of cryptosporidiosis. *Journal of the American Waterworks Association*, September:76–86.

Sonawane BR (1995) Chemical contaminants in human milk: an overview. *Environmental health perspectives*, 103(suppl6):197–205.

Spengler JD et al. (1996) Impact of residential nitrogen dioxide exposure on personal exposure: an international study. In: Yoshizawa S et al., eds. *Indoor air '96: proceedings of the 7th International Conference on Indoor Air Quality and Climate, Nagoya, Japan, 21–26 July 1996*. Tokyo, Institute of Public Health.

Speth JG (1996) Two worlds in counterflow, or 358 = 2.3 billion and counting. *Herald tribune*, 23 August.

Stanners D & Bourdeau P, eds (1995) *Europe's environment: the Dobrís Assessment*. Copenhagen, European Environment Agency.

Steinglass R Brenzel L & Percy A (1993) Tetanus. In: Jamison DT et al. *Disease control priorities in developing countries*. New York, Oxford University Press (A World Bank Book).

Steinhart CE, Doyle ME & Cochrane BA (1995) *Food safety 1995*. New York, Food Research Institute/University of Wisconsin-Madison/Marcel Dekker, Inc.

Stoll BJ (1997) The global impact of neonatal infection. *Clinics in perinatology*, 24:1–21.

Stoltzfus RG et al. (1997) Epidemiology of iron deficiency anaemia in Zanzibari school children: the importance of hookworms. *The American journal of clinical nutrition*, 65:153–159.

Tarimo E & Webster E (1994). *Primary health care concepts and challenges in a changing world*. WHO, Geneva.

Tengs T (1996) Enormous variation in the cost-effectiveness of prevention: implications for public policy. *Current issues in public health*, 2:13–17.

Tesh RB (1994) The emerging epidemiology of Venezuelan haemorrhagic fever and Oropouche fever in tropical South Africa. In: Wilson ME, Levins R & Spielman A, eds. *Disease evolution: global changes and emergence of infectious diseases*. New York, New York Academy of Sciences (Annals of the New York Academy of Sciences No. 740).

Thériault G et al. (1994) Cancer risks associated with occupational exposure to magnetic fields among electric utility workers in Ontario and Quebec, Canada and France: 1970–1989. *American journal of epidemiology*, 139:550–72.

Timaeus IM & Lush L (1995) Intra-urban differentials in child health. *Health transition review*, 5:163–190.

Tobler W et al. (1995) *The global demography project*. Santa Barbara, National Center for Geographic Information and Analysis (Technical Report TR–95–6).

Tomasevski K (1993) *Women and human rights*. London, Zed Books.

Trichopoulos D Li FP & Hunter DJ (1996) What causes cancer? *Scientific American*, September:50–57.

Tronko ND (1997) Personal communication.

Tseng WP et al. (1968) Prevalence of skin cancer in an endemic area of chronic arsenicism in Taiwan. *Journal of the National Cancer Institute*, 40(3):453–463.

Tsouros D, ed. (1992) *World Health Organization Healthy Cities project: a project becomes a movement. Review of progress 1987–1990*. Published for the WHO Healthy Cities Project Office. Milan, SOGESS.

Tsyb et al. (1996) Thyroid cancer in children and adolescents of Bryansk and Kaluga regions. In: Karaoglou A et al., eds. *The radiological consequences of the Chernobyl accident*. Brussels, European Commission (EUROPE 16544EN).

UN (1948) *Universal declaration of human rights*. New York, UN (document E.DPI/876).

UN (1977) *Report of the United Nations Water Conference, Mar del Plata, Brazil, 14–25 March 1977.* New York, UN (E/CONF.70/29).

UN (1981) *UN statistical yearbook 1981.* New York, UN.

UN (1990) *UN statistical yearbook 1990.* New York, UN.

UN (1993) *Agenda 21: the United Nations programme of action from Rio.* New York, UN.

UN (1995a) *World population prospects: the 1994 revision.* New York, UN, Department for Economic and Social Information and Policy Analysis, Population Division (document ST/ESA/SER.A/145).

UN (1995b) *Report of the International Conference on Population and Development. Cairo, 5–13 September 1994.* New York, UN (document A/conf. 171/13/rev.1).

UN (1995c) *UN statistical yearbook 1995.* New York, UN.

UN (1995d) Partnerships for poverty alleviation in Cebu City, The Philippines, case study. In: *Dubai International Conference for Habitat II on Best Practices in Improving the Living Environment.* Dubai, UAE. 19–22 November 1995.

UN (1995e) *The challenge of urbanization: the world's large cities.* New York, United Nations (ST/ESA/SER.A/151).

UN (1996a) *Indicators of sustainable development: framework and methodologies.* Report for the UN Commission on Sustainable Development. New York, UN Department for Policy Coordination and Sustainable Development.

UN (1996b) *The Beijing declaration and the platform for action. Fourth World Conference on Women, Beijing, China, 4–15 September 1995.* New York, UN Department of Public Information.

UNCHS (1995) *Human settlements interventions addressing crowding and health issues.* Nairobi, UNCHS (HS/374/95/E).

UNCHS (1996a) *Report of the United Nations Conference on Human Settlements (HABITAT II), Istanbul, Turkey, 3–14 June 1996.* New York, UN (A/CONF.165/14).

UNCHS (1996b) *An urbanizing world: global report on human settlements, 1996.* Oxford, Oxford University Press.

UNCHS/UNEP (1996) *Implementing the urban environment agenda: report on the Global Meeting of Cities and International Programmes during Habitat II, Istanbul, Turkey, 3–14 June 1996.* New York, UN.

UNCTAD (1995a) *The least developed countries: 1995 report.*

UNCTAD (1995b) *Comparative experiences with privatization: policy insights and lessons learned.* New York, UN (document UNCTAD/DTCI/23).

UNDP (1991) *Human development report 1991.* New York/Oxford, Oxford University Press.

UNDP (1994) *Human development report 1994.* New York/Oxford, Oxford University Press.

UNDP (1995) *Human development report 1995.* New York/Oxford, Oxford University Press.

UNDP (1996) *Human development report 1996.* New York/Oxford, Oxford University Press.

UNEP (1988) *Assessment of chemical contaminants in food: report on the results of the UNEP/FAO/WHO Programme on Health-related Environmental Monitoring,* Nairobi, UNEP.

UNEP (1991a) *Freshwater pollution.* Nairobi, UNEP (GEMS Environmental Library No. 6).

UNEP (1992a) *The world environment 1972–1992: two decades of challenge.* London, Chapman & Hall.

UNEP (1993) *Environmental data report 1993–1994.* Oxford, Blackwell Publishers.

UNEP (1995a) *Global programme of action for the protection of the marine environment from land-based activities.* Nairobi, UNEP (document UNEP(OCA)/LBA/IG.2/7).

UNEP (1995b) *Water quality of world river basins.* Nairobi, UNEP (UNEP Environment Library No. 4).

UNEP (1996a) Industry and environment, 19(3).

UNEP (1996b) *The state of the marine and coastal environment in the Mediterranean region. Mediterranean Action Plan.* Athens, UNEP (MAP Technical Report Series No. 100).

UNEP (1996c) *Management of industrial accident prevention and preparedness: a training resource package.* Paris, UNEP, Industry and Environment Office.

UNEP (1997a) *Global environmental outlook.* New York, Oxford University Press.

UNEP/IETC (1996) *International sourcebook on environmentally sound technologies for municipal solid waste management.* Osaka/Shiga, UNEP IETC.

UNEP/WHO (1992) *Urban air pollution in megacities of the world.* Nairobi/Geneva/Oxford, UNEP/WHO/Blackwell publishers.

UNFPA (1997) *Task managers' report for the 1997 special session of the General Assembly: demographic dynamics and sustainability.* New York, UNFPA.

UNHCR (1995) *State of the world's refugees: in search of solutions.* Oxford, Oxford University Press.

UNICEF (1990a) *The state of the world's children 1990.* Oxford, Oxford University Press.

UNICEF (1990b) *First call for children: world declaration and plan of action from the World Summit for Children. Convention on the rights of the child.* New York, UNICEF.

UNICEF (1994) *Central and Eastern Europe in transition public policy and social conditions: crisis in mortality, health and nutrition.* New York, UNICEF (Economies in Transition Studies. Regional Monitoring Report. No. 2).

UNICEF (1997) *The state of the world's children.* Oxford, Oxford University Press.

UNIDO (1995) *Industrial development: global report 1995.* New York, Oxford University Press for the United Nations Industrial Development Organization.

UNPF (1989) *The state of the world population 1989.* New York, United Nations Population Fund.

UNSCEAR (1993) *Sources and effects of ionizing radiation.* New York, UN (document E.94.IX.2).

UNSCEAR (1996) *Exposure from man-made sources of ionizing radiation.* New York, UN (document A/AC.82/R.556).

USDA (1994) *World grain situation and outlook.* Washington DC, USDA.

USEPA (1978) *Preliminary assessment of the sources control and population exposure to airborne polycyclic organic matter (POM) as indicated by benzo a pyrene (BaP).* Research Triangle Park, NC, USEPA Office of Air Quality Planning and Standards.

USEPA (1992) *Respiratory health effects of passive smoking: lung cancer and other diseases.* Washington, DC, USEPA (EPA/600/6–90/006F).

USEPA (1994) *Pesticide industry sales and usage: 1992 and 1993 market estimates.* Washingon DC, USEPA (EPA 733–K–94–001).

USEPA (1996) *National air quality and emissions trends report, 1995.* Research Triangle Park, NC, USEPA, Office of Air Quality Planning and Standards, Emissions Monitoring and Analysis Division, Air Quality Trends Analysis Group (EPA 454/R-96-005).

US Department of Health and Human Services (1991) *Healthy people 2000: national health promotion and disease prevention objectives.* Washington DC, US Department of Health and Human Services (DHHS Publication No. PHS 91–50212).

US Department of Health and Human Services (1995). *Healthy people 2000: midcourse review and 1995 revisions.* Washington DC, US Department of Health and Human Services.

Unidad de Análises de Políticas Sociales (1993) *Inversión en capital humano y focalización del gasto social.* La Paz, Bolivia, Ministry of Human Development.

Van de Walle D & Nead K, eds. (1995) *Public spending and the poor: theory and evidence.* Baltimore, Johns Hopkins University Press (A World Bank Book).

Victora CG et al. (1988) Water supply, sanitation and housing in relation to the risk of infant mortality from diarrhoea. *International journal of epidemiology,* 17(3):651–654.

Vineis P et al. (1988) Proportion of lung cancers in males due to occupation, in different areas of the USA. *International journal of cancer,* 42:851–856.

Vogel RJ (1988) *Cost recovery in the health care sector: selected country studies in West Africa.* Washington DC, World Bank (World Bank Technical Paper No. 82).

WCED (1987) *Our common future: report of the World Commission on Environment and Development.* Oxford, Oxford University Press.

WHO (1946) Constitution of the World Health Organization. *Official records of the World Health Organization,* 2, 100.

WHO (1978) *Primary health care: report of the International Conference on Primary Health Care, Alma Ata.* Geneva, WHO (joint publication with UNICEF).

WHO (1979) *Formulating strategies for health for all by the year 2000: guiding principles and essential issues.* Geneva, WHO ("Health for All" Series No. 2).

WHO (1981). *Global strategy for health-for-all by the year 2000.* WHO, Geneva.

WHO (1986a) *Intersectoral action for health: technical discussions, Geneva, May 1986. Background document.* Geneva, WHO (unpublished document A39/Technical Discussions/1).

WHO (1986b) *Health promotion: Ottawa charter. International Conference on Health Promotion, Ottawa. Canada, 17–21 November 1986.* Geneva, WHO (unpublished document WHO/HPR/HEP/95.1).

WHO (1987a) Diarrhoeal diseases morbidity, mortality and treatment surveys. *CDD update,* 1:1–3.

WHO (1987b) *Air quality guidelines for Europe.* Geneva, WHO (WHO Regional publications, European series No. 23).

WHO (1988) *Guidelines for healthy housing.* Copenhagen, WHO Regional Office for Europe (Environmental Health Series, 31).

WHO (1989a) *Report on the meeting on the early diagnosis and treatment of pneumoconiosis.* Manila, WHO Regional office for the Western Pacific (unpublished document WP-OMC/ICP/OCH/001-E).

WHO (1989b). *Environment and health: the European charter and commentary. First European Conference on Environment and Health, Frankfurt, 4–8 December 1989.* Geneva, WHO (WHO Regional Publications, European series No. 35).

WHO (1989c) *New approaches to improve road safety: report of a study group, Geneva, 14–18 December 1987.* WHO, Geneva (WHO Technical Report Series No. 781).

WHO (1989e) *Health principles of housing.* Geneva, WHO.

WHO (1990a) *The public health impact of pesticides used in agriculture.* Geneva, WHO.

WHO (1990b) *Diet, nutrition and the prevention of chronic diseases: report of a WHO study group.* Geneva, WHO (WHO Technical Report Series No. 797).

WHO (1991a) Towards a framework for urban health development. *World health statistics quarterly,* 44(4):241–244.

WHO (1991b) *Livestock management and disease vector control: report of the tenth meeting of the joint WHO/FAO/UNEP Panel of Experts on Environmental Management for Vector Control.* Geneva, WHO (unpublished document WHO/CWS/91.11).

WHO (1991c) *PEEM medium-term programme 1991–1996.* Geneva, WHO (unpublished document CWS/91.7).

WHO (1992a) *Report of the Panel on Urbanization of the WHO Commission on Health and Environment.* Geneva, WHO (unpublished document WHO/EHE/92.5).

WHO (1992b) *Report of the Panel on Industry of the WHO Commission on Health and Environment.* Geneva, WHO (unpublished document WHO/EHE/92.4).

WHO (1992c) *Indoor air pollution from biomass fuel*. Geneva, WHO (unpublished document WHO/PEP/92.3A).

WHO (1992d) *Report of the Panel on Food and Agriculture of the Commission on Health and Environment*. Geneva, WHO (unpublished document WHO/EHE/92.2).

WHO (1992e) *Report of the Panel on Energy of the Commission on Health and Environment*. Geneva, WHO (unpublished document WHO/EHE 92.3).

WHO (1992f) *Our planet, our health: report of the WHO Commission on Health and Environment*. Geneva, WHO.

WHO (1993a) *The urban health crisis: strategies for health for all in the face of rapid urbanization. Report of the technical discussions at the Forty–fourth World Health Assembly*. WHO, Geneva.

WHO (1993b) *Report on solar energy and health for the World Solar Summit, Paris, 1993*. Geneva, WHO (unpublished document WHO/EPI/LHIS/93.2).

WHO (1993c) *WARDA/PEEM proposal for a consortium research project on the association between rice production systems and vector-borne diseases in West Africa*. Geneva, WHO (unpublished document).

WHO (1993d) *Guidelines for drinking-water quality. Vol. 1: Recommendations*, 2nd ed. Geneva, WHO.

WHO (1993e) *Environmental health criteria 137. Electromagnetic fields (300 Hz–300 Ghz)*. Geneva, WHO.

WHO (1993f) *Health, environment and development: approaches to drafting country-level strategies for human well-being under Agenda 21*. Geneva, WHO (unpublished document WHO/EHE/93.1).

WHO (1993j) *Foodborne trematode infection. In point of fact*, 80.

WHO (1993k) *Human rights in relation to women's health: the promotion and protection of women's health through international human rights law*. Geneva, WHO (unpublished document WHO/DGH/93.1).

WHO (1994a) WHO *Scientific Working Group on Monitoring and Management of Bacterial Resistance to Antimicrobial Agents, Geneva, 29 November–2 December 1994*. Geneva, WHO (unpublished document WHO/CDS/BVI/95.7).

WHO (1994b) *Declaration on occupational health for all*. Approved at the Second Meeting of the WHO Collaborating Centres in Occupational Health, Beijing, China, 11–14 October 1994. Geneva, WHO (unpublished document WHO/OCH/94.1).

WHO (1994c) *Environmental health criteria 160. Ultraviolet radiation: an authoritative scientific review of environmental and health effects of ultraviolet radiation, with reference to global ozone layer depletion*. Geneva, WHO.

WHO (1994d) *Declaration on action for environment and health in Europe*. Copenhagen, WHO Regional Office for Europe (unpublished document ICP/CEH/212 Rev. 1).

WHO (1994e) *Développement agricole et santé au Bénin: rapport d'un séminaire national, Cotonou, 23–26 novembre 1993*. Geneva, WHO (unpublished document WHO/CWS/94.1).

WHO (1994f) *Managing medical wastes in developing countries: report of a consultation, Geneva, 15–18 September 1992*. Geneva, WHO (unpublished document WHO/PEP/RUD/94.1).

WHO (1994j) *Public health and coastal tourism (sea, tourism and health): report from a WHO symposium, Rimini, Italy, 26-28 May 1994*. Geneva, WHO (unpublished document WHO/EOS/94.39).

WHO (1995a) *World health report 1995: bridging the gaps*. Geneva, WHO.

WHO (1995b) *Health economics: WTO what's in it for WHO?* Geneva, WHO (unpublished document WHO/TFHE/95.5).

WHO (1995c) *Indoor air pollution database for China.* Geneva, WHO (unpublished document WHO/EHG/95.8).

WHO (1995d) *Air pollution and its health effects in China.* Geneva, WHO (unpublished document WHO/EHG/95.21).

WHO (1995e) *Case studies: community water supply and sanitation project.* Sri Lanka, Ministry of Housing, Construction and Public Utilities (unpublished report).

WHO (1995f) *Control of foodborne trematode infections: report of a WHO study group.* Geneva, WHO (WHO Technical Report Series No. 849).

WHO (1995g) *Food safety issues: food technologies and public health.* Geneva, WHO (unpublished document WHO/FNU/FOS/95.12).

WHO (1995h) *Criteria for the derivation of toxic equivalency factors for dioxin-like PCBs.* Copenhagen, WHO Regional Office for Europe (unpublished document EUR/ICP/PCS 211).

WHO (1995i) *Global Strategy on Occupational Health for All.* Geneva, WHO (unpublished document WHO/OCH/95.1).

WHO (1995j) *Lead and health.* Copenhagen, WHO Regional Office for Europe (Local Authorities, Health and Environment Briefing Pamphlet Series No. 1).

WHO (1995k) *Acute respiratory infections in children: case management in small hospitals in developing countries.* Geneva, WHO (unpublished document WHO/ARI/90.5).

WHO (1995l) *The healthy route to a sustainable world: health, environment and sustainable development.* Geneva, WHO (unpublished document WHO/EOS/95.21).

WHO (1995m) Yanuca Island declaration. Manila, WHO Regional Office for the Western Pacific (unpublished document WHO/HRH/95.4).

WHO (1995n). *New horizons in health.* Manila, WHO Regional Office for the Western Pacific (unpublished document).

WHO (1995o) *Health consequences of the Chernobyl accident: results of the IPHECA pilot projects and related national programmes. Summary report.* Geneva, WHO.

WHO (1995p) *Concern for Europe's tomorrow: health and the environment in the WHO European Region.* Report from the WHO European Centre for Environment and Health. Stuttgart, Wissenschaftliche Verlagsgesellschaft.

WHO (1995q) *Environment, health and sustainable development: the role of economic instruments and policies.* Geneva, WHO (unpublished document WHO/TFHE/95.2).

WHO (1995s) *Renewing the Health-for-All Strategy: guiding principles and essential issues for the elaboration of a policy for equity, solidarity and health.* Geneva, WHO (unpublished document WHO/PAC/95.1).

WHO (1995t) *Water resources development and vector-borne diseases in Zambia: report of a national seminar, Kafue Gorge, 6–10 November 1995.* Geneva, WHO (unpublished document WHO/EOS/95.23).

WHO (1995v) *Women's health: improve our health, improve the world. WHO position paper prepared for the Fourth World Conference on Women, Beijing, China, 4–15 September 1995.* Geneva, WHO (unpublished document: WHO/FHE/95.9).

WHO (1995w) *Building a healthy city: a practitioner's guide. A step-by-step approach to implementing healthy city projects in low-income countries.* Geneva, WHO (unpublished document WHO/EOS/95.10).

WHO (1995x) *WHO report on the tuberculosis epidemic, 1995.* Geneva, WHO (unpublished document WHO/TB/95.183).

WHO (1996a) *World health report 1996: fighting disease, fostering development.* Geneva, WHO.

WHO (1996b) *World health statistics annual.* Geneva, WHO.

WHO (1996c) *Equity in health and health care: a WHO/SIDA initiative.* Geneva, WHO (unpublished document WHO/ARA/96.1).

WHO (1996d) *Investing in health research and development: report of the Ad Hoc Committee on Health Research Relating to Future Intervention Options.* Geneva, WHO (unpublished document TDR/GEN/96.1).

WHO (1996e) *International perspectives in environment, development and health: priority setting for research and intervention. Report of the Joint Meeting of the WHO and the Rockefeller Foundation, 12–15 September 1995.* Geneva, WHO (unpublished document WHO/EHG/96.2).

WHO (1996f) *Cholera and other epidemic diarrhoeal diseases control: fact sheets on environmental sanitation.* Geneva, WHO (unpublished document WHO/EOS/96.4).

WHO (1996g) *A case study of community participation in solid waste management, Kalabagan,* Dhaka (unpublished report).

WHO (1996h) *A methodology for estimating air pollution health effects.* Geneva, WHO (unpublished document WHO/EHG/96.5).

WHO (1996i) Radon. Copenhagen, WHO Regional Office for Europe (Local Authorities, Health and Environment Briefing Pamphlet Series No. 10).

WHO (1996j) *Health consequences of the Chernobyl accident: scientific report.* Geneva, WHO (unpublished document WHO/EHG/95.19).

WHO (1996k) Cholera in 1995. *Weekly epidemiological record,* 21:157–163.

WHO (1996l) *Levels of PCBs, PCDDs and PCDFs in human milk: second round of WHO-coordinated exposure study.* Copenhagen, WHO Regional Office for Europe (Environmental Health in Europe No. 3).

WHO (1996m) *WHO Panel of Environmental Health Indicators. Meeting of the International Society for Environmental Epidemiology, 17–21 August 1996.* 8th Annual Conference of the International Society for Environmental Epidemiology, Edmonton, Alberta, Canada.

WHO (1996n) *Beirut declaration on action for a healthy environment.* Alexandria, Egypt, WHO Regional Office for the Eastern Mediterranean.

WHO (1996o) *Creating Healthy Cities in the 21st century. Background paper, United Nations Conference on Human Settlements, 3–14 June 1996, Istanbul, Turkey.* Geneva, WHO (unpublished document WHO/EOS/96.9).

WHO (1996p) *Building a healthy village: concept and practice. A step-by-step approach to implementing "Healthy Village" projects.* Geneva, WHO (in preparation).

WHO (1996q) *GEENET progress report.* Geneva, WHO (unpublished document WHO/EHG/96.21).

WHO (1996r) *Global burden of disease and injury due to occupational factors.* Geneva, WHO (unpublished document WHO/EHG/96.20).

WHO (1996s) *Tobacco alert.* Special issue, World No-Tobacco Day 1996.

WHO (1996t) *Safe motherhood.* Geneva, WHO (unpublished document FRH/MSM/96.14).

WHO (1996u) Creating healthy cities. *WHO environmental health newsletter,* 26.

WHO (1996v) Healthy Cities. *World health,* 49(1).

WHO (1996w) Issyk-Kul Resolution on actions for environment and health protection in Central Asian Republics. Copenhagen, WHO Regional Office for Europe (unpublished document EUROPE/ICP/NEAP 03 01 11).

WHO (1997a) *World health report: conquering suffering, enriching humanity.* Geneva, WHO.

WHO (1997b) *Health for all for the 21st century.* Geneva, WHO (draft for review).

WHO (1997c) *Technology for health in the future.* Geneva, WHO (unpublished document PAC/97, in press).

WHO (1997d) *Indicators for decision-making in environmental health.* Geneva, WHO (Unpublished document WHO/EHG/97.7).

WHO (1997e) *Intersectoral actions for health: addressing health and environment concerns in sustainable development.* Geneva, WHO (unpublished document WHO/PPE/PAC/97.1).

WHO (1997f) *Air quality guidelines for Europe.* WHO, Geneva (in preparation).

WHO (1997g) *Health education in food safety.* Geneva, WHO (in preparation).

WHO (1997h) *CTD progress report.* Geneva, WHO (unpublished document CTD/PR/97.1).

WHO (1997i) *Health and environment library modules.* 2nd edition. Geneva, WHO (unpublished document WHO/EHG/97.2).

WHO (1997j) *Approaches to human resources planning in environmental and occupational health.* Geneva, WHO (in preparation).

WHO (1997k) *Neurology in public health: proceedings of a Meeting on Neurology in Public Health, Tokyo, 26–28 September 1995.* Geneva, WHO (unpublished document WHO/MSA/MNH/NRS/96.3).

WHO (1997l) *Child friendly schools' initiative.* Geneva, WHO (unpublished document MNH/PSF/97.1).

WHO (1997m) *Weekly epidemiological record, 72(1/2):1–8.*

WHO (1997n) *Report of a WHO Consultation on Medicinal and other Products in relation to Human and Animal Transmissible Spongiform Encephalopathies, Geneva, 24–26 March 1997.* Geneva, WHO (unpublished document in preparation).

WHO/UNEP (1987) *Global pollution and health: results of health-related environmental monitoring.* Geneva/Nairobi, WHO/UNEP.

WHO/UNEP (1995) *Protection against exposure to ultraviolet radiation.* Geneva, WHO (unpublished document WHO/EHG/95.17).

WHO/UNICEF (1992) *Water supply and sanitation sector monitoring report 1990: baseline year.* Geneva, WHO.

WHO/UNICEF (1993) *Water supply and sanitation sector monitoring report: sector status as of 31 December 1991.* Geneva, WHO.

WHO/UNICEF (1996a) *Water supply and sanitation sector monitoring report: sector status as of 31 December 1994.* Geneva, WHO (unpublished document WHO/EOS/96.15).

WHO/UNICEF (1996b) *State of the world's vaccines and immunization.* Geneva, WHO (unpublished document WHO/GPV/96.1).

WMO/UNEP (1995) *The global climate system review: climate system monitoring.* Geneva, WMO (Document 819).

WRI (1992) *World resources 1992–93: a guide to the global environment. Toward sustainable development.* New York, Oxford University Press (joint publication with UNEP and UNDP).

WRI (1994) *World resources 1994–95: a guide to the global environment. People and the environment.* New York, Oxford University Press (joint publication with UNEP and UNDP).

WRI (1996) *World resources report 1996–97: a guide to the global environment. Urbanization.* New York, Oxford University Press (joint publication with UNDP, UNEP and the World Bank).

WSSCC (1996) *People and water: partners for life. Meeting report. Biennial Forum of the Water Supply and Sanitation Collaborative Council, Third Global Forum, Barbados, 30 October–3 November 1995.* Geneva, WSSCC.

WTO (1996) *Report of the Commission on Trade and Environment.* Geneva, WTO (unpublished document WT/CTE/1 96–4808).

Wagner GR (1996) *Screening and surveillance of workers exposed to mineral dusts.* Geneva, WHO.

Wagner EG & Lanoix JN (1958) *Excreta disposal for rural areas and small communities.* Geneva, WHO (Monograph Series No. 39).

Walsh M, ed. (1997) *Car lines.* Arlington, VA.

Warren KS et al. (1989) Helminth infection. In: Jamison DT et Moseley WH, eds. *Evolving health sector priorities in the developing countries.* Washington DC, World Bank.

Warren KS et al. (1993) Helminth infection. In: Jamison DT et al. *Disease control priorities in developing countries.* New York, Oxford University Press (A World Bank Book).

Washino RK & Wood BL (1994) Application of remote sensing to arthropod vector surveillance and control. *American journal of tropical medicine and hygiene,* 50, supplement 6:134–144.

Weiss R (1993) Rat-borne virus may take secret toll. *Science,* 135:292.

Whelpdale DM & Kaiser MS (1997) *Global acid deposition assessment.* Geneva, WMO (unpublished document WMO-TD No. 777).

Wigley TML (1995) Global mean temperature and sea level consequences of greenhouse gases stabilization. *Geophysical research letters,* 22:45–48.

Willett WC Coldit GA & Mueller NE (1996) Strategies for minimizing cancer risk. *Scientific american,* 275(3):88–91.

Williams ED et al. (1996) Effects on the thyroid in population exposed to radiation as a result of the Chernobyl accident. In: *One decade after Chernobyl: summing up the consequences of the accident. Proceedings of an International Conference, Vienna, 8–12 April 1996.* Vienna, IAEA.

Williamson JD (1996). Promoting environmental health. *British medical journal,* 312(7035):863–864.

Winblad U (1996) *Towards an ecological approach to sanitation.* International Toilet Symposium, Toyama, Japan, 9–11 October 1996.

World Bank (1992) *World development report 1992: development and the environment.* New York/Oxford, Oxford University Press.

World Bank (1993) *World development report 1993: investing in health.* New York/Oxford, Oxford University Press.

World Bank (1995a) *World development report 1995: workers in an integrating world.* New York/Oxford, Oxford University Press.

World Bank (1995b) *Mainstreaming the environment: the World Bank Group and the environment since the Rio Earth Summit. Fiscal 1995.* Washington DC, World Bank.

World Bank (1996) *Towards environmentally sustainable development in sub-Saharan Africa: a World Bank agenda.* Washington, World Bank.

World Bank (1997) *Pollution prevention and abatement handbook.* Washington DC, World Bank (in press).

Wu W (1988) Occupational cancer epidemiology in the People's Republic of China. *Journal of occupational medicine,* 30:968–974.

Wyndham CH et al. (1986) Mortality of middle-aged white South African goldminers. *British journal of industrial medicine,* 43:677–684.

Xuan XZ et al. (1993) A cohort study in Southern China of tin miners exposed to radon and radon decay products. *Health physics,* 64:120–131.

Yach D & Harrison D (1995) Inequalities in health: determinants and status in South Africa. In: van der Walle K et al., eds. *Health matters: public health in North–South perspective.* Amsterdam, The Netherlands, Houten–Diegem (Health Policy Series, Part 9).

Yoshimura T (1974) [Epidemiological study on Yusho babies born to mothers who had consumed oil contaminated by PCB]. *Fukuoka igaku zasshi,* 65; 74–80.

Zvekic U & Alvazzi del Frate A, eds. (1995) *Criminal victimisation of the developing world.* Rome, UNICRI (General series No. 1).

Index

96, 127
refineries, 64, 68, 79, 82
reforestation, 59, 104
refrigeration, 32, 36, 125
refugee, 23, 27, 93, 133
remote sensing, 33
reproductive disorders, 118, 120, 172
reproductive hazards, 120
reproductive health, 170-171
reservoir, 55, 57, 76, 106
resource-intensive industries, 65-66
rheumatic heart disease, 160
risk assessment and management, 179
risk transition, 7-8
road-traffic accidents, 149-151, 154
rotavirus, 106, 139, 141
rubella, 171
safe food, 93, 113, 139
safe water, 1, 45, 52, 96-97, 113, 131,
    193, 200
salmonella, 106, 108, 139, 141
sandfly, 147
sanitary facilities, 24, 113
sanitation, 1-4, 7-8, 11-13, 15, 20,
    24, 26, 38-39, 46-49, 53-54, 78,
    93-96, 98-99, 103, 112, 115,
    118, 125, 129, 131, 138-139,
    141, 143-144, 148, 163-164,
    173-175, 181, 183, 190-193,
    198-201
scavengers, 95
Schistosoma haematobium, 49
Schistosoma mansoni, 57
schistosomiasis, 46-47, 56-58, 93, 98-
    99, 104, 124, 131, 139, 145, 147-
    148, 163, 183, 199, 201
schizophrenia, 155
SCOPE, 58, 127, 183
SDI, 10
sea level rise, 27, 122, 124-125, 201
selenium, 64, 75
settings, 13, 16, 19, 81, 84-88, 128-
    129, 141, 168, 190, 193, 195
settlements, 5-7, 9, 26, 39, 45, 48,
    53, 59, 95, 114, 143, 181, 189-
    192, 198
sewage water, 141
sewerage, 46-48, 55, 93, 148
shellfish, 93, 100, 106, 108, 110,
    140, 153
shelter, 9, 15, 45, 113-115, 198
shigella, 106, 139
sick building syndrome, 39, 168

silica, 64, 112, 120, 162, 168-170
silicosis, 120, 169-170
skin cancer, 96, 101-102, 126, 131,
    160, 165-167, 201
skin disease, 172
sleeping sickness, 139, 145
small-scale industries, 66, 118
social justice, 177
social services, 6, 15, 23, 27, 37, 113
socioeconomic group, 28
soil erosion, 13, 23, 27, 60-61
solar energy, 31-32, 71
solar ultraviolet radiation, 201
solid waste, 7, 46, 49-51, 94-95, 104,
    193,
soot exposure, 162
South-East Asia, 59, 76, 104, 107-108,
    147
SSA, 136
steel, 34-35, 63-64, 68, 79, 82
steroid compounds, 36
stomach cancer, 161, 163-164
stoves, 30-31, 72, 75, 84, 115, 117,
    150, 168
stratospheric ozone depletion, 7, 30,
    122, 125-126, 166
streptococcus pneumoniae, 138
stroke, 130, 157
structural adjustment, 37
sub-Saharan Africa, 3, 20, 58, 78, 87,
    104, 135-136, 138, 145, 151,
    155, 160-161, 168
subsistence agriculture, 39
sulfur oxides, 73
sulfuric acid, 37, 82
sulphur dioxide (SO2), 83, 159
supportive environments, 13-14, 194
surface water, 53-54, 64, 100, 113,
    165
suspended particulate matter (SPM),
    81, 88
sustainable cities, 189, 192
sustainable development, 2, 4-8, 10,
    12-17, 19-20, 22, 24, 26, 28-30,
    32-34, 36-43, 46, 48, 50, 52, 54,
    56, 58, 60, 62, 64, 66, 68, 70, 72,
    74-76, 78, 82, 84, 86, 88, 90, 92,
    94, 96, 98, 100, 102, 104, 106,
    108, 110, 112, 114, 116, 118,
    120-122, 124, 126, 128, 130,
    132, 134, 136, 138, 140, 142,
    144, 146, 148, 150, 152, 154,
    156, 158, 160, 162, 164, 166,

Annex A
Country Groupings by Development and by Geographic Region

Abbreviations:

UN Classification by Development Level:
DCO = developing countries other than LDC
DME = developed market economies
EIT = economies in transition
LDC = least developed countries

WHO Regions (based on geography):
AFR = Region for Africa
AMR = Region for the Americas
EMR = Region for the Eastern Mediterranean
EUR = Region for Europe
SEAR = Region for South-East Asia
WPR = Region for the Western Pacific

World Bank Regions (based on development level and geography):
EME = established market economies
FSE = formerly socialist economies of Europe
LAC = Latin America and the Caribbean
MEC = Middle Eastern Crescent
OAI = Other Asia and islands
SSA = sub-Saharan Africa
CHI = China
IND = India

UN Regions (based on geography):
Africa
Asia
Europe
Latin America
North America
Oceania

Annex B

Countries Providing Data for WHO/UNICEF (1996a)

Africa (38 countries)

Angola, Benin, Burkina Faso, Burundi, Cape Verde, Central African Republic, Chad, Côte d'Ivoire, Djibouti, Egypt, Equatorial Guinea, Gambia, Ghana, Guinea, Guinea-Bissau, Kenya, Lesotho, Liberia, Madagascar, Malawi, Mali, Mauritania, Mauritius, Morocco, Mozambique, Namibia, Niger, Nigeria, Senegal, Sierra Leone, South Africa, Sudan, Swaziland, Togo, Tunisia, Uganda, Zaire, Zambia.

Asia & Pacific (23 countries)

Afghanistan, Bangladesh, Bhutan, China, Federated States of Micronesia, Fiji, India, Indonesia, Iran, Kiribati, Lao PDR, Maldives, Myanmar, Nepal, Niue, Pakistan, Papua New Guinea, Philippines, Sri Lanka, Tokelau, Tonga, Tuvalu, Vietnam.

West Asia (5 countries)

Iraq, Jordan, Lebanon, Oman, Syrian Arab Republic.

Latin America & Caribbean (18 countries)

Belize, Bolivia, Brazil, Chile, Colombia, Costa Rica, Cuba, Dominican Republic, Ecuador, El Salvador, Guyana, Haiti, Honduras, Mexico, Nicaragua, Panama, Peru, Venezuela.